"A most challenging reflection about the presence of the past in society, Panourgiá's new book relates the singular story of the Greek Left, bringing out its multiple voices and often conflicting narratives. In this ethnography, based both on the author's experiences and on extensive fieldwork in Athens, the narrator/anthropologist explores the tension between individual voices and collective representations and boldly confirms—again—that the writing of anthropology can always be an innovative experience."

—Maria Couroucli, Research Fellow CNRS,
University of Paris–Nanterre

"*Dangerous Citizens* assembles paradoxical evidence of leftist formations in Greece. . . . A multi-scaled history of political violence suffering, this fascinating text is plain-spoken yet gnomic, with adroit comparative asides to wrap nonspecialist readers in drastic episodes artfully unfurled. Neni Panourgiá resists sanitized geopolitical generalization; she lodges patently nationalistic loci (e.g., war-waging) in radically skewed intimacies of experience. Revisiting fabled scenes of violent encounter and more-than-traumatic memory, this gifted critic offers uncompromising ethnography of manifest dissidence, everyday resilience, and specificities of terror (sometimes unwitting) endlessly difficult to fathom."

—James A. Boon, Princeton University

"*Dangerous Citizens* is a simultaneous indictment of the 'liberal' nation-state's blithe pretensions and willful self-ignorance, of the political and discursive relegation of modern Greek history to the historical margins of the colonial 'civilizing mission,' and of inhuman simplifications of the past everywhere. . . . Neni Panourgiá writes with the ethical passion of a partial witness who nonetheless claims no special privilege other than that of the common humanity denied by the state to those it repeatedly configures as its enemies. In posing this appealingly controversial challenge to the liberal self-imagination, moreover, Panourgiá—who has honed her distinctive writing idiom into a compelling mix of careful scholarship and stylistic adventurism—calls anthropology itself to account."

—Michael Herzfeld, Harvard University

D0878308

NENI PANOURGIÁ

DANGEROUS CITIZENS

THE GREEK LEFT AND THE TERROR OF THE STATE

FORDHAM UNIVERSITY PRESS / *New York 2009*

Fordham University Press has no responsibility for the persistence or accuracy of URLs for external or third-party Internet websites referred to in this publication and does not guarantee that any content on such websites is, or will remain, accurate or appropriate.

Library of Congress Cataloging-in-Publication Data

Panourgiá, Neni.
Dangerous citizens : the Greek Left and the terror of the state / Neni Panourgiá.
    p.   cm.
  Includes bibliographical references and index.
  ISBN 978-0-8232-2967-3 (cloth : alk. paper) — ISBN 978-0-8232-2968-0 (pbk. : alk. paper)
  1. Greece—Politics and government—1935–1967. 2. Greece—Politics and government—1967–1974. 3. Greece—Politics and government—1974- 4. Greece—History—Civil War, 1944–1949. 5. Political persecution—Greece—History—20th century. I. Title.

DF949.P36   2009
949.507'4—dc22   2009007059

Printed in the United States of America

12   5 4 3 2

First edition

For my son Petros,

and his friends
Telemachus,
Hector,
Thodoris,
Alexis

Και οταν θα 'ρθουν οι καιροι	And when the time comes
Που θα 'χει σβησει το κερι	That the candle goes out
Στην καταιγιδα	In the storm
Υπερασπισου το παιδι	Defend the child
Γιατι αν γλυτωσει το παιδι	Because if the child escapes it
Υπαρχει ελπιδα	There is hope

—Pavlos Sidiropoulos, through Mikis Theodorakis and Lefteris Papadopoulos

CONTENTS

ILLUSTRATIONS

Yáros (between pages 96 and 97)

Makrónisos (between pages 102 and 103)

PREFACE

This book had its origins in less turbulent times, before 9/11, when the ascending neo-liberalism of the Clinton years gave the false impression of a placid and prosperous future, carefully obscuring politics and neutralizing dissensus. The question that I was asking then concerned the collusion of the political and the existential subject as it appears in the character of Oedipus. How can we configure the location where a person becomes a political subject, I wondered, as I was looking at the problematics raised by Oedipus in his multiple subject positions—within kinship, the state, the location of authority and sovereignty, but above all in that tattered body of his, multiply mutilated, always intentionally, once aiming at the erasure of his lineage, then attempting to inscribe onto his body accountability for acts that he had performed unknowingly. And how can we see this ethnographically?

Oedipus seemed the perfect critical metaphor for the landscape of sovereignty after 9/11, where responsibility and accountability became notions so controlled and malleable by the sovereign power that they became distorted idealities. In an environment where power refused to account for its excesses and where structures (of governance, secrecy, security) were given priority over the humanity that lay beneath them, the paradigm of Oedipus seemed more apt every day. When I read how in their memoirs prisoners and exiles tortured in the concentration camps of Greece threaded together their experiences as political subjects with the character of Oedipus, I realized that there is a kernel of mutual recognition between the myth of the political in antiquity and the realities responsible for today.

Upon further reading of the histories of the Left (or what counted as the "Left") in Greece, rifts upon rifts, splits, heroisms and paranoia, the chasms between the Left and the Right that had seemed so clearly delineated and charged with emotions and affects that have shaped generations—all started becoming muddled and treacherous. Distinctions did not disappear, but the further I researched, the more, not less, occluded they became. Binary oppositions (if any ever really existed) exploded their binarisms into seemingly infinite layers of significance and significations, littering the landscape with inexplicable contradictions: mistrust of the state but reverence for authority; proclamations of self-determination and independence but need for the security provided by a position in the public sector; nostalgia for one's pristine home village but total disregard for the environment. But there, unspoken, was the civil war—always, everywhere present, silently brought to mind though never spoken of, wounds that never really healed.

And if anyone thought that they had, the December Events of 2008 would have proved him wrong. The uprising of the high-school students, sparked by the murder of one of them, fifteen-year-old Alexis Grigoropoulos, by a Special Forces policeman after yet another demonstration against the excesses of the government, brought center stage the festering wounds of the modern Greek polity. The high-school students, along with university students, immigrants, anarchists, "antiestablishmentarians" (the best word I have found to translate the inimitable Greek term *antiexousiastes*, where *exousia* stands for sovereign power), urban guerrillas, the lumpen, the poor, occupied the University, the Law School, the School of Public Governance, burned stores and rubbish bins, overturned police cars, threw stones and Molotov cocktails, burned the municipal Christmas tree three times over, looted, wore balaclavas and surgical masks, were attacked by the police with tear gas, smoke bombs, and baton beatings, turned Athens first and Greece shortly thereafter into an ongoing demonstration for three weeks, demanding, demanding nothing in particular and everything in general. "Fuck '68, Fight Now" became the slogan of the Events; "You have destroyed our lives" was the charge by the students toward everyone: their parents, their teachers, their schools, the government, the state, society, the church.

Trying to create a cogent narrative of the experience of perpetual resistance to the state has been a challenge both because of the trenchant critique that my generation of scholars has articulated against the production of grand and seamless narratives and because of the ethical impossibilities of forcing such a narrative onto this experience. What I have tried to do, both epistemologically and ethically, is to lay open its seemingly endless layers, where what appears as stable at one level collapses under its own weight at another level. In this attempt I have turned to the wisdom of others, who have generously agreed to lend me their eyes and ears, and to act as sounding boards for my ideas. I am grateful to each and every person who has lent me his or her thoughts and criticisms in the long time that it has taken me to complete this project.

First of all, I owe everything to the people who talked to me about their own histories in the long twentieth century. In some cases I have promised them anonymity, so I can only thank them here in this manner, knowing that they know I know my indebtedness to them. Others allowed me to use their names, so deep thanks go to Antonis Liakos, Stergios Katsaros, Titos Patrikios, Vardis Vardinogiannis, Yiannis Papadopoulos, Mimis Beis, Giorgos Angelakopoulos, Apostolos Papageorgiou, Thymios Karagiannakidis, Mimis Gourgouris, Fotis Provatas, Yiannis Reggas, Dimosthenes Dodos, Sotiris Vogiatzis, Othon Iliopoulos, Aleksa Djilas, Hara Tzavella-Evjen, Katerina Tsoucala. How can one thank one's parents? But I do want to thank my mother Demetra Tsakalou and my late father Konstantinos Panourgias, who died in October 2007, as this book was being submitted to the publisher, having endured eleven years of cancer and other hideously debilitating attendant diseases.

I could not have asked for a more supportive department than the one created by my colleagues at Columbia University. I want to thank especially Lila Abu-Lughod, Partha Chatterjee, Valentine Daniel, Nicholas Dirks, Claudio Lomnitz, Mahmood Mamdani, Brinkley Messick, Elisabeth Povinelli, David Scott, Lesley Sharp, Michael Taussig, and Paige West, who read or discussed my work with me and provided invaluable feedback. Columbia colleagues and friends, in general, have been more than kind with their time and energies in responding to my queries and requests for comments, either institutionally or personally, by inviting me to speak at or be affiliated with the various fora that fall under their care. I have presented material from this book at the Modern Greek Studies University Seminar, the University Seminar on Memory, the Harriman Institute, the European Institute, and the Institute of Comparative Literature and Society Seminar Series (previously CCLS). I want to thank those who invited me and everyone who participated in those seminars and offered comments, especially Vangelis Calotychos at the Seminar on Modern Greek Studies and Marianne Hirsch and Sonali Thakkar at the University Seminar on Memory. At the Harriman Institute, I would like to thank Gordon Bardos, who has made possible everything that seemed impossible, and Mark von Hagen, who answered my questions about the KGB and its predecessors, put me in touch with colleagues working on Yugoslavia and Titoism, and asked questions that I had not considered until then. Karen Van Dyck, Victoria de Grazia, Janaki Bakhle, Marc Nichanian, Andreas Huyssen, Rashid Khalidi, Anupama Rao, Marianne Hirsch, Leo Spitzer, Patricia Dailey, Reinhold Martin, Felicity Scott, and Elena Tzelepis have all offered comments and critique that have honed my argument and streamlined my writing. Research for this project has been generously supported by Columbia University, through two Humanities and Social Sciences Council Summer Grants (2001, 2003), a Chamberlain Fellowship for Junior Faculty Development Leave (2003–4), a University Seminars Schoff Publication Grant, and two Harriman Institute Publication Grants (2007, 2009).

A portion of Chapter 5, "1946–1949: Emphýlios," was published in an earlier form as "Desert Islands: Ransom of Humanity," *Public Culture* 20 (Spring 2008): 395–421. The section of Chapter 8 entitled "Freud's Remnants" was published in an earlier form as "Fragments of Oedipus: Anthropology at the Edges of History," in Neni Panourgiá and George Marcus, eds., *Ethnographica Moralia: Experiments in Interpretive Anthropology* (New York: Fordham University Press, 2008), 97–112.

I have profited greatly from having presented this material in various forms when I was invited to give lectures and seminars at the following anthropology departments: Princeton University, Rutgers University, New York University, Goldsmiths College, the London School of Economics, Duke University, University of California at Irvine, University of Michigan (with the Department of Classics), and the Department of History, Archaeology, and Social Anthropology (IAKA) at the University of Thessaly. I also want to thank the colleagues who invited me to present my work outside of the context of anthropology: in particular, Eleni Varikas during my stay as University Professor at the Department of Political Science at the University of Paris VIII, St Denis in the spring semester of 2007; Janet Halley and Philomela Tsoukala at the Harvard European Law Association and the European Law Research Center at Harvard University; and Ali Behdad at the Department of Comparative Literature at the University of California, Los Angeles. Equally important have been my interactions with my colleagues and fellow members on the Advisory Board of the Anthropology Section at the New York Academy of Sciences, especially Jane Schneider and William Mitchell, who read parts of this book in manuscript form and offered invaluable comments. I would like to thank my colleagues at the NYAS for providing me with a most supportive and collegial environment.

Along the long way that this book has followed, I have been very fortunate to have the ideas in it hammered out in discussions with many friends and colleagues, both from within and from outside the fields of anthropology and Modern Greek Studies. We did not always agree; I did not always convince them; and they did not always convince me. But I learned from their comments, and I hope that I have reciprocated. My deep thanks go to João Biehl, Carole Browner, Elizabeth Ann Davis, David Sutton, Constance Sutton, Antonio Lauria, Yopie Prins, Edmund Burke III, Webb Keane, Maria Couroucli, Michael Herzfeld, George Marcus, Vassilios Lambropoulos, Artemis Leontis, Thomas Gallant, John Iatrides, Margaret Kenna, Kirstie McClure, Susan Slyomovics, Sherry Ortner, Vincent Crapanzano, Michael Wood, Yael Navaro-Yashin, Dimitris Papanikolaou, Steven Reyna, Nina Glick-Schiller, Steven Luke, Maria Koundoura, William Ayers, Bernadine Dorn, Chris Fuller, Harold Evjen, Rashid Khalidi, Dimitris Vardoulakis, Ilias Nikolakopoulos, Hagen Fleischer, Abdellah Hammoudi, Sondra Hale,

Dusan Bjelic, Obrad Savic, Andreas Kalyvas, Kath Weston, and the late Begoña Aretxaga and Clifford Geertz. Adam Liptak, the Supreme Court correspondent for the *New York Times*, tracked down articles and information that had appeared in the paper and discussed with me the implications of the Welch assassination by 17N for the enactment of legislation protecting covert agents in the United States. Lawrence Downes, of the *New York Times*, was kind enough to discuss with me the production of *Oedipus Rex* by the inmates at Sing Sing. David Binder, the *New York Times* correspondent to the Balkans, talked to me about his meeting with Markos Vafeiades and his experience of Greece and the Balkans in the 1960s. Dorothy Lauterstein Doppstadt read the manuscript and offered me her critical journalistic eye.

In Greece, I want to thank the Collective of the Journal *Historein*, especially Antonis Liakos, Efi Gazi, Ioanna Laliotou, Polymeris Voglis, and Yiannis Papatheodorou. Eleni Papagaroufali has tirelessly discussed anthropology with me. Vasilis Karydes made certain contacts possible and gave me a way to look at the complexities of police surveillance. Dimosthenes Dodos helped me understand key concepts in the legislation concerning political prosecution. I want to thank the director and staff at the American School of Classical Studies in Athens for their generosity and hospitality during my tenure there as Senior Research Fellow in 2003–4. Special thanks are owed to the Head Archivist, Ms. Natalia Vogeikoff-Brogan, who helped me look through the papers of Oscar Broneer in pursuit of any material pertaining to Broneer's visit to Makrónisos in 1948. The staff at the Society for the Preservation of Historical Archives (EDIA) and its director, Mr. Vardis Vardinoyiannis, gave me invaluable material. Thanks of the same order go to the Secretary General of the Association of Imprisoned and Exiled (SFEA), Mr. Protopsaltis, and the President of the Association Yáros–Historical Memory, Mr. Kostas Katsimbinis. Similar thanks go to Nota Pantzou and (my old student) Katerina Stefatou, at the Museum of Political Prisoners Ai-Stratis. Mss. Aliki Tsirgialou and Eirini Boudouri, at the Photographic Archive at the Benaki Museum in Athens, made the archive available to me. I thank them for granting me permission to publish some of the photographs from the archive. Leslie Morris, Curator of Modern Books and Manuscripts at Houghton Library at Harvard University, found the unpublished Upton Sinclair note to *The Nation* with the letter on "The Greek Dachau" and granted me permission to publish them. Susannah Verney, at the University of Athens, sent me at lightning speed photocopies of obscure and forgotten articles that I needed and that she managed to find for me, often having only one name as a lead. Christina Agriantoni encouraged me in my political reading of Oedipus. Iason Handrinos read the entire manuscript for inaccuracies (and found many). The remaining ones are my responsibility.

Apostolos Papageorgiou gave me more than I can count and thank him for; he talked to me about his imprisonment during the junta, found books that had been out of print for three decades, photocopied them and sent them to me, sent me articles, photographs, videos, and accounts of the visits to Yáros by survivors, talked to me about the most obscure details that occupied my mind. The same is true of Nikos Karagiannakidis, who, in addition, read the manuscript more than once, combing through it for missing items and hanging arguments, and made his father's unpublished manuscript available to me.

The poet and graphic artist Dimitris Kalokyris created the artwork on the cover, based on a series of paintings by Eleni Kalokyri. The haunting faces on the tiles of the series *Ostraka* convey perfectly the ghostly lives lived by people under persecution for so many decades in Greece. Marios Pontikas graced me with his Laius. Yiorgos Chouliaras kept sending me poems, read the manuscript, and kept telling me stories. Constantinos Tsoukalas has been a constant inspiration in my life, and Fotini Tsalicoglou, a constant source of friendship. Eleni Varikas and Michael Löwy made a home for me in Paris, discussed Hannah Arendt's theory of totalitarianism with me, and talked to me about the Stalinist persecution of the Trotskyists in prewar Greece. Athena Athanasiou, *ouk ea me katheudhein*.

Throughout the writing of this book, ever since its inception, my students in my graduate seminars at Columbia were astute co-thinkers and unsparing critics. In the seminars "The Culture of Oedipus," "Dangerous Citizens," "Other Tribes," "Death, Terminable and Interminable," and "Exiles, Enclosures, Dystopias," but also outside the context of the classroom. Adriana Garriga-López, Dejan Lukic, Rodney W. J. Collins, Richard Kernaghan, Ronald Jennings, Christina Sornito, Morgan von Pelle-Pecelli, Shahla Talebi, Khiara Bridges, Ana Miljanic, and Patrick Higgins engaged with the ideas that I presented and offered me their intellectual jouissance.

There is a constellation of people whose intellectual agility, commitment to thought, and passionate engagement with ideas is only paralleled by their ethical position in life, and I am in their debt for their willingness to share both with me. Gil Anidjar, James and Olivian Boon, Carlos Forment, Virginia Jackson, Allen James, Martin Harries, Lawrence Hirschfeld, Antonio Louriar-Pericelli, Saloni Mathur, Meredith McGill, Aamir Mufti, Nauman Naqvi, Andrew Parker, Anupama Rao, Kitty Ross, Nermeen Shaik, Ann Stoler, Connie Sutton, Joel Whitebook, and the late Edward Said have all been with me when I wanted to discuss anything and debate everything. It is a rare privilege to have friends who never tire of moving deeper, to the core of an idea, a position, an argument, late into the night with the certainty that the morning will still find the friendship intact and the exchange inexhaustible.

Helen Tartar, my editor at Fordham University Press, stands in a category by herself. Her vision for the project, her perseverance when the text seemed to be getting impossibly large and complex, and her constant encouragement brought the book into existence. It is the ultimate fortune to have an editor who is an intellectual and understands the depth of a project from beginning to end, and who is willing and unafraid to push harder for the best possible expression, the most precise word, the clearer formulation of an idea.

I have dedicated this book to my most beloved son, Petros Konstantinos, and his friends, Telemachus Christopoulos (who bears the nom de guerre of his partisan grandfather), Thodoris Pappas, Hector Klonaris, and Alexis Verney-Provatas. These children, whose parents and grandparents have found themselves caught in the political web of Greece, in some occasions on opposite sides, share a deep friendship that transcends space and time. This book is a gift to them, with the wish that through it they may acknowledge that life is worth nothing without friendship and the sense of responsibility that makes it possible. To Petros goes my deepest gratitude for having endured and thrived in years when the most common response to his utterance "Mommy" was the locution "Not now, I am writing." My nephews, Orestis and Iason Charchalakis, have shared their lives with me and have shown me the bankruptcy of the grand political narratives and the new meanings of autonomy that make life possible for their generation.

Nothing would be possible without the brilliance, friendship, camaraderie, love, and devotion of Stathis Gourgouris, my fellow traveler in life. There has not been an idea, a claim, an argument that appears in these pages that has not been argued, fought over and about, discussed exhaustingly and passionately from morning until late into the night between us. I cannot thank him for this any more than I can thank him for his existence, again.

New York City
January 29, 2009

FROM NOW ON . . .

This is a text split into two parts. They do not take up the same space, although they both have things to tell, stories to recount and account for, histories that refuse to be forgotten. They bleed into one another; they cannot stand independently of one another. That was the greatest challenge I faced in writing this book: How could I allow these stories, which have been bleeding for so long (into each other, onto themselves, spilling out of all bounds), to retain their infectiousness, to stay there, crowding each other, while remaining singularly meaningful?

This is a book that tells a story and a history, simultaneously: the story is one of abjection, of multiple abjections, of miasmas, danger, and dehumanization. It is the story of the Greek Left, or, rather, of the Greek Leftist as a paradigmatic figure of abjection. Or, rather, of how the Greek Left has been constituted by the Greek state. It is the history and the story of how a zone of danger was instituted in the early years of the twentieth century and how it was both populated and inhabited by what came to be construed, understood, conjured up as "the Left." The history is of how the run-of-the-mill democracy that Greece has been throughout the twentieth century, with breaks for the occasional dictatorship, through systematic ideological positions, managed to create a zone of danger that it then populated with this new paradigm of danger, the Greek Leftist. The first part is the story/history. The second part, *parerga*, is a shadow text to the main one. I would suggest that you familiarize yourselves with the *parerga* before you continue with the main text. You can read the two independently of each other; you can read the *parerga* as notes; or you can read them together.

In the printed version of this book, the parerga short enough to be set in the margins have been placed there, so that they can be read in spatial proximity to the text. They are keyed to the text by superscript number. Those too long for that treatment have been put in the back, with cross-reference in the text. This has resulted in two sets of numbering: in-text superscripts for parerga in the margins, and numbering by chapter (e.g. 1.1) for those in the back of the book. The intent of both sequences is the same—to open the possibility of a layered and somewhat aleatory reading experience, through which the reader can be repeatedly reminded of the many different voices and discourses brought together in the years of fieldwork and research done for this volume. The print version will be followed by an electronic version (www.dangerouscitizens.columbia.edu), prepared in conjunction with the Columbia Center for Digital Research and Scholarship, that will further explore new possibilities of reading via the unique opportunities made available in the electronic medium, including the addition of new visual and audio materials.

How you proceed from now on is up to you.

A NOTE ON PARERGA

Parerga are not simply notes; they should be thought of as the extremities of a body, without which the text is truncated. They are notations to the text that make the text show its complexities, as they bring into the main narrative the realities of multiple positions, make interventions that show that there is no stability in this history, that the story itself constantly shifts ground, that any attempt to produce a cohesive narration, an Ur-text of the history of the Left in Greece, will always draw voices from the margins that will demand to be heard and will demand that the nuances they offer be taken into account. Parerga are not commentaries. They do not interrogate a stable main text or invite further commentary. Rather, they are, in a sense, what Derrida has called a "lean on," a space where I, the author, offer you, the readers, the chance to hold onto something: an idea, an explanation, a question, an interrogation, a dissent. They are a metatext that seeks to unseat any certainties that might exist in the main text, any convictions that might have developed in the narrative about the Left. Parerga offer a means of engaging with the main text's "imponderabilia of actual life"; they are the hand I offer you to proceed with the reading of this book.

Parerga are intimately connected with the development of the Western critical tradition, encompassing the historical and discursive development of social and philosophical thought that is the backdrop for the entire discipline of anthropology, indeed, that has engendered anthropology as an inquiry and a discipline, from its methodology to its epistemology and content. The term initially appeared in Greek in *Philotheou Parerga*, a text conceived between 1716 and 1718 by the Voivode of Wallachia, Nikolaos Mavrokordatos, as a guide to conduct for his son. (*Voivode* was an Ottoman rank bestowed upon high-ranking individuals in the occupied lands.) It next appeared in Ayliff's *Parergon Juris Canonici Anglicani; or, A Commentary by Way of Supplement to the Canons and Constitutions of the Church of England* in 1726. Both texts make clear that *parerga* denote a supplemental and instructional gesture that accompanies a main text or narrative but does so in a resolutely critical manner. In Kant's *Critique of Practical Reason* (1788) and later in a very long note in his second edition of *Religion Within the Limits of Reason Alone* (1794), the *parergon* is developed as adornment, embellishment, ornamentation (*Zierathen*) of the main *ergon*, the work. In his *Religion* Kant thinks further about the parergon. His very long note is appended to a "General Remark" at the end of the second part. Each part constitutes a parergon that concerns a parergon. Kant describes these four "General Remarks" as "in some measure *parerga* . . . they are not integral parts of [the work] but they verge on it [*aber strossen doch an sie an*: they touch it, they push it, press it, press against it]," as explained by Jacques Derrida (1987: 53). Thus, the parergon participates in the act of reflective thought, in the act of reflective faith, through the seemingly endless segmentation of the commentary on religion by Kant.

Half a century later, in 1851, Arthur Schopenhauer published his *Parerga and Parelipomena*, a work that, Schopenhauer explained, was subsidiary to his other, more systematic works, could not find a place in those other works, and dealt primarily with philosophical issues that positioned the subject with regard to the legal system, death, and existence.

Derrida has brought the idea of the parergon one step closer to anthropology by threading together anthropology and the logic of the supplement in Claude Lévi-Strauss's *Tristes Tropiques*. Lévi-Strauss, placing his work in a direct line of descent from Rousseau, makes *Tristes Tropiques* "at the same time *The Confessions* and a sort of supplement to the *Supplément au voyage de Bougainville*," Derrida notes (1976: 107). The supplement, Derrida continues, replaces and intervenes (*tient-lieu*), as its presence is as dangerous to the structure as is its absence (1976: 141–64, 216–69).

It is precisely this critical texture of the parergon, its capability to contain text that is both explanatory and indispensible, that raises the stakes of the reading experience that I am exploring here.

A NOTE ON
TRANSLITERATION

I have looked at many attempts to create a systematic approach to transliteration, and the one that I find most convincing and agreeable (with minor adjustments) is the one proposed by Robert Fitzgerald in his translation of the *Odyssey*, because it retains the complexities of Greek orthography and shows the affinities between Greek and Romance-based words. I have kept most of the Greek diphthongs and two-lettered vowels, double consonants, and long and short vowels. Accent marks indicate what they connote: the accent stress on a word. I do not use accent marks on two-lettered vowels (such as *ei* or *ai*), as these are single utterances. I use accent marks on all proper names, and I follow these rules of transliteration, except for names that have an already-established spelling in European languages (hence, for instance, Oedipus, not Oidipous, Aegean, not Aegaean). Toward the end of writing the book, a computer meltdown forced me to change programs. A glitch in the new program did not allow for the addition of certain diacritics. You will notice this inconsistency, and I apologize for any difficulties it might present in deciphering the correct Greek spelling, grammar, and pronunciation.

e : (short *e*) as in m*e*n (not accented)

é : (short *e*) as in *E*dgar (accented)

ê : (long *e*) as in s*ee*k (accented)

ē : (long *e*) as in r*e*tain (not accented)

o : (short *o*) as in O*r*éstēs (not accented)

ó : (short *o*) as in *au*to (accented)

ō : (long *o*) as in *au*tomaton (not accented)

i : (short *i*) as in *i*n

yi : (soft and long *g*) as in the Spanish *fuego*

ABBREVIATIONS

In transliterating acronyms, I have stayed as close to the Greek spelling as possible, so that the abbreviations will be more apparent in English.

Political parties

AKE	Agrotiko Komma Hellados (Agrarian Party)
EDA	Enomene Demokratike Aristera (United Democratic Left; Left coalition)
EK	Enosis Kentrou (Center Union)
EON	Ethnike Oragnosis Neon (National Organization of Youth; fascist youth)
ERE	Ethnike Rizospastike Enosis (National Radical Union; radical Right party)
HPE	Henomene Parataxis Ethnikophronon (United Patriotic Party; extreme Right party)
KKE	Kommounistiko Komma Ellados (Communist Party)
KKE-ES	Kommounistiko Komma Ellados—Esoterikou (Communist Party of the Interior; Eurocommunist party)
PASOK	Panhellenio Socialistiko Kinema (Panhellenic Socialist Movement)
SKE	Socialistiko Komma Hellados (Socialist Party)

Resistance groups

EAM	Ethniko Apelftherotiko Metopo (National Liberation Front)
EDES	Ethnikos Demokratikos Ellenikos Syndesmos (Greek National Republican League)

EKKA   Ethnike kai Koinonike Apeleftherose (National and Social
        Liberation)

ELAS   Ethnikos Laikos Apeleftherotikos Stratos (National Popular
        Libration Army)

OPLA   Organismos gia tin Prostasia tou Laikou Agona (Organization
        for the Protection of Popular Struggle)

PEEA   Politike Epitrope Ethnikes Apeleftheroses (Kyvernese Vounou)
        (Political Committee of National Liberation; mountain
        government)

Antiresistance organizations

TA   Tagmata Asphaleias (Security Battalions; collaborationist
        forces)

"X"   Chi (royalist forces)

International committees

UNSCOB United Nations Committee on the Balkans

USCOB   United States Committee on Borders (investigating border
        incidents)

Government organizations

KYP   Kentrike Yperesia Pleroforion (Central Intelligence Service)

Archives

ASKI   Arheia Syghrones Koinonikes Istorias (Archives of
        Contemporary Social History)

EDIA   Etaireia Diasoses Istorikon Arheion (Society for the
        Preservation of Historical Archives)

ELIA   Elleniko Laografiko kai Istoriko Arheio (Greek Folklore and
        Historical Archive)

SFEA   Syllogos Fylakismenon kai Exoristhenton Antistasiakon
        1967–1974 (Association of Imprisoned and Exiled Resistance
        Fighters 1967–1974)

DANGEROUS CITIZENS

1

1963–2008

History, Microhistory, Metahistory, Ethnography

The Bookseller

It was late one evening on a winter preceding the junta. The day the junta came to power was April 21, 1967, when I was about to turn nine years old. This incident happened two or three winters before, in 1964 or 1965. There was a knock on the door, and when my mother answered a middle-aged man (or so he seemed to me) was standing there, dressed in not tattered but certainly old-fashioned clothes, a dark suit and white shirt, no tie, with a light sweater underneath his suit jacket, no overcoat, but a scarf around his neck, and a leathery, deeply furrowed face, whose seriousness fell on me like a weight.[1]

He was holding two large, very heavy canvas bags, one in each hand, half holding them, half resting them on our doorstep. He looked at my mother and said, "I am selling books, madam." He looked at me and said again, "Buy one, please, for your daughter." My mother asked him to come inside, where, from her salary as a high-school teacher, she bought four books, two bound in green fabric, two bound in black fabric, all with golden letters on the spine and the front: Foivos Grigoriadis's *To Andártiko* (*The Partisan Warfare*), a four-volume history of the

1. When I interviewed the Greek historian Antonis Liakos in March 2006, he also commented that, when he was a child, he and his friends would flock around the parents of friends, primarily fathers, returning from extended periods of exile or prison not so much because of the excitement of their return as for the oddity of their appearance. "They would wear these suits with oversized lapels and high-cut vests, which we had never seen before because they were in vogue before we were born."

Greek organized armed resistance to the German* occupation during the Second World War (Parergon 1.1). The books were curiously numbered: the first volume had no number on the spine; the second, third, and fourth had

---

*Throughout this text, in reference to the Second World War occupation, I will use the term *Germans* to denote the Nazis or the Third Reich, as this is the locution commonly used in Greece, both in official historiographic documents and in everyday discourse.

3

Figure 1. 1959: High Heels. Private photograph.

their numbers. At some point, many years later, when I actually read the books I realized that the first, numberless, volume was really the fourth. That we had had no volume one, but two copies of volume four, one numbered, one not, all the result of a low-budget, clandestine production of the books, no doubt. This was by no means the first time that I had encountered a clandestine procurement of books. When I was even younger, from when I was four until I was six or seven years old (so, around 1962–65) my mother would take me with her to downtown Athens, to a basement apartment that served as a contraband bookshop, beneath the Opera House. She would carefully balance her high heels on the winding metal staircase descending to the shop, where we would buy copies of Nikos Kazantzakis's censored books. Walking to the shop, my mother would hold me by the hand and make me whisper to her what she had taught me to tell the police if they stopped us: "We are going to buy underwear" (nearby there was a shop that made underwear to order). We would buy one book at a time, as much as my mother's purse could accommodate, so as not to arouse suspicion. In this way we managed to get the complete works of Nikos Kazantzakis.* I opened one of those books, *The Fratricides*, to read again recently. It is a novel that Kazantzakis wrote about the civil war in Greece. It was originally published in 1963, but ours was the second edition of 1965. Binding pages 13 to 18 my mother had left a bookmark, a cheap, utilitarian bookmark, which has, nevertheless, marked this book forever: she used a tailor's pin. This makeshift bookmark probably marks page 18, a page where Kazantzakis writes about the experience of the forced exchange of populations in 1922 between Greece and Turkey after the Treaty of Lausanne. The specific passage describes the last gesture that the villagers of this Greek-speaking, Christian village make before they have to leave it forever: they visit the cemetery, where they bid farewell to their dead.[2]

2. "The people got up from the graves, with soil still clinging to their hair and faces; they found their courage; they opened their arms and held one another, as if they wanted to comfort one another; without thinking, they started serenely, slowly, to dance around the graves; and their eyes filled with tears that ran down to their necks" reads the paragraph that straddles pages 18 and 19 (my translation).

*For opposition to Kazantzakis's books in Greece, see Antonakes 1996.

I can't remember now when I learned who this man, Mr. Kosmás, was, but he continued to come around, once a month, selling books. At some point, though, during the junta, I came to know that Mr. Kosmás, the man selling books, like many other men selling books in the evening, "had been at Yioúra,"[3] where my Uncle Stéphanos also had been.[4] Although at the time we did not really talk about it as a common encounter in our lives (although maybe the adults did), a large number of "non-Leftist but democratically minded families [*Ohi aristeroi, alla demokratikon pepoitheseon*]" had the same experience. Only later did these bits of knowledge start becoming available and freely offered.

One day, a few years ago, at the house of a new friend, I saw a book that I needed, which my family used to own but which had disappeared from our library. I asked if I could borrow it for a few days.

As Aléka handed it to me, she said, "We had bought this from Mr. Kosmás." She looked at me intently and added, "You know . . ."

I said, "from Yáros . . ." as she nodded, "Yes."

I am certain that it was probably not the same Mr. Kosmás, but at the moment this was immaterial. Although this was the first time that I had been told openly by someone about the phenomenon of the traveling booksellers, the knowledge of their existence was both widespread and unspoken in the 1960s and 1970s.

I had known about my Uncle Stéphanos for years, around the time that Mr. Kosmás started coming to our house, certainly ever since I was old enough to understand that the whispers and muffled comments, the concealed eye contacts and the sighs of my grandmother held not a tantalizing, juicy secret (like my other uncle's sexual escapades, which also burdened her) but something of a profound sadness, a secret that implicated in different and perplexing ways various strands of my family that had never known or imagined they could be entangled, a skein

3. Yioúra (either in the feminine, hē Yioúra, or in the neuter plural, ta Yioúra) is the name used by the interned, their families, and anyone who had any connection to anyone interned on the island. Its official name is Yáros, which is also the name used by everyone during the last phase of internment there, during the junta. I use both names here: Yioúra largely for the first period of internment and Yáros for the second. It is not entirely clear why the generation of the junta detainees used the official name of the island, but one can determine, with a great degree of certainty, whether a title of an article or a book by one of the actors refers to the first or the second period depending on which name is used. All books that come from the first period use Yioúra, such as the 1950/1951 *Yioúra Hypomnema Kratoumenon Pros ton Hypourgo Dikaiosynes tes Kyverneses Plastera* (*Yioúra Memorandum of the Detainees to the Minister of Justice of the Plasteras Government*), sent to the government to expose the conditions of detention on the island; the 1952 *Yioúra Matōménē Vivlos* (*Yioúra Bloodied Bible [or Book]*); the 1964 *Apagorevetai: To Hēmerológio tēs Yioúras* (*Forbidden: The Diary of Yioúra*), by Andreas Nenedakis; the 2005 *Yioúra "To Áparto Kastro" ston Emphýlio kai tēn Junta* (*Yioúra "The Indomitable Castle" in the Civil War and the Junta*), by Demetres Manousos. The 1969 book by Tzavalás Karousos about his detention there during the junta is entitled *Yáros*, as is the photographic album put together immediately after the fall of the junta.

4. I have used pseudonyms for all names of persons whom I interviewed except where otherwise noted. In deciding what pseudonyms to use, I have kept in mind class, religious affiliation, and place-of-origin markers. Obviously, as Clifford Geertz has pointed out (in Panourgiá 2002), when people read what we write, people try to match pseudonym with true name, and I have no illusions that no matter how diligently I employ pseudonyms

and mix up lines of descent, the identity of some characters will be obvious to their prototypes.

My grandmother was suffering because this particular political adventure of Stéphanos was causing immense heartache for her sister, Stéphanos's mother-in-law. My uncle Stéphanos was married to my father's first cousin on his mother's side. My father's mother and Stéphanos's mother-in-law (my great-aunt Eleni) were sisters. Eleni married a man from the Cyclades, a Catholic who had converted to Orthodox Christianity, and they had four children, two boys and two girls: Rosa, Marios, Marinos, and Lucia. My uncle Stéphanos was married to Lucia and had two daughters, roughly my age. There were many children in the neighborhood, all of us cousins of varying degrees, and most of us about the same age. For a detailed account of the naming patterns in Athens, see Panourgiá 1995; on naming patterns in Greece in general, see Herzfeld 1982b.

of relationships whose last strands I was able to pull apart only in the early years of the twenty-first century.

But how can I lay all this open for you, so that you can sense what this thing we call a "civil war [Emphýlios Pólemos]" really means on the ground, for children who are not old enough to understand that there is a realm in their lives called *politics* (let alone that this politics organizes their lives in brutal and inexplicable ways) and for adults who find themselves in the vortex that produces a political DNA of sorts (Parergon 1.2), which organizes not only their lives but also the lives of generations to come and has been organized by kinship lines that extend into the past? How can I lay out for you the intricacies of meaning in "being a Leftist" (even when simply "democratic") in Greece of the twentieth century, which have organized the meanings of political being in the twenty-first century? I can only pick a point and call it a beginning.

Flesh and Light You Breathed into the Golden Rocks (Parergon 1.3)

We (Parergon 1.4) often rest comfortable in the notion that we, *ánthropoi*, humans (Parergon 1.5), are interminably engaged in an attempt to understand the world around us, to make meaning out of garbled symbols. I would argue, with Yiorgos Cheimonas,[5] for the opposite: that the farther away we are from power and its mechanics, the more we try to make ourselves understood by the world that surrounds us; that each of us is crying out to be heard and agonizes over the process of translating this cry, a process that often takes on a violent form, the more violent, the more desperate; and, further, that if this effort is at the center of the project of humanity, then the project of anthropology is to make this process of translation intelligible. It is to provide a map of the circuits that are traversed in the walk toward this translation.

Imagine that you find yourself in an old, walled city, with narrow, winding streets, dead ends, windows that open and close unexpect-

5. Yiorgos Cheimonas (1936–2000) was a prose writer and psychiatrist. His writings comprise prose, inquiries into the nature of logos, translations of ancient Greek drama and Shakespeare, articles, television interviews, and writings on psychiatry. On January 12, 1985, in what became *Ta Taxidia mou (My Journeys)*, Cheimonas writes that, if the philosophical and scientific explorations of the human (*ánthropos*) aim at an understanding of the world by the human, the frightening demand of art is for the human to be understood by the world.

edly. A city inhabited by humans who have experienced terror and mistrust, hatred and joy, deep passions and frightening desires. At its vortex resides an *ánthropos*, a human being whose locations are always contested and interconnected: she is someone's parent, someone's child, someone's sibling, someone's friend and, perhaps, even someone's comrade; she is claimed by her family, by her state, by her party as an object of their want and desire, perchance she is a (their) subject too.

This central *ánthropos* (whose centrality lies only in the fact that, unbeknownst to her, she has been claimed as the subject of this project, too), who has desires, passions, needs of her own, acquires (or is given) dimensions that are beyond her physical capacities, is endowed with intentions, thoughts, ideas, and capabilities that could never materialize in one single human, becomes a specter that contains everyone she is made to stand for. She becomes *dangerous*.

Not only does she become dangerous, but she inaugurates a category that is made to fit her and she is made to inhabit: the category of the *dangerous person*. A person who posits a danger not because of the acts that she commits and the gestures that she makes, but because she (and those like her) thinks such acts and imagines such gestures. Her body, as flesh and bone, enfleshes the danger that she has come to embody and represent. Her presence becomes dangerous for the polis, as she is always suspected of thinking up thoughts of exploding (the categories, the borders, the classifications, the complicities, the secret treasuries of) this city. She becomes a suspicious enemy; she cannot be located in any specific class or neighborhood; she transcends the polis; she becomes a part of it; she knows its inner workings, makes hiding places in its buildings, learns and produces a topography that is also a topology completely unimagined and unsuspected by the sovereign who suspects her. She becomes one with the polis, a *Homo politicus*, hence dangerous, to whom we can, perhaps, give a name, let's say a "Lucy" or a "Rosa" or an "Oedipus."

But she certainly belongs to the new (as in modern) category of the person,[6] which is always being dreamt up as singular, monolithic, cohesive, and coherent, all "part of statecraft that depends on taxonomies of simplification for control," as Ann Stoler has put it in Foucauldian terms (2002: 648), thus conjuring up a governmentality with a twist. This is a state that not only wants to control its population but wants to define the resistance to its own existence, so it produces the late-nineteenth- and early-twentieth-century category of the *dissident*, the anarchist, the Marxist, the Communist, the Leftist.

Can this topology/topography be traced?

6. I am echoing here Clifford Geertz's critique of the discourses that have conflated the modern self (self-contained, bounded, autonomous) with the universal notion of the self as an existential, but also social, category. The critique that Geertz articulated is, obliquely, included in the "modern" category of the monolithic, cohesive, and coherent persona that I am animating here.

Can we map the little streets and alleys, the dead ends, the secret passage-
ways, stone arcades, overpasses, and underpasses through which she finds
herself walking, crawling, slithering as she feels the breath of the sovereign on
her nape? Can we map how and in what way she has been made dangerous
and, even more, what sorts of daily realities, lived experiences, memories,
thoughts, and speech acts this construction has produced for her? How it has
organized her life, and everyone else's?

   This is what this book seeks to do. It seeks to be a map of this city that is the
conceptualization (by the sovereign) of the dangerous person as she becomes
accountable for the collapse of political categories, right where the political
sphere of engagement meets the demands of social and cultural order. There is
no Baron Haussmann here; there are no wide boulevards, no direct, cohesive,
unobstructed lines that lead from point to point, because the ways by which
this polis has produced its own *classes dangereuses* are through the back alleys,
dark corners, and dead ends of democracy. In these times, when dictatorships
in "the West" no longer happen as a result of military coups and interventions
but rather through the hyper-legalization of the minutiae of everyday existence
(where the law deigns to regulate the amount of hair gel carried by passengers
in an airplane cabin), the process of the gradual tightening of the juridical
system that happened in Greece over the course
of the first two-thirds of the twentieth century
and the cultural, social, and political specificities
that it has produced, the experience of history on
the ground and the type of citizen that has been
made possible or imperative, can help us read the
experience of the citizen in the vortex of history
in such times as these, when the Law becomes
the skin of the state.[7]

   This is also to trace what happens to political categorical ascriptions (i.e., the "Leftist,"
the "patriot," the "traitor," the "law-abiding
citizen") when this particular political danger
is animated and "the dangerous and criminal"[8]
elements (the *epikindyna kai kakopoia stoiheia* of
Greek legislation from the 1920s to the 1970s) are
expelled from the body politic and enclosed in a
(phantasmatic or actual) space of exclusion. Not
what Veena Das and Deborah Poole have called
"a simple story of exclusion" but what they, too,
seem to be after, to try to elucidate, namely,
what constitutes the margin, what passes for the
margin in the story that wants to pass itself as

7. The significance of this legal tightening
for the Left will become evident later on.
For the moment I need only acknowledge
that, as the state sought to place an ever-
larger segment of its citizen body under
tight control through the constriction
of the law, the same legality allowed the
Left to challenge the actions of the state
and use the law as a means of resistance
to the state. I am indebted to Abdellah
Hamoodi, who pressed me to articulate
this point.

8. Historically the term *dangerous persons*
was used for the mentally ill, who were
housed in special psychiatric units within
general hospitals as early as the beginning
of the nineteenth century in Europe. See
Foucault 1978. Around the notion of the
"dangerous person" spun rather rapidly
an interwoven thread of risk and danger,
so that the pre-emptive restriction of
these persons from interaction with the
general public became legitimized as the
duty of the state. The term was initially
formulated in Greece during the Metaxas

the center, the matrix.* I am speaking of specific spaces of exclusion, of camps where these citizens were concentrated, camps with names: Makrónisos ("long island," but also, Long Island, in Yiorgos Chouliaras's felicitous word play), Yáros (or Yioúra, intimately known in that incongruity of the intimacy of terror), Trikeri, Chios, all of them names, topoi, locations known since antiquity, laden with significations independent of the project of national rehabilitation thought up in the twentieth century.

These were concentration camps established with the expressed aim of reeducation and rehabilitation of the actual or suspected "enemies of the state,"† by and under *democratically elected governments*, in the context of a parliamentary democracy, of active parliaments that included parties of the Right and the Center.[9] What is it that makes such a conceptualization and actualization possible? And what happens not only to these interned bodies but to the body politic in its entirety when such a possibility is initially conceptualized and eventually actualized? If the aim of these camps was to produce Foucault's "virtuous" men (1974: 154), can we set the question "What was produced there?" against Foucault's certainty that in such spaces (like Attica, in New York, or Auburn, or Philadelphia, or in what we will be reading here) "nothing is produced" (155)? Can we, in the end, say that, since Attica, Philadelphia, Auburn, or Makrónisos and Yáros did not manage to produce "virtuous" men or "nationally minded citizens," they did not produce anything at all? Can we say that the negation of virtuousness\

dictatorship of 1936 as "dangerous and suspicious persons" to denote: (1) carriers of infectious diseases and (2) declared members of the Left and their kin (though otherwise uninvolved), or even persons merely suspected of belonging to the Left or being sympathetic to it. The term was employed as part of a discourse that sought to offer to the public a solution to the problem of "managing" this category of citizens, a management that took place through the establishment of concentration and rehabilitation camps.

9. When it appeared in Greece, the project of re-education was not new. In July 1944, the U.S. Army produced a "Draft Directive on the Re-education of Germany," which later came to be known as the Morgenthau Plan. The directive outlined two phases: a period of coercive and repressive measures immediately after the end of hostilities, and a second, larger phase, during which "interest in the ideas of popular democracy, such as freedom of opinion, speech, the press and religion" would be promoted. In 1947 Great Britain tried to put this plan into effect, although the assessment of the State Department by that point was that "it is difficult to educate; it is more difficult to re-educate; it is well-nigh impossible to re-educate a foreign nation." For an assessment of the importance of the plan for the *mentalité* that made the idea of re-education possible, see Marcuse 2001. For the text of the Morgenthau Plan and its contextualization within U.S. and British foreign policy, see David Irving, http://www.fpp .co.uk/bookchapters/Morgenthau.html.

---

*Das and Poole (2004) have brought the margins of the state to the forefront of anthropological discourse. They focus on the notion of the state and its development in anthropological literature, and the notion of the margins of the state, especially as it complicates the relationship of the state to its margins as an anthropological problem. Daniel (1996) has specifically addressed the methodological problems that arise from ethnographic study on the margins of the state.

†I will return to this point of the "enemy" later, but for now I need to note what Anidjar (2003) has developed, namely, that "we don't have a theory of the enemy," a lacuna that Anidjar craftily fills through his reading of Carl Schmitt and Edward Said. See also Anidjar 2004.

produced in these places, the negation of the nationally minded ideology, is indeed a nothingness?

Such questions need to be addressed with more questions, which I lay open here. How is the *human* (*ánthropos*) conceptualized as a cultural category opposed to the animal and the divine, while being foreclosed as a categorical ascription for certain classes of citizens (here, the Leftists)? How is this human an object of biopolitics—meaning, how is it that he becomes a citizen and, as a citizen, submits to the rule of law that seeks to rule over his life, body, and mind?

How does this life, circumscribed by its legal definition, become an object of contention as to its ownership, and how are the synapses of the state and its law articulated through the presumption of this ownership? What is the nexus of life, law, and the body of the citizen? What is the point where a perceived illegality becomes metaphorized through medical references? In other words, where does medical discourse become intelligible to legal discourse? Where does the medical become part of the imaginary of the political?[10] As Athena Athanasiou points out, "there is no such thing as the human . . . there is only the dizzying multiplicity of the cut human, the human body as interminably cut, fractured" (Athanasiou 2005: 125), and it is this fragmentariness and its attendant hesitancy about the possibility of producing a whole subject that I want to map.

At the heart of all this pulsates the following question: What are the parameters within which a state categorizes a portion of its citizens as "dangerous and suspicious," and what are the long-term effects of this categorization for how that specific society comes to understand itself as a cultural and political entity? The state has reserved this right of deciding who among its citizens is dangerous so that it can then engage in recognizing human rights as privileges or entitlements, Judith Butler has noted. Once the state has deemed that someone is dangerous, it is enough "to *make that person dangerous* and to justify his indefinite detention," she continues (Butler 2004: 59; my emphasis).

"The state [*to krátos*]" (Parergon 1.6) is the term used on the ground. It is the "local" term for what Max Weber (after Engels and Lenin) has described as the cluster of administrative

10. The easiest of these deployments to observe is, of course, the recent proliferation of the use of medical discourses in war operations. ("Surgical precision" is often invoked for operations for which, had they been really surgical, the surgeons performing them would have been prosecuted for criminal negligence.) In the case of Greece, however, Prodromos Yannas has shown how, in the containment discourses produced by the Truman administration regarding the reconstruction of Greece after the civil war, clear distinction was made between medical discourses referring to Greece and to Europe. For Europe, the terminology employed was biomedical, whereas for Greece the terminology was psychiatric. Yannas has drawn our attention to the fact that, whereas Europe was "medicalized," Greece was "psychiatrized." Yannas argues that the Truman administration relied upon "hearing" in the Greek case and "seeing" in the case of Europe, delineating thus the different epistemological approaches that produced the diagnosis of the post–World War II European landscape. Yannas quotes Paul Porter, head of the first United States Economic Mission to Greece, who, in an article in *Collier's* magazine (later republished in *Reader's Digest*), referred to Greece's "national psychosis" and "psychological paralysis"

and authoritative practices, gestures, and archi-
tectonics that make possible the preservation of
class structure and relationships over, above, and
outside the specificities of any particular government or political party. *To krátos* in Greece
is often extended and expanded to include the
administration, the government, the state mechanism, and the sovereign, a
conceptual and semantic expansion that includes both the official designation
of Greece as a sovereign country, as the "Hellenic State [*Hellēnikón Krátos*]"
and the disdain that permeates the relationships of citizens with the mechanisms of this state. This disdain, paired with a deeply seated suspicion of the
state, acquires texture in the expressions "There is no *krátos*" or "What kind of
krátos is this?" when the state is perceived as having failed to provide citizens
with the (assumed as) necessary and indispensable services that they demand
(ranging from adequate control of drinking water quality or medical coverage
to prompt and efficient snow removal, or cleaning up after floods that have
occurred at neighborhoods built illicitly and illegally—but with the tolerance
of the state—in river beds, ravines, wetlands, on the beach, or on mountain
slopes). Conversely, the invocation of the absence and lack of *krátos* in cases of
blatant law breaking (such as illegal parking on sidewalks and ramps for the
disabled, the occupation of sidewalk-guiding strips for the blind by outdoor
cafes and restaurants, or smoking in public hospitals) almost always indexes
the speaker as a Leftist, further underlining the peculiar, particular, and intimate relationship of the Left with the law.) Tzavalás Karousos underlined this
dialectic of the law and the (Leftist) citizen when he commented, at the height
of the dictatorship (1967–74), after he had been released from the concentration camp of Yáros, at the age of sixty-four, for a grave health matter:

(Yannas 1994: 118). Emmanouela Mikedakis, in her dissertation, has traced the use
of biomedical and psychiatric tropes in
the language used by the dictator George
Papadopoulos (1967–73) in his political
speeches. See Mikedakis 2007.

> A people [*laós*], without arms, without newspapers, without schools,
> without radio, without anything, armed only with its desire to fight in
> order to make the Law stand up on its own feet. A Law that, neverthe-
> less, it has not authored. And it was a meager Law, one that could not
> secure a relief in its life. And on the other hand, there was a *krátos* that
> did nothing but break its own Laws, break them each day more, until
> it arrived at plain murder. (Karousos 1974: 15)

This notion of the *krátos* complicates the means by which the experience
of history, even when seemingly forgotten, organizes the ways people respond
to their current, lived realities, as these register "on their very bodies," as the
expression goes.* It also means that this conceptualization of *krátos* organizes

---

*This is not simply an expression but a robust and tight theoretical and epistemological position
developed and expanded in feminist theory and critique, primarily by Minh-ha 1989, Butler 1990, and
Grosz 1994. Loraux 1986 addresses the issue of the construction of the body as a body of inscription for
the city in her seminal reading of Pericles's funeral oration.

the modes in which the experience of the body becomes translated into the experience of history through the collectivization of the memory of persecution, torture, and exile.

Asinen te (Parergon 1.7)

"Everything is unified," Yiannis Filis submits in his autobiographical sketch, which traces his trajectory starting in the small, largely Right-wing (by his account) village of Asine in one of Greece's most ancient and famous areas, the Argolid, where Mycenae, Ancient Epidauros, and the obscure Homeric Asine lie. Asine appears only as a name in Homer's catalogue of the ships that participated in the Trojan War.[11]

> Everything is unified. Education from the day of Sunday School to the Polytechnic School, where I start studying in 1968, constitutes a cogent unit [enótēta]. Emphýlios [the civil war], the Special Security guy [asfalitēs] with the thin mustache and the angry face at the gate of the Metsoveion [the Polytechnic School], the party meetings of the decade of the sixties, the battles in the school yard, the history lesson from grammar school to high school, every lesson, the maps showing the as yet unliberated homelands, the sketches of the faces of the Greek warriors of the War of Independence and the Turks, the pious and the sinners of the village, the serious ones and the frolickers, the normals and the homosexuals, everything is a cogent unit. Nothing is left to chance. Nothing allows for margins. They inscribe in our mind the foundational theory of us and the rest. We, the good ones; the others, the bad ones. (Phillis 2006: 100)

The story of the Left in Greece has a very idiosyncratic history (as the Nobel Prize laureate George Seferis noted about the entirety of Greek history, which, for him, probably did not include the Left). It is a history written in fragments and intervals, within a larger history that has not always included it. From the beginning of the labor movement in Greece (which included the beginning of the agricultural labor movement and its significant event, the massacre at Kilelér on March 6, 1910) to the return of the last exiles in 1963 (a return that proved to be ever so brief, as the junta of 1967 opened the exile and concentration camps once again, and most of those who were released in 1963 were interned and exiled again at that point), the history of the Left was not being written as a conscious historiographic endeavor; in fact, it was expressly prohibited from being written, a

---

11. *Asine* becomes just a place name again in Stathis Kalyvas's *The Logic of Violence in Civil War* (2006), in which Kalyvas tries to show that the entire area of the Argolid had been politically homogeneous and without political rifts before the civil war. Filis's account, however, shows that such rifts existed even within the cloak of fear and silence. For a critical review of Kalyvas, see Panourgiá 2008b.

censorship that concerned only the Leftist historiographic act and was based on the premise that writing this history would "stir up passions [*anamóhleusis pathón*]" (Parergon 1.8).

The first scholarly conference to mention the civil war in its title took place in Greece in 1995,* when, on the occasion of the fiftieth anniversary of the end of the Second World War, the historian Hagen Fleischer decided to organize a conference on the civil war that would consider the preceding decade to be constitutive of it. Fleischer argued, as I do here, that since the war in Greece neither ended in 1944 (since this was the beginning of the civil war) nor started with the Italian attack in 1940 and the German invasion in 1941, but bore the burden of the 1936–41 Metaxas dictatorship, the time of the Second World War needs to be examined within its rightful context, which, for Greece, was intimately connected with the story and the history of the Greek Left.† Right-wing historiography did not concern itself with either of these contentious events—the Metaxas dictatorship or the civil war—except in publishing accounts of the latter that maintained and supported the official state position that the Greek Left (and later the Communist Party)[12] had always been a treacherous tumor, a carcinoma within the Greek polity, having as its aim the forceful overthrow of the (or any) legitimate Greek government. Hence, the civil war would be codified as nothing more than the latest attempt at such a forceful change in political formation. The history of the Greek Resistance was gauged according to this reading, which forcibly collapsed within it the history of the civil war. Curiously, the historiography of the civil war has from the beginning employed sports metaphors (the First Round, the Second Round, the Third Round; Parergon 1.9) engendering, in effect, an *emphyliol-ogy*,‡ a long and sustained discourse on the *emphýlios* that has managed to produce as much as to analyze its content.

12. The ironic fact that the Communist Party of Greece was never a revolutionary party aiming to take over political power has been lost on everyone (most of all on itself) save for its critics located to its left (the Trotskyists and the Maoists).

The mid-sixties, before the junta, witnessed a tentative attempt by the Left to initiate a coherent, cogent, and systematic account of the Left and the actions taken by the Greek state (of Right-wing or Centrist leanings)

*See Chouliaras 2003. I do not mean to imply that there had been no research done or publications on the civil war prior to the conference in 1995, nor that conferences on the civil war had not taken place outside of Greece. Hagen Fleischer mentions, in the introduction to the volume of essays he edited in 2003, that when he and the historian Nikos Svoronos organized, in 1984, the first conference ever to take place in Greece on "those years of the great contrasts," they dealt only with the Metaxas dictatorship, the Resistance, and the German occupation. When Fleischer suggested that they include the civil war, Svoronos said to him, "Be patient" (Fleischer 2003: 12). Conferences and publications on the matter had been taking place abroad for about twenty years before one could be attempted on Greek soil. The bibliography is not very long, but it is significant. See, e.g., Iatrides 1972, 1981; Sarafis 1980; Baerentzen, Iatrides, and Smith 1987.

†See Fleischer 2003; also Chouliaras in the same volume.

‡I am consciously echoing James Boon's notion of Baliology.

to suppress it. Apart from Foivos Grigoriadis's *To Andártiko* (the first book mentioned in this study), Nikos Margaris's *History of Makrónisos*, published in 1963, was such an attempt, as were two books by Spyros Linardatos on the Metaxas dictatorship. During the junta, Constantine Tsoucalas's *The Greek Tragedy*, published in London in 1969, was the first attempt to provide a cohesive narrative of political developments in Greece from the inception of the modern Greek state to the dictatorship of 1967 while delineating the measures that were taken by the state to eliminate all critical political discourse.

What such attempts were trying to do was to put in writing, to bring up to the level of public discourse, indeed, to make public and discursive something that the whole of Greece was experiencing as private and unspeakable: the reality and the specter of all those who had spent anything from two or three to twenty-two or twenty-three years in prison, in the army, in concentration camps, in exile, or in plain fear. These were attempts to explain the fear that permeated the air, despite the "democratic" government in place,[13] the whispers and the silences, the circuitous explanations about why someone who held a university degree and was fully qualified to teach, work at a bank, or in the public sector was, instead, employed at a small factory, selling books from door to door, surviving by giving private lessons, being a private accountant, or renting a small hole in the wall, off the beaten track of downtown, selling souvlaki and gyro sandwiches. Obviously the Right wing was oblivious to (and, occasionally, even ignorant of) all this, seated comfortably in the seat of the right and the correct, content in its satisfaction that this only happened elsewhere, to other people, to "the others," who had been asking for it. Thus all discussion was stifled; the cards were drawn, East was East and West was West, and that was the way it would be.

13. The feminist political philosopher Eleni Varikas insists that I put the appellation "democratic" in quotation marks when I refer to this period. I do want to insist, however, that, however rigged, forced, and disingenuous the elections that produced those governments were, there was an insistence on the performativity of the rule of law, on the constant iteration and reiteration of the discourse of legality as producing legal order, that is of primary importance to my project overall. I am trying to show that the performance of the legal speech act, the invocation of law at the very moment the same law was being broken, was the ground on which the violation and abuse of civil and human rights took place at that time.

(Speaking of Method)

How can fear, terror, pain, torture, and the dialectic that always accompanies them—hope for poetry, love of life, stubbornness, endurance, the desire to have children—how can they be written (of, about, against)? Where can one start writing? And if we understand this dialectic as resistance to hegemonic forms not only of power but of underwriting processes of subjectivities, how can such a resistance be written? The stakes for the anthropologist are great, Sherry Ortner tells us, when she reminds us that as anthropologists we position ourselves not only as engaged intellectually and morally but in a "bodily process in space and time" (Ortner 1995: 173). Therefore the writing that will result from this bodily process called "fieldwork" ought to recognize (if not tremble in the face of) the intellectual and moral responsibility that we have in the encounter of this dialectic.

Theory seems to be a good place to start, although, as Valentine Daniel has warned us, nothing is transparent to theory, not "even ordinary life" (1996: 6), especially when the ordinariness of this everyday life contains within it the torturers and the tortured, the maimers and the maimed, the fearsome and the feared, or, as Begoña Aretxaga has put it, "people who are too close and whose lives we know, and whom we cannot disregard so easily because they form part of the intimate social framework" (Aretxaga 2005: 166). And one could very well posit the legitimate question of why attempt to write about a terror that took place so long ago, why now, when the bodies of the tortured have been healed, their psyches have been soothed, now that some of those persecuted and brutally tortured for being dissident (to social order, to political submission, to normalization) have become ministers, and deputies, and full professors, directors of powerful organizations in the public sector, recognized and revered poets, novelists, filmmakers, architects, jurists, painters—who, in other words, have largely become what they were denied to be. What, one might ask, is the merit of writing a story that now has become history?

I officially started fieldwork for this project in May 2003 for fifteen months, followed by additional fieldwork in the summers of 2005 and 2006, with follow-up interviews in the summer of 2007. This was the time-frame of my experience in "the field." But what could "the field" mean for me, a "native," a person known among my family, friends, acquaintances, and colleagues as a "native anthropologist"? Where does the field end and where does unmarked, daily experience begin, and what can the two tell us about one another? Many different levels of identities and identifications are claimed in this book, all of them problematic and problematized simultaneously. There is no fixed identity of the "Leftist," an identitary ascription that is as slippery as the ground of the "Left" on which it walks. At times all "Leftists" were counted in with the "Communists," who were counted in with the "labor unionists," who were counted in with the "anarchists," all ascriptions used by the state in the process of legislating their persecution, although occasionally a flicker of differentiation would accompany the desire that "our" people not "really" be Communists, as oftentimes happened when people on the Right would draw a distinction between the "Communists" and the "Leftists." Zina, a friend whose father was a chief justice for the Special Military Courts until 1963, always joked about how her father would say of Leftist members of the family: "Ah, he's not a Communist; how would he know to be a

Communist? He's just a Leftist [*aristerós*]." Within the "Left" these identitary ascriptions become even more fraught, and the delineations among Marxists, Marxists-Leninists, "true" Marxists-Leninists, Trotskyists, *Archeiomarxistés* (Archive Marxists; Parergon 1.10), Maoists, Guevarrists, Eurocommunists, Revolutionary Marxists, and Fourth-Internationalists have produced not only friction within the "Left" on the level of revolutionary dogmatism but have organized the lived, everyday experience of individual Leftists throughout the history of the Left movement in Greece.[14] At times the persecution of members of these groups by the official Party has been as fierce as their collective persecution by the state. "Is he a Stalinist?" the mother of a friend whose father, an *Archeiomarxist* who had lived in hiding for years out of fear of both the official Communist Party and the police, would ask in a whisper, about people she did not know. Identities of the "Right" are a little less slippery and better fixed, as they have always been associated, in many ways, with the state and its representations and self-presentations, thus have been both reified and institutionalized in ways in which any internal or external nuances have lost their force.[15] Slight differentiations persist across the spectrum of the Right, and they distinctly separate the "Right" from what is commonly called the "extreme Right," which, in Greece, has always been associated with totalitarianism, Fascism, and the terror of the state (it includes, for instance, the *parakrátos*, the paramilitaries, and armed civilian militias).

My identity as a "native anthropologist" in this context and these encounters is no less slippery and no more fixed. I belong to the "Left" but not to the "aristocracy" of the Left. I do not come from a family that has sprung from the long history of the Leftist movement in Greece; no one in my family ever held any position of importance within the movement; our family name is not recognizable as a "Leftist" one. There are other families, families that have experienced the constant persecution of the state from the beginning of the Left movement, families whose members had been sent to Moscow to study at the KUTV[16] (derogatorily named *Koutvides* by the Greek Special Security); there are other families that saw three generations of their members imprisoned simultaneously, and yet other families who have intermarried within the Party. In that sense my "nativeness" becomes frustrated. Indeed, members of my family have

14. I would argue that this is true of the international Left movement, but that falls outside of the scope of this particular project.

15. Except, of course, when even the identity of the "Right" was questioned from within, as during the junta, when officers of the Greek National Army who had fought against the Communists during the civil war found themselves in the same prisons and places of exile as the Leftists.

16. The Communist University of the Toilers of the East, also known as the Far East University, established in April 1921 in Moscow and closed in the late 1930s. The curriculum included Marxist theory, Party organization and propaganda, law and administration, theory and tactics of proletarian revolution, trade union organization, and problems of socialist construction, among others.

been imprisoned, have been sentenced to death, many more have voted for the Party, but the family as a whole has been Centrist. That certainly has not sheltered the family from suspicion, but it has created an added level of complication, both of what we understand as "native anthropology" and what we generally understand as fixed political ascriptions. This frustrated identity, however, would have a greater importance had this been a project on the self-identification of the "Left" or had the history of the Left not organized the experience of modern Greek history in its entirety. As there cannot be an examination or an understanding of modern Greek history outside the context of the relationship between the modern Greek state and the Greek "Left," there cannot be a space within that history where one can claim that the "Left" is not part of her or his particular, personal, and perhaps even private history. In that sense, this claim of "nativeness" becomes necessarily both expanded and constricted.

In many ways, conscious and unconscious, this research started a long time ago, maybe when I first started thinking about the question of the Left, about who is a Leftist, who is this creature who, as I was growing up, was constantly on the run, persecuted, hunted down, and, after I had grown up and the Left was made legal again, claimed a piece of the national fantasy, demanded to be included in the national imaginary, finally setting the terms of the debate by collapsing story and history into a narrative that could not separate the one from the other. But it is research that has other starting points and locations, or debates and disagreements that came up within the Left, which constantly tried to determine, for different reasons and through different rationales, who was a dissident, what it is to be a Marxist, who or what can claim to be the true Left (with or without quotation marks). In this sense, this work traces not only the processes by which the "dangerous" are constituted as such but also the ways in which one is delineated and identified as a Leftist, a process that is inevitably tautological and homological.

I am a trained anthropologist, a training that demands that even if I do not follow certain protocols, at least I must acknowledge them. So here I acknowledge the need for historical diagrams (you will find them in an appendix). But I also recognize the need to acknowledge the contentious and problematic delineations of structures of interiority and exteriority, the constant need to walk the dialectic between being here and being there, being simultaneously a daughter, a sibling, a niece, a friend, a colleague and a researcher.* There are no claims to privileged or interior knowledge and understandings in this

---

*I want to acknowledge Weston's brilliant points in articulating the difficulties that arise when we engage in fieldwork among colleagues, in her case in the context of the U.S. academy, in my case in the context of colleagues and friends in Greece, with whom I don't have a constant institutional engagement but with whom I am in constant intellectual and political exchange. See Weston, "The Virtual Anthropologist," in her *Long, Slow Burn.*

work, any more than would be staked out by anyone else conducting the
same research. What is claimed, though, and even this not as privileged or
interior but simply as particular, is a longitudinal experience of the events and
circumstances described here. There is a group of men and women who had
similar upbringings. I don't want to say the "same," but I will claim that they
are "selfsame" in that they animate and produce a fiction of the self as same.
The fact that we are not all of us, at all, at the same place in life now is only
another crude refutation of the determinism of history. The fact that there
were countless other groups of men and women with "similar" or even the
same upbringings is only a testament to the commonality of the experience
of history. Why it is that this history is only now rising up, and why it is only
now that it can be commonly acknowledged and, for some of us, equally
claimed, will become evident in the course of these pages.

17. As James Clifford argued in 1986, even
though such attitudes were "diminish-
ing," the "allegory of salvage [was] deeply
ingrained" in anthropological discourse,
even at a time when the discipline thought
of itself as not being concerned with the
"salvage business." As he wrote, this
allegory "is built into the conception and
practice of ethnography as a process of
writing, specifically of contextualization,"
because the transfer of orality to textuality
constitutes a re-enactment of the "structure of 'salvage'" (Clifford 1986: 112).

Anthropology is often accused of being in
the salvage business, of concerning itself with
dying populations, almost extinct, with trying
fervently to take down notes on histories that
will have no importance or meaning for anyone
after the person recounting them has died, that
all this is nothing more than Edmund Leach's
"butterfly collecting."[17] I found myself, in the
course of this research, in animating encounters,
engaging with people who had long thought of
themselves as intellectually and emotionally
dead, as having abandoned their psyche somewhere while waiting to die. One of those people
was my mother. From the time that I became an anthropologist, hence from
the time that there was a legitimacy in my asking questions about the past,
about herself, questions to which I ought to have had answers already available, known to me, her encounter with herself did not seem self-indulgent
and self-centered, and her stories and her history acquired some value beyond
one she understood as trivial in the sense of "telling stories to the children."
This woman, who has lived in the isolation of her dementia for several years
now, who cannot remember not only what she had for lunch but whether
my mother-in-law ever had children, this woman effortlessly reached deep
into her psyche and came back with names, places, circumstances, events
that finally explained to me that she is also part of this history that I am
researching; that the stories that she had been telling all these years, clipped,
fragmented, unfathomable, and almost clinical, were stories based on the
specificity of that experience. While I interviewed her in the summer of 2006
(and at one point in these interviews, when I intervened in her narrative to

ask for a clarification, she gave me the clarification, but not without saying, "Don't interrupt me, because, you know, my mind isn't all there, and I'll forget what I want to finish telling you"), her eyes had the spark that I remembered, but that I also saw in the eyes of so many older friends, acquaintances, and relatives whom I have been interviewing all these years. Though they would never have written their histories themselves, that spark validated the act of preserving those stories within them.

It is curious how ethnography and its practice, fieldwork, operate in the case of old friends, friends about whom you think you know almost everything there is to know in their biography: where they were born, where they grew up, what school they graduated from, what political organization they belonged to, whether they came from a Right or a Left family, etc. From the time many of these old friends found out what my research was about, a whole new dimension of their lives was opened up to me and for me, not one of transparency but one of epiphany. One after the other they would say: my father was in Makrónisos; or my mother sheltered that person; or (as with my mother) for three days I did not have a place to sleep at night because they were on my heels and no one could hide me.

These are not the stories of the heroic resistance against the Germans that I overheard and was told repeatedly when I was researching my first book, stories that my mother (primarily) but also my father (occasionally) would tell at the dinner table. These are stories that hurt so much, stories of persecution of Greeks by Greeks, of a fratricidal history, that have lain below the heroism and the commonality of Greek experience, and they span almost the entire twentieth century, certainly its first two-thirds. In the vortex of this tension, Resistance versus fratricide, is the reason why the tortures that the Gestapo and the SS used on the Greek Resistance fighters and partisans they caught were always named, even put in a grid of classification: "the torture of the falling drop" (where a drop of water was let fall rhythmically in the middle of the forehead of the tortured); "the torture of hot boiled eggs in the underarms"; "the torture of the ice block" (where the head of the tortured was put in a noose and she was made to stand on blocks of ice; as the ice melted the noose tightened around her neck); "the torture of the crown" (a medieval torture, where a metallic band was placed around the head and gradually tightened); beatings, whippings, burnings with hot irons. We children were never told of the sexual tortures, which also abounded. But we were never told of the tortures by the Greek state on the torture islands either, islands that had not been used as exile places since Roman times. The Greek tortures on the islands always remained only cartographically noted: "the *islands*" someone would say, and everyone knew exactly what and which islands these were and what had happened on them. Often sarcasm would appear in these mentions:

"they took him for a cruise of the islands" my mother said of the parents of a student of hers, who had been taken to Makrónisos.*

"Why are you asking me these questions?" my mother asked me.

"For the book I am writing," I said.

"What do I have to do with your book?" she asked again.

"It's about how you lived during the war, and the *emphýlios*, and afterwards, and under Metaxas," I said clumsily.

"Ah, how I lived during the *emphýlios*," she said, sighing, picking that one out, "only my little heart knows. To go by the Avérōf [Averof Prison]† and listen to their voices, as they were singing before they were executed. You know, they were singing 'Good-bye wretched world, good-bye sweet life [Parergon 1.11].' But you should be very careful writing about these things."

"Why?" I asked.

"Eh, you never know, time takes turns [*éhei o kairós gyrismata*], who knows what can happen," she said, meaning that there is still danger of political upset that could, potentially, lead to my demise.

I was given this advice repeatedly during my research, from both Left and Right, but not for the same reasons. Once I was talking with an uncle of mine who had been a very powerful person in the Special Security (*Eidikē Asfáleia*), the branch of the police put together for the management (i.e., persecution) of Communists in 1936 (not unlike the Bureau of Homeland Security that President George W. Bush put together after 9/11). We were discussing a particular person and whether he had participated, as some other people had told me, in the execution of a neighbor.

My uncle, who was in charge of prosecuting that particular case, was very cautious. "I don't recall him being a part of this particular operation," he said, "but why are you asking, again?"

I went through the same explanation about the book and the memory of the experience, things that I had said repeatedly to him.

"Well, he was not part of that operation, but since you are writing a book you should be very careful in what you write because, you know better than I do, *scripta manet* and there are still a lot of people alive from that time."

How can one go on, writing this dialectic as one is walking it? There are no clear interiorities and exteriorities here; at any given moment you are within and without; you are a comrade and you are not; you are a researcher and you are also the daughter who is called to make tea while the narrative is left

---

*Banac and Lukic both mention similar expressions used in reference to Goli Otok and Sveti Grgur, two of the exile and torture islands opened by Tito in 1949 for the re-education of Stalinists. As Banac notes, the two islands "have entered Yugoslavia's folklore as 'the Marble Isle,' 'Hawaii,' and/or 'Alcatraz'" (Banac 1989: 247; also Lukic 2007). *Goli Otok* has been translated as "Bare Island" (Djilas 1985: 235) or as "barren island" (Markovski 1984: ix).

†The main prison in Athens, where those on death row were kept and executed. It was on one of the major thoroughfares, where the building of the Supreme Court now stands.

hanging. "You'll get pummeled from every angle," many friends have warned me about this project. Doubtless. But I need to understand, and I need to explain what it means to be this generation of post–civil war Greeks, of how it has been possible for this generation, my generation, to go to demonstrations and rallies and demand "Americans Out of Greece For Ever" and accuse "Americans, Slaughterers of Peoples" while wearing blue jeans, listening to Bob Dylan, and reading Noam Chomsky and John Steinbeck.

This is an anthropography, again, for reasons I have set out elsewhere, as has Valentine Daniel, each independently of the other.* It is an anthropography because it has writing at its core, as an act of making public, of bring up to the point where discourse is located, the writing of *ánthropos*, of the human being as the only universality of experience that can be claimed, as its main location. And it is an anthropology and not an ethnography, as Daniel has rightly argued, because, given that the political and sociocultural experience of Greece is paradigmatic of the excesses of democracy, it applies beyond that specific location. It is, then, a concern with the human and with the excesses of sovereignty that makes this an anthropography. There is no recipe for this, James Boon has pointed out (Panourgia 2002); just a willingness to engage in its telling.

So, "What Is a Camp," Indeed?

"What is a camp?" asks Giorgio Agamben, only to answer, "the camp is the place in which the most absolute *condition inhumana* ever to appear on Earth was realized: this is ultimately all that counts for the victims as well as for posterity" (Agamben 2000: 37). But Agamben slips out of the historicity of the "camp," which he himself constructs, by moving almost effortlessly from the Spanish camps in Cuba in 1896, to the British camps for the Boers at the turn of the twentieth century (without any mention of the camps in the Andaman Islands), to the Nazi camps, noting that in the Spanish and the British camps, within the context of a colonial war, "entire populations were placed under the state of exception" (38). Of course, we know that "entire populations" were not placed under the state of exception. This generalization in fact occludes the process of exception. When the Mau Mau insurgency (and subsequent civil war) broke out in Kenya in 1950, only the nonloyalist Kikuyu were placed in camps. The descriptions that we have of the camps in Kenya are disturbingly similar to those from Makrónisos and Yáros, perhaps not surprisingly, if we keep in mind that both sets of camps were set up by the same colonialist logic and technologies of oppression and

---

*See Panourgia 1995 for a detailed discussion of "anthropology at home," "native anthropology," "ego-histoire," and other such categories of exclusion from mainstream anthropology; and Daniel 1996.

18. This is one of the most disturbing points made by Eichmann, if one can engage in such prioritizations. Wilhelm Kube, an old party member and *Generalkommisar* in occupied Russia, apparently wrote an outraged letter to Eichmann in December 1941, opposing the transport to Minsk of German Jews with the Iron Cross for "special treatment": "I am certainly tough and I am ready to help solve the Jewish question but people who come from our own cultural milieu are certainly something else than the native animalized hordes." Eichmann apparently admitted in court that he "knew that the *Einsatzgrouppen* had orders to kill but did not know that Jews from the Reich evacuated to the East were subject to the same treatment. This is what I did not know" (Arendt 1963: 96).

19. The camp at Goli Otok, in Yugoslavia, provides a sharp, even jagged, contrast to Agamben's position. Dr. Gojko Nikoliš, a retired general and former head of the army's Health Administration, has noted that what happened at Goli Otok was "much more amoral than the death penalty, more difficult to bear than a bullet or a guillotine blade. I am no pacifist; I am for the 'sword of the revolution'; let it cut where and when it is necessary. But I am a humanist and wish to remain one, at least to the extent of not being obliged to hold that the sharp edge of the sword ought to be exchanged for the systematic humiliation of people, in fact below

exclusion.* In Malaya, shortly after the establishment of the Makrónisos camp, we find the institution of similar camps from 1948 to 1960, where approximately six hundred Communist partisans were interned by the U.S. forces with the explicit aim of being re-educated.† In the case of the Boers, the families of fighters were placed in the camps, not the fighters themselves.‡ Even in the "final solution" under Nazism, a fine tuning of identity ascription took place, so that the Jews of the Reich would be separated from the rest of the arrested and interned Jewish population.[18]

What needs to be exposed, then, is not the totalization of the experience of the camps but the process (legal, conceptual, administrative) by which a specific segment of a population can be exempted.[19] The beginnings of this process of exception in Greece are narrated differently according to the political position of the narrators: each position produces the narrative of a different beginning. Nicos Poulantzas has noted that concentration camps are a particularly modern invention, since they concretize the same "spatial power matrix" as does national territory, thus making possible the notion of an "internal enemy" by internalizing "the frontiers of the national space at the heart of that space itself" (Poulantzas 2000: 105). Poulantzas correctly notes that concen-

---

*For two well-documented accounts of the insurgency and the establishment of the camps in Kenya, see Anderson 2005 and Elkins 2005. For a review of both Anderson and Elkins that seeks to produce a nuanced and segmentary account of the dynamics among the various groups that participated in the Kenya uprising and a critique of the hegemonic position that the Kikuyu resistance has acquired, see Ogot 2005. For a review that seeks to produce a textured account of the British colonial involvement and the complexity of the historicity both of the insurgence and of the technologies of counter-insurgency employed against it, see Mamdani 2006. The Kenyan insurgency had been amply documented before this new wave of historiographic writings. Kenyata 1971 is one such account, severely critiqued by Ogot, since Kenyata managed to procure a leading political career for himself. For an indicative, but certainly not exhaustive, bibliography of such accounts by survivors, see Ogot 2005.

†See Clutterbuck, 1963, 1966, and 1973.

‡Hitler was taken with the paradigm of the British camps for the Boers. In September 1920, he said: "In South Africa, England deported 76,000 Boer women and children to concentration camps, thus forcing the men to return to their homes" (Tuchel 1991: 36, quoting Jäckel and Kuhn 1980: 233, quoted in Marcuse 2001: 408n.8).

tration camps are constructed in order to hold "anti-nationals" within the national space.

Hyper-legality

The civil war (*emphýlios*) in Greece, which followed the Second World War and lasted from 1946 to 1949, provided a pretext for the systematic use of camps by Greek governments starting in 1947. The camps both exploded and expanded an already-existing concept of exile that had been used under the dictatorship of Ioannis Metaxas, from 1936 to 1941, and that had been prepared for through small-scale exiles and a number of legislative gestures by the parliamentary democratic governments of the mid 1920s, specifically, the Papanastasiou government of 1924. All this, in turn, rested on the 1871 Law Concerning Brigandage and the Prosecution of Their Relatives. This law provided the death penalty for brigands and the *ektopise* (Parergon 1.12) of their families and "everyone *suspected* of providing coverage" for them.[20] The law was introduced as a means of managing the problem of brigands in the countryside, especially after the Délesi Affair, when a group of English travelers were taken hostage by a group of brigands, who demanded ransom. The government refused, and the hostages were executed. Later the brigands were captured, tried, and executed, and their heads were publicly displayed.*

The law remained intact and was not amended until the democratic government of Anastasios Papanastasiou introduced a Legislative Decree (*Nomothetikó Diátagma*),[21] the 19–21 April/1924, whereby it decreed the insti-

the zero point." To this, Ivo Banac points out, the defenders of the system respond that "if there had been no Goli Otok, the whole of Yugoslavia would have been a Goli Otok" (Banac 1989: 253). Matthew Mestrovic, in his Introduction to Venko Markovski's *Goli Otok, The Island of Death: A Diary in Letters*, attributes this assessment to a commentator from Zagreb, Milika Sundic (Markovski, 1984: ix). This response, which seems to anticipate Agamben's position, is precisely what makes Agamben's totalization so much more problematic.

---

20. Here we can see local understandings of kinship (*syggeneia*) playing into the production of a local theory of danger. In Greece (as is evidenced in literature and ethnography) the family has always been thought of as the most intimate and private space in which the negotiation between the sovereign and the subject takes place. But it is also where the possibility of mobility becomes actualized, as family members engage in a simultaneous process of proximity (by performing the act of belonging) and distance (primarily through exogamy and migration, both internal and international) with regard to it. With this law, however, family and kinship collapse, denying any possibility of mobility from the family and treating kinship like a sort of unity of essence, a conceptual and analytical DNA for producing deviant, criminal, dangerous, and antisocial behavior. Certainly the law originally aimed to cut lines of support for brigands, but as it was taken up into the later legislative network, it came to invest kinship with almost metaphysical dimensions rather than operate pragmatically to contain crime.

---

21. I have translated literally the terminology for a form of legislation that seems to

*See Herzfeld 1982a on the Délesi Affair. For a very nuanced analysis of the issue of social brigandage in Greece and its relationship to the tradition of agrarian revolt and the development of the nationalist state see Damianakos 2005. On the impact that brigandage continued to have in the development of policing and the establishment of the gendarmerie see Mazower 1997. On the question of brigandage as political act see Hobsbawm 1965.

be unique to the Greek legal landscape. The executive branch can produce a decree (and order) that can then institute a law without being passed through the deliberative process of Parliament. It is not, strictly speaking, an executive order because it does produce a legal act within the juridical framework. See Alivizatos 1981.

22. The Greek term is *Epitropai Demosias Asphaleias*. *Epitropes* (noun, plural) is translated as "committees"; *Demosias* (adjective, feminine genitive) is translated as "public"; *Asphaleias* (noun, feminine genitive) can be translated as either "security" or "safety." I have opted for "security," for the following reasons. The term *safety* does not conjure up the official contours that the term *security* does (especially after 9/11 in the ominous U.S. Department of Homeland Security). But I also want to keep the genealogy of *security*, which can be traced back to the French Revolution.

23. Two constitutive events contributed to the construction of the Left in general, and the Communist Party in particular, as enemy and suspect. The first was the internationalist position that the Communist Party took against the First World War, and the second was the support for self-determination and sovereignty demanded by certain circles for the territories in Macedonia newly acquired as a result of the Balkan Wars of 1912 to 1913. If we keep in mind the fact that Franz Boas was censured by the American Anthropological Association in 1918 for taking a similarly internationalist approach toward the First World War (a censure that was not lifted until 2004), then the position of the Greek state acquires an international context.

tution of Committees of Public Security.[22] These committees were charged with the administration of *ektopismós* by first identifying the suspicious elements in a community and then deciding on a place and duration of exile. The dictatorship of Pangalos (1925–26) introduced an amendment to this law (article 2, paragraph 7) whereby the 1871 Law Concerning Brigandage was specifically applied to the persecution and prosecution of the Communist Party.[23] It amended the provision for the *ektopismós* of "everyone suspected of harboring brigands" to simply "everyone suspected [*pantós hypóptou*]." Both 19–21 April/1924 and Pangalos's amendment retained the principle of administrative *ektopismós*, effected by the Committees of Public Security without intervention by the court system. A new law, however, Law 4229/1929, which came to be known as *Idiónymon* and which was introduced in Parliament by a well-known liberal democratic parliamentarian, Eleutherios Venizelos, shifted the weight of the production of the dangerous person from the executive (the Committees) to the legislative (the courts). The law, without mentioning Communism or Marxism specifically (thus allowing the broadest interpretation of its articles), decreed that those ideas that have at their basis the violent overturn of the political system constitute a danger "to the quiet [*dia ten hēsyhian*]" of the citizens and ought to be "preemptively prosecuted [*prolēptikē diōxis*]," since the pursuit of their objectives by any means (not only violent attempts to change of the political system, but also nonviolent means, such as the development, dissemination, and application of theories and ideas) constituted a unique crime (an Idiónymon crime, a crime that had no parallel, no precedent, no affinity to any other), punishable by imprisonment and *ektopismós* (Parergon 1.13). The Idiónymon cancelled the already-existing administrative *ektopismós* and turned the process over to the court system, introducing judicial *ektopismós*. (This was presumably a more democratic measure, since a court decision theoretically allowed for a process of appeal through the legal system, although such appeals were rarely heard. Even when they were, the decision of the committees was rarely changed.)

Law 5174/1931 reinstated the Bill of Law of 1926 and reinstituted the Committees of Public Security, and the Bill of Law of 12–16 July/1932 decreed the
ektopismós of those harboring brigands (*lēstotróphoi*) and all those resisting
Law 4229 (the Idiônymon).

An Obligatory Law (AN) was introduced by the dictator Georgios Kondyles
on 21–23 October/1935 and 19–20 December/1935, seeking to establish the
parallel operation of both administrative and judicial *ektopismós*. The 21–23
gave the Minister of Security and the Minister of Interior Affairs the power
to effect exile on the recommendation of the committees, or even on their
own initiative. The 19-20 ordered the parallel operation of both modalities
of exile. Obligatory Law (AN) 117/1936 replaced the Idiônymon, concerning the persecution of Communism and the results of the dissemination of
its ideas, and it was supported by AN 375/1936, concerning espionage. This
was the law most commonly invoked by the prosecution in seeking sentences
for Communists, even when the charge of espionage could not be proven.
Sentencing for 375/1936 had a very narrow range: the lightest sentence was
life imprisonment and the harshest was the death penalty. The law was carried out only by military tribunals, even when the accused were not military
personnel. It was valid during both war and peace, and being a special law, it
transcended both common and military penal laws. On top of this juridical
nexus, AN 1075/1938, "regarding security measures for the social order and
the protection of the citizens," codified the articles of 117/1936, reiterated the
criminality of disseminating Communist ideas, and set the punishment for
transgressing the law: at least three months of imprisonment followed by exile
from six to twelve months. AN 1075/1938 also set parameters for the systematic breakup of Communist organizations and the parallel establishment
of incentives for cadres to leave the party and, through a process of reform
(*anánēpsis*), become members of bourgeois society again.

Particularly important is the decision of the Council of State, which decreed,
in its decisions 763 and 765, that "the clustering of the exiled (*ektopisménōn*)
under disciplined existence at the building of the old prison in Akronauplia
does not constitute deprivation of their freedom." The 1871 law was reinstated from July to December 1945 and from August 1950 to August 1951,
and the Bill of Law 4 May/1946, introduced by the democratic government
of Konstantinos Tsaldares, reinstated administrative *ektopismós* by establishing Committees of Public Security at each prefecture. The Third Resolution
of Parliament of 18/6/1946 and Obligatory Law 509/27/12/1947 introduced
military *ektopismós*, which gave complete power to military authorities to
effect any *ektopismós* they deemed necessary. Both the resolution and the law
instituted lengthy sentences for disseminating ideas. Article 15, paragraph 2
of the Third Resolution ordered that such sentences range from temporary or
prolonged incarceration to the death penalty and made provisions for exile
as additional punishment if the sentence ordered by the court was a light one

(i.e., included only imprisonment). Article 7, paragraph 2 of the AN 509/1947 gave the military courts authority to change an order of imprisonment into one of exile for an equal time. Legislative Decree 392/18/8/1947 changed the temporal limit of exile from twelve months (as had been decreed by 19-21/4/1924) to twenty-four months and decreed obligatory police surveillance of the exiled and heavy punishments for even temporary transport from the place of exile. AN 511/31/12/1947 (put in effect by Law 539/3/2/1948) organized and systematized the institution of "disciplined existence" and transformed all places of exile into concentration camps. It imposed: (1) regular appearances before the executive power, (2) a ban on transport beyond a specific radius around the camp, (3) curfew, (4) declaration of any change of address and unexpected house searches, (5) a ban on the establishment of clubs, societies, etc., (6) a ban on the circulation of printed or handwritten material, (7) a ban on the pursuit of one's profession, (8) a monetary allowance, (9) search of all packages, (10) censorship of correspondence. Legislative Decree 687/7/5/1948 gave the committees the authority to extend the length of exile indefinitely. Legislative Decrees 21/2/1949 and 9/2/1950 lifted martial law, and Decree 1/1/1952 restored the Constitution.

The restoration of the Constitution did not bring with it the expected end of executions. That came only in the wake of international outcry over the execution of Nikos Beloyiannis. Beloyiannis, known as the "man with the carnation" after a portrait of him done by Picasso, was a lawyer and member of the KKE (Kommounistiko Komma Ellados; Communist Party of Greece), who had been in and out of prison and exile since the Metaxas dictatorship and had participated in the civil war. Beloyiannis was accused of treason and executed, along with Nikos Kaloumenos, Demetres Batses, and Elias Argyriades. The execution, the last political execution in Greece, took place on Sunday, March 30, 1952. "Not even the Germans carried out executions on Sundays," wrote Maria Rezan, a journalist and wife of the undersecretary to the prime minister, Andreas Iosef, who was the only member of the government to resign on account of the executions (Rezan 2006: 282). To judge from political accounts at the time, later political analyses, and small talk recorded during interviews that I conducted in 2004, the general feeling was and still is that the execution took place because "the Americans" (an entity not as spectral and phantasmatic as such an invocation might initially appear[24]) wanted to replace Prime Minister Plasteras with Field Marshal Alexandros Papagos. The replacement was successful. The Plasteras government fell, and Papagos became the new prime minister.

24. This assessment is explicitly mentioned by Andreas Iosef, a person who was as far away from Communism and the Left as one could be, having been a Chites (by his own account). His article entitled "You Don't Kill a Human for His Political Beliefs," in Kouloglou, ed. 2006, is a testament to his political and personal integrity. The American Ambassador to Greece, John Peurifoy, participated at that time in the sessions of the Greek National Security Council.

Two days before the execution, Iosef mentions, there was a meeting of the small council of ministers, among whom were Iosef and Minister of the Interior Konstantinos Rendis. By Iosef's account (2006: 286), the discussion concerned the outcome of the trial and what course of action ought to be taken. Rendis, according to Iosef, posed the question of executions by asking, "How many should we send to the firing squad? Four or six?" Iosef responded that these were executions that they were discussing, human lives, only to receive a "murderous [*foniko*]" look from Rendis. Iosef resolved to resign if the executions were to take place, and he did so when they did.

The executions apparently took everyone by surprise, not least of all the government itself, with a handful of exceptions. The minister of justice must have known about it, and officials at the American embassy, especially Ambassador John Peurifoy, must have known, as well.[25] At the last moment, King Paul rejected the granting of a stay of execution, but since it was Saturday, everyone was expecting that the weekend might produce something positive. But the executions did take place, despite the fact that it was a Sunday, despite the government's promises that there would be no more executions, and despite assurances given to the lawyers for the defendants that the executions would be stayed. Moreover, there had been an international outcry about the staged and prearranged trial, convictions, and sentences, and for Demetres Batses a morally hefty bribe had been paid. According to Iosef, the information about the bribe came from an independent source: a well-respected journalist, Kostas Triantafyllides, had telephoned him and said that he had a message from Papagos to be transmitted immediately to Prime Minister Plasteras. When Iosef and Triantafyllides met later in the day, the latter revealed that the previous day Minister of the Interior Rendis had violated (*viase*: meaning "raped")[26] Batses's wife Lilian, while a high-ranking policeman named Panopoulos photographed the whole incident from behind a glass closet. Iosef says that he did not believe Triantafyllides's account (and for good reason, probably, since it was coming from Papagos to Plasteras) but Batses's wife confirmed

25. In 1950, Kevin Andrews described John Peurifoy as "one of the architects of the hard-line policy toward Greece gradually formulating in the State Department, that was soon to see the establishment of Marshal Alexander Papagos as Prime Minister at the head of a strong Right-wing government" (Andrews, 1980: 294). Constantine Tsoucalas mentions that in March 1952 Peurifoy intervened in the Greek parliament's discussion concerning the electoral system that would be used for the upcoming elections. Most politicians favored proportional representation. Prime Minister Plasteras ("either through senile miscalculation or in a gesture of throwing down the gauntlet," Tsoucalas comments) favored a majority system. Peurifoy then publicly declared, "'The US Government believes that the re-establishment of the simple proportional system, with its unavoidable consequences of the continuation of governmental instability, would have destructive results upon the effective utilization of U.S. aid to Greece. The US Embassy feels itself obliged to make its support publicly known for the patriotic position of Prime Minister Plasteras on this subject.' Lest this should not prove to be enough, he also threatened behind the scenes to suspend US aid if the proportional system were accepted" (Tsoucalas 1969: 125).

26. An interesting and disturbing set of meanings needs to be interrogated here.

First, one might ask whether the violation of Lilian Batses by Rendis was indeed a "rape," since she had agreed in advance to the sexual encounter in exchange for her husband's life. Such a question, however, would be misplaced. Rendis was on multiple levels in a position of power over Batses: he was the minister of the interior and held in his hand (potentially, if he and his government had not been under the thumb of the American Embassy) the power to stay Batses's execution; he was considerably older than Lilian Batses; and he was a man, in 1952, when rape had a less inclusive reference, if it was recognized at all. To question whether this was a case of rape would do injustice both to Lilian Batses's desperation and to the structures of gender, class, and power inequalities securely in place at that particular time. But there is also a violation of a different order: Rendis did not keep his word. He violated his own word as he was engaging in the violation of Batses (not to mention the more general violation of the ideas of justice and national sovereignty.)

it the day before the execution, saying that despite the fact that she had kept the terms that Minister Rendis had made with her in exchange for saving her husband, Rendis would still have her husband executed (Iosef 2006: 287).

All this indicated that the executions would not take place. But they did, to everyone's astonishment. They happened at 4:10 A.M. on a Sunday morning, before sunrise, so that the headlights of police and military vehicles had to be used to light up the place of execution. One of those taken by surprise was the chief justice of the special emergency military court, whose daughter, my older friend Zina, remembers the moment clearly. "We were at a gala on Saturday evening," she said in 2006, going back almost fifty years. "All four of us: my father, my mother, my sister, and myself. I think it was a gala ball of the military academy cadets, and it seemed that everybody was there. It was a very important ball, because we were dressed in evening gowns and my father had his most formal uniform on. At some point, fairly late, someone came up to my father and whispered something in his ear. My father, I remember it so clearly, as if it were now, turned to my mother, whispered something in her ear, and then got up and left. I asked my mother what he had said, and she replied that he had just told her that, if he wasn't back by the time we were ready to go home, we should go on without him and he would come home on his own. We left the gala, went home, and the next morning saw on the front page of the paper the announcement of the Beloyiannis execution. And there it was, too, a photograph of my father descending from the jeep that had taken him to the execution site."

"What was it like," I asked, "to live in a household where your father had been so deeply involved with so many executions, so many trials, so many sentences, so deep a belief in understanding what was right and what was wrong?"

Zina shrugged her shoulders and closed her eyes in a gesture of bafflement. "We never knew what it was like for him," she said. "Sometimes I would approach my mother with the question. She would sigh and say, 'Only I, who sleep with him every night, only I know . . . how he tosses and turns and moans . . . ,' but she never finished the phrase. Did she mean that he felt remorse? ambivalence? fear? I don't know," Zina said.

We were standing in her kitchen, and I could almost see the weight she was bearing. She moved her hand as if to shift the moment or dispel the memory. "Let's have breakfast," she said.

With the reasoning that the insurgency had not ended, the state, using the *Trite Syntetagméne Exousia*, the legislative branch of the executive power, managed to keep all who had been exiled at their places of exile. The Council of State decided, in its decision 724/1954, that the exiled were being detained legally because "the insurgency has not ended, since the legislator has not declared it ended with an explicit Legislative Decree."* Nearly a decade later, Legislative Decree 4234/30/7/1962 abolished the decisions and decrees that allowed for the indefinite *ektopismós*. At the same time, it retained *ektopismós* as an institution for the persecution of ideas, and it extended its twenty-four-month duration for an additional twenty-four months. The requisition for the extension would be submitted by the police, who were obligated to produce articles of proof for the necessity of the extension being requested.

The law that underlay all this and made possible the persecution of the politically radical was Obligatory Law DEK/1912, "On the State of Emergency," drafted during the First Balkan War of 1912 to 1914. This law brought all state power into the hands of the military and made it possible for ordinary, non-military citizens to be indicted in military tribunals both for transgressions of the penal code and for military insubordination. According to article 91 of the Greek Constitution (prior to revisions that followed the general plebiscite of 1974 and changed the form of government from parliamentary monarchy to parliamentary representative democracy), the king had the administrative discretion, in consultation with the Council of Ministers, to suspend specific articles of the Constitution,[27] as well as to institute special military tribunals in case of war, general mobilization of the army, or concerns about the stability and internal order of the country. The Obligatory Law required endorsement of a state of emergency by Parliament. In the event that Parliament was not in session, it was to be convened within ten days. The decision to declare a state of emergency could not be extended beyond the war that made its invoking imperative or beyond two months after the eruption of internal strife without the validation of Parliament. It was often used interchangeably with 375/1936, the law concerning espionage, in the legal prosecution of the Left. Thus Communists and Leftists in general were accused either of inciting internal strife or of engaging in espionage. These laws all remained intact through the junta of 1967 to 1974. They were abolished only with the restoration of parliamentary democracy in 1974, so that every government between 1924 and 1974 could make use of them.

"In detaining some prisoners indefinitely, the state appropriates for itself

27. Articles 5, 6, 8, 10, 11, 12, 14, 20, 95, 97, all referring to civil liberties and the responsibilities of the citizen and the government toward the country.

*Decision 724/1954 Supreme Court, published in the *Gazette of Greek Jurists*, issue 21 (1954): 1087, quoted in Anonymous 2003: 2.23n.2.

a sovereign power that is defined over and against existing legal frameworks, civil, military, and international," Judith Butler writes (2004: 57). But the Greek state both disregarded existing legal frameworks and at the same time, by introducing new laws, demonstrated recognition of a need for the performativity of the law, a need to articulate in law the epiphenomenal structure that makes sovereignty and the state complicitous and necessary to each other's existence. The state, in other words, announced its recognition of the fact that it cannot exist without the law (even a law that is performed, perforated, disarticulated, duplicitous, fabricated).

Sunset

"What sort of legal innovation is the notion of indefinite detention?" asks Butler, as she contemplates the indefinite extension of sovereign power and legal jurisdiction in the United States post 9/11 (2004: 51). The legislative net that I have just described shows that indefinite detention is not a "legal innovation" that appeared with the Bush administration but has a history that reaches back to a space and place used as a laboratory for neo-colonialism at the outset of the imperial expansion of U.S. power after the Second World War: namely, Greece after the Truman Doctrine and under the Marshall Plan.[28] This legislative net produced a system that transformed inaccessible corners of Greece into a web of fenced and strictly disciplined spaces of existence. In the early years of the twentieth century, the only securely inaccessible places were the thousands of islands strewn throughout the Greek seas.

Amorgos, Kea, Thera, Gavdos, Corfu, Folegandros, Hagios Eustratios (Ai-Stratis), Anafi, Paros, Andros, the North and South Aegean, the Ionian Sea, the Cretan Sea, the Libyan Sea, the Saronic Gulf: some of these places are now cloaked with the glamour of leisure, wealth, ostentation, and the kitsch of the nouveaux riches (Greek and non-Greek alike); some are now only an airplane or a hovercraft hop away from Athens; some are still quiet, requiring a ten- or twelve-hour ride on a thirty- or forty-year-old boat; others, in the years before the explosion of tourism that came with the junta of 1967 to 1974, could require days of travel. Some, such as Thera, Amorgos, Folegandros, Ai-Stratis, and

28. Greece marks the beginning of the cold war. As Michael McClintock notes, quoting Lt. Col. Robert Selton of the U.S. Army, the Greek Civil War constitutes "the formal declaration of the cold war" between the "Free World . . . and the forces of communism" (McClintock 1992: 11). It was on the occasion of the beginning of the civil war in Greece that President Truman articulated his famous (or infamous) doctrine about the necessity for intervention on behalf of other countries to prevent infiltration by ideologies originating elsewhere. As McClintock notes, as of November 1961, starting with an initial allotment in 1947 of $400 million through the Marshall Plan, Greece was granted $3.4 billion for postwar reconstruction, out of which only $1.2 billion went to economic aid. The rest was used for military aid and defense support, including the establishment and maintenance of the concentration camps and the containment of Communism. (See Selton 1966: 68; McClintock 1992: 466n.31.) James Becket

Anafi, could be reached only once a fortnight in the summer, once a month in winter. Ships and naval vessels could not dock at their minuscule ports, which were constructed only for fishing boats. They would remain "at road" offshore, while service boats ferried supplies, people, letters, and sometimes books (which were strictly forbidden in the camps but nonetheless were regularly smuggled in).

Surveillance of the exiles by the gendarmerie on those islands exceeded the act of policing. After all, in these places no criminal act ever took place, and only the presence of the exiles made surveillance necessary. Everything considered a human and not an animal activity was forbidden: reading books or newspapers, contacting local residents, taking a stroll outside the village, staying out past sunset, listening to the radio.[29]

notes about the Truman Doctrine that "Greece was the first country of the Old World to experience the full impact of *Pax Americana*. Aid and advisors of every kind arrived: agronomists, soldiers, teachers, spies, businessmen, diplomats" (Becket 1970: 12). For an incisive analysis of the beginnings of the cold war in reference to the civil war, see Gerolymatos 2004.

29. Venko Markovski, interned at Goli Otok in Yugoslavia between 1956 and 1961, mentions similar conditions of everyday existence: "Everything is forbidden at Goli Otok. It is forbidden to look around, to listen, and, of course, to speak. Even sighing is forbidden us" (1984: 47).

In 1948, the director of one of the American schools in Greece, an American philologist, took a trip to one of those islands, Thera, to visit a newly excavated site. An old acquaintance of hers had been exiled there, an architect who had already served time on Makrónisos. She saw him sitting alone at the coffee house in the main square late in the afternoon and she went up to talk to him, since they had known each other in Athens. She had lost track of him completely, and her surprise at seeing him was immense. They sat down and started talking. After she got up to leave, on her way to the house where she was staying, a gendarme stopped her. "Why were you talking to him?" he asked. She said that she had known him as a colleague, that she was an American, and that she was surprised to see him here, so she had stopped to say hello. The gendarme said that he would have to file a report about what he had witnessed. She was a woman, talking to an exiled Communist, and there were only two categories available for a report: he could write that she was either a Communist or a prostitute. Which would she prefer? "Prostitute," she said, and that's how he wrote his official report: so-and-so has been visited by a prostitute.*

We know the terrible effects of a combination of civil war, concentration camps, and oppressive and authoritarian governments on the everyday lives of citizens. We know of the dismantled families, the maimed relationships, the broken bodies, the poverty, the devastated infrastructure. A civil war, however,

---

*I am indebted to Hara Tzavella-Evjen for this story about a common acquaintance.

has lasting effects that are not so immediately apparent. It produces psycho-pathologies, mistrust, and resentment in addition to economic and political devastation. There is nothing civil in a "civil war." In such a war, siblings fight against each other, children are tortured in front of their parents, parents are killed in front of their children. When it ends, no one can get up, dust off his clothes, and shake hands. The effects are lived for generations, long after the war has ended and decades after the winners and losers have settled down (curiously comfortably) in their respective positions.[30] The Greek paradigm acquires particular importance here, because in Greece, though the civil war ended in 1949, its effects are only now being discussed. The case of Greece gives us the texture of the *longue durée* of this particular historical experience, sitting, as it does, on the cusp of cultural and political memory.

In Greece, the collective experience of history seems to be located in a deep-seated mistrust of the political sphere, a mistrust that can be traced by turning over the folds of recent social and cultural history when it is viewed as an anthropological problem. In the many interviews I have conducted with people who lived in the camps, their families, and their wider network of friends, this historical experience manifested itself along a double axis. One pole of this axis is factual: the reintroduction and expansion of the camps in Greece from 1947 to 1958 (or, even, 1963) and from 1967 to 1974. The second is discursive: the biomedical metaphors that pervade what is said about dangerous and suspicious persons.

In terms of public understanding, the watershed event organizing this experience of history was the Second World War. In Greece, the war segued into the period of White Terror (1945–46), in which the Resistance fighters against the German occupation (*Katohé*) were persecuted by paramilitary gangs, whereas the collaborators of the Germans were rewarded with promotions, positions in the much-coveted public sector, and pensions.[31] This period of terror led Greece into its civil war (1946–49), which, in turn, led to the reopening of the concentration camps (1947–58). The effects of both the civil war and the camps were solidified by the Junta (1967–74), and were felt until the beginning of the 1980s.[32] But if the

30. In Greece, the side that lost the civil war, the Left, has engaged in a prolific production of meanings and symbolic constellations concerning the "generation of the defeat" (as it has come to be known), from literature to historiography. Nothing is monolithic, and the "defeat," as a locus of symbolic subjectivity, is not felt by the Left in its entirety. Rather, it tends to characterize (again, not collectively) the political subjectivities of what is known in Greece as the Revitalized Left, or what we would generally call Eurocommunism (namely, Communism with a decidedly European orientation, deeply critical of Stalinism and Sovietism and adhering to the "historical compromise" between the Communist and the bourgeois political parties that had been developed by Enrico Berlinguer in Italy as the new strategy for the preservation of Communist ideology and the possibility of participation in government).

31. *Collaborators* denotes people who collaborated with the occupying forces against the occupied country. The Greek term is *synergates*, which after the war ended and *synergates* were tried in courts of law changed to *dosilogoi*, meaning those who had to give an account of themselves and their actions.

32. Certainly we can say that the effects are still being felt today, if not on the level of

world war publicly organized the experience of Greek history, so that, in a gesture of national and statist colonization of the experience of history (after the total defeat of the Left), the heroism of the Resistance came to be acknowledged as a collective one, the civil war was the unspoken but deeply felt trauma of Greek history. Like all civil wars, it did not just erupt one day, nor did it end on the date that the calendar says it did.[33] (The civil war has always lasted its length and a day.) *I don't like these kinds of statements*

I am writing this in mid-morning on August 4, 2006. Early in the morning our friend and neighbor Eleni came by. It is the anniversary of the deaths of her husband and my uncle. They died years apart, but since they were close friends we always remember the anniversaries together. Eleni joked, "All the 4th Augustans [*Tetartoavgoustianoi*; "followers of the ideology of August 4," the locution that came to represent Metaxas's totalitarian ideology] die on the same day [*mazi*]."

Eleni's daughter and my cousin (my uncle's son) cracked the same joke as we were leaving the cemetery after my uncle's funeral. "All the *juntikoi* [supporters of a junta] die the same day," they quipped about their fathers, even though the two deaths were some fifteen years apart. August 4 (*Tetártē Avgoústou*) is also the anniversary of the Metaxas dictatorship or, as Metaxas himself was fond of calling it, the Third Hellenic Civilization. The allusion to the Third Reich, however, is as incorrect and misguided as it is obvious (Parergon 1.14). Despite the fact that Metaxas would have liked to have created a system closer to his own ideology and akin to Nazism (and we will see what steps he took toward that), as he conceded at some point, his regime was closer to Salazar's in Portugal (Parergon 1.15).

Metaxas's dictatorship was not the first ever to appear in Greece (there had been Plasteras's coup in 1922, Pangalos's in 1925–26, and Kondylis's in 1926),* but we can safely argue that Metaxas was the first to try to enforce totalitarian thought in Greece in the sense that he was the first dictator to understand

the experience of history by its actors, then at the level of historical, anthropological, and political epistemologies that are currently being debated. The debates among a number of researchers who are trying to rehabilitate the Right and apologize for its actions during the occupation and the civil war, a number of aging Leftists who are attempting to assume a critical positionality toward the period, and a newer hermeneutical approach that attempts to dispel the attempts of the former and contextualize those of the latter is instructive here. For a whole year this debate raged publicly through inserts in the three major dailies in Greece (*To Vema, Eleutherotypia, Ta Nea*), and in the end the exchanges were published separately.

33. Dionyssis Savvópoulos has marked the difference between the two periods as lived historical experience in his sad, introspective, but ultimately conciliatory verses about Greece:

*ki an ston emfýlio
sernótan san tsoúla
sten katohê
êtan lyménē psychoúla*

even if during the civil war
she was dragging herself
like a whore
during the occupation
her little psyche was unleashed

---

*See Mazower 1997, which traces the engagement with anticommunism and the specter of fear that Kondylis and Pangalos created in Greece prior to the Metaxas dictatorship. See also Marketos 2006.

34. Both Hannah Arendt and Cornelius Castoriadis succumbed to the seduction of the cold war imaginary in their disappointment at what became of the "True Existing Socialism" of the Soviet Union under Stalin and, eventually, in all of Eastern Europe.

35. I use the Greek term *psyche* instead of its common translation "soul" in order to avoid the temptation to read into it any Christian meanings. *Psyche*, in Greek, predates Christianity by many centuries. It has been picked up by Christianity (without linguistic change, nevertheless) in a (failed, I would say) act of appropriation and has been the object of serious theologico-philosophical debate in Greece for the past twenty years. The failure of Christianity to fully appropriate the meaning of *psyche* is nowhere more evident than in the Greek expression *ki auta psyche ehoun* ("even animals have a *psyche*").

36. The "Greeks" of Metaxas were a rather nebulous and forced category of persons who resided within the geographical parameters of Greece and subscribed to a common imaginary that had as its points of orientation classical antiquity (curiously enough, including *both* ancient Greece *and* ancient Rome) and Byzantium. From such a scheme, obvious and natural exclusions were readily constructed: the ethnic minorities, primarily in the newly acquired territories in the north, in Macedonia and Thrace, to the extent that the use of local languages and idioms was strictly prohibited even within the private sphere (see Karakasidou 1997). Curiously enough, given his hellenocentric and christianocentric ideology, Metaxas never developed (nor did he ever express) a racist or anti-Semitic discourse.

that social change can be effected only when the totality of the sociopolitical structures manage to change the totality of the sociopolitical imaginary.[34] Metaxas, by all accounts, was not simply interested in political power (as had been true of all previous political formations in Greece), instead, he was interested in form(ulat)ing whatever it was that he understood as "the Greek psyche"[35] and "the Greek mind." Metaxas held that both these entities, psyche and mind (*psyche* and *pneuma*), ought to constitute a monolithic,* monadic, singular articulation of an imaginary shared by all "Greeks,"[36] an imaginary that started in Greek antiquity, extended through Rome, and developed into the Byzantine Empire. The specter of imperialism hovering over the Metaxas project is not a rhetorical one. It underlies a certain imperialist totalitarianism in his thought, despite the fact that he never had any desires or plans for territorial expansion. His was an imperialism of the mind and the psyche, an imperialism as aggressive as it was brutal, aimed at totally annihilating the citizen by demanding his mind. A citizen could not placate this project through mere compliance. It required not only total submission but total agreement. It could not tolerate or absorb dissent and disagreement but demanded complete agreement and subscription.

Metaxas conceptualized, and tried to enact, a total reorganization of the sociopolitical and cultural landscape of Greece that would, in effect, re-educate Greek society. Education and political indoctrination, he reasoned, were the two nodal and structural points on which his project would rest. One of the first acts of the Metaxas Office of Propaganda was to invite Joseph Goebbels (the secretary of propaganda of the Nazi Party) to visit Greece in September

---

*Lefort reminds us that: "at the foundation of totalitarianism lies the representation of the People-as-One. It is denied that division as constitutive of society" (1986: 297).

1936, merely a month and a half after the dictatorship had come to power.

In November of the same year, Metaxas, following Hitler's example, auspiciously after Goebbels's visit, was the first Greek politician to create a youth organization, the EON (National Organization of Youth). The organization was divided into two groups, the *skapaneis* (literally, the "toilers," those who work the land with an axe, *skapánē*), comprising children from six to thirteen years old, and the *phalangites*, adolescents and young adults from fourteen to twenty-five. By October 1939, through the systematic coercion and terrorization of the country, EON numbered seven hundred and fifty thousand members. Their uniform was distinctive, with blue shirt and riding trousers, white tie, white gaiters and belt, and a little two-pointed hat. The EON absorbed, forcibly, the Greek Boy Scouts,[37] one of the acts that brought Metaxas to a point of friction with young Prince Paul, whose pet project was the Boy Scouts. In the end the prince became the head of EON, just as his young bride, Frederica, had been a member of Hitler's Youth. The stated objective of EON was the patriotic education of Greek youth, so EON administratively belonged to the Ministry of Education. Metaxas himself took charge of the Ministry of Education in order to oversee the project of re-educating the youth, a youth that he called his "pride [*to kamari mou*]."* As in Hitler's Nazism, belonging to EON was not a matter of choice, or, rather, it was not altogether a matter of choice (indeed, in the end it was not a matter of choice at all). As Manolis Anagnostakis, the famous Greek poet of the Left,[38] has noted, he joined EON, against strong objections from his family, who were all Centrists, because in the beginning EON gave away free tickets to movies and football matches. But his case was not

37. This matter resurfaced during the junta. At some point the junta established its own youth organization, the Alkimoi (literally, "those at the height of their youth"). At a large party given by my parents, I once overheard my mother (the eldest of all present and the only one who had experienced EON) telling the guests (all of whom had children the same age as my sister and myself) that maybe they should all register us with the Scouts so that we would not be conscripted into the Alkimoi. Such conscription never took place during the junta, since the junta was never the totalitarian regime that the Metaxas dictatorship was, but rather a brutal, authoritarian stratocracy haphazardly constituted of colonels interested in the exercise of power. Their lack of a project (in the sense that Metaxas had one) did not go unnoticed by the old Metaxians. "Those were shadow puppets [*karaghiozides*, meaning literally the figures of the shadow puppet theater in Greece and metaphorically inept, uneducated, but cunning]," one of my interlocutors said. (He had been a Chites himself during the German occupation). A more self-reflexive and self-critical appraisal of the junta was the common saying "Everyone has the junta that befits them." On EON, see Liakos 1988, Balta 1989, Varon 2003. Of great importance is also the self-representation of latter-day followers of Metaxas as it is performed on their Web site, www.themetaxas project.com.

38. Manolis Anagnostakis (1925–2005) was a poet of "the generation of the defeat," although he called himself a poet of silence. Born in Thessaloniki and educated as a physician in Greece and in Vienna, Anagnostakis gave up writing altogether when he decided that he had written enough. He was particularly disenchanted by the ways in which the Left kept destroying itself in vortices of

*Diary, IV, 769–851. Quoted in "Metaxas on EON," www.themetaxasproject.com.

paranoia and self-immolation, and most of his poetry deals with that disenchantment. The last poem in this book, entitled "Epitymvion" ("Epitaph") was written for an old Leftist friend of his. On Anagnostakis see Calotychos 2003, also Lambropoulos 2006, Gourgouris 2006, Theodoratou 2006, the last three papers delivered at a conference in Anagnostakis's honor at Columbia University.

39. As Metaxas himself said at the First Congress of Regional Commanders of EON: "The schools, at the outset, were hesitant. Only the primary schools joined with a great, a magnificent enthusiasm. The secondary schools hesitated at first to aid us. . . . The reason for this is that at the national ministry of education there was originally a defiance, which gradually disappeared, but the tone was set. But the youth, little by little, without threats or violence, and only by persuasion, managed to win over and conquer the secondary schools almost entirely, teachers and pupils alike. . . . In the universities we encountered at the outset much resistance . . . as much from students as from a large proportion of the teaching personnel. Did you know this? Of all those who fought and who gave us our liberty in 1821, not one was an intellectual leader. I do not wish by this to belittle the value of intellectual work. But allow me to say that I consider it a secondary question in comparison to the importance of character. (Applause.) As for the teaching personnel, I admit that I found a certain resistance, not on the part of all, but of some. But since I assumed the portfolio of public instruction, I have found a greater comprehension and conviction, and even enthusiasm, so that I am certain all will go well" ("Metaxas on EON," from the Metaxas Project, www.themetaxasproject.com, edited for grammar and spelling). The means of producing compliance in adults (and older adolescents) included beatings, torture, confinement, and exile.

unusual—most children and adolescents were required to join. [39]

There is hardly a bourgeois family in Greece that does not have a photograph of one of their (then) young members in the EON uniform, often giving the Nazi salute. As a friend, now in her eighties, said: "It was almost impossible to avoid it. If you were not already organized in one of the movements of the Left [thus, already old enough to have been marked by the Special Security Police and already otherwise preoccupied through imprisonment, torture, and or exile], then there was no getting away from them."

I had the same conversation with another friend of my parents, Mimis. "We were spared all that," Mimis said, "because our father was a moderate." He baffled me.

His wife, much younger than him, who was also present at the discussion, asked, "So, were you ever drafted into it or not?"

"We were spared all that," he repeated.

I said that I knew from my mother (who was old enough at the time to be forced to join, whereas my father, who was seven years her junior, was barely old enough to be starting school) that the leadership of EON would go through school registers and systematically force children to join, although some, maybe a lot, joined of their own volition.

I mentioned the Anagnostakis story about free tickets for movies and football matches. "Oh, tickets, schmickets, they would come to pick you up and you had no choice but to join them," he said.

"So, you did join," his wife said.

"Yes, but only very briefly," he replied.

This is exactly what Anagnostakis testified: EON would conscript youth forcibly, but because it lacked deep structure, after a while it lost track of its members, although its ranks were forcibly replenished with new conscripts, to

Figure 2 (left). Dated November 28, 1939, Thessaloniki. My interlocutor, his younger brother, and their father. On the back, the photograph is inscribed to the children's grandmother, who lived in Athens: "To our beloved grandmother Julia, to see us in our first caps. With kisses, your grandchildren." Until the 1950s caps were an obligatory part of school boys' uniforms and a marker of passage from early childhood to school age. Disciplinary action was taken against children not wearing their caps, although rules were less strictly enforced in major urban centers beginning in the 1950s. Private collection.

Figure 3 (right). Undated, but temporally very close to Figure 2. My interlocutor with his two younger brothers and their father. The children are dressed in the EON uniform. The youngest of the boys is not included in Figure 2 because he was not old enough to wear a schoolboy's cap, but he was old enough to be drafted to the EON. Private collection.

the extent that in 1940, when EON was dissolved after the Italian invasion, it numbered close to one million youths.

Metaxas also authorized the publication of an anonymous pamphlet distributed free to the members of EON and entitled *Ho Kommounismos sten Hellada* (*Communism in Greece*), published by a "National Society" in 1937. The pamphlet had a motto by Metaxas, a foreword by his undersecretary of public security, Konstantinos Maniadákis, and an introduction by the editors of the National Society. In this pamphlet Maniadákis and the National

Society expose the rationale behind the need for a thorough knowledge of "the enemy": "We first need to see and understand and then we must strike the enemy," the editors wrote (Anonymous 1937: 7). They continued: "The first is called enlightening. The second, unified institution of all National forces, regardless of social class, gender, intellectual or other differences. . . . But there is no hope of a successful outcome to this struggle if we do not, all of us, first get to know the enemy in depth, meaning how he thinks, how he acts, and through what satanic methods he tricks the populace so that he can win them over for his revolutionary plans." The National Society undertook to "expose the whole conspiratorial revolutionary plan," on the basis of the confiscation of the archives of the Communist Party by the undersecretary of public security. This pamphlet, said Undersecretary of Public Security Maniadákis, in his foreword, constituted "the safest means of self defense" for those who had been blinded-sided and had not realized how "satanic and dangerous the enemy is" (4). The pamphlet was, indeed, invaluable in teaching everyone the structure of the Communist Party and the elements of Marxism, and not only those whom it hoped to influence. A number of people have noted to me, both in interviews or informal discussions and in writing—notably Manolis Anagnostakis—that this pamphlet was their introduction to Marxism, Communism, and (most important for their survival at times of crisis and persecution) their template for existing underground. As might be expected, nowhere in its pages could one find any hint concerning the means, contexts, and circumstances under which the Leftist was produced as dangerous and as the enemy, even as a means of mapping a relationship between the state and its dangerous elements.

2

1936–1944

The Metaxas Dictatorship, the Italian Attack,
the German Invasion, German Occupation, Resistance

Epitaphios (Parergon 2.1)

On May 8, 1936, a major strike and demonstration by tobacco workers was organized in Thessaloniki. The response of the gendarmerie was immediate and brutal. The next day the strike spread to other professions, and a new demonstration took place. This time the response of the gendarmerie, aided by the army, which sent in an equestrian force and a motorized unit, was not only brutal but lethal, leaving twelve dead and thirty-two seriously wounded, all of them demonstrators. The photograph of the mother of Tasos Tousis, one of those killed by the gendarmes, leaning over the body of her dead child as it lay stretched out on a makeshift stretcher that his co-workers had put together, has become emblematic of the brutality of the time. The poet Yiannis Ritsos, whose poem *Epitaphios* is a lament alongside the lament of that mother, has noted how deeply shocked he was by that image, which brought to mind the lament of the Virgin over Christ. He wrote *Epitaphios* in ten days (Parergon 2.2).

On the same day, the army took over the policing of the city, but a number of soldiers joined the strikers. The Communist Party, much as it tried, did not manage to take advantage of this chaotic (and absolutely revolutionary) moment, but the strike galvanized the labor movement in prewar Greece. The brutality of the police during the strike has remained legendary and has informed expectations concerning police action, especially since it revealed, again, the means that the liberal state is willing to use in order to remain in power. The strike was over on May 11, after all the demands of the strikers were satisfied—mainly, the establishment of an eight-hour work day and a state system of pensions and medical coverage. Although both measures had been in the works for some time, Metaxas came to be credited with them. The political fallout from the strike was long-lasting, and it precipitated Metaxas's ascent to political power and his determination to produce a pliable and compliant body politic.

This event is one of the revenants of history. In 1958, Ritsos sent *Epitaphios* to Mikis Theodorakis, then a young composer. As a musical setting for the poem, Theodorakis followed Ritsos's lead and blended folk themes into his learned endeavor. In 1960, he finished the composition *Epitaphios*, using folk instruments, such as the bouzouki, and untrained musicians and singers (Grigoris Bithikotsis) to produce a haunting lament. Like all of Theodorakis's work *Epitaphios* was banned from being publicly performed on and off until 1974, but the music circulated clandestinely, thus helping further the mystique and romanticization of the Left and of antiestablishment culture, producing *topoi* where the rift between those who were "with us" and those who were "against us" could crystallize.

Perfectly Nice People

"Did you ever get a chance to meet Maniadákis?" my interlocutor, a lovely woman in her sixties, asked as I was interviewing her husband. I said no, I never had, failing to note the number of times I had heard my parents and everyone else I knew say that one would never really wish to meet him.

"He was such a gentle, nice man," she continued, "very civil and such a gentleman . . ." while at the same time herself recognizing and acknowledging the complete terror that Maniadákis had brought to the country as undersecretary of public security.

I recounted the story to my friend Zina, whose father had been a judge of the Special Military Court. She started to laugh. "One day, during one of the summers that Stephen [her husband] and I were in Greece," she said, "Stephen went out to buy the newspaper. It took him longer than I had expected. When he got back, he said that it took him so long because he had chanced upon my father at one of the coffee shops on the square, sitting with a charming old man. He had a strange name, Stephen said, Manitakis? Manatakis? I understood immediately," Zina continued laughingly, "and I said to him, look, from now on you'll take the upper road to go buy the paper; I don't want you gallivanting with Maniadákis."

---

1. At the beginning of the pamphlet *Ho Kommounismos sten Hellada* (*Communism in Greece*), published in 1937 by an Ethnike Hetaireia (National Society), Metaxas articulates his nightmare: "Above the whole of Greece a big red flag was being raised and many more smaller red flags were being prepared to be raised at the appropriate moment in the most vital points in Greece, in the military barracks, in the ships, in the schools, in the universities, in the factories, in the house of the farmer. And some day this land would

Perfectly nice people can produce perfectly total terror. Metaxas claimed that the events in Thessaloniki indexed the bankruptcy of parliamentarianism and, using the spread of Communism as a point of fear, he prepared the political environment for the dissolution of Parliament.[1] When on August 4 King George II agreed to the suspension of the Constitution and turned over the country to Metaxas, no politician in Greece was either surprised or felt the urge to resist. Metaxas moved quickly to destroy any democratic presence in Greece. He deemed the Idiónymon of 1929 (the law that established the persecution of ideas and convictions) inadequate and reasoned that only through the complete and total destruction of the Communist Party and the parallel indoctrination of the population from the youngest age on could the political landscape he envisioned be produced. Exile was used systematically for members of the Communist Party and for the Left in general, although many of the politicians of the Center did not fare much better.[2]

With Maniadákis at his side as undersecretary of public security, Metaxas embarked on the project of destroying not only the Greek Communist Party but the Leftist movement in general. In Metaxas we see the danger of the Left fleshed out through two main actions by the state. The first was the destruction of the Communist Party through infiltration[3] and persecution of the Left in general, utilizing forms of imprisonment, enclosure, and administrative banishment that were already in existence during the Centrist governments that preceded Metaxas's dictatorship, going back as early as 1924. Four modalities of enclosure were available to the Metaxas regime: krátēsis ("jail"), fylakê ("prison"), kat'oikon periorismós ("home confinement"), and exoria ("exile") or ektopismós. The destruction of the Left, however, was not achieved (and could not have been achieved) through persecution alone.[4] As we know all too well, persecution causes ideological positions to intensify, not collapse. The most effective measure against the

drown in the red color of blood." This Ethnike Hetaireia is different from the organization of the same name that was implicated in the nationalist movement of the latter part of the nineteenth century and financially and morally supported both the Cretan Revolution of 1896 and the failed Greek expedition of 1897 against the Ottoman Empire. As Papadimitriou states, according to its bylaws, the new Ethnike Hetaireia was formed by Metaxas to "strengthen the status quo as it had been formed by the developments of August 4, 1936, and to disseminate its political, economic, and moral principles" (Papadimitriou 2006: 168; bylaws of the Ethnike Hetaireia found at ELIA). Papadimitriou further writes that the Metaxian period was a time when the terms *ethnikóphrones polites* ("nationally minded citizens") and *ethnikophrosýne* ("the state of thinking nationally") were coined in order to denote "the bourgeois consciousness and anti-Communist mental disposition of the Greeks *regardless of their partisan identity*" (ibid.: 15, my emphasis).

_____

2. George Papandreou was exiled to Andros. George Kafandaris, Andreas Michalakopoulos, Panayiotes Kanellopoulos, Ioannis Theotokis, and Panayiotis Mylonas were exiled to other islands. Some movement of resistance developed in Crete, led by Emmanouel Tsouderos (who later became prime minister), but it ended before the navy arrived to suppress it—namely, within six hours.

_____

3. The infiltration of the Communist Party by snitches (*hafiedes*) has since the time of Metaxas been an issue for the Left. The particular moves undertaken by the Metaxas regime, which managed to bring the Party into such disarray that the Left considered it completely broken by the time Greece entered the Second World War in October 1940, were not made systematically available from the viewpoint of the Right until the publication of Theodoros Lymberiou's *The Communist Movement in Greece* (2005), in which all the measures taken by Maniadákis and Metaxas are gleefully detailed. (On the Metaxian issue of propaganda, see Petrakis 2005 and Varon 2003.)

_____

4. As the editors of the anonymous pamphlet *O Kommounismos sten Hellada* (*Communism in Greece*) note in their introductory remarks:

"Someone needs to arrive at a state of great panic and intellectual confusion in order to believe that simply through the use of persecution, imprisonment, exile [*exories*], in other words, with the state's forceful imposition, can an enemy who appears in the state, social, and educational structure, that is, in the middle of public and private life, in myriads of manners, threatening and organized, be effectively battled."

---

5. *Retsinolado* is a concoction produced from the oil of the poisonous seeds of the bush *Ricinus communis*, commonly known in the United States as castor oil. *Ricinus communis* seeds contain the toxin *ricin*, which enters the intestinal wall and causes severe diarrhea, abdominal pain, and vomiting. If the victim survives the first three days, then death has been averted. *Restinolado* was administered via a funnel (not unlike what we see nowadays happening at fraternity parties during spring break, or the force-feeding of geese and ducks to produce fois gras). The person to whom it was administered was usually placed on a block of ice and left there for several days. See Figure 4.

Left launched by Metaxas and Maniadákis was the process of indoctrination, upon which the state embarked on a number of different levels. First, once the Left had been conceptualized and solidified through the Idiónymon as a political entity that was opposed ideologically and politically to statism, to the transformation of labor into human capital, and to the structures of exploitation, the enemy of the state had been invented. Whereas previous regimes had sought to eliminate this enemy, Metaxas demanded her transformation. He realized that only by thoroughly knowing the enemy could the state force her to acquiesce in its designs.

Second, a number of measures were introduced to put the Idiónymon into effect as it was originally conceived. Lymberiou scornfully notes: "they [previous governments] thought they were going to manage the communists the way they had managed the brigands," underlining the effectiveness of the new measures that the Metaxas government undertook (Lymberiou 2005: 165). The persecutions of Metaxas were so brutal that they have become a synecdoche for political oppression and persecution. *Retsinolado* (castor oil) and the expression "they put ice on him [*tou'valan pago*]" have become metonymies for punishment and reprimand, respectively.[5] Since the Idiónymon prosecuted *ideas*, Metaxas (through Maniadákis) sought to debunk ideas by introducing two measures: the "declarations of repentance [*dēlôseis metanoias*]" and the "certificates of social convictions [*pistopoiētiká koinōnikôn phronēmátōn*]," or *certificats de civisme* (Parergon 2.3).

Obligatory Law 1075/1938, introduced by Maniadákis, set the legal framework and the specific procedure to be followed for the institution and extraction of the *dēlôseis*, although *dēlôseis* were being extracted long before there was a specific law about them. Over and above creating a legal platform that would have to be challenged in court, something absolutely impossible during the dictatorship, the law delineated the process through which the *dēlôsis*, having been extracted from the accused by any means whatsoever, would then be announced publicly through the press in the daily newspapers of Athens, through the press in the signer's place of origin and residence, and by the priest at the signer's parish. In this manner, the act of repentance

Figure 4. The plant *ricinus communis* (castor oil plant), from which the concoction *retsinolado* was produced. The plant grows wild everywhere in southern Greece, on road sides and in open fields. It is a sight as common as that of hemlock, although rarely recognized for what it is. Photograph by the author.

would not remain an empty gesture of complicity between the state and the party member but would place the state in the position of intermediary agent between the repentant and his newly produced social context. The secrecy that had hitherto organized the daily life and social contacts of the Communist would be publicly repudiated, and the signatory would be publicly recognized as law-abiding, both "being safe and certain reasons for his dismissal from the Party, while he becomes useless and suspect of counterintelligence against them," as Maniadákis noted in the explanatory memorandum that he circulated (Lymberiou 2005: appendix).

The legalization of the *dēlôseis* was met with apprehension. It produced a number of reactions within government circles, where people asked the logical question: What would prevent the Party from directing its members to sign the *dēlôseis* so that they could be released and return to Party work? On February 8, 1938, the undersecretary for security (that is, Maniadákis himself) immediately drafted, issued, and circulated the aforementioned internal explanatory memorandum 18/106/2, "On the exact meaning of the *dēlôseis metanoias* submitted by the Communists," which was sent to all general directors and prefects, the chiefs of the gendarmerie and the city police, the high commands of the gendarmerie, and the directors of the city police and the gendarmerie, and which sought to explain exactly what those documents were by presenting the position of the Communist Party toward them and the corresponding governmental position. Maniadákis explained that the Party had already formulated the position that under no circumstances should Party members sign the declarations, since it would be impossible afterward for the Party to be able to discern among those who signed as a strategic move, those who signed because they found themselves in a momentarily weak position, and those who signed because they had genuinely reconsidered their position. This reasoning by Maniadákis does not take into account the fact that the Party had indeed instructed a number of its members to sign the declarations so that they would be able to return to the Party, although he does concede that of the two thousand released repentant Communists the state had recaptured only four for having returned to Party activity.[6]

Maniadákis's logic was perfectly redemptive: he was convinced that the Communist Party was a transient location for all save its professional members, especially for the young and those who lived in a state of social disappointment and disillusion. On that basis, he argued that if the state made it possible for members of the Party to emerge from underground without repercussions and reenter the social sphere, such a gesture would further undermine the authority of the Party, would encourage the "natural" seepage of Party membership, and would produce for the state an invaluable fund of information about the organization, membership, activities, and structure of the Party, while contributing to the Party's fear of infiltration by snitches (the infamous *hafiedes*).*

6. The poet Titos Patrikios, who had been sent to Makrónisos as a drafted soldier, mentioned that one thing that contributed to his not signing a declaration was the story of one of his uncles, who during the Metaxas period had been instructed by the Party to sign a declaration so that he could then be released and return to Party activity. This uncle was later accused by the Party for having signed the declaration, dismissed, and shunned. There are, obviously, no Party records on this practice, although some cases of high-ranking members who were directed to sign a declaration are well known (personal communication).

Recognizing that the *delôseis* might become an empty gesture, with its form maintained while its content of repentance was evacuated, Maniadákis instituted a further measure to prevent signers from retracting their act. This was clause 11 of Obligatory Law 1075/1938, which declared that: "(1) No one will be eligible for a position in the public sector or receive a state scholarship without being able to produce a certificate relating to his social beliefs issued by the undersecretary of security and (2) that the aforementioned certificate is required for hiring at corporations whose funds are in the excess of 20,000,000 drachmas and in companies that have underwritten contracts

* See Lymberiou 2005: 176. Lymberiou, a nephew of Maniadákis, does not quote him directly, but many of the opinions that he expresses about Maniadákis's motives, thoughts, and convictions come from his intimate acquaintance with him.

with the state whose object is directly or indirectly connected to the security of the finances of the country" (Lymberiou 2005: Appendix). With internal explanatory memorandum 15/6/20, Maniadákis delineated the process to be followed in issuing the certificates.

The burden of collecting the information required to issue a certificate fell to the local police, except in areas where there was a branch of Special Security, under whose jurisdiction the investigation would then fall. Once all the information had been collected in "a meticulous and careful manner . . . based on specific and proven information so as to avoid the possibility of unfairness . . . since often false information is provided for reasons that are self-centered, irresponsible, or even vindictive," as Maniadákis noted, the National Security Office should issue the certificate and send it to the requesting authority, keeping in mind that "the disclosure of the contents of the certificate should not be communicated to its subject or to anyone else *even if there is nothing objectionable stated therein*" (my emphasis).

As Maniadákis noted, the reason for these measures was to prevent the infiltration of the public sector and of the corporations mentioned in Law 1075 by individuals who "on account of their social beliefs not only should not occupy positions at specific points of the state mechanism but are not even worthy of any special protection by the state." Further on, Maniadákis delineated the categories of citizens who should not be permitted to come into contact with the management of any branch of the public sector. These categories were: (1) everyone who has been proven to adhere to Communist or other revolutionary principles, even if he does not express them on account of the punitive measures already established; (2) whoever does not believe in the national ideology and is so indifferent toward it that even inadvertently he might be lured into supporting revolutionary ideas, in other words, everyone who has a positive view of Communism; (3) everyone who, despite the fact that he might believe in the national ideology, is opposed to the legal form of government of the country and engages in expressions that suggest that he intends to spread rancor and disrupt social cohesion.

What this taxonomization of citizens in accordance with their "social beliefs" did, of course, was to profile everyone who was opposed to the regime of August 4. Not only were active members of the Communist Party denied the possibility of a certificate, but certificates were also to be denied to anyone who might be a sympathizer, anyone who might be considered a potential sympathizer, or anyone who might have no objections to nationalism and nationalist ideology but might object to the August 4 regime specifically. Because the certificate was required for any position in the public sector and in large organizations (meaning the educational system, banks, utilities, corporations, telecommunications, the transport system, the merchant marine, etc.), anyone who could fall into any of the above-mentioned categories was in effect barred from the sectors of education, security, the military, offices in municipalities and prefectures, social services, and medicine. The system of certification fell into the hands of public servants who were devoted to the regime, had rudimentary education, and suddenly found themselves with immense power over their fellow citizens.

One of the most commonly misused portions of the directive regarding the process of collecting information was the segment about beliefs that one might hold, even when not expressing them openly. This became the linchpin on which the certificate would or would not be issued. As an old director of Special Security mentioned during one of our conversations, "This was the point that we could use in order to establish the family's devotion to nationalist ideas, asking and finding out about their parents, if they were Venizelists or royalists."[7] On this point hinged the dangerousness of dissidence, and it extended both to the past and to the future, including not only past and current generations of political resistance but also bequeathing the idea of danger as inherent and innate to generations to come. This produced a political DNA of sorts, a discourse on the inevitability of one's constitutive politics. A dissident was simultaneously the offspring and the parent of a suspect until both had been reformed, in a helix that stretched to the past and to the future until the whole citizen body was to have been refashioned by Metaxas's political engineers.[8] In the hands of crafty government employees and civil servants, left to the loyalty of each one of them to the state (rather than to the citizen whom they had been called to serve), these certificates came to index citizenry itself. Given that each of these public servants could add his (and occasionally her) own desire to produce a completely loyal citizen body, demands piled up and up. Over time, slowly but surely, these certificates, by the time of the junta in 1967, came to be required for every dealing of the citizen with any aspect of the state: for the issuance of a driver's license, for the issuance of a passport, certainly for the issuance of identification cards, for admission to the university system, for remaining in the university system, for supplying electric power to a new building, for getting a bank loan. Even

7. I cannot expose the social and professional identity of my interlocutor beyond saying that he is my uncle (my mother's cousin). He was placed in the Special Security Office immediately after its establishment in 1936, when he was a relatively fresh graduate of the Police Academy. He remained at his post until the junta of 1967, when, because of his royalist disposition, he was moved to the branch of the police responsible for the protection of antiquities. After the junta fell, he claimed Resistance status and was promoted to being the director of special security until he retired with the rank of general.

8. A homologous gesture is the attempt to find miasmatic kinship ties via surnames. The surname of the director of the camp on Yáros, Bouzakis, also happens to be the surname of the publisher of the *Memorandum of the Detainees to the Minister of Justice of the Plasteras Government*. In a note at the beginning of the book, Manolis Bouzakis, signed simply with his initials, wrote: "A Note from the Publisher. The Publisher, having conducted an exhaustive research into the family tree from 1740 to today, wishes to state that the Bouzakis mentioned by the detainees of the infernal Yioúra as the director of the camp has no relationship to the publisher's family or his ancestors." Likewise, on the electronic

though such directives were never committed to paper, it was always left to the discretion of each public servant whether to require the certificate. In actuality and in real time the certificates proved handy to all governments, parliamentary or not, until their use was repealed in 1974 when Obligatory Law 509/1947, which had outlawed the Communist Party, was repealed.

Such rifts do not appear in a vacuum. They reflect deep divisions that persist over time, not in the facile way in which the popular press has come to talk about "ancient hatreds" or "ancient feuds" but as lived experience. If we tease out an end in the skein that is twentieth-century Greek history, we find ourselves at the beginning of the Greek state, when a king was imposed on Greece in 1832, largely by the Great Powers and their collaborators from within the newly formed Greek state. Why the Great Powers wanted Greece to be a kingdom, and a weak one at that, having as king the nineteen-year-old son of a Bavarian king, are difficult neither to imagine nor to understand.[9] Why Greek politicians themselves accepted such a form of government is far more interesting and complicated, and beyond the scope of this inquiry. But it was a decision that was to organize Greek history for the two following centuries, producing a rift between royalists and republicans (called *demokratikoi*, democrats, in Greek) that reached its apex in the time of *Ethnikos Dichasmos*, the National Split, when the democratic Eleutherios Velizelos, the architect of the unification of Crete with Greece, clashed violently with King Constantine I over Greece's involvement in the First World War. Venizelos wanted the country to remain neutral, while Constantine, whose wife Sofia was Kaiser Wilhelm II's sister, wanted to enter the war on the side of Germany.

In 1916 a coup against the royalist government by Ethnikê Amyna (National Defense), a secret Venizelist military organization based in

list EUI-CIVILWAR, dedicated to discussing studies of the civil war in Greece, the surname of one of the participants, Stathis Kalyvas, a political scientist and the author of a line of revisionist histories, became a point of discussion. *Kalyvas* happens to be the name of one of the torturers on Yioúra and one of the torturers of the junta. (Whether or not this was the same person has not been determined.) A question was posted on the list: Is Stathis Kalyvas related to "that" Kalyvas? Stathis Kalyvas responded by asking, "Is the name a miasma?" (He has no kinship ties to the torturer.) A sustained discussion and analysis of family names in Greece does not exist in anthropological literature, but the crux of this story is not why and how Stathis Kalyvas came to share the same family name as the torturer but whether that sharing taints the innocent. The deeper question lies in the historicity that has made necessary this need for distancing oneself not from a name but from the history that the name animates.

---

9. The Great Powers were instituted after the Congress of Vienna in 1815, when the Concert of Europe was formed as a means to bring peace and stability after the Napoleonic wars. The Concert of Europe comprised five main political and military powers: Great Britain, Prussia, the Austrian Empire, France, and Russia. Of these, only France, Great Britain, and Russia intervened in the Greek War of Independence, so much so that the first modern Greek political parties post-Independence were actually called the Russian, the French, and the British. Prussia remained on the sidelines, providing assistance in forming the new national army, and Germany (or rather, Bavaria) supplied the first king of Greece, King Otto, and an army of architects who reconfigured the face of modern Greece. The Greek royal line (nominally Greek, and marginally royal) was, until the end, primarily British and German.

Thessaloniki, succeeded in establishing a second, provisional government in Thessaloniki, which was eventually recognized by Great Britain and France. In response to Amyna, the royalists organized a paramilitary organization led by Metaxas, which brutalized Venizelists, liberals, and democrats in general, primarily in Athens and a few other large cities. The political climate of fear, danger, and persecution thus formed in Greece not only made the rise of Metaxas to power possible but also allowed a glimpse, for the first time in Greece, of the experiences such excesses of power could produce.

Cyclades

Greece entered the Second World War after an attack by the Italian navy on August 15, 1940, when an unidentified submarine torpedoed the Greek Navy Frigate *Hellē* in the harbor of the Cycladean island of Tēnos during the festival of the Assumption of the Virgin, which is celebrated officially there every year (Parergon 2.4). On October 28, 1940, after having asked and been denied free access for the Axis powers through Greece, Italy declared war on Greece. Metaxas became a hero overnight. His reported one-word response to the Italian Ambassador—*Ohi* (also transliterated *Ochi*), "No"—became the motto of the Resistance and to this day is celebrated yearly (as *Ohi* Day, on October 28). An entire mythology has been created around the moment of resistance, a heroic and patriotic stance by Metaxas that seems incongruous with his political position vis-à-vis both Axis powers. The fact that he was awakened at 3:00 A.M. by the Italian minister, that he opened his door wearing his pajamas, housecoat, and slippers, that the moment he heard the Italian demands he immediately pronounced the denial—all this has made it into the official historical imagination.

Figure 5. Pencil drawing by an eleven-year-old boy (one of my interlocutors) a few weeks after the Italian invasion of Greece in 1941. The original was initially published in one of the Athenian newspapers. Collection of the author.

Count Galeazzo Ciano, Italian minister for foreign affairs and Mussolini's son-in-law, mentions in his diary what has not been taken up into historical memory—namely, that when the Italian minister to Greece, Emanuele Grazzi, returned from Athens on November 8, 1940, as the war in the northern mountains raged between the Italian and the Greek armies, he reported a very different encounter between himself and Metaxas. According to Grazzi, Ciano claims, "Metaxas, receiving our ultimatum in his nightshirt and dressing gown, was ready to yield. He became unyielding only after having talked with the king and after the intervention of the English minister" (Ciano 1947: 308). Greek forces fought the Italian army in the mountains of Epirus from October 1940 to April 1941, at which point the German army attacked, entering Greece through Bulgaria. On April 19, 1941, the Bulgarian army entered Yugoslavia and Greece, and on April 27 German tanks entered Athens. By Hitler's decree, no Greek fighter who had participated in the battles against the invasion was taken as prisoner of war, an act that Mussolini resented deeply.[10]

King George II (a cousin of the British royal family) and the Metaxas government (Metaxas himself had died on January 29) escaped to Egypt, where they proclaimed a government-in-exile with a seat in London and Emanuel Tsouderos as prime minister.* This government was initially recognized by the Allies and considered legitimate by the majority of the Greek population. Through the insistence of Great Britain that the king appoint moderate ministers, George II appointed Centrist ministers, but he also included two members of the Metaxas dictatorship. The fact that the government in exile included members of the Metaxas government delegitimated the king's gesture in the eyes of the Greek population, most of whom then refused to recognize it. This government-in-exile did not officially dissolve the Metaxas regime until February 7, 1942. Meanwhile, on April 30, 1941, three days after they entered Athens, the Germans set up a collaborationist government under the premiership of George Tsolacoglou, one of the three chiefs of staff, who appointed officers of the Metaxas dictatorship to serve in various posts.

Tsolacoglou issued orders that decreed the conduct of the Greek population toward the occupying forces. A "Daily Address of the President

Figure 6. The front page of *Life* magazine, four months after the naval attack on Helle and two months after the Italian ultimatum to Greece. The soldier, called *tsioliàs,* belongs to the Royal Guard. The costume was later used to dress the paramilitaries and the collaborationist forces, which came to be known as *Germanotsoliàdes.* Collection of the author.

10. Apparently the Italian plan, also attempted in Croatia, was to "win the hearts and minds" of the local populations. Ciano says about the Croats, "Our humane treatment of them, *as compared with inhuman treatment by the Germans,* should attract to us the sympathy of the Croats. The Duce is also resentful of the German attitude in Greece. The Germans have practically assumed the air of protectors of the Greeks" (1947: 343, my emphasis). This protection of the Greeks by the Germans lasted merely a few days, until General Tsolacoglou ("or some such name," Ciano

of the Government to the Army," issued in the first days of May 1941, announced: "Now that, on account of the magnanimous gesture of the Führer, Leader of the German Nation, freedom has been granted to all military officers and soldiers, I must address the following matters to all those who fought on my side and those who fought on the side of my collaborating generals. . . . The German army has not come here as an enemy, as an adversary. It has come as a friend. It occupied our land in order to expel the English from mainland Greece. They, an evil fortune, had been invited to our national land by our criminal government. We are obligated to exhibit our friendly feelings toward the Germans, to submit to the new order of things, and to take to heart the great dogmas and the great principles of national socialism, this new political religion, which has been created by the luminous mind and great psyche of the Führer. Returning now to your homes, maintain your gratitude to the Führer and apply yourselves to your peaceful endeavors . . . G. Tsolacoglou, Lieutenant General."[11] This was not the only directive at collaboration to be issued. Among others, the "People's Committee of the Prefecture of Chania" (headed by the Bishop of Kydonias and Apokoronou, the ecclesiastical administration of the area), issued a communiqué that was published on September 22, 1941. It exhorted the people of Crete to work hard and with "conscientious loyalty to the law," so that, with the help of the German authorities, they could rebuild Crete. In order for such a fast return to civilian life to take place, the communiqué continued, it would be imperative that the people of Crete surrender their arms, as had been requested by the German authorities and the Greek government in Athens.[12] In the eyes of the population, the government was immediately exposed for what it was, and then some. It was a government both unable and unwilling to protect the population from German atrocities; it handed all the political prisoners from the Metaxas dictatorship over to the Germans, who sent many of them to the German concentration camps (primarily Dachau and Buchenwald), while keeping the rest in prisons in Greece;[13]

notes) decided to establish a Greek government in Athens "to save the national and ethnic unity of Greece" (ibid.: 344). Hitler, according to Ciano, considered this "a heaven-sent favor," while Mussolini hoped that the Italians would at least be allowed the civil government (ibid.: 344).

11. The decree can be found in Methenites [2007]: 485. This work is the most complete study of the area of Markopoulo, in Eastern Attica. It includes the most exhaustive account of the period from the Metaxas dictatorship to 1950. Methenites has searched the municipal archives of Markopoulo and has reproduced original documents, some of them for the first time.

12. The communiqué was signed by the members of the committee, one of whom was Kyriakos K. Mitsotakis, the father of later Prime Minister Konstantinos Mitsotakis and grandfather of the minister of foreign affairs under the government of Kostas Karamanlis, from 2004 to the present (2008).

13. There were 1,983 interned Leftists of various hues (members of the Communist Party, Trotskyists, Archive Marxists, Socialists, and active members of labor unions) in the Greek prisons when the Germans entered Athens: 630 in the Akronauplia Prison; 500 in Tripolis; 170 in Aigina; 220 in Anafi; 230 in Ai-Stratis; 130 in Folegandros; 36 in Kimolos; 17 in Asvestochori; 50 in Ios, Amorgos, and Pylos (Lymberiou 2005: 352).

Figure 7 (left). A document of food stamps, yet another palimpsest. The photograph was taken sometime in the summer of 1940 and submitted to the authorities in Thessaloniki on August 23, 1940. The seal in the upper left corner of the photograph was applied at a later date. The photograph initially certified that the persons appearing in it are members of the family of the man in the photograph, a tax inspector, and it is signed by the director of the tax service. Each person in the photograph is named (parents, three sons, and the maid of the family, who does not appear in the photograph). During the war, the photograph (by then an official document) was used as proof of family membership for receiving food aid.

Figure 8 (right). On the back of the photograph, in the upper right corner, it is noted that the family received stamps for bread on October 31, 1941, a year after the war had started and six months after the Germans rolled into Athens. On the front of the photograph, in the upper left corner, a stamp states that the old stamps had been exchanged for new ones. Private collection.

its corruption and financial mismanagement created galloping inflation and food shortages that, on top of the blockade imposed by the British in order to cut German lines of support and the German appropriation of Greek products, led to a famine that lasted from the autumn of 1941 until the spring of 1942 and that both decimated the Greek population and produced a rampant black market.[14] All these

14. There is as yet no agreement on how many people died from the food crisis. The figure of one-tenth of the population seems high, and it has been disputed by people who have read this book prior to publication. Hionidou 2006 is the most comprehensive study on the question of the famine and food shortages in occupied Greece, but mainly for the islands of the Eastern Aegean; see also Hionidou 2004. Fleischer

(n.d.) argues that the casualties from the famine did not exceed one hundred thousand. Konstantinos Doxiadis, the minister of reconstruction in 1946, preparing documents on the collective deaths during the war and occupation, maintains the figure of one-tenth. The numbers vary even more if one considers strictly the period of the famine in Athens and Piraeus in the winter of 1941, or instead employs a more nuanced periodization over the course of the occupation, as does Hionidou. By all accounts, in my interviews, in stories that have been circulating, and in the documents on the intervention by the International Red Cross on behalf of Greece, the famine was not only severe but was observed and acknowledged by the occupying Italian forces. Ciano mentions that Mussolini was incensed by the German position toward Greece, saying, "The Germans had taken from the Greeks even their shoelaces, and now they pretend to place the blame for the economic situation on our shoulders. We can take the responsibility, but only on condition that they clear out of Athens and the entire country" (1947: 387).

circumstances not only incited hostility toward the government among the Greek population but also rendered imperative the need for active resistance against both the occupation forces and the collaborationist government.

The lack of a national government willing to fight the Germans opened the political and symbolic space for several Resistance movements (*Antistasē*) to form shortly after the beginning of the occupation. The largest was the Ethnikó Apeleftherōtikó Métōpo, or EAM (National Liberation Front), founded on September 27, 1941, by representatives of four left-wing parties: Lefteris Apostolou for the Communist Party of Greece (KKE), Christos Chomenidis for the Socialist Party of Greece (SKE), Elias Tsirimokos, for the Greek Popular Republic (ELD), and Apostolos Voyiatzis for the Agricultural Party of Greece (AKE). The acting leader was Georgios Siantos, a member of the Central Committee of the KKE ever since the KKE's Secretary General, Nikolaos Zachariadis, had been handed over to the Germans by the Metaxas government and was interned in Dachau. EAM had approached the liberal parties for a broader collaboration, but they had all refused. Finally, EAM built a broad coalition that included and won the support of many non-Communists and came to be thought of as a democratic republican (as opposed to monarchist) movement. In February 1942 EAM founded its military wing, the Ethnikos Laikos Apeleftherotikos Stratos, widely known as ELAS (National Popular Liberation Army), and one year later, February 23, 1943, founded the youth organization EPON. The university students established their own branch of EAM called Lochos Lord Byron (Battalion Lord Byron, not to be confused with the battalion Hieros Lochos, later established in the Middle East by career officers under the command of Lakis Tsigantes).

Following EAM and ELAS, other political constituencies founded other Resistance armies and movements, most of them short lived and rather insignificant either in their impact on the general population or in the outcome of their actions. The most important such forces were the Ethnikos Demokratikos Hellenikos Syndesmos, or EDES (Greek National Republican League), led by a former army officer, Colonel Napoleon Zervas, and a minor Resistance force, Ethnike kai Koinonike Apeleftherosis (National and Social

Liberation, or EKKA), led by Colonel Demetrios Psaros. EKKA was a liberal, antimonarchist movement, and its importance lies only in the fact that its leader, Psaros, was executed in 1943 by members of ELAS on suspicion of collaboration with the Germans, an act that provided the British with an excuse to declare ELAS a Communist organization interested in power, to cut off their funding, and to encourage antagonism between ELAS and EDES. EDES's initial democratic and republican ideology was soon eroded after 1943, when Zervas morphed into a royalist and collaborated closely both with the Germans (in a common attempt to eradicate the ELAS) and with the British Foreign Office in preparing the return of the king to Greece after the expected collapse of the Axis powers.

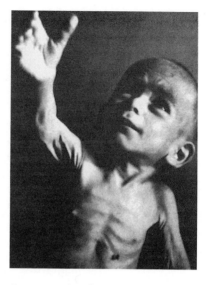

Figure 9. A less fortunate child during the famine. Photograph by Voula Papaioannou, Athens 1941–44. Reproduced with the permission of the Benaki Museum.

The geographical structure of Greece, a mountainous country with thousands of islands, and the lack of any infrastructure that would have permitted effective communications favored guerrilla operations. By 1943 the Axis forces and their collaborators controlled only the main towns and connecting roads, whereas the rest of the country was controlled by the Resistance. At that time, ELAS had an army of over thirty thousand men and controlled large areas of the Peloponnese, Crete, Thessaly, and Macedonia (a territory of thirty thousand square kilometers and 750,000 inhabitants). EDES had about five thousand men, nearly all of them in Epirus. EKKA only had about a thousand men. There is no question that the brunt of the Resistance was carried by ELAS, and this explains the large numbers of those interned in the camps later. But let me say no more about this now.

The Allies initially contributed to the Resistance by supplying all Resistance organizations with funds, equipment, knowledge, and agents for covert operations. When the British Foreign Office realized that ELAS was developing into a regular army and was no longer a small and insignificant force, however, fearing a further strengthening of the Communist Party, it started withdrawing support from ELAS, with all the consequences that such a gesture meant—no funds, no equipment, no agents, no collaboration whatsoever—while it turned exclusively to EDES. ELAS managed to take control of the armament of the Italian army after Mussolini's government collapsed in the summer of 1943 and Italy joined the Allies. In 1944, after the Germans retreated from Greece, ELAS took over most of the armament and equipment left by the Germans.

Chthonic Adorations of Orthodoxies (Parergon 2.5)

Acts of resistance intensified as the occupation went on, always calling down savage reprisals by the Germans. Places became emblematic of atrocity: Kalavryta, Kaisariani, Haidari, Distomo. Camps, prisons, open fields, villages, towns. Bombardments, motorcades, the sound of the military lorries, the sound of the voice of the German commander, the sound of German, keep appearing in the stories told.

"The great truck road across the Boetian plain divides at Livadia. To the left it continues north past the Lion of Chaeronea to the mountains behind which lies Thessaly; to the right, after crossing the Alpine district of upland meadows, where in the spring the large number of Judas trees strike a curiously exotic note, it follows the barren valley dividing the two great massifs of Parnassus and Helicon. Less than an hour from the town the latter route divides again at a depressing wind-swept cross-roads where, according to tradition, took place the unfortunate meeting between Oedipus and his father, *hinc illae lacrimae*, whence the main road continues on to Delphi and the fork to the left winds its wretchedly surfaced way to Distomo. This village, which must always have worn a sufficiently poverty-stricken aspect, is now a terrifying monument to human barbarity. In 1943 [actually in 1944, as the Germans were leaving] it was the scene of the most savage act of German reprisal and almost every house still standing amid the ruins exhibits crosses scrawled in blue paint beside the door, together with the names of its inmates whom the Germans took out and shot in the market-place" (Lancaster 1949: 151). This is how Osbert Lancaster saw Distomo in 1945, through the eyes of a humanist American journalist.

Willie Snow Ethridge, the wife of the chief of the American delegation to the United States Committee on Borders (USCOB), visited Distomo in the spring of 1947. Her account tells us that poverty and desolation, the deepest sadness and mourning imaginable, were still the texture of the place. Only a few women and children had been spared by the German battalion, and now the area was filled with women and children in black, going to the cemetery, coming from the cemetery, lighting candles, trying to preserve a life that was barely worth living.

This is what the Germans did in Distomo, as was countless times recounted to me by my mother when I was growing up in Athens: a German company of Waffen (armed) SS was ambushed by a guerrilla company that happened to be stationed a few kilometers outside Distomo. On their way to Athens after the attack, the Germans chanced upon some Greek farmers tending their fields. The German commander thought this suspicious, turned around, went to Distomo, and ordered his men to shoot and kill everyone in sight. Very few people lived to tell the story (although the story was told, in the form of conflicting reports, by the German commander and an accompanying member of the military police; see Mazower 1993).

Lancaster, in an ingenious conceptual sweep, fixes in the Greek experience of history the management not only of space and time but also of tropes of alterity and selfhood by bringing into the memory of Distomo and the barbarity of the German troops the story of Oedipus and the barbarity of his father Laius. The indeterminacy of the existence of Oedipus (who is he, whose is he, who is the old man on the vehicle whose arrogance and violence causes the wrath of Oedipus and his eventual violent retaliation) and the incongruity of the serenity of the landscape, with Judas trees and calmly curving slopes, brought out by Lancaster, underscore not only the barbarity of the moment in 1944 but also the painful collusion of myth, history, and memory. From the chance encounter of Oedipus with his father Laius to the chance encounter of the German soldiers with the Partisans, the stratigraphy of violence and the constructions of the social and the metaphysical (who is to whom what and why) circumscribe the experience of the place. But the paradigm of Oedipus—as myth, text, and narrative, thus as it has lent a syntax to the interrogation of the fixity of identity (no one can pretend to occupy even the suspicion of a stable existence after Oedipus has lain open the instability of existence)—also places the experience of the Left within the somatization (literally) of the tension between *zóe* and *bios* and the constant problematization of the notion of the human (*ánthropos*).[15]

Figure 10. A survivor of the Distomo massacre (1944) tending a grave in 1945. Photograph by Voula Papaioannou, reproduced with the permission of the Benaki Museum, Athens.

15. The myth of Oedipus has constituted the inaugural moment not only of the modern subject, as read through Hegel and Nietzsche, but also of anthropology as an interdisciplinary project. The myth of Oedipus, received by Freud through Nietzsche and transformed into the universal Oedipal complex with the aid of Jones, Ferenzci, and others, made the debate between Malinowski and Westermarck, on the one hand, and Freud, on the other, imperative. It also authorized anthropological fieldwork as the pivotal point on which a theory of humanity, a meta-knowledge of human action, could be articulated, while raising the problematic issue of the accountability of theory in the triangulated relationship among knowledge, truth, and method.

And Then Came the One with the Erased Face (Parergon 2.6)

"I remember the *bloko* [the round-up] very well," my interlocutor said. "They gathered us all in the square across from your father's house. First, through an interpreter the Germans asked our names. I don't know how they sorted us, because it wasn't alphabetical, it wasn't by age, it wasn't by height—all of us were there, every boy and man of the district. I was fifteen at the time, but my father was there, too, your uncle Tassos, Spyros, Odysseas, Nikos (both of them, actually), everybody. And then the hooded-one came [*aftos me tin koukoúla*] and started pointing, without saying anything, not a word."

"Did you know who he was?" I asked.

"Of course I did, everybody did . . ." he didn't finish the sentence.

"He was the apprentice of the baker, wasn't he?" I asked.

He looked at me in utter surprise. "How do you know this?" he said, "You are too young to know this."

I said that I had heard it.

"Yes," he said, "he was the apprentice of the baker, Klémes, down the street from your father's house."

I knew this story very well, but it was not until the last summer of my research, a few weeks before this encounter took place, that I was told by my father, who was also there during the *bloko*, who the hooded person was. "He would come around," my father said, "and he had the hood on, a black one, you could see only his eyes, but he would come around and he would stand in front of us and lean over, close to our faces, and we would whisper to him 'I know you [*se xéro*].' "

I asked if the baker knew.

"Of course he knew," my father responded. "How wouldn't he know? Everybody knew."

"Is that why you did not let us go to that bakery for bread?"

"What do you mean?" my father said.

"You didn't want us to buy bread from him because he knew about his apprentice."

"Nothing of the sort whatsoever," he said. "I didn't want you do go there because he didn't make good bread; but Klémes was the one who pointed at your uncle and they took him to the camp."

That was my father's eldest brother, who was picked up by the Gestapo in the *bloko* at age sixteen and kept in a concentration camp in Athens for a few months. It took my grandmother a few thousand English gold pounds to get him released by the Germans, money that no one knows how she was able to procure. What is remarkable about this story, though, is how this collaborator managed to escape execution later by the OPLA,[16] some-

16. On February 12, 1943, EAM called the first political strike against conscriptions of forced

thing that my original interlocutor's father did not.

The brutality of the German occupation cannot be overestimated. Torture and executions were part of daily life. Constant famine forced many Athenians to move to villages in the hope that local orchards would provide them with the rudimentary nutrients that they needed. A division of labor that reconfigured not only gender roles but also understandings of age appeared, as childhood disappeared.[17] Young adolescents would be sent with a wheelbarrow to the area around Athens, to the Mesogeia, or to Eleusis, fifteen, seventeen, twenty kilometers away, to gather dandelions or olives, or to beg for an egg or two, and then return to Athens so that their families could eat. Somewhat older adolescents formed groups called *saltadoroi*. Five or six of them would accost a German lorry and occupy the driver's attention while others would pilfer as much of the lorry's contents as possible. Sometimes the lorry was carrying food, at other times petrol, at other times spare parts. Anything and everything would be used. Even if these small acts of resistance were not much more than the proverbial fly on the lion's nose, the Germans took them very seriously, and no distinctions were made between the children *saltadoroi* and the older adolescents who were involved in more systematic and organized resistance. If captured, they were all summarily executed. As one of my interlocutors—a man who grew up to become the headmaster of one of the public high schools in Athens, though not before he was exiled on Yáros at the age of sixteen—told me: "We grew up much too fast."[18]

When the Resistance started causing serious problems for the Germans, on June 18, 1943, the collaborationist prime minister, Ioannis Rallis, created the Tágmata labor to be sent to Germany, an action that the Germans had taken with the support of the collaborationist government. German forces attacked the strikers and left three dead, but the strike managed to prevent the conscriptions. During the strike EAM announced the formation of Enomeni Panellenia Organose Neon (United Panhellenic Organization of Youth, or EPON) and the armed Organose gia tin Prostasia tou Laikou Agona (Organization for the Protection of Popular Struggle, or OPLA), whose express objective was to protect the members of the Resistance from the militias and paramilitary thug groups, and to expose and punish collaborators.

17. In Greece at this time, we find a configuration of segmentations like that E. E. Evans-Pritchard describes in *The Nuer*, namely, differentiation between "age group" and "age set," where the classification of youth according to age is superceded by classification according to social involvement. The Greek term *synomêlikos*, meaning "commonly shared age," deepened to include not only biological age but a radical reconfiguration of social age. In this sense, a "ten-year-old" was a child (in terms of biology) but could very well be counted among Resistance fighters. There has been no study as yet of how age became a fluid marker of socialization in Greece between 1940 and 1950.

18. Lesley Sharp has convincingly shown the inherent difficulties present when we attempt to produce clearly delineated age demarcations and, more importantly, how problematic the tendency to pathologize different age stages is. Sharp argues that viewing adolescence as a deeply traumatic stage in human emotional development is a culturally informed position by showing that what traumatized adolescents in Madagascar was colonization. See Sharp 2002. What we see in Greece at the time of the war, what the comment of the old Resistance fighter underlines, and what made the sudden muddling of age stages painful and traumatic was the very experience of the war.

Figure 11. Makeshift shoes during the war. Photograph by Voula Papaioannou, Athens 1941–44. Reproduced with the permission of the Benaki Museum.

Asphaleias (Security Battalions—TA, in short, their members being known as *Tagmatasphalētés*, or, in a play on words, *Tagmatalētes*, "battalion ruffians"), a paramilitary force armed and clothed by the Germans, comprising mostly local ideological fascists and Nazi sympathizers, royalists, and criminal convicts. The TA were formed to fight the Communist partisans and reduce the strain on the German army, so that "precious German blood would be spared" (Parergon 2.7). At their peak in 1944, the TA had twenty thousand men. Not only were the Tágmata not part of the Resistance, but they collaborated with the Germans to exterminate partisans, albeit only ELAS partisans. They also engaged in general terrorist attacks on villages thought to be sympathetic to the Resistance. After the war was over, the members of the Tágmata were absorbed into the armed and security forces, as well as into the general public sector, and they were later used extensively as torturers at the camps on Yáros and Makrónisos.

The TA operated mainly in the periphery, whereas in Athens Rallis organized the Tágmata Evzônôn (Battalions of the Royal Guard), which operated in addition to and in collaboration with the main paramilitary organization "X" (Chi), an organization that was heavily subsidized by the British, that had no active participation in the Resistance (or systematic collaboration with the Germans, for that matter), and whose only objective was to ensure the return of the king after the war had ended. "X" was a notorious terrorist organization, involved in the relentless and brutal persecution of all nonmonarchists, especially the Left. It did not engage in any act of resistance against the Germans at all. It had strongholds in certain areas of Athens, primarily in neighborhoods of internal immigrants in the old historical center of the city (in the area around Colonnus, in Petralona, and in Theseion).

Members of "X" were so notorious, and their involvement in the White Terror so extensive, damaging, and lasting, that Athenians still think about "X" as a runaway, lawless, and fearfully criminal organization. My interlocutor, though, was quick to distinguish between "X" and the Tágmata. "You can't put them together," he said sternly. " 'X' was *not* a collaborationist force; they were just royalists [*vassilophrones*]. They did not engage in criminal activities." The fact that the activities of "X" were not considered by this particular person to be criminal reveals that the Chites and, eventually, the Greek state, had a notion of criminality that did not extend to include acts of political terrorism. But this is a misleading statement on many levels. "X" was only one of the notorious paramilitary militias that sprang up in Athens in the spring of 1943, organized and directed by the collaborationist government of Rallis. These organizations—the armed-vehicle group belonging to the Security Police led by Nikos Bourandás (sporting helmets, not caps), the "X" of Grivas, and the Mandouvalos gang in Piraeus—all operated within a peculiar system of alliances that can be explained only by the communisto-phobia that oriented the British presence and intervention in Greece: these organizations collaborated simultaneously with the Germans and the British, so that when the Germans withdrew from Greece they were ready to be uti-lized by the provisional government set up by the British Foreign Office.

The systematic extermination of the Left and antiroyalist elements through brutal beatings and assassinations did not constitute criminal activity in the eyes of this man, as in the eyes of those holding executive power, because the Leftists and antiroyalists were, according to his logic, criminal elements who needed to be eliminated in order for the country to be governed by a legiti-mate government. He continued: "It's incomprehensible to me! Everywhere else in the world, history is written by the winners. In Greece it has been writ-ten by the losers, and we [the winners, the royalists, the Right] have found ourselves in the apologetic position."

On an opposite end a friend mentioned to me the reaction of her father (a Centrist) when she mentioned to him the name of her lover's grandmother: "I had always known about this family because when my mother was study-ing at the university she lived in the same house as Elias's aunt, during the *Dekemvrianá* ("events of December"; see Chapter 3). She was there when the andártes (partisans of ELAS) came and took out the four sons of the family and killed them in the courtyard. So I had always known about this family, and especially about Mary, my mother's friend and Elias's aunt. Actually, one day when I was young, about twenty years old, it was around the late seventies, I was a university student myself—one day I was in the streetcar, standing in front of a middle-aged lady who was sitting down. She looked at me, and at some point she said, 'You are Demetra's daughter, aren't you?' When I said, yes, I was, she said, 'I am a friend of your mother's, you look so much like her. Give her my best regards, from Mary, tell her.' So, I went home and told my mother this, and she repeated the whole story about how they were such close friends as university students, especially after the andártes killed Mary's brothers who 'nevertheless, were Chites, let's not forget that,' my mother said.

Figure 12. Mary (left) and Demetra, as university students, in front of the Grande Bretagne a few months before graduation, in 1946. Private photograph.

19. This is further evidenced by the voting patterns of the area. Laconia is the only place in Greece that has consistently voted over 80 percent for the Right. See Nikolakopoulos 2007.

My father, who had been in the Resistance, though not in any organized way, had fought the Chites in the Dekemvrianá, when they tried to take over the neighborhood where he lived. When I went to him in 1990, saying that I had met Elias and, I said, you know, he is a nephew of Mary's [and added the last name], my father looked at me incredulously and said, 'Child, they [the family] are Chites.' He said they *are*; he didn't say they were."

At yet another end, given that fratricidal stories have many ends that never close off anything, I remember a story that has stayed with me for many years. One evening in the summer of 1981, a friend of my parents' came to visit them, visibly upset. This woman was from Laconia, at the southern tip of the Peloponnese, an area that is historically royalist and Right wing. It has traditionally staffed the state mechanism, both on the level of surveillance and law enforcement and on the level of the civil service: the king's personal guard came from recruits from the area, and the gendarmerie was initially made up of Lacones. This, of course, does not mean that there are no republicans in the area or that the area is exclusively Right wing, but the general expectation is that if someone is from Laconia he is probably on the Right.[19]

This woman (let's call her Eleni) was married to a man, Pavlos, who was also a Rightist but whose brother was a Leftist and had died of torture on Makrónisos in 1948. That evening Eleni was very upset because her son, who was about my age, whom I had known all my life, and who was a rather quiet and not politically involved or aware person, had fallen in love with a young girl. I walked into the room and saw Eleni crying. I asked what the matter was, and my mother said, "Don't ask, Pavlos [the young boy had, uncharacteristically, the same name as his father] has fallen in love." She looked at me as if she wanted to tell me not to ask any more. But ask I did.

"She is a Communist!" Eleni screamed, collapsing in tears. I shrugged and said something to the effect that if they fell in love and they were happy together, what difference did it really make in 1981?

Eleni looked at me as if I had come from another planet. "But don't you understand?" she said as she composed herself and dried her eyes. "What does it *mean* that they are in love? She is a Communist! They killed my cousins, bam, bam, at Pegada."

"They," of course, were the Communists. I knew the case, where the partisans of Aris Velouchiotes in September 1944 executed a battalion of TA at Pegada, in Meligalas (in the Peloponnese), after the TA had collaborated with the Germans in reprisals against civilians when the andártes had attacked a German detail. I was stunned. Never before had I seen anyone react so passionately to something that to me was history, something that neither I, nor her son, nor her son's beloved had witnessed, since we were born nearly fifteen years after the incident in question. What was even more disturbing to me at the time—and it took me some years to appreciate its depth—was the fact that not only did this particular young woman have no involvement with the war and the andártes of Aris but that no one knew what her family's involvement was in the Communist (or just the Resistance) movement, since they came from a different part of the country and had no prior acquaintance with Eleni's family.

In 1943 EAM accused (the now royalist) EDES of collaboration with the Germans, a gesture that led to battles among ELAS, EDES, and the Germans that continued until February 1944, when British agents in Greece negotiated a ceasefire (the Plaka Agreement). On March 10, 1944, EAM, now in control of most of the country, established the Politikê Epitropê Ethnikês Apelefthérōsēs (Political Committee of National Liberation, or PEEA), a third Greek government to counter the collaborationist one of Athens and the absentee one in Cairo. Its aims were "to intensify the struggle against the conquerors . . . for full national liberation, for the consolidation of the independence and integrity of our country . . . and for the annihilation of domestic Fascism and formations of armed traitors." PEEA's authority was significantly reinforced after the National Congress (Ethniko Symvoulio) recognized it as a legitimate government. PEEA's first president was Euripides Bakirtzis, the military leader of EKKA. On April 18, PEEA was reorganized when a new group of people joined it, including Alexandros Svolos, a professor of constitutional law at the law school of the University of Athens, who replaced Bakirtzis, and Petros Kokkalis (Parergon 2.8). PEEA consisted not only of Communists but also of progressive bourgeois, who had little to do with Communist ideas.

The democratic aims of the PEEA (known as *Kyvernisi Vounou*, the Mountain Government) won wide support in Greece and even among Greeks in exile. A delegation of resistance leaders met in Cairo in 1943, asking that the question of the monarchy be addressed before the king returned to Greece after the projected defeat of the Axis, on the grounds that the king had collaborated with the Metaxas dictatorship before the war. Winston Churchill backed the king. In April 1944 the Greek armed forces in Egypt revolted against the Allies (primarily the British, who had the greatest authority over them), demanding that a government of national unity be established based on PEEA principles and that the issue of the republic be resolved. The revolt was suppressed by the British, who arrested approximately eight thousand Greek officers and soldiers and sent them to prison camps in Libya, Sudan, and Egypt. Later on, through political screening of the officers, the Cairo government created staunchly anti-Communist armed forces, such as the Third Mountain Brigade (also known as the Rimini Brigade, since it fought in the battle at Rimini, in Italy), and the Hierós Lóchos (Sacred Battalion), headed by Lakis Tsigantes.

20. These figures are given by Constantine A. Doxiadis, the urban planner and architect who was the minister of housing and reconstruction from 1945 to 1946. Doxiadis resigned his post shortly before the elections of 1946, but he remained as director of the project of reconstruction until 1949. Tsoucalas gives slightly different figures. He says that 8 percent of the population (550,000 people) died and 34 percent of the national wealth was destroyed (rather than Doxiadis's 40 percent): 401,500 houses were destroyed, leaving over a million people homeless; 1,770 villages were burned; harbors, railway tracks, bridges, steam engines, telephone networks, and civil airports were destroyed; 73 percent of the cargo ship tonnage was gone, as well as 94 percent of passenger ships, 65 percent of private cars, 80 percent of public buses, 60 percent of trucks, 60 percent of horses, 60 percent of cattle, and 80 percent of domesticated small animals; 25 percent of the forests had been burned; and the Greek national product was at 40 percent. The aftermath of the war took its impetus from these realities: a population that was broken, starved, unclothed, and barefoot (Doxiadis 1946; Tsoucalas 1969: 90–92).

In May 1944, representatives from all political parties and resistance groups came together at a conference in Lebanon, seeking agreement about a coalition government of national unity. Despite the mutual mistrust between EAM and the rest of the resistance forces, the conference ended in agreement on a government of national unity, to consist of twenty-four ministers (six of whom were EAM members). But the issue of the disarmament of the armed Resistance forces after liberation was not resolved.

On October 12, 1944, the Germans left Athens. A few days later they crossed the borders and dispersed into the chaos of the collapsing Reich. Greece was left with 250,000 dead from famine, 15,700 dead from the Italian war, 8,000 dead from the week-long German invasion, 3,000 dead from the German bombings, 50,000 dead from Allied bombings, 40,000 dead from the Bulgarian forces, 30,000 dead from German and Italian retaliation to acts of resistance, 4,000 military deaths abroad, 1,000 dead in the merchant marine, 60,000 disappeared Jews. In a country of fewer than eight million, there were 415,300 dead between October 28, 1940, and October 12, 1944.[20]

3
1944–1945
The Battle of Athens

Athens, December 3, 1944

Early one morning in the summer of 2005, at our summer house, where my entire family was spending a few days together, I went downstairs and outside to the garden to have coffee. My uncle-in-law Kostes and his wife were already there. Before I could get any coffee, Kostes, who was reading a hefty book, looked up from it and said, "I am reading about the involvement of Aris Velouchiōtēs in the civil war, and I am amazed . . ."

I interrupted him, still half asleep and without thinking too much, saying, "Aris had no involvement in the civil war; he died in 1945."

I could not have anticipated the reaction. "And you mean to tell me that in 1945, when he died, there was no civil war? And what were the Dekemvrianá?"* he said.

I replied that the Dekemvrianá was a clash between the British army, the police, and the andártes, which started because the British and the police fired upon an unarmed crowd at a peaceful demonstration.

"I was there, I saw it," he said. "And you can't tell me that that was not a civil war, when Greek kills Greek. I was there, I still can't eat garbanzo beans,[1] they repulse me, because I was there, on the roof of our house, and my mother was making garbanzo soup when the andártes came looking for my father, and my mother said, 'He's gone, he is not here, we haven't seen him in a few days.' The garbanzos were there, and now even

1. Sutton 2001 engages in a nuanced and in-depth analysis of the experience of food as an experience of history in Greece. Sutton shows why it is important to pay attention to stories, sentences, and phrases that start out "I was cleaning squid . . . when the mailman came" or "The whole family was together, we were eating lentils when . . . ," since the invocation of the

*For the history of the civil war and its historical and political context, two recent publications are invaluable: Margarites 2001 and Iliou 2005.

acts and gestures that surround narratives of food always index a deeper historical statement. Garbanzo beans are not the only food that many Greeks will refuse to eat even nowadays because it reminds them of the war; polenta and anything associated with corn is another. Indeed, *bóbota*, "cornbread," has come to be a synechdoche for the occupation. After the war, parents would not allow their children to buy souvlaki, out of fear that it might have been made with cat meat, as (allegedly) it often was prior to liberation.

Garbanzo beans present an interesting case, since they appear frequently in both written testimonials (see Oikonomakos 2006) and in interviews as being ubiquitous in civil-war Greece. No study of alimentary conditions, the famine, or provisions in Greece mentions the proliferation of garbanzos immediately after the retreat of the Germans. Thymios Karagiannakidis, who spent time on Makrónisos in 1950 and had worked as an agricultural engineer before the war and briefly during the emphýlios, remembered during an interview that immediately following the retreat of the Germans Greece received a large shipment of garbanzos from Morocco, the first shipment of pulses to be clean of leaves, dirt, and vermin. This might explain the ubiquitousness of this particular pulse in postwar Greece.

the smell of them makes me nauseous. My mother sent me to my uncle's house [their own house was in Metaxourgeio, one of the areas of Athens where there was heavy fighting], which was right on Constitution Square, and the andártes were shooting from everywhere. I had to slither from building to building until I got to Solonos Street. There I could go no further, because there was no protection from the 'X.' I was there, I saw it," he repeated.

I said that I wasn't there but that both my parents were. My mother lived in the same neighborhood as he did. She actually lived in his cousin's house, although the two did not know each other then, but my father lived in "Red Athens," a neighborhood that was heavily EAM, and he too had told me that the andártes would make forays to fight off the *Bourandádhes* (the vehicular branch of the collaborationist police force) and "X." Both my parents had told me, however, that this was the doing of the British, over and above everything that I had read about the Dekemvrianá.

"Leave out of this anything that you've been told and you have read," he yelled, "because I am telling you, because I was there and you were not."

By now we were both yelling and screaming, to the point that his wife left the garden, my husband and my son were both awakened by the sound, and my brother-in-law came outside, saw us, and without saying a word walked straight out of the garden and the house. We were all a bit unhinged by this encounter. My uncle and I quickly regained our composure and made up. The incident did not become part of my research until much later, when I was able to sit down, pen and paper in hand, and record it. Once again, my reasons for conducting this research, which seemingly deals with a fifty-year-old history, came back to me: it does not deal with a fifty-year-old history; it deals with the story that is modern Greece.

By the summer of 1944, as the Soviet army was advancing toward Romania and Yugoslavia, it became obvious that the Germans would soon withdraw from Greece rather than risk being cut off and left behind enemy lines. The government-in-exile, now led by a prominent liberal, George Papandreou, moved to Cava dei' Tirreni, close to Naples, in preparation for the return to Greece. Very close to Cava dei' Tirreni is Caserta, where an agreement was signed in September 1944. It stipulated that all the Resistance armies in Greece were to be disarmed and placed under the command of a British officer, General Ronald MacKenzie Scobie.[2]

British troops (including forces from the colonies—South Africans, New Zealanders, and Nepali Ghurkhas*) landed in Greece in October. Resistance by the Germans was minimal, since they were rapidly retreating and most of Greece was under the control of ELAS or EDES. The only significant German presence, assisted by "X" and Bourandas forces, was in central Athens. ELAS numbered about fifty thousand men at that moment, and it was effectively restocking from supplies left behind by the Germans. On October 13, British troops entered Athens, and Papandreou and his ministers followed six days later. The king stayed in Cairo, in accord with the agreement, awaiting a referendum on the future of the monarchy.

At this point, there was little to prevent ELAS from taking full control of the country. They did not do so. When ELAS forces approached Athens, they waited at Eleusis until the Papandreou government had come back from Egypt. ELAS did so partly because a forcible takeover of Athens had never been part of the KKE project (for which KKE was criticized by the Trotskyists as having abandoned the principles of revolutionary ideology), and partly because the KKE leadership was reluctant to undertake action that would not have the support of the Soviet Union, as Stalin had expressly mentioned the need for the unity of the Allied front.[3] Greece was not part of

2. Scobie became so hated in Greece for his involvement in Greek domestic policy and the role that he played in the Dekemvrianá that songs ridiculing him circulated in Greece until the 1970s. The last time that I heard one of them, *He Psole tou Scobie*, was during the last years of the junta, sung by a friend of my mother's at our house as she was having coffee. It was sung to a swing tune, and its first verse (perhaps the only verse that has survived) referred to Scobie's member:

He psōlé tou Scobie
Einai kómboi-kómboi
Ki an te lysei tha fanei
He megálē tou politikê

Scobie's dick
is tied up in knots
and if he lets it lose
his grand politics
will be shown.

Vervenioti 2000 also mentions the song, as one sung by the women prisoners on Trikeri, but does not give the lyrics.

3. According to Nikos Pharmakes, an ex-deputy of the Right who was recruited by the "X" at the age of fourteen, the reason why ELAS did not attack Athens was of purely military nature. Pharmakes says that in October 1944, when ELAS was voluntarily stationed in Eleusis, the collaborationist Prime Minister Rallis had mobilized five to six thousand Tagmatasphalétes from various garrisons that had been defeated by ELAS as the Germans retreated. In addition, there were about five hundred Chites, who were heavily armed, since they had started buying the German arms stock as early as mid 1944. They did so through an intermediary, Christos Zalokostas, who, Pharmakes mentions, was able to procure the necessary funds. They continued buying arms until September 1944.

In addition, the British sent "X" three shipments of automatic weapons, which

---

*Ghurkha or Gurkha, the first being the British, the second the Nepali latinized spelling.

arrived at the port of Porto Rafti in September 1944. Pharmakes mentions that he participated in one of those operations himself. Half of the Athens police force was also present (the other half, Pharmakes claims, had joined EAM), as well as the Mountain Brigade, with twenty-five thousand men. ELAS could not have expected to win against such a force. So, Pharmakes claims, ELAS made a tactical move, correctly assessing the situation and biding their time. Whether Pharmakes's analysis is correct or not no one can know, since it is intuitive and not factual. What is invaluable in his account, however, is the (unwitting) admission that the collaborationist government forces, along with the British, had planned for a battle (Pharmakes 2006). I am indebted to Stella Litou and Kostas Spiropoulos of ERT (Greek National Television) for making the transcript of this interview available to me.

4. A Greek journalist who interviewed Milovan Djilas late in his life mentioned to me that during the interview Djilas told her, off the record, that Greece should declare Stalin a national hero for not having included the country in the Warsaw Pact.

5. The Third Mountain Brigade had managed to expel ELAS partisans from Mt. Hymmetus, in Athens, by creating an ecological catastrophe: they cut and burned the thick pine forest that covered the mountain so as to expose the hiding places of the partisans. Only recently is the forest beginning to recover from the napalm that the brigade dropped. In the foothills of the mountain lies my parents' house, on Third Mountain Brigade Street (Hodos Trites Oreines Taxiarcheias), which was renamed thus from Plethonos Street, in honor of the brigade, some time in the mid 1950s.

Stalin's postwar project.[4] KKE's leadership tried to avoid a confrontation with the Papandreou government, and ELAS considered the Allies to be liberators, although not without some suspicion by KKE , particularly Andreas Tzimas and Aris Velouchiotis, who did not trust them.

The issue of disarmament was a cause of bitter disagreement between George Papandreou and the EAM members of his government. Prompted by the British ambassador Sir Reginald Leeper, Papandreou demanded that a National Guard under government control be constituted and all forces bearing arms be disarmed with the exception of the Hierós Lóchos and the Third Mountain Brigade, or Rimini Brigade,[5] both units that had been formed by the British after they suppressed the revolt in Egypt. EAM, having faced the anti-Communist brutality of "X" and the Tágmata, and fearing that disarmament would leave the Left in a vulnerable position and its members in real danger of liquidation, counter-proposed the total and simultaneous disarmament of all armed groups. Papandreou, who by then was considering the Tágmata a possible ally in the event of a further strengthening of the Left, rejected the EAM plan. On December 1, Scobie issued a directive demanding the dissolution of ELAS, a gesture that he had neither the legal nor the political mandate to make. ELAS (and KKE) decided that such a demand was not only unwarranted but also beyond the scope of Scobie's authority and decided to resist the dissolution. The EAM ministers resigned from the government on December 2. Meanwhile, the leader of "X," Georgios Grivas, had instructed his Chites to fortify themselves in central Athens against possible EAM and ELAS violence, until the British troops arrived, as Grivas had been promised. The Chites obeyed and joined forces with the Bourandádhes.

Amputated Bodies . . . Broken Statues, etc. etc. (Parergon 3.1)

On Sunday, December 3, during a peaceful and unarmed but nevertheless banned EAM demonstration of approximately 250,000 people in central Athens, members of "X," policemen, and the newly instituted Mountain Brigade (LOK) started shooting at demonstrators in Constitution Square (Syntagma, the square located in front of Parliament). This resulted in twenty-eight deaths and heavy fighting between ELAS and the government in the following days.[6] According to Nikos Pharmakes (later an MP in the Right-wing government, but a member of "X" at the time), the leader of "X," Georgios Grivas, had already, as early as October 1944, "put out a plan of the center of Athens for the protection of the city, starting at the garrison at Theseion, passing through the regiment of the gendarmerie at Makryianni, then to Solonos Street, the first garrison at Solonos and Harilaou Trikoupi, the second garrison at the end of Solonos, where I was, the Special Security, the general security, the gendarmerie. On the other side were the red apartment buildings at Vassilis Sophias Avenue . . . That was the circle . . . And we shouldn't place great importance on the demonstration of December 3, I mean political importance. Of course deaths occurred, but in wartime you don't take such things into consideration. Even if there had been no dead, something else would have happened, given the decision by the KKE to take over Athens. What I mean to say is that *the attack* [by "X," the gendarmes, the British, and the gangs] *in Athens did not happen because of the demonstration.* I was here and saw how the situation developed . . ." (my emphasis).

On the day of the demonstration, Pharmakes arrived around 10:00 A.M. and was stationed at the Old Palace (the Parliament Building), which on one side faced the Tomb of the Unknown Soldier, Constitution Square, and the Hotels Grand Bretagne and King George, and on the other side faced Vassilis Sophias Avenue and police headquarters. The chief of police, Angelos Evert, was on one of the balconies facing the headquarters with no view of the square. At about 10:30 the demonstration was approaching the Tomb, waving banners asking that collaborators be punished and a government of national unity be established, praising the British and Winston Churchill in particular, and demanding the official deposition of the king.[7] Pharmakes saw Police Chief Evert take a white handkerchief out of his pocket and wave to the police across the street. From a restaurant next to police headquarters, he saw fifty to sixty police officers come out. Some of them placed machine guns on the sidewalk, while others attacked the main body of the unarmed demonstrators.

6. For an incisive description of the Dekemvrianá, see Elephantis 2008 and Gerolymatos 2004.

7. Gitlin mentions that the correspondent of the *Chicago Sun* heard them shouting "Long Live Churchill! Long Live Roosevelt! Down with Papandreou! No King!" (1967: 152). The eyewitness accounts of the events at Constitution Square on

Sunday and Monday all concur about the initial enthusiasm of the demonstrators for the British, the fact that the police opened fire unprovoked, that the British joined in the firing after an initial attempt to stop it, and the number of casualties: 28 dead and 150 wounded, the majority of them women and children. An invaluable account is that of *Life* photographer Dmitri Kessell, whose photographs and account were first published in 1994, initially in the Sunday magazine *Seven Days* of the daily *Kathimerini,* and subsequently in an album published in Athens by Olkos.

8. Pharmakes also says, though rather obscurely, that, as Evert motioned with his handkerchief to headquarters, Pharmakes saw a dismembered body come flying by. He surmised that the body must have belonged to a policeman because the legs and feet were clad in gaiters of the type that the police used. He says, "I understood that it was a policeman whom they had dismembered," but there is no indication of who those "they" might have been, since he does not mention any presence on his side of the street other than the police (Pharmakes 2006). This is the only account that we have of this incident, as it appears in no other accounts of the Dekemvrianá, either published or in the interviews that I conducted.

"The demonstrators stopped moving. In the midst of all this chaos there was silence. Some of them fell to the ground, and I didn't know whether they were dead or not . . . But two minutes later I remember that a young girl across from me, who was holding a red flag, bent over, dipped the flag in the blood of one of those who had fallen, and raised it. And as she raised it, the blood that had soaked it made a red line through the air. I was stunned, watching all this. Then they started chanting again, and they pressed on. And then a second blast, and a third blast, and what happened then was unprecedented. These 250,000 people turned, threw the flags on the ground, threw the placards away, and started running toward Hermes Street, toward Stadium Street, toward Philhellenes Street . . . I was really impressed . . . I was fifteen years old and was very impressed by this massive retreat. I mean, in under fifteen minutes the whole square was empty. That's all I saw, for whatever it's worth."[8]

The British supplied "X" with artillery and aircraft to supplement the armament of the government forces, which had only a few policemen and a brigade without heavy weapons. The Battle of Athens had started. The ELAS was fighting with its own forces, and the Greek police were aided by the British. Heavy fighting continued throughout the day, with many dead and many more wounded. The next day the fighting intensified. That day, December 4, 1944, Papandreou wanted to resign and approached Themistocles Sofoulis (a moderate politician who had signed a pact with the KKE in 1936) to ask him to form a government with the agreement of EAM. But on December 5 Leeper informed Sofoulis that Churchill opposed a change of government, and Sofoulis turned the government over to Papandreou (Gitlin 1967: 156, extensively quoting McNeill 1947). The thirty-six hours at Constitution Square resulted in twenty-eight dead and over a hundred wounded on December 3; one hundred dead on December 4; and a broken body politic that has never recovered.[9]

The fighting went on—between the British forces, the Greek nationalist forces, and the para-

9. In 2006, intense opposition from the university community in Greece to the educational reform proposed by the Right-

militaries, on the one hand, and ELAS, on the other—throughout December. The British and government forces, having at their disposal heavy armament, tanks, aircraft, and a disciplined army, were able to make forays into the city, burning and bombing houses and streets and carving out segments of the city under their control.

The actor Mimis Fotopoulos has described first his mother's and then his grandmother's utter disbelief at the fact that British bombs had burned down their house.*

"But, really, the English[10] burned our house? What have we done to the English and they burned down our house?"

"Nothing," Fotopoulos replied, "quite the opposite, we even had a picture of Winston Churchill hanging on the best wall of our house."

The Fotopoulos house was on Hippocratous Street, almost on the line that separated "X," the Bourandádhes, and the British from the ELAS, which was in control of the rest of the city. Fotopoulos witnessed how British tanks had stood at the crossroads across from his house and were shelling it. He and his family huddled in the laundry room, waiting for the shelling to stop. When it was over, they got one blanket and, "through innumerable check points of soldiers, policemen, militias, and *hafiedes* ('snitches')" they were able to get to Kolonaki, an affluent neighborhood a few blocks up from Hippocratous Street, where a distant relative of his mother, who was a concierge in one of the apartment buildings there, let them stay for a few days in one of the rooms of his basement apartment.

Fotopoulos's grandmother got into the discussion, asking why, exactly, had the British come all the way from England to burn their houses. "Don't they have houses closer to them to burn?"

wing government of Nea Democratia (New Democracy) revived the intensity of the student movement. Throughout its tenure, this government has attempted to overhaul the tertiary educational system, calling for it to be more competitive, to conform and respond to the needs of the market, and to be subjected to evaluation by outside entities. In addition, the government has been trying to pass an amendment to the Constitution that would change Article 16 (which safeguards tertiary education as a public institution, to the exclusion of private universities) and allow private colleges, universities, and the equivalent of community colleges to operate legally and grant degrees equivalent to those granted by the state-owned universities. In February 2007 a student demonstration at Constitution Square ended in brutal intervention by SWAT and antiriot police, leaving students wounded and leading to many arrests. One blogger took the mini-video that the student organization Youth of the New Democracy has put together and interspersed it with footage of police attacks on students. The last shot of the blogger's video is that of an armed English soldier peeking from behind the wall of the parliament building on December 4, 1944.

10. The common term for the British in Greece, even today, is "the English," reflecting the dominance of England in Britain itself.

*Fotopoulos 1984; originally published in English in 1964 by Alvin Redman (Hellas) under the title *El Daba'a: A Chronicle*. All excerpts from Fotopoulos are taken from the third edition, which is out of print, even after its third printing. I had been looking for this memoir for at least four years and was unable to find it anywhere. I thank Apostolos Papageorgiou, who tracked it down, photocopied it, and mailed it to me in time for me to be able to use it, and Yiannis Patilis, who tracked down the first edition.

"They are idiosyncratic, and they prefer burning down houses that do not belong to them and that are very far away," Fotopoulos replied.

The general strike was answered with martial law, imposed by General Scobie on December 5. There was a strict curfew, and movement from neighborhood to neighborhood was almost impossible. "The hunger was unimaginable," Yiorgos, a man who was an adolescent then, said. "Because there was no way for any of us to have kept any provisions, because what provisions could one have when food was procured day by day, and we couldn't even go up to the mountains to gather dandelions or mushrooms, or anything. No bread, no milk, I couldn't remember the last time that we had had meat to eat, no cheese, nothing." The Athenian landscape was once more a war zone, only now with the incongruity of occupation by a friendly force. The German tanks had been replaced by British ones, the SS and Gestapo officers by British soldiers, Nepali Ghurkhas ("with their white turbans," Yiorgos Angelakopoulos writes), and various other armed groups not readily identifiable. Open markets would spring up at various places, but no one could know exactly where, or how long they would stay. Navigating the streets proved dangerous because of government and British snipers, who would fire at will. "You would be walking in the street and suddenly someone would fall next to you, all bloodied, and you didn't know if he was dead or just wounded. All you could do was run for cover," Angelakopoulos said to me. At night you would hear weapons crackling and neighborhoods being bombed.

On December 6, under Scobie's orders, British aircraft bombed Metz,[11] a poor neighborhood by the palace, resulting in numerous civilian casualties. Even after that, McNeill mentions that the Communist leader, Siantos, was "relatively conciliatory." By December 12, ELAS had gained control of most of Athens and Piraeus. The British, outnumbered, flew in the Fourth Infantry Division from Italy as reinforcements. During the battle with ELAS, "X" fought alongside the British, triggering an open confrontation throughout the greater Athens area. The conflict did not spill over to the rest of the country. It remained an Athenian affair, and it continued through December (hence the term *Dekemvrianá*), with the British gaining the upper hand at the end.

The outbreak of fighting between the British army and the Resistance groups, while the war was still being fought outside of Greece, created a serious political problem for Churchill and his coalition government, causing much protest in the British and American press and in the House of Commons. To prove himself the peace-maker he wanted to be thought to be, Churchill arrived in Athens on December 25 and presided over a conference to arrive at a settlement, with the participation of Soviet representatives. EAM asked for an appointment with him, but he refused to meet with them. EAM then

11. This was the first time that Athens had been bombed. Athens was never bombed by the Germans, presumably out of concern for its antiquities, or so the legend goes, although Piraeus was bombed repeatedly and catastrophically.

demanded full participation as a political force in the government, a demand that was considered excessive by the British and was summarily rejected.*

And They Took Us to Al Dab'a (Parergon 3.2)

As we all know, writing (at least recent writing, done by people who do not have the luxury, or the disadvantage, of a stay-at-home spouse who raises children, manages the household, puts dinner on the table, and acts as a social secretary) is a profoundly social act. Despite the fact that what finds itself on the page at the end bears the responsibility of our decision to put it there, what makes the decision possible is the constant *fort-da* of the exchange with other minds, encounters with objections and approbations of the object/subject at hand.

Al Dab'a has stayed with me for a very long time. Maybe because there is so little mention of it in almost all of the historical analyses of the period. Maybe because not too much importance has been given to it. Maybe because of the ways in which the operation was carried out, in scattered mentions, here and there, in testimonials by people interned on Yáros, about a place on Yáros called "Ntámpa," an encampment of punishment within the encampment of punishment that the place was, tickled my propensity for minutiae. But Al Dab'a cannot, and ought not to be, considered minutia. Perhaps, as Angelakopoulos says, "compared to the other horrors, the experience of this particular British camp would not merit great attention." But in the larger scheme of things, in the overall assessment of the processes that have made the enfleshment of the danger of the Left possible, Al Dab'a opens the space of barbed wire for Greece.

The place (also known as El-Daba'a, and later, among Greek detainees in Yáros, simply as Ntámpa) is a Bedouin Awlad 'Ali village on the Egyptian coast, which was also a station and goods siding on the railway.[12] It is located approximately 60 kilometers from El-Alamein, 200 kilometers from Alexandria to the east, and 600 kilometers from Tobruk to the west, and it should not be confused with the oasis Tell El Daba'a, which lies further to the east and slightly to the south, where a major Hyksos

12. I am indebted to Lila Abu-Lughod and Timothy Mitchell, who helped me decipher the name *Ntámpa*, which I kept reading and hearing about in testimonials by Yáros detainees, and identify it as Al Dab'a. Abu-Lughod (2000) has shown how such stations became the nuclei of towns where the Awlad 'Ali sometimes settled or were used as markets. For a detailed account of the Al Dab'a camp during the Second World War, see http://www.nzetc.org/tm/scholarly/tei.

*For a full, exhaustive, but nonetheless brief account of political contingencies at this time, the detrimental role played by the British Foreign Office and Winston Churchill, personally, and the circumstances that led to the involvement of the United States Department of State and the Truman Doctrine, see Gitlin 1967. Gitlin's more recent and very problematic positions toward not only the role of armed struggle in the context of parliamentary democracy but also the war in Iraq do not (should not) obscure the clarity with which he approached the issue of foreign involvement in Greece between 1941 and 1949, or his positions on the war in Vietnam.

13. The Hyksos were invaders or migrants from the Near East (some suggest that they were probably Canaanites) who ruled the Delta region of Egypt from 1720 to 1570 B.C. Some have argued that they were Minoans. See Shaw 2000; on the excavations at Tell El Daba`a, see Bietak 1996.

settlement has been recovered.[13] The British had an RAF base in Al Dab`a, established in 1938. It included a prison that was then nothing more than a space open on all sides, called by the British "the tented encampment," encircled by barbed wire, or, as a New Zealander Axis prisoner there called it, "a cage." According to Karrer (2004: 55), Camp 381 was 1.5 kilometers long and about 800 meters wide, broken up into twenty-four cages placed at intervals of about 15 meters and separated by three lines of barbed wire. Every five meters there was a lamppost and every two cages there was a watch-tower covered with a tin roof. The camp was captured by the Germans under Rommel during the first battle of El-Alamein in June 1942 and used as a prisoner-of-war camp. It was retaken by the British under General Montgomery in September of that year, during the second battle of El-Alamein.

A friend in Athens, knowing my insistence on the importance of Al Dab`a, kept looking for references, comments, anything to do with that place. In one of his e-mail messages, he sent me the press release for a small, privately published pamphlet entitled *381 Camp El Ntampa*, by Georgios Angelakopoulos, who had been taken to Al Dab`a "at the age of eighteen, sometime in the middle of December" of 1944. When I spoke with him, he could not remember the exact date. He had been stopped for a random check in Athens, while he was going from his uncle's house to his parents'. In tattered clothes, a jacket that he had been wearing for a few years, full of mended and unmendable holes, he was searched over and over by the police, and there, fallen through a hole in his jacket pocket, was a poem that he had written against King George II. He was immediately arrested and taken to the police station. On the way, he yelled his address to some bystander, asking him to notify his parents that he had been arrested.

The press release placed Angelakopoulos's experience within a wider context, mentioning names of three more well-known Greeks who had also been taken there. Two I knew about: Vassilios Kokkinos (later chief justice of the Greek Supreme Court) and Mimis Fotopoulos, whose account of his experience I had already read (thanks again to the friend who had looked for months for a reprint). The third name startled me. I knew this name only too well. It belongs to a very old and close friend of my family, a man only a couple of years older than my father, who had grown up in the same neighborhood as my father and whom I had not seen for fifteen years. This man is Dimitris Beis (Mimis to his friends), former mayor of the Zographou municipality in Athens, where we lived and where my father had been born, subsequently mayor of the city of Athens and member of PASOK (the Socialist Party, established by Andreas Papandreou in 1974). I called my parents immediately to see if they knew about this. They did not. My mother remembered when Mimis had been imprisoned by the junta, but nothing about Al Dab`a. My father remembered that he had been picked up by the English but could not remember what happened to him after that. As a matter of fact, I found out that neither of my parents could recall anything about Al Dab`a, although they remembered very well the prison camps in Syria, Palestine, and Egypt (Tobruk and Asmara). But they did not know about the hostages of December 1944.[14]

"They picked me up on St. Nicholas Day," Mimis told me. St. Nicholas Day is December 6, so he was picked up three days after the first demonstration, the same day as Karrer was picked up (2004: 14).

"Why did they pick you up?" I asked.

"Probably because I was in EPON," Mimis said. "The funny thing is that, a few hours before they picked me up, OPLA had come to the house looking for my brother, who was on the Right." (My mother had already mentioned this to me: "Mimis had always been democratic; but his brother was really Right wing, although later he changed, too, and became democratic also.") "We managed to hide my brother; he went into the *rema* [the creek], and he left from there, all the way down to the bridge. So I went out to play ball with my friends [Mimis was sixteen years old at the time], and they caught me right outside of your house."

I asked who had arrested him. "The Third Mountain Brigade, the Rimini," he said.

14. Were they hostages? Alexis Karrer, a journalist who was picked up on December 6 and sent to Al Dab`a with the second shipment on December 19, says that, when they arrived at the camp, the Scottish colonel announced to them that they were hostages of the Greek government (2004: 56). A few days later they asked a British lieutenant for more food and cigarettes but were denied both because they had been classified the same as German prisoners of war. The lieutenant promised them that he would intercede with Middle East Headquarters to change their classification to that of Italian prisoners of war, so that they would be entitled to more cigarettes and more and better food. The prisoners wrote memorandum after memorandum telling him that they should not be considered prisoners of war because they had not been indicted for having been arrested in battle or bearing arms, as international laws of war require. The colonel admitted that they were not prisoners of war but rather "refugees." But Karrer notes about the colonel: "He does not know what we are, he is confused. He has received orders and he is carrying them out. But we know very well what we are: HOSTAGES. Nothing else. Not even political prisoners" (2004: 58–59).

15. Fotopoulos, Angelakopoulos, Beis, and the songs about Al Dab`a all mention that an English soldier went around with a soup tureen collecting the valuables of those arrested.

"Right there, in the middle of the street, they caught me and they took me to the police station; from there to Hasani, do you know where Hasani is?"

I did. Hasani was the name of the old airport of Athens, later named Hellenikon, which the British had commandeered.

"And from there to Goudi [the military camp on the other side of Zographou]. There they stripped us of all our valuables—wrist watches, money (though what money did we have? no one had any money with him), billfolds, pens, whatever we had that had some value.[15] They kept us for a long time. First we were guarded by the English, but then the National Guard joined them."

We talked about their treatment at the camp, whether he could see any others that he knew, how they were transported to Al Dab`a.

"We had no idea where they were taking us," he said. "They put us all in huge transport ships, and we were sailing for days, in the middle of the war, right? I am still amazed that we did not get attacked by the Germans. At some point they let us out, and we were at Port Said."

"How did they get you to Al Dab`a?" I asked.

"By train, by lorries, anything they could. They took us there and I can't tell you . . . The whole camp was just a huge area with barbed wire all around it. Three deep. There were no tents, no buildings. There were watchtowers everywhere, but the thing that gave me a jolt was the fact that there was nothing green around. Nothing at all. No trees, no shrubs, no bushes, nothing. On the right was the sea, and on the left the desert. Well, this was in the desert anyway." When they arrived at the camp, they were ordered to shower and wear gray pajamas with a large black rectangular patch on the back (Karrer 2004: 51). I asked again if while there he saw anyone he knew, wondering out loud how could he in the midst of eight thousand people?

"It wasn't eight thousand," Mimis said. "There were at least twelve thousand of us, probably closer to fifteen thousand. I calculated the number because there were fifty cages and each cage held three hundred of us." This is the number that Angelakopoulos has also estimated, although Karrer stays closer to the official number of eight thousand.*

"Is there a list, do you think, of people who were taken there, at least of the numbers?" I asked.

"What lists?" Mimis said. "I told you, this was a human roundup [*anthropomázema*].† They just rounded up people. They rounded up little children ten, eleven, twelve years old. They accused them of running news errands between the partisans."

This is exactly the same narrative Angelakopoulos has given. He added that the children were frightened and kept crying for their parents, so that the actors who were there would put together little skits to calm them down. No one had informed the families of the arrested what had happened to them, and no one could find out anything about them. "Such awful days were those," Karrer writes, "that if anyone went missing unexplainably or unexpectedly from home he had to be considered dead, or wounded, or taken hostage, and all meant the same" (2004: 37). The families tried to find out

---

*Karrer 2004: 63. Karrer's son Aris, who wrote an introduction to his father's memoir, calculates the number to have been 12,000 (2004: 19), although Karrer's own arithmetic adds up to 14,400, when he mentions that he was put in charge of organizing his cage of 600 people and that there were twenty-four such cages at Camp 381. Probably Karrer counts subdivisions of the cages, whereas Mimis and Angelakopoulos count whole segments.

†This is exactly the word used by Karrer, also. Mimis did not know of Karrer's memoir when I spoke with him, so the term has been used by both of them independently.

the whereabouts of the arrested, but it was impossible. The narratives are very similar, and I would be inclined to believe them commonly invented (in Benedict Anderson's sense of inventing) and shared among Al Dab'a prisoners, but Mimis and Angelakopoulos did not know about each other's being there until I told them both. These narratives coincide independently. Angelakopoulos knew that the actor Mimis Fotopoulos was there but did not know that he had published his memoirs of the place.

Fotopoulos has given a slightly different chronology of his arrest and detention, although his account of his arrest is just as absurd as the rest that I have heard. On that New Year's Eve day, Fotopoulos had been down the street to Hippocratous to look once again at his destroyed house. On his way back to the apartment, he stopped at Kolonaki Square, where some peddlers were selling toys. As he stopped to look at the toys, wearing his pajamas underneath his clothes to keep warm, someone tapped him on the shoulder. When he turned, he saw an usher from one of the theaters, who, accompanied by an army lieutenant, asked him to follow him to the police station "for a little interrogation." At the station he was first asked what the red cloth that kept peeking out from underneath his trousers was. He said that it was his pajama bottoms, to keep him warm. He was then accused of having yelled "Power to the People [*Laokratia*]"[16] during the demonstration on December 3. He denied it, but the interrogator had a witness: the usher.

"But he was a member of the theater division of EAM," Fotopoulos protested. "He was, but now he has recovered" was the response of the interrogator.[17] From there Fotopoulos was taken to Goudi, where he realized the extent of the operation, and from Goudi to Al Dab'a. He was not seen or heard from until June 3, when the same navy ship brought the last group of those who survived back to Greece.

16. *Laokratia* means literally "the *krátos* of the people," *krátos* in its ancient Greek meaning of power, sovereignty, *puissance*.

17. Pharmakes mentions that, after the Dekemvrianá, people whom he knew had been members of EAM would say, "We? at EAM? never. We were with EDES, we were with these, we were with those . . . Because, as you know, the Greeks are always on the side of the winner" (Pharmakes 2006).

By December 29, two days before the New Year, in Athens the British, aided by the Greek Security Police, had rounded up most of the men they would eventually transport to the camp at Al Dab'a. By early January ELAS had been pushed out of Athens, through the operations of the Rimini Brigade. With Churchill's intervention, given that he considered Papandreou soft on Communism, Papandreou resigned and was replaced by the staunch anti-Communist General Nikolaos Plasteras. On January 15, 1945, Scobie agreed to a ceasefire in exchange for ELAS's withdrawal from its positions at Patras and Thessaloniki and its demobilization in the Peloponnese. This was a severe defeat, but ELAS remained in existence and the KKE had an opportunity to reconsider its strategy. The defeat was mainly military, but as it was retreating ELAS took along close to eight thousand hostages from various parts of Athens, in a manner not unlike the one used for the hostages that were sent to Al Dab'a: people picked up in the middle of the street or pulled out of their homes in their pajamas, some in their slippers, with no food, no provisions. Some of them died on the long march out of Athens. An eye for an eye leaves the whole world blind.

OPLA re-imagined itself at this point as a self-appointed vigilante and salvationist body. The scope of its operations extended far beyond the protection of individual fighters and the exposure and execution of collaborators. Nearly twelve hundred people were executed for various political crimes, mainly collaboration, but also simply on suspicion. KKE, attempting to reorganize its forces and avoid the clear oncoming terror of the Greek fascist and royalist organizations, turned inward. A painful culture of mistrust and fear of informers or "snitches [hafiédes]," what Talal Asad (2005: 186) has termed "organized suspicion"—something that had existed since the Metaxas dictatorship—was solidified during this period. It would endure for a long time to come.[18] OPLA executed Leftists and non-Leftists alike as it became an organization of fear and paranoia, and it managed to produce an image of the Communist as a bloodthirsty villain who would use the cut-off tops of tin cans to execute his victims, an image that permeated the social imaginary of Greeks until at least the beginning of the 1980s. The cut-off tops of tin cans, collectively named konservokoutia, became a common point of reference, almost synecdochically, for the Left in general. Athens, and Greece in general, entered a phase of terrorism by the militias and paramilitaries that led to the period known as the White Terror.

The danger from the Right-wing paramilitaries was so great that in December 1945 Octave Merlier, director of the École Française in Athens, arranged for fellowships to be granted to a number of young university graduates for postgraduate studies in France. Merlier, with the support of Deputy Director Roger Milliex and his wife Tatiana Gritsi-Milliex, chartered the New Zealand military transport boat Mataroa to take these students, most of them belonging to the Left, though a few of them belonged to the Right, to France in order to save them. And they needed to be saved: some had participated in the Resistance and the Battle of Athens; some were Trotskyists and needed

18. The Metaxas government, especially Maniadákis, had systematized the use of infiltrators (hafiédes) into the Central Committee of the KKE. As Maniadákis himself noted, the benefit was double: not only would the state manage to have complete control of the organization and (eventually) the operations of the Communist Party but it would create an environment of such distrust within the Party that it would, in effect, collapse. Maniadákis nearly succeeded on both counts. At the beginning of the war in 1940, the Party was in disarray, as many of its members were interned or exiled and a climate of deep distrust hampered the operations of the members who were still underground. Maniadákis seems to have thought that, in time, with the right maneuvering, patience, and skill, he would be able to infiltrate even the Communist International. See Lymberiou 2005: chaps. 11, 12, 13.

to be protected from the KKE and OPLA; some were members of the Party and needed protection from the paramilitaries. Some (very few) were Right-wing, and they were probably offered the fellowship for political reasons. The students came from every faculty of the University of Athens and the Polytechnic School: philosophers, sociologists, economists, architects, engineers, painters, sculptors. They later became leading intellectuals and artists in France: among them the philosophers Cornelius Castoriadis, Kostas Axelos, Kostas Papaioannou, and Mimika Kranaki; the historian Nikolaos Svoronos; the composer and architect Iannis Xenakis; the artists Kostas Koulentianos and Iason Molfessis; the cinematographer Adonis Kyrou (Parergon 3.3). Forty-five of them boarded the *Mataroa*, and another hundred or so were sent by train. The *Mataroa* sailed from the port of Pireaus to Taranto and from there on "undependable trains, through a desolate Italy" (Castoriadis 1990: 3), the young Fellows were taken to Paris through Switzerland. As Dimitris Papanikolaou notes in his review of Mimika Kranaki's memoir, the *Mataroa* does not index "only the trauma of each one who left Greece on it in 1945, or perhaps the traumatic experience of any migrant in the modern world; it becomes metonymically the collective trauma of History. . . . Kranaki seems to be saying that the traumatic experience does not emerge the moment when History invades each person's life and turns it upside down. Quite the opposite: History is precisely what happens when one's trauma gets indelibly mixed up with the trauma of everyone else" (2008: 30). But the *Mataroa* is also the beginning of the brain drain from Greece.

Officially called *stasis* at the time, later called "the second round" of the civil war by Rightist historiography and Dekemvrianá by everyone else, the twenty-eight days of December 1944 foretold of the impending darkness. "At the end of the war we counted ourselves and we were found fewer," Georgis Maratos says, announcing, in 2003, for the first time the killing of his father by OPLA on December 3, 1944.

4

1945-1946

White Terror

I Want to Speak of the Great Silence (Parergon 4.1)

Following the Dekemvrianá and the retreat of ELAS from Athens, the vacuum in policing and surveillance in the country became acute. It was felt not only by the Greek government but also by the British, who, as Mazower notes, needed their troops elsewhere as quickly as possible (1997: 143). In haste they expanded the already formed National Guard (Ethnophylake), a body that had been set up in November 1944 and manned primarily by conscripts from the "class of 1936," called to military service during the Metaxas dictatorship (and hence by definition anti-Communist and largely anti-Republican), a move that EAM considered to be explicitly aimed against the Resistance. Mazower further notes that the British officers were urged by Royalist officers to rearm the Tágmata (whose members, being collaborators, were being held in various prisons awaiting trial) and that the British police officers largely "sympathized with them who were 'out of a job through no fault of their own'" (1997: 143). During the Battle of Athens, former gendarmes, Tagmatasphalétes, and various collaborators were armed and incorporated in the National Guard. In February 1945 the political parties, ELAS, and EDES entered into negotiations under the auspices of the British in a southern seaside suburb of Athens, Várkiza, and arrived at what has come to be known as the Várkiza Agreement. The agreement demanded the complete disarmament of ELAS and all other paramilitary groups, amnesty for all political offences,[1] a referendum on the question of the monarchy, and a general election as soon as possible. The KKE remained legal, and its leader, Nikolaos Zachariadis, who returned from Dachau in May 1945, said that the KKE's objective was now a "people's democracy," to be

---

1. Close attention ought to be paid to the wording regarding the amnesty. The provision was made for amnesty for all *political* offenses. This wording allowed for a legal loophole that was utilized in the eventual criminalization of the Resistance.

achieved by peaceful means. There were dissenters, of course, like former ELAS leader Aris Velouchiotis. The KKE renounced Velouchiotis when he called on the veteran guerrillas to start a second struggle: shortly afterward he died in such a struggle.[2] Of the demands of Várkiza (as the occasion has come to be known), the only one that was kept was the disarmament of ELAS, a condition that amounted to its termination.

The disarmament of ELAS made possible the unchecked persecution of all EAM/ELAS Resistance fighters, just as everyone had anticipated, despite the fact that the KKE was, nominally at least, a legal political party and despite the fact that the majority of EAM/ELAS fighters were not Communists. The amnesty was not comprehensive, especially since many of the actions by the Resistance during the German occupation were classified as criminal and therefore excluded from the amnesty.[3]

2. Velouchiotis was either killed when he was surrounded by the TA or committed suicide so that he would not fall into their hands.

3. As we will see, the Yáros camp was established specifically for those indicted and sentenced for crimes punishable under criminal law and not for political reasons. This gesture of the state to categorize actions by the Resistance as criminal facilitated the legal prosecution (along with the persecution) of the Left and provided the legal framework for the establishment of the Yáros camp.

During 1945 and 1946, the National Guard militias and paramilitaries killed about 1,190 pro-Communist and Leftist civilians, and tortured thousands of others. They released German collaborators from prisons, terrorized suspected Leftists and their families, and attacked entire villages that had helped the partisans during the occupation and the Resistance. According to the Right wing, they were retaliating for what they had suffered from ELAS during the German occupation.

The British, fearing that this indiscriminate terror would force the Left back underground and feeling an urgent need to get out of Greece, decided to rebuild the Greek gendarmerie and appointed Sir Charles Wickham to head this mission. Wickham was not an uncontroversial choice, as he was the founder and head of the Royal Ulster Constabulary, having cut his military teeth at the age of twenty during the last two years of the Boer War (he served there from 1899 to 1901). As Mazower notes about the role of policing in the defense of the empire, Wickham was one of the persons who traversed the empire, establishing the infrastructure needed for its salvation. After the Boer War and before being sent to Ireland, during the Russian Civil War Wickham was sent with the British Expeditionary Force to support the White Russians. In 1919 he was stationed in Ireland, and from 1922 to 1945 he was the head of the Royal Ulster Constabulary. Wickham arrived in Greece in 1945, where he remained until 1952, when, as Mazower notes, he "traveled as an adviser to Palestine."*

*Mazower 1997: 250. Interestingly (or, rather curiously) Mazower does not discuss Wickham's involvement in the establishment of the Yáros concentration camp in 1947.

Wickham announced that he wanted to train the Greek police to be impartial and professional. During his seven-year tenure in Greece, Wickham failed to build the nonmilitarized, impartial, and professional police force that he had been asked to produce (and which, by all accounts, had been his elusive dream since the times of the Royal Ulster Constabulary). Hence, the White Terror continued in Greece and finally led many ex-ELAS members to form self-defense troops, without the approval of the KKE.

In July 1945, Papandreou informed the government that the dissolution of the Comintern was only a sham. Although Stalin still did not support a resumption of armed struggle in Greece, thereby showing his respect for the Yalta agreement, in February 1946 the KKE leadership decided that, taking into account domestic circumstances and the wider Balkan and international situation, armed struggle was the only means for self-preservation. The KKE boycotted the March 1946 elections as being rigged (predetermined by backstage manipulations by the British, the Right, and the Palace) and as excluding de facto a vast portion of the electorate, which had gone into hiding out of fear of the paramilitaries—in effect anyone to the Left of the Right.[4] The elections were won by the monarchist United Patriotic Party (Hēnōménē Parátaxis Ethnikophrónōn, HPE), whose main member was the People's Party (Laiko Komma) of Konstantinos Tsaldaris. In September, in a climate of continued terror, a manipulated referendum decided to retain the monarchy,[5] and despite the protests of the KKE, which disputed the results, King George II returned to Athens.[6] From February to July 1945, 20,000 persons had been arrested, over 500 had been murdered, and 2,961 had been condemned to death. According to the minister of justice, in December 1945 "the number of imprisoned persons is 17,984. Of these 2,388 have been legally condemned and 15,596 are detained preventively . . . 48,956 are being prosecuted for their activities as EAM/ELAS members. The total number of persons to be charged, including those already detained is, according to our estimate, over 80,000" (Tsoucalas 1969: 94).

4. Eventually even the KKE itself deemed the decision to boycott the elections a grave mistake.

5. The referendum was so rigged that it produced more votes than there were voters, something that came to be standard practice in almost all Greek elections until 1974. When I asked people about this particular election, the most common response was that "every body and every thing [*oi pántes kai ta pánta*]" voted: the dead, trees, empty houses. Pharmakes (2006) attempts to rehabilitate these elections by saying that, when electoral representatives of the KKE tried to substantiate the votes through the electoral catalogues by visiting the specific addresses, "of course, after such a long time, things had changed; they went there and where a house used to be they found a tree." Yet the attempts to substantiate the votes were made only a few months after the referendum took place.

6. King George II had been deposed and reinstated in Greece twice, and had to flee the country at least as many times, a situation that, allegedly, led him to declare that the most important possession for a king of Greece was a suitcase.

5

1946–1949
Emphýlios

One Night When the Houses Drowned under Snow (Parergon 5.1)

In a letter written in 1972, Foucault mentions in passing that his real interest was not "to analyze the phenomena of power, nor to elaborate the foundings of such an analysis" (2003: 284). In a sense, Foucault was not interested in producing laundry lists of where power can be found and what that power did. He was far more interested, he says, in producing a "history of the different modes by which, in our culture, human beings are made subjects" (ibid.). As a way of arriving at this genealogy of subjectification, Foucault mentions that he wanted to analyze power relations, relations that produce subjects out of human beings, through the act of "the most disparaged of all wars: neither Hobbes, nor Clausewitz, nor the class struggle: civil war" (ibid.: 282). In setting civil war (*emphýlios pólemos*, in Greek) apart from the contours of both the "absolute war" of Clausewitz (where the enemy has to be obliterated militarily and politically) and the Hobbesian notion of war as the means for entering civilization, Foucault recognizes that only civil war engages with the project of biopolitics in that it engages in the production of a new type of citizen.

What is an emphýlios, then? Is it civil war? And what is so civil about it? *Emphýlios Pólemos* has been translated into English as "civil war." In Greek the term is unambiguous, but translation into Latin-based languages is not without its dangers. Attempts have been made, both Right and Left, to name as "civil war" all forms of armed battle that happen within a singular ethnic group. Under this understanding, the French Revolution, the October Revolution, and the Battle of Athens in 1944 are as much civil wars as are the Russian Civil War, the Spanish Civil War, and the Greek Civil War. But time is, among other things, a political "thing" (perhaps even a "site" in Alain Badiou's terms) that determines the naming of events.

The Bush administration was as adamantly opposed to calling the war in Iraq a "civil war" as was the United Nations Special Committee on the Balkans to name the Greek war a "civil war" in 1947, for exactly the same reasons: so that the involvement of neighboring countries and outside sources would not be disputed. The U.S. delegate to the Committee, Mark Ethridge, charged Greek Prime Minister Tsaldaris with "monumental stupidity" because he had managed to succeed in doing exactly what the commission had been trying to undo: "Namely, focusing attention upon Greek domestic affairs only." But what is a civil war, really, and how has it developed, conceptually, over time?

Emphýlios Pólemos literally means "interracial war," a war between races, although this is not an unproblematic translation. First, one should resist at all costs the temptation to think about race as a biological category here, as the term has been developed and received in Romance and Anglophone languages. The problems of translating the Greek term *phylē* into English are immensely complicated. As Liddell and Scott, the lexicographers of antiquity, note, the term *phylē* primarily meant "a congregation of people by nature distinguished from each other," but, as they also note, this very general and broad meaning was almost never used. The term was most often used to denote the equivalent of the Latin *tribus* and means "a body or sum of people united by an assumed kinship and common ancestry, such as the *phylai* of the Dorians." In ancient Athens, the *phylai* comprised the different groupings delineated by Kleisthenes according to their place of residence, not unlike (later) European boroughs.[1] As *phylon* (the neutral of the noun), it means simply any segmentary delineation other than the one to which the speaker belongs, as, for instance, when Sophocles, in *Oedipus Tyrannus* talks about the *phylon* of the birds, or Hesiod about the *phyla* of singers or the *phylon* of women. In a much more restrictive meaning, *phylon* means "nation," such as the *phylon Pelasgōn* (the nation of Pelasgeians), and, even more restrictively, a segment that is related by blood ties, what in anthropological jargon one would call "cognates," as it appears in Homer in reference to the blood relatives of Helen (*phýlon Helénēs*). In Greek antiquity *emphýlios* had the meaning of belonging to the same *phylē*, to the same *genos*; therefore, *emfýlioi* were blood relatives, cognates. *Gē emphýlios*, in *Oedipus at Colonnus*, denotes the place of origin, the homeland. Both in *Antigone* and in Plato's *Laws*, *emphýlion haima* means the murder of a cognate, of a blood relative.

The term *emphýlios* as a term to denote a war between Greeks appears in Plato's *Republic*, in reference to the Peloponnesian War, in Theognis, in

1. Kleisthenes, being given the mandate to form a government after the excesses of the Peisistratids, introduced the first substantive reforms to the old Solonic laws, so that the form of government became democratic: being based on the *demos*. In 508–507 B.C. Kleisthenes broke up Attika into 136 municipalities (*demoi*), which then reorganized from the existing four tribes (*phylai*) into ten, without regard to ancestry, so as to produce a more equitable distribution of power.

Oedipus Tyrannus, in Aeschylus's *Eumenides* (as *Arēs emphýlios*), in Theocritus as "men's *emphýlios* battle [*machen emphýlion andron*]," and in Polybius as war (*pólemos emphýlios*). In Plutarch, it means mutiny (*stasis,* also "partisanship, faction, or sedition") although Nicole Loraux distinguishes between *stasis emphyl(i)os,* the term used for a war that happened within the city when the city understood itself as belonging to the same *phýlon,* and *oikeios pólemos,* a civil war in the city when the city understood itself as part of a *maison,* in the sense that James Boon has used the term in his reading of Claude Lévi-Strauss, to denote all the segmentary categorizations that are produced when a common ancestry of a large kin group including both affines and agnatics is deployed. (See Loraux 1997a; Boon 1990: 96–114; Lévi-Strauss 1983: 187.)

In Latin we find the term for "civil war" transformed. Rather than centering on the notion of the *phylē,* it acquires a political dimension that centers on the idea of the polis: *civita.* Hence *Comentarii de Belli Civili,* the famous account of the war that Julius Caesar waged against Pompey and the Roman Senate. European languages, with the exception of Greek, have adopted this political formulation (*Bürgerkrieg* in German, *guerre civile* in French, *guerra civile* in Italian). Loraux sees in the term *emphýlios* the Greek notion of *stasis* ("sedition, faction, partisanship," but also "stopping, cessation of movement and motion") and, in a short-hand motion, translates it into "civil war": "what the city experiences as *stasis,* to use the Greek term for what is simultaneously partisanship, faction, sedition, and—as we say in an expression with very Roman connotations—civil war" (2006: 10). But I would like to press a bit further this small aside by Loraux, this gesture of rendering *emphýlios,* within dashes, as if parenthetically, as "civil war." As a term *emphýlios* announces two points: (1) the phyletic self-sameness of those involved and (2) the impossibility of evacuating it. Hence, while the term *civil war* introduces the importance of the city, it evacuates the notion of kinship, with which *emphýlios* (linguistically and as an act) is impregnated and which legitimates the characterization of *emphýlios* as fratricide.

In the context of post-Ottoman Greek history, we find the term used to refer to the two civil wars that erupted during and after the War of Independence from the Ottomans, which broke out in 1821, and then for the *emphýlios* after the German occupation. The two civil wars of the Greek Revolution occurred from November 1823 to June 1824 and in November 1824. Ioannis Makryiannis, in his memoirs, uses the Latin-derived term *fatria* ("counter-party, clandestine resistance," but originally "clan") in reference to the First Emphýlios when he writes that:

> in the Peloponnese, Koliopoulos and others had opened a *fatria* on the side of the government, whereas Deligiannes, Zaimes, Londos, and others went to the other side. . . . We asked what sort of thing this

fatria was (where we came from we didn't know this word, although we knew other things that the *kapetanioi* ["captains of the revolution"] were doing). They ordered me to go and try this good thing, to eat *fatria* with my people. I told them, "I did not take an oath to pick up my arms and fight other Greeks; I took an oath to fight the Turks." And we did not go. (Makryiannis 1972: 71)

He uses the term *emphýlios* in reference to the Second Emphýlios when he recounts the offer made to him by Andreas Zaimes (one of the leaders of the revolution) of one thousand grosses a month as a salary in exchange for his allegiance to the party that Londos, Notaras, Zaimes, and Mavrokordatos had formed, fighting Kolokotronis, Deleyiannis, and Sisines. Makriyannis mentions that he rebuked Zaimes by saying: "Even if you give me fifty thousand I will still not sell meat for a civil war [*kreas dia emphylion polemon den poulo*]" (ibid.: 70). The term also appears in the Greek translation and edition (by Yiannis Kordatos and Tassos Vournas) of George Finlay's *History of the Greek Revolution*.

The First Emphýlios, also called the War of Kolokotrones, because the famous hero Theodoros Kolokotrones was a central figure in it, broke out on the pretext of the future disbursement of the loan that the British government had approved as financial support of the revolution. Of the 800,000 British gold pounds that the government had approved, only 336,000 finally arrived in the hands of the Greek government, the rest having been appropriated by various warlords (also known as *kapetanioi*, "captains") who were leading the revolution. The war ended when the son of Kolokotrones, Panos, who had besieged and taken the city of Nafplion, turned it over to the Executive Power when he found out that the first installment of the loan had arrived in Greece and he was given the portion that he had requested. At the beginning of 1824 Great Britain, suspecting that Theodoros Kolokotrones, Odysseus Androutsos, and Demetrios Ypsilantes, who had formed an alliance, were agents of Russia, ordered the extermination of Kolokotrones. While this internal strife, supported by the intervention of the British, was taking place, Sultan Mahmood provided the necessary incentives to Mohamed Ali Pasha, governor of Egypt, to attack Greece. The Greek revolutionaries, embroiled in their own struggle for power and financial gain, paid no attention to these preparations by Mohamed Ali and the sultan, so that the sultan and Ali were able to take advantage of this oversight and attack with disastrous results. Or so goes the interpretation given by historian George Finlay, who sought to exonerate the British from any responsibility for interfering in the management of internal Greek affairs.

The Second Emphýlios is known as the War of the Elders (*Pólemos tōn Proestôn*). It was fought briefly and with the single objective of taking over power from the *proestoi*. These were the leaders of the communities, initially appointed by the Ottomans as agents and mediators of political power between the Ottoman administration and the members of the community. Unsurprisingly, they did not, from the beginning or at all times, support the revolution against the Ottomans.

The Left used the term *Emphýlios* (along with *Deutero Andártiko*, "the Second Partisan War") for the war fought between 1946 and 1949, whereas the Center and the Right used the term *Symmoritopólemos* ("Brigand War").[2] *Rizospastis*, the official newspaper of the Greek Communist Party, used the term *emphýlios* as early as 1947 in its leading articles. The emphýlios has been periodized by the Right, by the British, and by U.S. historiography from the beginning: the First Round (1943), the Second Round (the Battle of Athens in 1944), the Third Round (1946–49), a gesture that left no doubt as to the specificity of its timing: when it started, when it ended, and how time was spent in between. Such a specific allocation of time, however, bespeaks the desire to set specific beginnings and specific ends to the event of the emphýlios: it started in 1943, when the competing Resistance armies of ELAS (of democratic, antiroyalist, and Left forces) and EDES (of Right and, eventually, monarchist elements) fought for the right to claim exclusive power over the movement of Resistance to the Germans, and it ended on August 29, 1949, when the National Army (EES) triumphed over the Democratic Army (DS) at the decisive battles in Grammos and Vitsi.

Such a periodization, however, does not take into account the schism that had divided the country with *Dichasmós* (when monarchists and republicans, trying to settle the question of the form of government, engendered a deep and enduring rift), the trauma of the Metaxas dictatorship, the handing of political prisoners over to the Germans by the successor to the Metaxas government in 1941, and the creation of the Security Battalions by the Germans and the collaborationist government of Rallis. Nor does it take into account that the war could not have ended on August 29, 1949, given that the concentration camps at Makrónisos, Yáros, and Trikeri were in full operation, receiving the returning and captured soldiers of the Democratic Army, their families, friends, relatives, and fellow villagers, all of them *symmorites* ("bandits") to the government, its forces, and its mechanisms, and *andártes* ("partisans") for everyone else. Nor does it account for the fact that the term *post–civil war* does not denote a temporality that sets apart the civil war from the rest of time, is not a term of closure but an existential adjective, a term that has participated in the production of a political reality, the reality that did not end with the defeat on Vitsi but continued to exist until almost the junta.

2. At least one researcher, Nikos Koulouris, who has compiled a bibliography of the emphýlios that includes both Right- and Left-wing publications, has set its temporal dimensions between 1945 (post-Varkiza agreement) and 1949 (with the collapse of the front at Vitsi). See Koulouris 2000.

The term *metemphyliakos* ("post–civil-war"), always an adjective in Greek, delineates the specificity of the experience of living-while-Leftist after the end of the military struggle. It conjures up images of state-of-exception military tribunals and state-of-exception death sentences, laws against political engagement and against the peace movement, exile, imprisonment on false or no counts or on false police reports, political murder, political rape, political torture. Nothing is past in the post–civil-war site, because it produces a space that keeps time in a state of purgatory.

In 1989 the term *emphýlios* became the official locution, replacing the term *Symmoritopólemos* ("Bandit War"), and the term *Democratic Army* replaced the term *symmorites* ("bandits") through Law 1863 "Concerning Lifting the Repercussions of the Civil War 1944–49" after the restoration of parliamentarism in 1974, when the Communist Party was made legal again, and especially after the act of reconciliation by the socialist government formed when Andreas Papandreou's Panhellenic Socialist Movement (PASOK) won the elections in 1981. The files on dissidents kept by the Central Information Service were then burned in the furnace of the Athens Steel Mills, and the Left was finally forgotten (despite the fact that it entered Parliament). Nevertheless, during an interview that I conducted in the summer of 2006, a man whose father had been executed by OPLA on December 3, 1944, started by setting out the ground for me, when I mentioned to him that I was researching the emphýlios. "So that we don't misunderstand each other," he said, "I am Rightwing [*dexiós*]; for me there is no *Emphýlios* but only *Symmoritopólemos.*"

The periodization of the emphýlios into three rounds is particularly seductive, as it presents a coherent narrative seeking to justify the perception that Communism posed a perpetual threat, taking for granted the presumed revolutionary character of the Greek Communist Party and its perpetual struggle for power, a presumption that would be correct if the KKE were truly revolutionary. But everything points toward the opposite, toward the fact that, despite what the personal illusions of some of its leadership at times might have been, the Party itself (in its true, Marxist meaning of the people who comprise it) never really engaged in an attempt to engender a radical political reformation, not during the Metaxas dictatorship, not in 1943, not in December 1944, not in 1947. Therefore the tripartite periodization can only be a gesture that belies the common understanding that in Greece history has been written by the loser, to underline the fact that, in the final analysis, one way or another, history is always written by the winner.

Witness of the Mountains

Fighting started in March 1946, when a group of thirty ex-ELAS members, not yet organized as an army, attacked a police outpost in the village of Litochoro, about thirty kilometers south of Thessaloniki. In May the collaborationists who had been indicted and sentenced to prison terms were released by the Tsaldares government. The same month the first Emergency Military Tribunals (Ektakta Stratodikeia) were established. On June 18 the Third Parliamentary Vote took place (as we have already seen), decreeing the death penalty for anyone who engaged in or contributed to breaking up the Greek state. By the middle of August, thirty-three such sentences had been carried out, and about 3,250 Leftists, along with the majority of the leaders of ELAS, had been exiled. The escalation of violence by the Right-wing paramilitary forces became such a concern for U.S. Ambassador Lincoln MacVeagh that he made a formal complaint to the head of the State Department. The same concern was expressed by British Prime Minister Clement Attlee. (See Alivizatos 1981.)

In December the KKE announced the formation of the Democratic Army (Demokratikos Stratos Elladas, DSE), headed by Markos Vafiadis (known as "General Markos"), who operated from a base in Yugoslavia. He was sent by the KKE to align and organize the already-existing armed groups. By late 1946, DSE could deploy about ten thousand partisans in various areas of Greece, mainly in the northern mountains, although a report in September 1946 prepared by the Greek Communist Party for the Communist Party of the Soviet Union states that there are four thousand partisans, all of whom are under the control of the Party. Both the Yugoslav and the Albanian Communist governments supported the KKE fighters (primarily by supplying sustenance, not armament), although the Soviet Union kept a safe distance.

Throughout 1947 fighting intensified, as did the emergency measures taken by the government in the form of legislation, terror, and rigged elections. In December 1947 the KKE announced the formation of a Provisional Democratic Government (Prosōrinē Dēmokratikē Kyvérnēsē), with Markos Vafiadis as prime minister. In retaliation, the Athens government outlawed the Communist Party. The National Army now numbered about ninety thousand men. The British undertook the task of modernizing its equipment and training, but by early 1947 Britain, having spent eighty-five million pounds in Greece since 1944 and facing the rapid collapse of the empire, could no longer afford this enterprise. On February 21, 1947, the British government informed the U.S. State Department that the British Empire would have to withdraw all troops and support from Greece as of March 31, 1947, because they were direly needed elsewhere.

On March 10, 1947, President Harry S Truman announced what came to be known as the Truman Doctrine, in which he committed the United States to step in to support the government of Greece against Communist pressure (Parergon 5.2). This move opened the cold war and began a long and troubled relationship between Greece and the United States. For several decades, for

3. While walking in Central Park in the fall of 2005, I encountered a group of about five people, who had set out a small table and were distributing literature. One of the men handed me a little postcard that gave a brief description of the involvement of the CIA in the training of foreign police and paramilitary forces in techniques of interrogation. As I took the card, the man asked if I would like to stop and listen to him about this issue. I was in a hurry and said that I really did not need to, that I am from Greece. The man looked at me with contrition and, almost in tears, whispered: "I am sorry, I am really very, very sorry." The involvement of the CIA in Greek politics has been amply documented in recent years. The first book on the matter is Agee 1975, which states matter-of-factly something that was understood as truth by the Greek population but seen as Greek paranoia elsewhere—namely, that "in Greece, the CIA participated in bringing in the repressive regime of the colonels" (8)—before Agee goes on to talk about the millions that The Company [sic] spent to "destabilize" the Allende government in Chile and set up the junta of Augusto Pinochet (in addition to murdering Allende himself, something that has been confirmed by the recent declassification of the Kissinger archives by the National Security Archives). Agee does not discuss in depth Greece or any other country where he was not stationed himself, but he has published a partial list of CIA operatives throughout (primarily) Latin America.

4. If the war was declared to be a civil war, as the KKE had done as early as 1947, the Western states would have had no right to interfere. The United Nations Special Committee on the Balkans (UNSCOB) of 1947 to 1952, led by Mark Ethridge and ostensibly sent to Greece to document border incidents and Balkan involvement, was from early on torn between the fiction of neutrality and the tug of Ameri-

example, the American ambassador advised the king about important issues such as the appointment of the prime minister and intervened in other political matters—not to mention the fact that the CIA trained Greek officers in the art of counterinsurgency and interrogation techniques.[3]

Given the Truman Doctrine and the Marshall Plan, funds, advisors, and equipment started flooding into the country from the United States. Under U.S. guidance, a series of major offensives were launched in the mountains of central and northern Greece, especially after James Van Fleet took over as commander of the Joint United States Military Advisory Group (Parergon 5.3). The equipment of the National Army included U.S. agents, battalions, and napalm bombs, which were being dropped on villages close to the strongholds of the Democratic Army. This greatly exceeded the equipment of the Democratic Army, which mainly consisted of what ELAS had managed to salvage from the collapse of Italy and Germany (Parergon 5.4).

The emphýlios was fought in the countryside, where the majority of the population was caught in the crossfire and had little chance to resist. The DSE was in dire need of supplies, mainly foodstuffs, as its supply lines were precarious, coming over the border from Albania and Yugoslavia. Often the DSE would enter a village and requisition its supplies (its crops, beasts of burden, blankets). The very village that had been raided by the DSE would then be held accountable by the National Army, with its citizens being characterized as Communist sympathizers and suffering the consequences (imprisonment, torture, and exile).

As Anikam Nachmani states, "although the situation was tantamount to civil war, Western states were extremely hesitant to define it as such, in order to avoid camouflaging the Balkan involvement" (1990: 93).[4] As I was reading Nachmani's book, my mother phoned. She asked what I was doing, and I said I was reading about this in a book on the international intervention and how the Allies refused to call it an *emphýlios.*

"What do they mean?" my mother asked.

I said that they were reluctant to call it *emphýlios.*

"Yes," my mother said sarcastically, "it wasn't an *emphýlios* war, it was a loving war [*den êtan emphýlios pólemos, êtan agapéménos pólemos*]!" She added an expletive.

Human Islands (Parergon 5.5)

On February 5, 1946, the Sofoulis government issued Emergency Law 890, abolishing the concentration camps of the Metaxas period. A year later, on February 19, 1947, General Ventêrês suggested to the minister of defense, G. Stratos, the organization of three concentration camps: Makrónisos for those drafted into the Greek armed forces, Trikeri for "suspicious" men and women of the areas cleared out by the government army, and Yioúra for those convicted under criminal law.[5] The last were members of the Resistance against the Germans, members of OPLA, and low-ranking members of the Communist Party, all accused under criminal law of murder, espionage, and "having broken the peace and quiet of law-abiding citizens." Children fourteen to eighteen years old whose parents were either fighting with the Democratic Army or were imprisoned for being Communists were also held in Yioúra. These children had originally been placed in "rehabilitation" centers, primarily in the Rehabilitation Center for Juvenile Delinquents in Kephessia, a notorious place where organized torture, including systematic beatings, rape, and terrorization, sought to extract *délôseis metanoias* ("declarations of repentance") from them. (See Maragaris 1966: 43.)

In order to put this plan into effect, Gen-

can interests. As early as 1947 Ethridge reported that members of his committee had "canvassed in [their] minds a neutral commission of three, but [they] didn't know any neutrals except the King of Mog Mog" (quoted in Nachmani 1990: 103). A year later, in March 1948, the U.S. State Department spelled out that the function of the UNSCOB observers ought to be to supply the Greek National Army with intelligence on the guerrillas (ibid.). In August 1948, Karl Rankin, a counselor stationed at the U.S. embassy in Athens, was even more direct, noting that the "objective and historical function of the UNSCOB should be changed. It should not again be necessary to 'prove' the Greek case *nor to insist on the fiction of the possible compliance therewith of A[lbania], B[ulgaria], and Y[ugoslavia], although contrary to the plans of international Communism.* . . . The non-Communist world must realize that Greece is on 'our side,' or rather that we are on 'her side,' and that we are defending her *in our own defense*" (quoted in ibid.; my emphasis).

---

5. The issue of women prisoners is multiply complicated, and I cannot address it here adequately. Women were imprisoned for a variety of reasons: as members of the (eventually) outlawed Communist Party; as aiding and abetting Communists; as conspiring with Communists; and, based on the old 1871 law against brigandage, for their kinship ties to the partisans. Women's bodies, undisciplined and unruly, lacking the kind of order and discipline that could be recognized by the military, presented a particular challenge to the wardens, the military police, and torturers. With the exception of those who were captured as members of the DSE and had been trained as active soldiers, women had not encountered military discipline and training in their civilian lives. Military commands were not easily understood, and acts of resistance by women prisoners took a form completely different from those of men. They included singing, the sharing

of child rearing, and caring for each other. As Tasoula Vervenioti has noted, even the most simple of military commands, such as "Attention!" could be impossible to follow, since some of the prisoners were carrying their infant children or were wearing traditional clothing (with long full skirts or long wide trousers), which prevented them from moving freely (Vervenioti, 2000: 103). On the position of women in the Resistance see Hart 1996; on women in exile prior to the Second World War, see Kenna 1991 and 2001; the most comprehensive work on women in the concentration camps, and on Makrónisos in particular, remains Vervenioti 2000. A number of memoirs have been published over the past five years by women who were interned as young adults on Chios, Trikeri, and Makrónisos. No women were sent to Yioúra.

6. As Alivizatos (1981) notes, Greek governments before and during the civil war managed not to slide into an outright dictatorship, but maintained at least the façade of democracy. Thus they could claim that the strife was between the democratically elected government and a political minority motivated and guided from abroad.

eral Ventêrēs asked Colonel Bairaktáres to be in charge of the organization Anamorphotikos Organismos Makronisou (Makrónisos Reformative Organization; I have used the translation in Voglis 2002: 107), which would eventually establish the camp of Makrónisos. The stated purpose of the organization, as developed by General Ventêrēs, was (1) to concentrate all battalions of sappers (i.e., noncombatant conscripted soldiers) in one place, where they could be used "in fruitful occupations with an eye toward redirecting them to the Fatherland"; and (2) to come into contact with the directors of the prisons throughout Greece and discuss the alleviation of the problem of overcrowding. In actuality the interned included: the leadership of the Communist Party and the captured leaders of the Democratic Army; members of the Communist Party; uncommitted Leftists, suspected Leftists, and their families, at some point including women and children aged two to eighty; and countless people who had participated in the Resistance against the Germans yet were merely antifascist in their political convictions. Characteristically, an old man who was the president of a mountainous village and who gave food and shelter to the andártes as they passed by his village one night was court-martialed and sent to Yioúra with a life sentence.

The status of Makrónisos and the methods applied there were legalized on October 14, 1949, by Resolution 73, a Special Constitutional Resolution brought to Parliament by the democratic Diomidis government a month after the end of the actual hostilities of the civil war and after the majority of the fighters of the Democratic Army had been killed or captured, or had escaped to Albania and from there to the People's Republics and the USSR.[6] That was also the time when the island of Vidos, off the coast of Corfu, was opened to intern children aged thirteen to twenty-one whose parents had been either killed during the hostilities or imprisoned by the government. Those two prisons had been preceded on January 4, 1948, by the decree that established the civilian concentration camp on Makrónisos, terming it A Criminal Prison, and, on July 6, 1949, by a royal decree published in the *Government Gazette* on July 11 that relocated the Sophronestikon Katastema

Anelikon (Juvenile Reformatory) of Kephessia to Makrónisos.

The islands existed in a space where, as Begoña Aretxaga has noted, "the State was both the law and its transgression" (2000: 60). They were set up to receive the Left as the wake, the refuse, the dregs of humanity, as undesirable and "superfluous."[7] This refuse of humanity, the undesirables and the superfluous, was managed and manhandled by those who had repented. On Makrónisos, the Military Police, the infamous AM, was almost entirely composed of repentant Leftists who had already signed declarations of repentance. The original group of AM, who escorted the first group of soldiers there on May 28, 1947, must have been old members of the TA, or AM from other military prisons. It is not entirely clear, and every attempt I have made to elicit this information through interviews has been ineffectual. On the camp in Yáros, which was not a camp for the military but was nevertheless under the jurisdiction of the army, the torturers and wardens were primarily convicts under the common criminal law, not under the Idiónymon. As one of my interlocutors said, "They were all kinds of social sediment: rapists, pederasts, embezzlers, murderers."[8] (This also appears in the memorandum sent to the minister of justice in 1950 by the detainees.) Over the years, the operation of the Makrónisos camp constantly produced new AMs, for an ability and willingness to engage in the torture and terrorism of fellow detainees was required as proof of their own redemption into nationally minded soldiers.

The detainees at Makrónisos and Yáros (and to a lesser extent at Trikeri) lived in tents for the duration of their confinement, roughly from 1947 to 1963. These were tents sometimes placed on the hard ground, sometimes affixed to low stone walls, which the detainees not only had to build themselves but for which they also had

7. "Noxious and superfluous" is the locution used by Wolfgang Sofsky to characterize the Nazi progression of exclusionary ascriptions from "socially dangerous" to suspicious and, in the end, to superfluous. Hannah Arendt has shown how humans are construed as "superfluous" as they enter the process of tight capitalist production. Totalitarianism, she argues, received this notion of "superfluity" and applied it to different classes of people. (In early Nazi Germany those were, in order of appearance, the mentally ill and challenged, Communists, union leaders, Gypsies, homosexuals, beggars, vagrants, ruffians, the work-shy, asocials [*Asoziale*], prostitutes, those suffering from venereal diseases, psychopaths, "traffic offenders," "fault finders," and, in the end, Jews; see Sofsky 1997: 33). I find Arendt's flattening of "totalitarianism" in the contexts of Nazism and Stalinism highly problematic and restrictive, though I recognize the political significance of her critique of Soviet abuses of democracy. See Arendt 1968.

8. The distrust of political prisoners toward those indicted for criminal offenses is not restricted to prisoners on Yáros. Foucault says that Jean Genet once mentioned to him that when he was in prison for theft he had to be transferred to the Palais de Justice for sentencing and was to be handcuffed to another prisoner for transfer there. When the warden moved to handcuff them, the prisoner asked the warden what Genet had been brought in for. When the warden said that Genet was a thief, the political prisoner refused to be handcuffed to him. From that moment on, Genet said, he had "a certain contempt for all forms of political movements" (Foucault 1974: 159). Nenedakis mentions that the wardens and torturers on Yioúra were *dosilogoi*, collaborators with the Germans and some members of the Security Battalions who had been tried and convicted of

Figure 13. Photograph of detainees on Makrónisos, June 1950. Note the low tents in rows and the mainland and Lavrion beyond the strait. The man in the gray shirt in the middle of the photograph is Kostas Papaioannou, whose archive is kept at the General State Archives in Kavala. Reproduced with permission.

collaboration. Thus on Yioúra the wardens and the torturers were themselves convicts. They were even given official ranks taken from the ancient army (*hekatontarchos, hiliarchos,* etc.; Nenedakis 1964: 116).

to procure the needed stones, an endeavor that became part of the torture. In the technologies of punishment and rehabilitation, there seems to have been a preoccupation with the handling of stone (already well known in the chain gangs of nineteenth-century prisons). On Makrónisos and Yáros, on the Andaman Islands, on Goli Otok (Parergon 5.6), and in Dachau, the mindless, useless, and repetitive handling of stone became the syntagmatic modality of punishment and of resistance at once. The constant repetition of the Sisyphean act, of needlessly and mindlessly carrying stone, seeks to obliterate the political consciousness of the prisoner, emptying his conscience, as if time did not exist, as if time were endless, as if the carrying of stone were the syntax of the prisoner's life. The order was always very clear: take those rocks from up there and bring them down here. When the transport was done, the order was reversed: take the stones from down here and move them up there. This would take place all day long, in the heat of summer or the cold of winter, always under a relentless wind, without water, without rest, without shoes, in tattered clothes on tattered bodies (Parergon 5.7). At some point the torture acquired a target: make embankments for the tents. The tents were large enough for ten people but were occupied by thirty, forty, or sometimes fifty. Some had cots, most had nothing, as if the lack of objects would teach the Leftists the value of property, would infuse in them the merits of our "Western, democratic values" (to echo President George W. Bush, himself eerily echoing the torturers of Makrónisos and Yáros a lifetime earlier). Despite all proclamations to the contrary, Makrónisos and Yáros amounted to pure punishment in contradistinction to Metaxas's and Maniadákis's concept of discipline.

The torture of stone on Makrónisos became an exercise in a nationalist history lesson: make replicas of ancient structures, build and sculpt as if you were ancient Greeks.[9] The segments of the camp where repentant soldiers stayed, those who had signed the *dēlôseis*, became an open-air exhibit of small-scale replicas of the Parthenon and other classical buildings. As Yannis Hamilakis (2002) notes, on Makrónisos the project of rehabilitating the Communists into nationally minded Christians passed through the archaeolatry of the national state as its only point of reference. Over the years, Makrónisos as the "New Parthenon" has been attributed (probably erroneously) to Panayiotis Kanellopoulos, minister of reconstruction in 1945 and a legal scholar educated in Athens, Munich, and Heidelberg (Parergon 5.8). But even if the New Parthenon cannot be claimed by Kanellopoulos, the ideas that "Makrónisos is a sample of Greek civilization," as he announced in Parliament on July 14, 1950, or that "on this dry island Greece has sprouted today more beautiful than ever" (as he mentioned in an interview with *Skapaneus*) are certainly his (Bournazos 2000: 129). Perfectly rational intellectuals and scholars, educated in Germany and France, who had held prestigious positions at many prestigious universities, went through Makrónisos and pronounced it "a great educational institution that seeks to rest on pure reason, since it has managed, in a very short time, to put some order to concepts and consciences. . . . All of us ought to live a Makrónisos. . . . On Makrónisos training, habit, and treatment have been substituted for persecution." This is the opinion of the neo-Kantian philosopher Constantine Tsatsos, later president of the Hellenic Republic (ibid.: 121). The *New York Times* correspondent to Greece, M. I. F. Stone, went many

9. The architect Tasos Daniel, who had been interned at Makrónisos and held in the military prison there, spoke during the first conference on Makrónisos, in 1988, about the handling of stone. He stated that the little theater they built on the island "open, classical, . . . was endearing . . . for three reasons. First, because it was a faithful copy of the ancient theaters. Second, because mortar had been used for its construction. Mortar is a strange medium to be used for the construction of bleachers and an open classical theater. But we had an allergic reaction to stone. We saw stone as the most violent form of hard labor, the most bestial hard labor, when we saw our fellow soldiers on the Battalions be made to transport it" (Bournazos and Sakellaropoulos 2000: 264–65).

steps further when he announced to the readers of the newspaper on May 25, 1949, that Greece constituted a U.S. political laboratory, whose results could later be utilized elsewhere (quoted in de Villefosse 1950: 1288).

In the assessment of scholars, Makrónisos appears again and again as an intimate and integral part of modern Greek Bildung. The archaeologist Spyridon Marinatos, the excavator of Akrotiri, at Thera (among many other very important excavations) wrote in the guest book of the island, during a visit that he paid on October 21, 1949, "There is no school with a greater educational effect than the great National School of Makrónisos" (ibid.: 120). He was supported by the celebrated antiwar novelist Stratis Myrivilis, who termed Makrónisos "the island of Divine Knowledge [*Theognosia*] of wayward minds, the infirmary of tortured consciences . . . the island of a new Circe, the island of an Anticirce, who took the transformed victims of the bad witch, pulled them out of the mud and the hay of her stables, and gave them back their human dignity and Christian heart" (ibid.: 120).

Yáros left few literary traces, and it certainly had no replicas of classical buildings. The torture of stone on Yáros was even more ambitious: to level the mountain to build your own prison. The prisoners did. They leveled the mountain with axes and shovels, and they built the prison—a labyrinthine structure with long, wide corridors that ended in steep, wide staircases—with cement and seawater. The building was uninhabitable. Bitter cold in winter, scorching hot in summer, its walls started crumbling as soon as they were built because of the seawater. The prisoners mutinied and refused to move inside. So they stayed in the tents.

Hark! The Herald Angels Sing (Pareregon 5.9)

The guise under which the islands received *anepithymitoi* ("undesirables") was not exactly Nazi *Schutzhaft* ("protective custody") but preemptive arrest, which led to *peitharheméne diaviosis* ("disciplined existence"), presumably to allow the interned to experience the "healing effects of productive work and tight discipline" that the Nazis had proclaimed as the objective of Dachau when they opened the camp on March 22, 1933 ("Die Wahrheit über Dachau," *Münchner Illustrierte Zeitung*, July 16, 1933; quoted in Marcuse 2001: 28). Two conceptual categories are reanimated here from the Metaxas and occupation periods: (1) that of the suspicious individual, and (2) that of family and kinship as a separate category of danger.

I cannot remember how I found out that my uncle Stéphanos had been an andártēs, but I do remember him telling us stories from the Resistance, starting when we were very young. He was the only one from our large family who would actually come to our country house on weekends. In those days in Greece, in the early and mid sixties, the work week was still six days long. My mother and my uncle, with my sister and me in tow, would take a taxi from our house, go to my father's job, and then all get into our car and drive to the country. We would usually drive at dusk and get there by evening. The roads were treacherous, and the car could not go very fast, so it would usually take us a bit over two hours to cover the distance of 152 kilometers. That was when my uncle Stéphanos would tell us stories from the war.

One evening I asked him if he had been an andártēs with Zervas (the leader of the Right-wing Resistance army). He shouted at the top of his lungs, so violently that I thought we would have an accident: "Zervas, the traitor, the fascist, what do I have to do with Zervas? I was with Aris"—meaning, of course, Aris Velouchiotes. And he would tell us stories from the war: how they would capture the Germans, how they would torture them, how they would hide, how they would ride on their horses for days on end, without rest, always on the run, how Zervas's soldiers would capture the ELAS soldiers and torture them (and just how they would torture them), how (occasionally) their ELAS battalion would capture some of Zervas's andártes and torture them by skinning them and putting salt in the wounds. He would tell these stories in between stories of the tortures on Yioúra and Makrónisos, leaving my sister and me speechless with fear. He never mentioned that after Makrónisos he was sent to the front, to Grammos, to fight against the Democratic Army, nor did anyone ever mention that the only way in which anyone could be sent to Grammos was to have signed a declaration of repentance, *dêlosē metanoias*. I did not find out about the Grammos detail until many years after his death, from one of his in-laws, during fieldwork for this book.

Nor did I know that my uncle Stéphanos had a brother. During one of those trips, somehow his brother was mentioned. I said with an incredulity that I still remember vividly, "I didn't know you had a brother." He started shouting (my uncle Stéphanos had a very liberal relationship to what we call inappropriate language): "A brother? Do I ever have a brother? That faggot [*ho poústes*], that worm, that awful human [*o palianthropos*], he was the one who testified against me and they sent me to Yioúra." Much later I found out that his brother (whose name I was never told) was a gendarme.

Someone Saw a Skylark (Parergon 5.10)

"Damn wind," I said to my mother in the summer of 2006. "I've been trying to go to Yáros for three summers now, and I can't get there." "You were spared in the knick of time in 1973," my mother joked. "And now you want to go of your own volition." Unlike Makrónisos, which is easily visible from Lavrion on the mainland (where, people say, with the right—or wrong—wind one could hear the screams of the men being tortured) and from the boat that takes you to Kea (Tzia), Yáros is barely visible from the surrounding islands.

10. "Yáros (commonly Yioúra). Island of the Cyclades, Northwest and approximately 9 miles from Cape Trimeso of Syros, and almost across the straights of Andros and Tenos. Its surface area is 17.2 square kilometers. In the 1951 census it counted 7,139; in the 1961 it counted 244. It belongs to the municipality of Ano Syros, province of Syros, Prefecture of Cyclades. Place of existence of political exiles during Roman and Byzantine times. Similarly place of confinement of political prisoners (1947–1961). The buildings erected precisely for this purpose were turned over to the Ministry of National Defense in 1962, to be used as storehouses. Ever since then the area surrounding the island has been characterized as off limits" (*Papyros-Larousse, Greek Edition*, 1964, vol. 5).

11. The "torture of the fig tree [*to vasanisterio tes sykias*]" has been memorialized in drawings by exiles on Yioúra, either during their tenure there or after their release. A prisoner's shoulders would be tied together with thick wire or rope, drawing them together in the middle of his back, and he would then be suspended from the branches of the fig tree for several days. See Figure Y-7 for one such image.

On a clear day, when there is little evaporation off the sea, if one stands on a high spot on the eastern part of Syros or the western part of Tenos one can perhaps make out the shape of its mountain in the midst of the sea. It is a rock of twenty-three square kilometers, located almost on the thirty-eighth parallel, in the midst of a circle composed of the islands of Andros in the northeast, Tenos, Delos, and Renia in the southeast, Syros and Serifos in the south, Kythnos in the southwest, and Tzia and Makrónisos behind it in the northwest. The closest two islands are Tenos and Syros, about fifteen nautical miles away.[10]

Yáros has no fresh water, only some puddles of saltwater sludge that support scorpions, snakes, rats, tumbleweed, some thyme, laurels in abundance, and the occasional fig tree, a sight of delight everywhere in Greece except on this island, where the fig tree became the instrument of one of the most feared and horrifying tortures.[11] It has been reported that someone saw a skylark flying over Yáros in 1947 (Nenedakis 1964). There is no shade on the island, no soft ground where the eye can rest, no gentle slope where one can lie down. From its peak, the mountain slopes down to the sea at a precipitous angle of 45 degrees; the ground is strewn with jagged rocks; it is riven by gullies full of poisonous laurels. A small boat can approach the island by five coves, the largest of which came to be known as the Fifth Cove.

As Yáros is totally exposed to the elements, the only things found in abundance there, other than vermin and rocks, are the sun, which scorches, and a constant wind, which uproots. Because the soil is so thin, barely four centimeters deep, the slightest wind creates a dust cloud that penetrates everything: food, clothes, mouths, ears, noses, wounds. The common joke among detainees and seamen alike is that there are two windy seasons (*meltémia*) on Yáros: one that starts in May and ends in October and another that starts in October and ends in May. Under these conditions, one would be hard pressed to decide which is more difficult, reaching or leaving Yáros.

Yáros was established, at the recommendation of Sir Charles Wickham, as an open-air prison in order to alleviate the asphyxiating conditions of the

Figure Y-1. Approaching the island. The prison building. Note the precipice. To the left of the building is a watch tower. Photograph and caption by Apostolos Papageorgiou; reproduced with permission.

Figure Y-2. A ferryboat with visitors approaching the Fourth Cove for disembarkment. The prison building was designed by the engineer Metaxas and built by the prisoners between 1948 and 1951. To the left is the Fifth Cove. An old prisoner is looking at the dry island with obvious emotion. Photograph and caption by Apostolos Papageorgiou; reproduced with permission.

Figure Y-3. Giorgos Christodoulakis, the baker of the Fourth Cove, shows the base where his tent was, fifty years ago. Photograph and caption by Apostolos Papageorgiou; reproduced with permission.

Figure Y-4. The southern slope of the Fifth Cove. The watchtower guards the southern flank of the prison. Terraces are visible on the slope, which has some soil on top of the rock. They are probably remnants from the time of Sulla's Roman exiles, when the exiles were left without any help from the outside. They had to cultivate both for themselves and for the garrisons. Photograph and caption by Apostolos Papageorgiou; reproduced with permission.

Figure Y-5. The prisoners' cemetery on Yáros, with the Aegean and Tenos in the distance. Photograph and caption by Apostolos Papageorgiou; reproduced with permission.

The cemetery was created by the prisoners themselves. After intense torture, to which the prisoners did not give in, the administration allowed them to create the cemetery so that they could bury their comrades who had been tortured to death.

Figure Y-6. The small cemetery, with twenty graves. The relatives and friends or fellow prisoners of the interred tend the graves and try to find which one belongs to whom. The salty air of the Aegean has eaten away the iron, and the crosses have been destroyed. It is difficult to identify the graves now. The pieces are all mixed up (also by visitors, who have moved them out of curiosity). Only two or three graves have been positively identified. Photograph and caption by Apostolos Papageorgiou; reproduced with permission.

Figure Y-7. The fig tree of Glastras. One of the first directors of the camp on Yáros, named Glastras (which, curiously, means "flowerpot"), introduced this particular torture. He would hang prisoners from the tree by their shoulders and subject them to beatings. He would let them hang there for days, adding the insult that they could come down only after they had ripened (they had signed *dēlôseis*). The tree does not really exist any longer, as most of it has been destroyed by the rain runoff during the winter. This and the following drawings from Yáros are from Anonymous [1950]. They were done by artists who had been interned at Yioúra. In those that follow, the captions were given by the artists.

Figure Y-8. Humiliation at the stone torture.

Figure Y-9. Solar discipline—the "El-Tampa."

«ΕΛ·ΝΤΑΜΠΑ»

Τό ἡλιακό πειθαρχεῖο τῆς Γιούρας. Στήν
πιό φριχτή χαράδρα τοῦ νησιοῦ. Σέ καίει ὁ
ἥλιος τή μέρα καί σέ θερίζει τό κρύο τή νύ-
χτα. Ἑκατοντάδες δίνουν τή ζωή τους ἀκόμα
κλεισμένοι στήν «Ἐλ-Ντάμπα».

Figure Y-10. "El-Ntampa," the solar discipline of Yioúra. In the most
horrific ravine of the island, the sun burns you all day long and the
cold cuts through you at night. Hundreds are giving their lives still
locked up in "El-Ntampa."

overcrowded prisons that had resulted from the severe persecution of Leftists during the period of the White Terror in 1945 and 1946, and it was reserved for civilians.[12] These civilians were Leftists who had been indicted for political acts under criminal law; civilians awaiting trial for the same offenses; civilians who had been indicted and sentenced previously, had been imprisoned elsewhere, and had signed declarations of repentance; and civilians who had been indicted and had been serving sentences in other prisons for either having collaborated with the occupation powers or for having committed civil-law crimes (such as extortion, drug dealing, pimping, embezzling, black marketeering, murder, or incest).

12. Tony Judt laments that "The British had originally hoped to bequeath to liberated Greece a properly non-political army and modern police force; but in the circumstances of time and place, this proved impossible" (2005: 505). One wonders, however, about two things in this statement. First would it really have been possible to produce a "properly nonpolitical army" when the army was engaged in the political reformation of the country? And second, would Sir Charles have had the opportunity to create such a nonpolitical army had he not been sidetracked by pressure to establish and oversee Yáros and Makrónisos?

Each of the five coves accessible by sea was set up as a camp, under the jurisdiction of the general director. Dimitris Manousos, who was detained in Yioúra from 1947 to 1950 and again in 1967, gives a fairly clear account of the distribution of the prisoners and the coves (2005). The first cove contained the main camp, with five thousand prisoners, mainly political prisoners but also a small number of prisoners of common law, and the underaged. This is where the kitchens and various shops were positioned. At the same cove was the house of the director and all offices, along with the penitentiary and the infamous fig tree. The second cove contained two thousand prisoners, the bulk of the civil-law prisoners and civilians who had signed declarations of repentance prior to their arrival on Yioúra. The second cove also had the infirmary, the ill, the disabled, and the aged. Cove three, with one thousand prisoners, was the camp of the intellectuals and party cadres. The fourth cove had two thousand prisoners and was the camp where torture and forced labor primarily took place. The fifth cove was the area of solitary confinement and hardest torture, little more than an annex of the fourth, with five hundred prisoners. Manousos says that the camps also contained two tents for priests who had been assigned to the island and two tents for Jehovah's Witnesses who had refused to carry arms during the emphýlios. There was also one shipowner among the detainees (2005: 24). Eventually Yioúra acquired a cemetery for those who died under torture. There are twenty-two graves on the island marked with iron crosses with no names. There are also two graves with cement crosses, belonging to warders who died on the island. Within the conceptual space of the camp but not belonging to any one of the coves was set up a place of total abjection, which was named by the detainees *Ntámpa* and on Makrónisos was called *Syrma* ("wire"). Not solitary confinement but a space of extreme punishment, *Ntámpa* was an open cage surrounded by three barbed-wire fences. There incorrigibles were sent, after torture had not extracted *dêlosê*. The "Memorandum of Detainees to the Minister of Justice of the Plasteras Government" describes *Ntámpa* as:

> "*El-Tampa*," an open-air cage made of wire, where the patient [sic] is enclosed in order to be literally murdered by the hot spears of the sun. Given the current physical condition of the detainees, the use of this exhausting stockade indicates a clear intent of murder. Even a healthy person, if placed in it, could not avoid fainting or suffering damage from the effect of the solar rays, or at the least suffering sunstroke. One is punished and tortured inhumanly because one submitted a request to be seen by the director, or because one announced to the office the case of someone febrile and in need of immediate transport to the infirmary, or because one appeared in front of the director to complain after having been cruelly removed from the infirmary. Thousands more prisoners have been punished for other reasons. (Petris 1984: 86b [36])

The first boats to carry humans to the island in the early spring of 1947 were fishing boats. They had to battle waves that were sometimes six to seven meters tall and were packed with vomiting, shitting men, already wasted from previous imprisonment. Nikos Oikonomakos, one of the prisoners to have been imprisoned both in Yáros and Makrónisos, was transported in April 1949 to Yáros, after having been sent from Makrónisos to the Tzaneio Hospital in Piraeus with a fractured wrist. From the hospital he was transported, along with other prisoners, to the transport station in Syros (Tmêma Metagōgôn). The night before their transport to Yáros, they were fed garbanzo beans, and Oikonomakos reports that they ate them without realizing that they were spoiled. Diarrhea and vomiting started almost immediately and lasted through the night. The next morning, soiled and still sick, the prisoners were piled into the caïque to be transported to Yioúra.

"You never get three consecutive days of calm here," the fisherman who had agreed to take me to the island in the summer of 2005 said, after the wind picked up on the second day of my stay on Tenos. "The *bourini* [bad weather] lasts a long time; you won't be able to go." The *bourini* comes unexpectedly for those who are not acquainted with the ways of the sea. What to me looked like a perfectly calm sea, with just a faint breath on the water, to the captain of the boat was the beginning of the *bourini*.

Sure enough, in a few hours' time I saw realized before me a description by Tzavalás Karousos, who, at the age of sixty-two, had been transported there in April 1967, not on a small boat, as Oikonomakos describes, but on a navy transport ship: "Someone offered me his place to sit. I had to accept, I had no other place. Apart from the exhaustion, the boat had started moving back and forth. But where could I sit? People had already started vomiting. And everything, *ánthropoi*, packages, vomit, piss, all had become one" (Karousos 1974: 95). Karousos had been detained on Makrónisos during the civil war, but he wrote only of this second experience, his exile to Yáros. "The *bourini* has come. As suddenly as that, as we were looking at the little blue and white islands on the horizon, we saw it coming from the tip of Andros. It was frothing with anger, running maniacally. The playful sea had turned leaden as it passed over her and turned her around. The waves now fought among themselves like immense rams, frantically charging against each other, trying to see which one will kill the other" (ibid.: 132).

As every account of the island written by prisoners there mentions, Yáros was briefly inhabited during Roman times, but its inhabitants were driven away by rats and scorpions. After it was abandoned, it became a place of exile, although so abject a place that already the Romans considered exile there to be the cruelest of all punishments. They reserved it for the most dangerous of the "enemies of the empire." Around 80 B.C. the Roman general Sculla opened Yáros again as a place of exile for eighty thousand of his political adversaries (Parergon 5.11). They were left on the island with seeds to sow and some agricultural implements, but the soil was so sterile that the exiles died within a very short time of hunger, disease, and the bites of rats and scorpions. Remnants of attempts at cultivation are still visible as terraces on the hillside above the First Cove.

During the reign of Tiberius (14–37 A.D.), Yáros was still being considered as a place of exile, until finally the emperor vetoed its use. Tacitus mentions in 109 A.D. that Tiberius was present at the trial of Vibius Serenus, who had been accused by his son (also named Vibius Serenus, who served as both prosecutor and witness against his father) of having plotted against the life of the emperor and of inciting rebellion. Despite the fact that Serenus's guilt could not be proven, even when his servants were tortured, Tiberius brought up old charges of misconduct against him. The Senate decided that he should be punished *more maiorum* (according to the ancient mores), but Tiberius vetoed the vote. Gallus Asinius suggested that Serenus be exiled to *Gyaro aut Donusa* (Yáros or Donusa), but Tiberius interceded again, stating, "both of these islands were deficient of water, and that he whose life was spared, ought to be allowed the necessities of life" (Tacitus, Bk. 4 [30]). Serenus was finally sent back to exile on the island of Amorgos, from which he had been brought, briefly, to attend his trial.

Because of its lack of water and vegetation, and its proliferation of vermin, Yáros remained uninhabited between the time of Tiberius and 1947, when it

13. We can find the category of the "suspicious" both in totalitarianism and in liberal democracies. In the Third Reich we see it first institutionalized in the 1936 "A List" of suspicious persons to be arrested in case of situation "A," which Gestapo chief Reinhard Heydrich composed and which, in 1937, included 46,000 names (Marcuse 2001: 32). The case of the Greek liberal governments of the early twentieth century is not much different; neither are the FBI lists of dangerous individuals of the McCarthy and post-McCarthy eras. The first use of the category of the "suspicious" not directed at the political and ideological convictions of those involved was in the Internment Camps for Persons of Japanese Descent in place from 1942 to 1946 throughout the western, southwestern, and Pacific Coast states of the United States (NARA). The British used the term *suspicious* to refer to Kikuyu suspected of having taken the Mau Mau oath against the colonial government, and they interned every Kikuyu suspected of such an act in specially established camps from 1950 to 1958. The narratives of survivors from the British, Yugoslav, and Greek camps are uncannily similar, including their accounts of torture, although neither group of inmates could have known of the existence of the others. On the Kikuyu, see Chege 2004, Ogot 2005, Anderson 2005, Elkins 2005, and Mamdani 2006. On Goli Otok and Sveti Grgur, see Djilas 1985, Markovski 1984, Banac 1989, Jambresic Kirin 2004, and Lukic 2007.

14. When I tried to find out whether anyone in Markopoulo (the main town near Porto Rafti, where the first encampment of detained soldiers was set up before they were moved to Makrónisos) knew anything about this temporary encampment, not only did no one seem to remember, but no one seemed even to know about this fact. It might have been kept a secret by the army (which is doubtful but not

was set up as a camp, initially for twelve thousand political prisoners who had been indicted for infractions of the criminal law or who had been suspected of being dangerous, and thus possibly having committed such infractions.[13] The notion of the criminal law, however, takes on many more meanings in reference to Yioúra and the Greek Left. First of all, within the context of the authoritarian governments from 1945 on, "criminal law" was primarily distinguished from military law, a distinction that concerned only the particular legal body that would manage specific persons and the place of internment that would be decided for them. Yioúra was reserved for those whose actions fell under criminal law, in opposition to those whose actions fell under military law, who were sent to Makrónisos. The beginnings of the history of Yáros, however, not only locate it on a painful continuum of abjection but, even more disturbingly, locate that continuum within the context of internal strife, civil war, and fratricidal histories. Yáros has never been anything but the space of political abjection. And precisely the total abjection carried on in this wretched place has made the history of it so palpable and so relevant for the prisoners telling its story.

Poems Were Impaled on the Barbed Wire
(Parergon 5.12)

Soldiers started being taken to Makrónisos in January 1947, after being briefly detained in the temporary encampment at Porto Rafti, the port of Markopoulo, to the east of Athens, by the new airport.[14] Makrónisos is better known than Yáros. First of all, it was established by a specific act of Parliament, whereas the establishment of Yáros was unacknowledged and because of that, I would argue, more horrific. It was a secret that everybody knew and no one was at liberty to articulate. Makrónisos has also been more extensively analyzed. Conferences have been organized, papers have been written, dissertations have been directed and defended, and, more importantly, many testimonials, Communist Party publications, and oral histories have been published about Makrónisos. There is no question that Makrónisos had more detainees and lasted longer. While the three camps (Yáros, Makrónisos, and Trikeri) were established simultaneously in 1947, Makrónisos was continuously used until 1958. Until 1950, once they had signed *dēlóseis* prisoners from Yioúra were taken to Makrónisos, and from there some of them were sent to the front to fight against the Communist army. After 1950, some prisoners from Makrónisos, primarily conscripts who had not signed *dēlóseis* before the time of their military service was over (so had not been sent to the front) were sent to Yioúra. Yáros was emptied in 1953 and used again briefly in 1954. In 1955 it was reinstituted by a royal decree that reactivated decree 1137/1942, issued during the occupation, and was used for a few exiles in 1958 until 1963, when it was emptied. It was opened again by the junta in 1967 and in 1973 to 1974.

But Makrónisos is also the more spectacular of the camps, with its complexity, its structures, its ruins, its proximity to Athens, and its literary production.[15] What later became post–civil-war literature was initially produced on Makrónisos. Yiannis Ritsos, Aris Alexandrou, Tasos Leivaditis, Titos Patrikios, and Mikis Theodorakis wrote poems there. Often they committed these to memory, but occasionally they scrawled them on paper, which was almost impossible to find, and hid them in bottles or in crevices, trying to save them from the raids of the Military Police. Later, after the camps had been closed down, novelists wrote novels and short stories that, along with the poems,

impossible), or it might have been erased from local memory (which is possible but not necessary). After repeated inquiries, Stamates Methenites found a trace of memory in someone in Markopoulo and published it in 2007. There was, however, one episode that almost everyone in the town knew and remembered very well (it was also more recent, having happened early in 2000). A bakery had opened on the edge of the town sometime at the beginning of the sixties, owned by a man from the Ionian islands. After a few years, this man opened a second bakery closer to the port at Porto Rafti. "One day," my friend Kostes said, "there was a big commotion at the first bakery. They had to call the police and then an ambulance because a customer who had gone in to buy bread had seen the owner and had recognized him as 'his AM.' He got so enraged that he beat him to pulp, so bad that he had to be taken away in an ambulance." "His AM" means his torturer on Makrónisos.

---

15. One of the most elaborate projects of a mimesis of antiquity was undertaken on Makrónisos, where the administration of the island required "recovered" soldiers to build small-scale replicas of famous structures of antiquity, such as the Parthenon, the Helakleion, and a number of statues. The high level of craftsmanship that went into this project testifies to the many artists who had been arrested as Communists, Leftists, or suspected Leftists. When one high-ranking visitor to the island commented to Director Vassilopoulos on the quality of the structures, Vassilopoulos replied that "all Greek intelligentsia" had passed through Makrónisos. The weight of antiquity in the modern Greek imaginary cannot be overestimated. It is so great that the declaration issued by the Society of Aesthetic Saboteurs of Antiquities (Syndesmos Aisthitikon Sampoter Archaiotiton) on November 18, 1944, calling for the destruction of the

Parthenon, can be taken as only half serious. The declaration stated: "The blowing up and complete razing of the Parthenon is designated as our first act of destruction, because it has, literally, drowned us." The declaration was signed by Yiorgos Makris, and the society comprised himself and a few of his friends, among whom was the later Minister Anastasios Peponis (quoted in Daloukas 2005: 64). The ruins of the replicas, ruins of ruins, remained on Makrónisos for a few years after the camp had been abandoned, and their foundations can still be seen. On the project of the replicas, see Hamilakis 2002.

16. On the literary production of and on Makrónisos, see Papatheodorou 2000 and Argyriou 2000.

17. "Makrónisos (ancient Helene or Kranae) Island belongs to the township of Korresia, of the Kea island, of the prefecture of Cyclades. Its 38 inhabitants of the 1928 census, the 32 of the 1940 census, and the 12 of the 1961 census refer to the shepherds seasonally established there from neighboring Kea, or fishermen, i.e. non-permanent residents. At the 1951 census it numbered 4,484 residents, still nonpermanent ones. At a certain time it had reached the number of 10,000, primarily detainees and confined soldiers and civilians" (Greek edition of *Papyros-Larousse*, 1964).

completely changed the literary landscape of Greece.[16]

Makrónisos is a long island, 5 square kilometers in all, 10 kilometers from north to south (hence its name), and 500 meters at its widest point, from east to west. It is located off the coast of Attica, across the water from Lavrion, on the thirty-seventh parallel.[17] Its western flank looks at Athens; its eastern flank looks at Kea (Tzia). Between Makrónisos and Tzia sank the *Britannic*, sister ship to the *Titanic*. It is a dry island, although not as dry as Yáros, given that it has two small springs. Its terrain is not as precipitous, even though its highest peak is at 281 meters. It is an island of ravines and slopes, full of poisonous laurels, myrtle bushes, low-lying junipers, and the ubiquitous *afánes* ("tumbleweed"). It has five natural coves on its western flank, facing Athens, but its eastern flank is completely inaccessible. The two springs are located on this inaccessible eastern flank, which faces the island of Tzia.

In antiquity Makrónisos was named Helene, after Helen of Sparta (or Helen of Troy, depending on one's position in history), because that is where, legend has it, Helen and Paris found refuge after the fall of Troy, as Pausanias mentions in his *Attika*. The ancient ruins found on the island indicate that in antiquity it was used as a sacred place of worship, without permanent residents. Some itinerant shepherds occasionally brought their goats to the island, and at the end of the First Balkan War, in 1912, a group of Turkish prisoners of war ill with cholera and tuberculosis were abandoned there. Russian and "undesirable" Greek soldiers were brought there in 1922, as were briefly, in 1929, refugees from the Asia Minor expedition. During the war the Germans established watch towers there.

When established as a place of exile and internment in 1947, Makrónisos had a single purpose: to reeducate Greek Leftists into the principles of nationalism (*ethnikophosyne*) and Christianity and to obtain from them written declarations renouncing communism and submitting to legality, the famous *dēlôseis nomimofrosynis*. From 1947 to 1958, over one hundred thousand people

Figure M-1. Approaching Makrónisos. On the slope to the right is the open-air church of Hagios Antonios. The long white building in the center of the photograph is the main bakery of the camp. The occasion of the visit was a two-day concert of the music of Mikis Theodorakis on the poetry of Yiannis Ritsos. Ritsos and Theodorakis were detained on Makrónisos for a year (1949–50), within months of each other. Theodorakis was brought to Makrónisos from exile on the island of Ikaria, Ritsos from exile on the island of Lemnos. Theodorakis was so brutally tortured on Makrónisos that he had to be taken to Military Hospital 401 in Athens. He suffered broken bones throughout his body and a dislocated jaw. After several weeks at the hospital, he was sent back to Makrónisos. After more torture (and the collapse of DSE on August 29, 1949) his father managed to have him released and took him to Crete. For ten years after Makrónisos, he would wake up in the middle of the night drenched in sweat and shivering. In the summer of 2004, at an interview given to the Greek newspaper *Eleutherotypia*, he mentioned that Makrónisos still sends shivers down his spine. I watched as the police helped him leave the theater after the recital, amidst red revolving police lights and a convoy of police cars. I wondered how he must have felt at that moment, his first time back on Makrónisos since 1950, being taken away from the island again by the police. The question was answered the next day when a photograph of him taken during the recital was published in the newspapers—the face of a person in deep pain. The concert was organized by the Athens Festival and took place at various sites throughout Greece, including the exile islands Samos, Lemnos, Ai-Stratis, Lesvos, Leros, and Ikaria. The Athens Festival had arranged for transport buses from the small harbor of the cove of the First Battalion, where the ferry docked, to the theater of the Second Battalion. These are the buses visible in the photograph. Photograph by the author.

Figure M-2. Part of the classical structures on Makrónisos, or, better said, of what was thought to be classical. The only connection to classicism that this bas relief has is through the classical sensibilities of fascist and Nazi aesthetics. At the top of the photograph is a watch tower. Photograph by the author.

Figure M-3. The exterior of the sanctuary of the chapel of Aghios Georgios of the Second Battalion. The church was built by the detainees with whatever materials could be found, produced, and engineered on the island. Both the exterior and the interior of the church are plastered and whitewashed. Whitewashing requires fiber to stay on the plaster, but fiber could not be found on the island. The evening of the recital a tall Makronisiotes, sitting on the bench next to me, patted his still-thick hair and said, "Do you see this hair? When we needed hair for the whitewash and none could be found, the lieutenant ordered us all shorn and used our hair for binding." Photograph by the author.

Figure M-4. Part of the Second Battalion structures. Some of these structures were first erected for the Turkish POWs in 1912. Photograph by the author.

Figure M-5. Looking up the hill toward the main road that connected all the battalions and coves. The low vegetation is afàna (akin to sagebrush). The detainees had to clear out the area by hand and level the slope in order to build the structures or fix their tents. Without interference from humans, afàna takes over parts of the island. Photograph by the author.

Figure M-6. One of the arched entrances to the Second Battalion. Photograph by the author.

Figure M-7. The ruined administrative buildings of the Second Battalion. All the buildings on Makrónisos had wooden beams and roofs, but the wood was plundered after the camp was abandoned. The photograph is taken at the end of the recital, August 30, 2003.

were deported and tortured on Makrónisos, Yáros, and Trikeri before being transferred to exile on the other "small islands" or dying. As Polymeris Voglis has convincingly argued, the islands constituted a space where new political subjects were systematically produced by the postwar governments (Voglis 2002). This process of reformulating political subjects rested upon a form of governmentality convinced that populations (in this case, the population of Greek Leftists and dissidents) could be inscribed and reinscribed, almost ad infinitum, in new subjective positions through a process of reeducation and rehabilitation.

The distance between Makrónisos and Yáros is significant and is made even more so by the roughness of the seas. Communication between detainees in the two places was impossible. The prisoners of Yioúra knew about Makrónisos, so much so that in the Memorandum of 1950/51 Yáros is described as "the largest prison for democratic detainees and the most frightful place of annihilation after Makrónisos."[18] But the same cannot be said of the detainees of Makrónisos—or, better, the detainees of Makrónisos either knew very little of the conditions on Yioúra (as one of my interlocutors who had spent time on Ikaria, Makrónisos, and Ai-Stratis said when I asked him about this) or those who were sent to Yioúra after 1950 thought of it as "summer camp" (as another of my interlocutors said, a person who had been in exile starting in 1937 under Metaxas, had participated in the Resistance, had been jailed in the Middle East, and had been sent to Makrónisos, from there to Yioúra, and from there to Ai-Stratis before being released in 1963). Whatever Yioúra was, a "summer camp" it was not. The accounts in the Memorandum (Petris 1984), Nenedakis 1964, Mahairas 1999, and in interviews I have conducted with prisoners who were held on Yioúra between 1947 and 1950 all mention a dreaded place where torture was a technology of manufacturing compliance and submission.

18. The authors of the "Memorandum" coined a new word to denote Yáros and Makrónisos as places of existence: *exontōtérion.* It conjures up the horror of the total annihilation of the other on the level of existence as being (*ōn*) (Petris 1984: 66 [18]).

Dachau

Dachau was the concentration camp Greeks knew best (Parergon 5.13). It was the only name of a concentration camp that I knew when I was growing up, until I was old enough to listen to Mikis Theodorakis's *Mauthausen* and learn about Auschwitz and Belsen. "It is important not to forget that that the first concentration camps in Germany were the work not of the Nazi regime but of the Socialist Democratic governments, which interned thousands of communist militants in 1923 on the basis of *Schutzhaft*," Agamben reminds us (1998: 167). Dachau as a camp is almost that old. Originally built as a munitions factory during the Great War, it was used as a concentration camp in March 1933 to intern political prisoners. The camp was placed under the jurisdiction of the SS, and special laws were enacted to legitimate its existence. With the Nuremberg Laws of 1935, Dachau acquired the legal framework that it needed. Greek partisans, Resistance fighters, saboteurs, and Communists, along with members of the clergy of the Greek church who had harbored English and Greek Resistance fighters and some monks from Mt. Athos, started being sent there as early as 1941.[19] Some of them endured there until they were released in 1945, when U.S. troops entered the camp. Among them was the secretary general of the KKE, Nikos Zachariadis. Many died. Greek Jews were almost all sent to the camps, and most of them died.

19. I have not been able to find much material on Greek clergy sent to German concentration camps. One source is Cramer 2006. Cramer mentions that the majority of prisoners at Dachau were Christians (I think that he means non-Jewish, not necessarily practicing Christians), something that could be explained by the fact that Dachau was primarily used for Resistance fighters.

"There are those who claim they knew nothing, although the regime had instrumentalized the concentration camps, using them to intimidate the German people," Wolfgang Sofsky writes, exposing the falsity of the claim to innocence that has been erected about the camps of the Reich (1997: 6). He also exposes the use of fear as a means of manhandling the public. This is why so many arrested detainees at Yáros and Makrónisos started to sign their declarations of repentance so soon after they arrived on the islands. Despite the fact that the methods used on the islands to extract the *dēlōseis* always came as a "surprise" to the authorities in Athens, the rumors that were circulating were enough to produce a climate of intense fear that induced compliance. On December 2, 1949, an anonymous petition drafted in Athens made its way, in translation, to Upton Sinclair, in the United States. Sinclair sent it to *The Nation* on December 17, 1949, with a note telling the magazine to make use of it if they so wished. *The Nation* never published the letter, which was entitled "Makrónisos Island—The Greek Dachau" (Parergon 5.14 and Document 4). According to de Villefosse, the only dailies to publish protests against the existence of Makrónisos, other than the Greek *Mache*, were the French *L'humanité* and *La libération* (de Villefosse 1950: 1290).

A Life (Not) to Be Lived

Agamben has argued that "naked life" (or "bare life") is what life became in the concentration camps of the Third Reich. It is, he argues, life stripped of any value, any desire, any signification as life. Agamben opens his argument concerning naked life by producing a circuitous genealogy of the notion of life through "the ancient Greeks [who] did not have only one term to express what we mean by the word *life*. They used two semantically and morphologically distinct terms: *zoē*, which expressed the simple fact of living common to all living beings (animals, humans, or gods), and *bios*, which signified the form or manner of living peculiar to a single animal or group. In modern languages this opposition has gradually disappeared from the lexicon" (2000: 2).[20] Naked life, Agamben argues, is the life of the animal, life that is devoid of political meaning, life that belongs to the sovereign while being devoid of any sovereignty of its own. It is a life that contains no *bios*, and it is the life that belongs to *Homo sacer*, the sacred man, he who cannot be executed or sacrificed (thus falling outside of the provenance of both the Law and the Church) but can be killed with impunity.[21]

Agamben takes a certain license with ancient Greek terminology, and this could potentially undermine his argument.[22] Is ancient Greece the index of all humanity, so that the ancient Greek distinction between *zoē* and *bios* can acquire significance for the totality of human experience? Is there an uncomplicated kinship line between this undifferentiated *we* ("*we* mean by the word *life*") and the ancient Greeks? Who are these *we*? The subjects of the modern State? Europeans? Moderns? And which are these "*modern languages*" out of whose lexicon the "*opposition* has gradually disappeared?" (my emphasis). Which languages other than Greek ever contained this opposition, so that "we" can now lament its elision? Who is "we"? Who counts with whom? What is the economy of the "same" and the economy of the "other," the economy of the "friend" and the economy of the "enemy"?

Technologies of alterity are fundamentally technologies for inaugurating a self. Processes of recognizing alterity in the presence and existence of the self constitute this inaugural moment in the technology of alterity. Bodies—total, intact, contained—submit to the facticity of representation: they are whole bodies, healthy bodies, desirable bodies. Pestilent bodies are only fragmentarily represented, fragmentarily received, providing textual fragments obliterated by the erasure of any possibility of the recognition of an intersubjectivity. The question raised here, reading Agamben, becomes pressing: since racialism, racism, and eugenics provide the framework of alterity for Hannah Arendt's "banality of evil," what is the ideological structure that participates

20. In *Homo Sacer* the ancients have been ascribed a specific name: Agamben attributes the distinction to Aristotle.

21. Athena Athanasiou (2005) has shown brilliantly how the questions of humanity, animality, and the notion of bare life intersect in the biopolitical project that Agamben critiques.

22. Derrida was the first to point out that the distinction Agamben makes between *zoē* and *bios* is not as rigid in Plato and Aristotle as Agamben makes it out to be. He notes: "the distinction between *bios* and *zoē*—or *zēn*—is more tricky and precarious; in no way does it correspond to the strict opposition on which Agamben bases the quasi totality of his argument about sovereignty and the biopolitical in *Homo Sacer* (but let's leave that for another time)" (Derrida 2005: 24).

23. Lady Amalia Fleming, the Greek wife of the Nobel Prizewinner Sir Alexander Fleming, who has been credited with the invention of penicillin, was arrested by the Greek junta and accused of having participated in the escape attempt of one of the political prisoners, the soldier Alekos Panagoulis. Fleming says in her memoir that during interrogation by the chief interrogator of the Military Police, Theophiloyiannakos (an interrogation that did not involve physical torture, because the junta could not afford to run the risk of international outcry for having tortured Lady Fleming), the discussion came around to the topic of discipline. Theophiloyiannakos said to Lady Fleming that she needed to be disciplined and punished for having strayed from the right path, not because she was a bad person, but just like his "own [two-and-a-half-year-old] daughter. If she does something wrong, she has to be punished" (Fleming 1973: 175). When Lady Fleming said to him that no child under the age of six should ever be punished, but that children at such a young age should be comforted and must be made to feel "that you love her," Theophiloyiannakos looked at Lady Fleming with "a pitiful expression" and told her, "But I do love my daughter." Lady Fleming found this to be the utmost banality, so much so that she said "this again is one of the reasons why I could not hate this man. When I have repeated this conversation I have been told 'So what? Even tigresses love their children'" only to respond by drawing the line between animal and human that torturers cross, "Yes . . . but they do not torture" (ibid.: 176).

24. The first camps were established for the Communists and Socialists. Only after 1938 were these camps were used to intern "Jews" as a distinct *legal* category, over and above the existing category of *race* (if the racial can ever be distinct from the legal; I am using the distinction here catachrestically, as a heuristic tool).

in and facilitates the separation of self from same?[23] If metaphors of pestilence (lice, nits, pests) provide the trope for the extermination of the one who is situated outside of the circle of interiority of the national body, what allows the sovereign to articulate a *logos* introducing metaphors of biomedicine (miasma, the plague, cancer), in the process of exterminating the Communist? What allows the sovereign, not the law, to announce the need of a "purging 'pharmakon,'" one that will cure the organism of all those who, out of lightness, ignorance, weakness, emotionality, ideology, or silly calculation, have been infected by the communist microbe?" (Anonymous 1937: 4).

The annihilation of the "Communist" takes place in the same space as the annihilation of the "Jew" in the camp.[24] But whereas the latter has already been constituted as the "radical other," as that which can never be read as the self (and is, hence, metaphorized as something that belongs to a different form of life, something that comes from without, from the outside, hence can potentially be identified and exterminated, just as its metaphor, louse, allows), the former becomes the tragic self, the one who will never be an "other" but can never be selfsame, either, and for whom metaphors of interiority are deployed, such as cancer, internal danger, disease, miasma. In the words of Maniadákis, "Communism is a psychic and intellectual affliction that seizes each person who lacks the force of resistance and self-determination against this [agent] that upsets and destabilizes the social, political, and intellectual cohesiveness of our life" (Anonymous 1937: 3). Where the extermination of the Jew, the Gypsy, the non-Aryan constitutes annihilation, the extermination of the Communist (German, Greek, Italian, Slav) constitutes a self-annihilation that refuses to be recognized as such.

Of course, the place where all this once happened and still has retained these tensions, oppositions, and distinctions is Greece, both in language and in practice, a place to which Agamben does not turn in his genealogy of the concept of life. The linguistic distinction between *zoē* and *bios* is still vibrant in Greece, though it has never existed outside the Greek context.[25] Therefore it becomes increasingly difficult to understand exactly what this invented lack/lapse/absence, this voiding of meaning might mean (other than the fact that the *modern* Greek paradigm has nothing to present or offer to Agamben.) The one space/place/location where the distinction exists as an organic part of its lexicon is elided in the paradigm of Agambenian modernity (if it is, indeed, modernity that one attempts to index through the elucidation of this distinction).

25. Two modern Greek expressions are indicative: (a) *den einai zoē aftē* ("this is not life," indicating that life is so hard and abject that it has become a burden); (b) *bios abiotos* ("my life has been made unliveable"). I would argue, furthermore, that the very term used in modern Greek for the camps, *stratopeda peitharhemenes diavioseos* ("camps of disciplined existence/life") ruptures Agamben's claims that there is a deep distinction between *zoē* and *bios* and that *bios* is annihilated in the context of the camp. In modern Greek the word *zese* has been coined as a neologism to denote what the word *bios* does (life in its length and depth).

Sacrum

War, Roger Caillois reminds us (1959), is the ransom of civilization, the bloodright paid for humanity's exit from the state of nature to inhabit the state of culture. With its sacrifice, bloodright, and the disruption of the everyday by enormity, the horrific, and the transgressive, war, "this terrible ransom paid for the various advantages of civilization causes them to pale and proclaims their fragility" (Callois 1959: 178). There is no advantage of civilization, Callois tells us, on the heels of the Frankfurt School, without its dialectical disadvantages. The dog knows that the hand that caresses its back will soon strike it, Adorno warned. If, however, war circumscribes what civilization is, if civilization cannot emerge without the inaugural moment of war, if *polis* ("the city") and *pólemos* ("war") are as closely bound as their etymology suggests, then war also exposes what humanity is. Thus, the question of what the human is such that it requires war as an organizing principle, places war at the core of its polis, invites the anthropological project to encounter a political problem, a problem of the polis.

The political subject, the dissident, the Marxist, as simultaneously object and subject of the humanist state is the location where this circumscription of humanity happens as an event. Located in the space of the profane, deeply suspicious of the state's call to sacrifice, the Marxist calls to order the contradictions inherent in the humanist tradition that has produced her, as she stands resolutely antithetical to any sacralization of experience that does

26. I am asking you to follow a slippery path of thought here. My claim that the Leftist is suspicious of the state's call to sacrifice does not imply that the Leftist herself does not engage in a discourse of or a desire for sacrifice. It means, however, that the Leftist suspects a calculated move in the state's call to sacrifice.

27. I use the term *selfsame* to denote the fiction of the self *as* the same, which is the fiction implicated in the process of totemism as examined in anthropology.

28. This political theology is by no means confined to any single religion, as we have been witnessing recently in fundamentalist Christianity, Islam, Judaism, and Hinduism.

not include her (or, rather, explicitly excludes her).[26]

In response to this gesture, the state, always animating sacrifice as the constitutive history of itself (i.e., the state is always founded by the self-sacrifice of its founders, or so the narrative goes), re-produces the category of the Leftist as resolutely nonhuman, since the sacrifice of the Leftist can never be included in or accepted by the liberal state as constitutive. Christianity, through the instantiation of Christ as *human* (in addition to divine), dislodged the sacrificiality of the selfsame[27] from the realm of totemism, where sacrifice always involves the same animal even if this sameness is purely performative, and reterritorialized it within the realm of political theology.[28] Through that gesture, sacrifice of the self becomes circularly redemptive (Christ sacrificed his human self, which is the only reason why his body could die, in order to save humanity), so that sacrifice of the other becomes impossible because it becomes ineffectual. The other now can only be annihilated, not sacrificed. Therefore, the relegation of the Leftist to the realm of the nonhuman both presupposes and actualizes her untouchability and her unsacrificiability.

"We live in a sacrificial society" is a philosophical announcement whose weight cannot be lifted even by the critical positionalities of those who announce it, such as Irigaray, Derrida, Girard, or Lacan. Are the "desert islands," then, this sacrificial space par excellence? Are they where the delineation and delimitation of the "human" takes place, so that the act of sacrifice produces the circle of interiority needed by the state? Do the islands engage the Leftist in a sacrificial act that would bring them into the inner circle of the state? On the "islands" the categories of sacrifice collapsed completely, exposing the fissure between the linguistic and semantic appropriation of the concept of sacrifice by the state and the foundational premises of sacrifice as a religious ritual of inclusion. Even if there is any way in which the Leftist can be the subject of a sacrifice, it would be a sacrifice that has no relevance for the state. The state gains nothing by the bodily violence to which the Leftist is subjected for "his own good," for the attainment of his own purification, for the purge of his own plague, no matter where this Leftist exists, no matter where sovereign power can be located.

Panos Terzopoulos has written about the massacre on Makrónisos when, from February 28 through March 1, 1948, the military police, demanding *dēlôseis* from the unrepentant soldiers of the First Battalion, raided their tents. Thirty hours or so later, more than two hundred soldiers were dead, but Terzopoulos survived without signing. Perhaps not unexpectedly, it was the prison priest who exposed this fissure: "My child, through torture the human reaches purification," he would say after the AM had tortured the soldiers (Terzopoulos, in Geladopoulos 1994: 52).

In the words of Bruce Lincoln, "there are more ways than one to sacrifice a human being, and it is not those victims alone who are actually led to the altar who deserve our respect and compassion" (1991: 175). As he further points out, under any circumstances where the specter of sacrifice is raised (metaphorical, linguistic, allegorical, or actual, with the head on the butcher block, so to speak) "far greater sacrifices are required from some members of society than from others, while those who offer the most often reap the leanest rewards" (ibid.). Sacrifice presupposes the presence of a sacrificial victim, one that will be sanctified to the point of becoming untouchable. A pre-Christian *Homo sacer*, an impossibility.[29]

Polymeris Voglis (2000) has argued what might appear to be the exact opposite of my position, namely, that Leftists saw the executions imposed by the emergency court-martials of the civil war as a sacrifice that gave meaning to death. Voglis has looked at the correspondence of Leftists on death row between 1945 and 1950. In these letters, the pain of death is mitigated by the conviction that the condemned have not "done anything wrong to anybody." The writers ask their families and loved-ones not to mourn but to remember them and to be proud of them (85). What Voglis reads as sacrifice, though, is what he has correctly identified as self-negation. Self-negation, in this instance, means that the Leftists who were executed chose death—hence the negation of life by their own authority, therefore the negation of the self—over submitting to the humiliation of having their lives evacuated of meaning by signing a *dēlosē metanoias*. No matter how the Leftists saw their position toward death, however, the state did not acknowledge those deaths as sacrifice. It kept that concept as a prerogative for itself.

29. The sacrifice of Christ rendered any other *homo sacer* an impossibility, because the sacrifice of Christ colonized the signifying space of sacrifice while making a pre-Christ time impossible, given that time is counted anew with the moment of the sacrifice of Christ.

Sacrifice

Hubert and Mauss provide the anthropological definition: "Sacrifice is a religious act which, through the consecration of a victim, modifies the condition of the moral person who accomplishes it or that of certain objects with which he is concerned" (1964: 13).

The state, however, by naming its own secular practices as sacrifice, engages in an act of self-sanctification. By refusing to recognize the act of the Leftist as sacrifice, it not only desanctifies the Leftist but also refuses to recognize the Leftist as selfsame, meaning as *human*. It is in light of this twisted gesture of the state that Yiorgos Yiannopoulos writes, making a comparison to Dachau: "At the Nazi concentration camps extermination was primarily on the level of the body, whereas in Makrónisos the primary care was for the moral and psychic extermination of *ánthropos*" (Yiannopoulos 2001: 118; Parergon 5.15).

Louis de Villefosse triangulates this comparison between Dachau and Makrónisos by engaging with one more metaphorical gesture: "A regime that is larded with old collaborators [of the Germans] has been imposed through the military intervention first of the English, then of the Americans, during the course of a civil war, has instituted Dachau in the Ile d'Ouessant. A Dachau worse than the previous one, according to the testimony of a detainee who knew both" (de Villefosse 1950: 1298).[30] The detainee, a soldier named Vyron Perakis, was interned first in Dachau and then on Makrónisos. Describing his experience of both places as a political prisoner, Perakis brings together the question of what is human and the question of soundness of mind when he says, "at Dachau, we suffered from famine. But here, they torture us, they render us 'crazy'" (quoted in de Villefosse 1950: 1295).

30. The Ile d'Ouessant mentioned by de Villefosse is actually a cluster of deserted islands off the coast of Armorique in France. Only two of the islands are (very sparsely) inhabited, and they are colloquially known in France as "wild islands."

Suicide

A riveting and disturbing question shadows Agamben's *Homo Sacer*: Why does the Foucauldian formulation of biopolitics and governmentality not extend to the concentration camp? Why does Foucault look at the prison, the school, and the hospital, but not the place of containment that holds not dear but sacred life, in its barest form: life that does not deserve to be appropriated by the state (and thus executed) or the church (and thus sacrificed), but can be killed with impunity? One could extend this question even further, as Jehanne Gheith has done, to ask: Why, in the context of the concentration camp, do the camps of the Reich (and the Holocaust) "preoccupy the Western imagination and why does the Gulag [or so many other camps, I would add] barely inhabit it?" (2007: 159).

A central question is thus raised about the liberal state in a time of crisis or a state of emergency (such as Greece between 1936 and 1974): How does human life get constituted and instituted as existing *as if* in a prelegal space (in the Hobbesian state of nature), while being securely within the parameters of the law? In other words, what is the rupture in the law, the fragmentation in its very constitution that allows for the suspension of life during a case of emergency? Agamben locates this in the "happening" (in a sense, in the "Becoming") of the concentration camp, but I would like to argue that it takes place primarily in the space of the rehabilitation camp.

Agamben invokes the moment of non-Kantian ethics in the gesture made by Karl Binding and Alfred Hoche in a pamphlet entitled *Authorization for the Annihilation of Life Unworthy of Being Lived*, published in Leipzig in 1920 by the distinguished publisher Felix Meiner. (Binding was a specialist in penal law and Hoche a professor of medicine interested in medical ethics.) Binding and Hoche separate the act of suicide from the discourse of ethics and place it within a legal discourse of rights. Binding argues that suicide is the expression of the individual's sovereignty over his own existence. Agamben writes, following Binding, "suicide . . . cannot be understood as a crime (for example, as a violation of a duty toward oneself) yet also cannot be considered as a matter of indifference to the law" (1998: 136). Indeed, "the law has no other option than to consider living man as sovereign over his own existence" (ibid.). It is only when human sovereignty can be handed to the citizen in the specter of the law that this sovereignty can be taken away by the law. It is only through the annunciation of sovereignty, this solipsistic representation, that sovereignty and its annunciation can be constituted as existing, as Being, that they can then be questioned and become political objects of the legal state. Only when the citizen can announce, in the context of the law, "I am a legal subject" can her sovereignty over herself-as-being be questioned by the law and retained or revoked. It was decided in the Weimar Republic that suicide was not against the law.

The gesture that the Weimar Republic was so reluctant to make—the announcement that suicide is illegal—was made by Antonios Vassilopoulos, the military director of Makrónisos, on March 6, 1948. The massacre on February 28 and March 1 had been followed by a wave of suicides. On March 6, Vassilopoulos issued a memo to his subordinates (members of the Military Police who had participated in the massacre). In it he declared:

> A wave of suicides has occurred in the battalion under my command. Those attempting suicide are misled if they believe that they can dispose of their selves as they wish. From now on, it is decreed that a sworn interrogation will take place concerning any and all who attempt suicide, the results of which will be submitted to me immediately, along with the necessary suit for the indictment to special court-martial. (In Georgatos 2003: 45)

"It is forbidden for soldiers to commit suicide," concludes Yiannopoulos, who survived the massacre (2001: 80). Despite the difference in context, such statements in Nazi Germany and civil-war Greek camps are no more chilling than recent events in Guantánamo Bay. On June 10, 2006, Guantánamo

31. Officials at Guantánamo Bay have reported forty-one unsuccessful suicide attempts by twenty-five detainees since the United States opened the concentration camp there in January 2002. The numbers are telling: the same detainees must have attempted suicide more than once.

32. One needs to keep in mind, however, that in a note to a paper on strategy that she was writing in Stammheim Prison in 1976, a few months before her death, Ulrike Meinhof observed that "suicide is the last act of rebellion" (Aust 1987: 347). Meinhof wrote this note as an elaboration on strategy, but it was later used by the West German authorities to claim that her death was a suicide (when all evidence points to murder).

officials announced the first *successful* suicides at the camp.[31] Navy Rear Admiral Harry Harris told reporters about the men who had committed suicide: "They have no regard for human life. Neither ours nor their own. I believe this was not an act of desperation but an act of *asymmetric warfare* against us" (BBC News, June 11, 2006, "Guantánamo Suicides a PR Move"; my emphasis). If this gesture is interpreted by the military and Bush administration officials as an "act of asymmetric warfare," then one would have to conclude that, had the three men survived the attempts, the military would have the right to kill them *as if* in combat, albeit an asymmetrical one.[32]

In the conceptualization of "*life that does not deserve to live*," Agamben recognizes a pivotal moment in the construction of an ideology of biopolitics: it leads from the examination of suicide as a possible breach of the legal system in Germany through the institutionalization of euthanasia as a humanistic and compassionate practice, to the emergence of a discursive and legal system that made possible the extermination of dangerous and polluting life (that of Leftists, homosexuals, Jews, Gypsies, and those perceived to be mentally ill or of lower intelligence). Discussing the pamphlet by Binding and Hoche, Agamben rightly points out that they elide the distinction "between exteriority and interiority, which the juridical order can therefore neither exclude nor include, neither forbid not permit . . . like the sovereign decision on the state of exception" (1998: 136–37). The discussion concerning suicide would not, on its own, have acquired significance had it not rested upon the crushing structure of "euthanasia" within the program of German eugenics. So far so good. We are still only talking about bodies; we are still in the 1920s.

Prague 1968

When I was growing up in Athens, in the sixties and early seventies, my mother had a friend and colleague, Lina, much younger than any other, more beautiful than any other. Lina was unmarried but lived with a man nine years her junior in one of the modern apartments built in Athens by the junta on top of the hill of our neighborhood, an apartment that looked and felt like so many modern apartment buildings built in Eastern Europe after the Allied bombings had razed the old ones to the ground. Socialist realism in the heart of the junta, enacted by the junta. Lina would take me home with her, teach me French, cook dinner for me, and show me photographs of her life before Athens. Crisscrossing Europe with her lover, she had lived in Barcelona, in Paris, and in Prague during the days when the world was rocked with the realization that youth was a contingency to be reckoned with. One photograph, in particular, stuck in my mind: Lina leaning out of a window in Prague on a lovely sunny spring afternoon, a few days before Soviet tanks came rolling into that street.

Lina hadn't always lived in Athens. She was from the north, her father from Macedonia, her mother a Yugoslav brought to Greece by Lina's father. Lina's father was a Communist. He had fled to Yugoslavia when the Democratic Army collapsed in 1949, having been condemned to death in absentia by the military tribunal. There was something elusive about her. "You can't read her," my father would say. "She's like a ghost."

"She's got death on her hands," our mutual friend Katerina said. "You know, Lina, when she lived in Prague, she lived in a very old building with four stories, and on top of the building, in the attic, there was an old lady who lived there alone; Lina lived above her, in the rafters." Long afterward, Katerina finally finished the story. "The old lady was very frail and ill. She had no one in the world, and her fear was that she would die alone. So she asked Lina to kill her. And Lina did. She smashed her head with a brick. It was euthanasia; she didn't go to jail." Katerina stopped there, although later I found out that Lina was arrested and taken away in handcuffs, only to be released after she had been acquitted in court.

There: *Homo sacer* to *Homo sacer*, life in the rafters and life not worth living. Or is it? Certain questions are not asked. How, why, what happened exactly? Was Lina alone or not, did her lover help her? What did she do with the body? You don't ask questions, you don't get answers, you are just left there, with a specter of death that hovers over your beloved older friend, who takes you home, teaches you French, cooks for you, and shows you photographs of her life before Athens. But this is not the euthanasia that Agamben points us toward, nor the euthanasia that Binding and Hoche established as the second gesture toward the circumscription of biopolitics. There is no annihilation in this euthanasia, just a young woman with a brick in her hands.

Oedipean Humanity

"Behind the ravine he had been tortured cruelly, they did *phálanga* [Parergon 5.16] on him and he couldn't walk . . . Why did they hit him so much? When the 'polite' lieutenant asked him, 'Well, child, will you sign the declaration?' he responded, 'Why should I sign, and stay out of solitary, with the thieves?' In

33. Nicos Poulantzas has noted that concentration camps are a particularly modern invention in the sense that they concretize the same "spatial power matrix" as the national territory, thus making possible the notion of the "internal enemy" by internalizing "the frontiers of the national space at the heart of that space itself." Poulantzas correctly identifies the fact that concentration camps are constructed in order to hold "antinationals" within the national space (Poulantzas 2000 [1978]). Poulantzas's position further underlines what Gil Anidjar has explicitly pointed out and convincingly addressed, namely, that we don't have a theory of the enemy. See Anidjar 2003 and 2004.

this way he transgressed every boundary of . . . politeness and the lieutenant decided to repay him by making him King Oedipus [*Vassiliá Oidipoda*]" (Yiannopoulos 2001: 154–55).

It is instructive to look at the discourses that make the processes of constituting an "other" as such possible, especially in the case of the Leftists, who, being the target of biomedical metaphors, have been termed "pestilence [*miasma*]" and the "internal danger [*esoterikos kindynos*]" or the "internal enemy [*esoterikos ehthros*],"[33] but also, in curiously psychoanalytic terminology, "undesirables [*anepithymitoi*]. How is the ascription of this "otherness" mobilized to denote actors who had hitherto been included in the social and political body? What sorts of discourses and practices allow this transference into otherness to become possible and permissible? The articulation of this question, both by the state and by citizens, is not a new one, and it was certainly one that helped spark the construction of concentration camps to intern the Jewish populations of Europe. What I am pointing to, however, is not only the history of the camps but also the processes that made the conceptualization of the camps as a place of internment possible, as well as the classification of "self" as "other" (who can be exiled, interred, exterminated). Examining narratives about state violence and terror, Aretxaga hoped to "raise questions about the ways in which the state is imagined and produced as a subject" (2005: 51). In her footsteps, I look at narratives about state violence and ask, rather, how the subject of the state is re-produced as alien, as a radical *other* impregnated with the certainty of danger. (See also Foucault 1978.)

Agamben has, as I mentioned earlier, posed an unanswerable question to Foucault: Why does his analysis of biopolitics not include the concentration camp? Here, I think, it serves us well to distinguish between the notions of biopolitics (in its Foucauldian formulation) and of thanatopolitics. Biopolitics applies to the rehabilitation/re-education camp (which becomes an extermination camp only de facto, accidentally), and thanatopolitics applies to the extermination camp (where no one exists under even the faintest pretense of "reformation"). In that sense, biopolitics becomes, indeed, the paradigmatic space where (as Andreas Kalyvas has noted) the sovereign rules "over brains and bodies, politicizing and policing human nature, producing, administering, and managing life itself, and ultimately deciding on its value or non-value" (2005: 109). We see that, although this description of biopolitics resonates for the rehabilitation camps (where brains were, indeed, the object of sovereign intervention), it does not in the case of the extermination camps (where the intervention was on the level of life itself, as Yiannopoulos and Agamben have pointed out). The question, then, demands to be rearticulated and readdressed: Why does Agamben not note the fundamental difference between extermination and rehabilitation, wherein the notion of biopolitics really articulates itself?

[handwritten marginalia: but they are not genuinely being rehabilitated — so can we really call it that/or can we it as such?]

August 29, 1949

The collapse of the DSE came not simply because of the military supremacy of the National Army but primarily because of political developments outside of Greece. In June 1948, the Soviet Union broke off relations with Tito, after four years of a strained and forced relationship. Tito had been the KKE's strongest supporter, but now, with the dissolution of Yugoslav-Soviet relations and with the majority of the KKE having been trained at the Moscow School, the leadership of the Party had to choose between their loyalty to Stalin and their relations with Tito. The Party chose Stalin, and in January Markos Vafiadis was accused of "Titoism" and removed from his political and military positions, being replaced by Zachariadis. Since then, the Greek Communist Party has remained the most loyal Stalinist party in Europe, even after the destalinization of the Soviet Union and even after (or especially since) the collapse and self-dissolution of the Soviet Union at Christmastime in 1990.

After a year of increasing acrimony, Tito closed the Yugoslavian border to the guerrillas of the DSE in July 1949 and disbanded their camps inside Yugoslavia (although Tito publicly denied doing so in a political speech delivered at Skopje in 1949). Albania remained as a possibility for material support, but the decline of the DSE was rapid. The split with Tito sent the Party, once again, into a severe closing-in of its ranks, trying to isolate the Titoists, in a repeat of similar prewar and wartime attempts with the Trotskyists.

In August 1949, Field Marshal Alexander Papagos, the new commander in chief of the National Army, launched a major counteroffensive against DSE forces in northern Greece,

Figure 14. Nikos Zachariadis, the secretary general of the Communist Party of Greece, in an undated postcard from one of the Communist countries. The caption reads: "Nikos Zachariadis, leader of the Democratic Army." Collection of the author.

Figure 15. Postcard of an etching of the Democratic Army, including men and women fighters. It is signed by A. Stam and dated 1949. Author's collection.

code-named "Operation Torch." The plan was a major victory for the National Army and resulted in heavy losses for the DSE. Its army was no longer able to sustain resistance, and August 29, 1949, is widely accepted as the date of the collapse of the DSE, although the Party ordered the partisans to remain armed (*hóplo pará pódan*: with a gun by their foot, on the ready). By September, most DSE fighters had surrendered or escaped over the border into Albania, Tito having closed the border crossing to Yugoslavia. By the end of the month, the Albanian government, presumably with Soviet approval, announced to the KKE that it would no longer allow the DSE to perform military operations from within Albanian territory, thus effecting a "temporary cease-fire to prevent the complete annihilation of Greece," to be announced by the KKE in October. That truce marked the end of the Greek Civil War, although the Greek state retained the state of emergency and did not announce the end of the war until 1963. The camp at Makrónisos remained in effect for the "preventive detention of anyone whom those in power might define as opponents," as Sofsky has said of Dachau between 1933 and 1936 (1997: 30), despite repeated motions by the international community to effectuate its abolition.

6

1950–1967

Post–Civil War

Fucking Fifties (Parergon 6.1)

Western European governments saw the end of the Greek Civil War as a victory in the fight against world Communism, so much so that President Lyndon B. Johnson later considered Greece the Vietnam of the 1940s.[1] The greatest irony about both the British involvement and the Truman Doctrine was that the Soviets neither actively nor implicitly supported the Communist Party's efforts to assert its size and become by force part of political power in Greece. Quite the contrary, they repeatedly advised the leadership of the KKE not to undertake a military campaign and made it quite clear that there would be no possibility of material or other support from the Soviet Union. Nikos Zachariadis, a favorite of Stalin, was repeatedly humiliated at meetings with Zhdanov, Molotov, and Dimitrov when he insisted on requesting help and was repeatedly denied it. (The contemporary evidence for this is overwhelming. See Nachmani 1990, Close 1995, Gitlin 1967, Iatrides 2005, and Farakos 2000.) In other words, there never existed an actual Communist threat in Greece, and it certainly did not come from the outside, as the Truman Doctrine claimed (Parergon 6.2).

But this is exactly how Greek historiography of the 1950s, all written by the Right, treated the emphýlios, as an attempt by the KKE, supported by the Soviet Union, to take over the country.[2]

1. See Gitlin 1967. In 1967, when the junta arrested all the Leftists that it could find and transported them to various camps and prisons, Tzavalás Karousos, an actor who had been persecuted since the civil war and was being arrested again at the age of sixty-two, during his transport to the camp, thinking about U.S. involvement in the junta, called Vietnam "the hope and the anguish of the whole world" (Karousos 1974: 85).

2. To be fair, I should add that it is not only Right-wing historiography from the 1950s and 1960s that has adopted this position. Tony Judt, writing about the postwar period in Europe, without giving his sources, rehearses the same argument, while acknowledging that "despite a significant level of wartime collaboration among the bureaucratic and business elites, post-

war purges were directed not at the Right but the Left. This was a unique case but a revealing one. The civil war of 1944–45 had convinced the British that only the firm re-establishment of a conservative regime in Athens would stabilize this small but strategically vital country" (2005: 48). But, looking at the transition period between the postwar and reconstruction, Judt announces that "in the post–World War Two years, the Communist KKE terrorized villages under its control, leaving a legacy of fear and associating the radical Left in many Greek memories with repression and atrocity" (ibid.: 505). These years, of course, would be the years of the White Terror, when even U.S. observers testified to the persecution of the Left.

---

3. Kalyvas accuses the following researchers of engaging in an ideological representation of the Left and its violence (or lack thereof): (1) overlooked violence, in Tsoucalas 1969, Svoronos 1982, Collard 1989, Hondros 1983, Hart 1996; (2) minimized violence, in Smith 1984 and Fleischer 1995, who is also accused of dismissing Leftist violence as an aberration (In Mazower 2000: 142); (3) whitewashed violence, in Elephantis 2008 and Broussalis 1997.

Not until 1963 did books coming from the Left suggest a different reading of the events of the preceding three decades. And only since the mid 1990s, after the fall of the Berlin Wall and the collapse of the Soviet Union, have memoirs of those years and of the years spent on the islands started to appear.

The Right-wing position was reiterated in 2000 by Stathis Kalyvas (in Mazower 2000). Kalyvas redeveloped the thesis that "red terror" in Greece had been more intense than and just as calculated as "white" and "black" terror, especially during the last years of the occupation, and he accused "recent historical research" on the issue of systematically and programmatically tending to "overlook, minimize, or whitewash leftist terror." He further chastised "even serious scholarship" for having minimized Leftist violence by employing a "skewed vocabulary," such as that used by anthropologist Riki van Boeschoten, who characterized "the violence of EAM 'revolutionary violence' and the violence of the Right 'terrorism'" (in Mazower 2000: 142). The only historians whom Kalyvas cites as developing an argument about Left violence during the occupation comparable to his own are Mark Mazower (1993) and David Close

(1995), and even they only partially so (in Mazower 2000: 178n4).[3]

When historians from the Left criticized this position, calling it ahistorical and deeply ideological, Kalyvas accused them of "histrionics, witch-hunts, and conspiratology," since, he claimed, "it is widely accepted that on the level of public discourse the dominant theories about the Occupation and the emphýlios come from the blatantly partisan myths that were created in the context of the emphýlios struggle" (2003: 31). Kalyvas recognized that the narrative of the emphýlios was originally produced by the winners, while after the junta it was appropriated and changed by the "descendants of the defeated" (ibid.). He and Nikos Marantzidis, calling themselves "revisionists of history," laid down what have come to be called (with derision) "the Ten Commandments" of the proper study of the emphýlios (2004).

The first such injunction is to relocate the beginnings of the emphýlios from 1944 (as had been announced by the Greek state and published in the *Government Gazette* on September 18, 1989) to 1943, claiming that it has "finally been grafted onto consciousness" that, when referring to the emphý-lios, "we mean the entire period of 1943–1949" (2004, point 1), although such consciousness seems to exist only within the group of the "revisionists," since not even the old Right-wing historiog-raphy made such a claim.[4] Another one of the ten points is that "recent research has shown that violence was not the prerogative of only one party" (point 4). With a suspicious wink at postmodern discourses, they accuse the research produced thus far of looking for "one truth," for which should now be substituted partial, collaborative, and conjoined research that would "avoid attempts at large scale interpretive schemes if they are not supported by detailed and complete documentation" (point 5). Of course, the positivism of their entire project, with its reliance on numbers, mathematical models (especially by Kalyvas), and the need "to set the record straight" (in Mazower 2000: 142) reveals not a commitment to postmodernism but a deep commitment to finding not "one truth" but "the truth." It is a project as far removed from postmodernism as could be.

4. Even if Kalyvas and Marantzidis would like to raise our consciousness on this matter, as Peter Berger told us in 1974, "it is, in principle, impossible to 'raise the consciousness' of anyone, because all of us are stumbling around on the same level of consciousness—a pretty dim level" (13).

Kalyvas and Marantzidis have reverted to the earlier, Right-wing model of narrating the emphýlios even more than moderate historians and political scientists such as John Iatrides, who came to the conclusion, after decades of studying the phenomenon, that the KKE "as a genuinely revolutionary party was determined to seize power at the first opportunity, preferably by political means but by armed force if necessary" (2005: 9). This possibility of seizing power, "preferably by political means" has been lost in Kalyvas and Marantzidis (as Iatrides has overlooked that the Greek Communist Party was not a "genuinely" revolutionary party, since it did not attempt to create the conditions for revolution).

To study the emphýlios in its entirety, Kalyvas and Marantzidis have sought to form a revisionist school of thought that would prove the emphýlios to be not only a power struggle initiated by the KKE but one that neces-sarily and as a matter of tactics used violence. In the first article that he wrote to set the project in motion (in Mazower 2000), Kalyvas set out to prove: (1) that the Left had not been the main "(or even the only) victim of violence" in the civil war (Mazower 2000: 142), and (2) that the "seemingly straightforward instances of German terror and rightist 'white' terror prove misleading when not connected to the red terror and placed into the full sequence of events to which they belong" (ibid.: 143–44). He thus seeded the argument that German reprisals and German and collaborationist terror resulted from violence enacted by the partisans against the occupying forces. Because this argument needs documentation with examples from across the

Figure 16. Photograph of Kostas Papaioannou and other exiles on the island of Ai-Stratis, in the northern Aegean, taken in October 1950. In the center is General Stefanos Sarafis, commander in chief of ELAS during the Resistance. Sarafis was exiled in 1945 to the island of Ikaria and then transferred to Makrónisos, from which he was transferred again to Ai-Stratis in 1950. Next to him, with glasses and an open jacket, is Konstantinos Despotopoulos. They are surrounded by other political exiles, both civilians and captured military. What is remarkable about the photograph is that the exiles appear (after the tortures of Makrónisos and—possibly—Yáros) with the imprimatur of the social class to which they belonged before the war and the civil war started: suits, military attire, and peasant and lower-middle-class aesthetics mingle in this photograph. Kostas Papaioannou Archive, General State Archives of Kavala. Reproduced with permission.

country, a number of younger scholars have been drafted into the endeavor. This movement has caused a furor in historical and political circles in Greece, since it has reanimated many of the original political positions and debates of the emphýlios itself. Because the Left is not a uniform and monolithic entity in Greece, this debate has drawn criticism from many angles, many different ones from the Left itself.

A great many graduate students, in both Greek and European universities, are participating in this project, engaging in local-history research and trying to produce a complete picture of the political landscape of Greece in the decade of the forties and fifties. Apart from the methodological problems of this entire project, however (see Panourgiá 2008c), there are other, more serious epistemological ones, as the project is ultimately both an

Figure 17. Photograph of salute to the flag at the opening ceremony of the *gymnastikés epideixeis* ("performances of gymnastics") at the High School of Naousa, Western Macedonia, May 1956. At the front, to the left of the flag-bearing group, is the physical education teacher in charge of the performance. Private collection.

Figure 18. March of the High School of Naousa in March 1956 to celebrate the 1821 War of Independence. Leading the march is the physical education teacher. Immediately following her are high-school students dressed in traditional costumes. Behind them follows the entire high school, dressed in the formal high-school uniform. Girls precede boys. Note how demeanor in this photograph differs from Figure 17: a fascistic appearance gives way to the softness of the flowing silk costumes and the smartness of the teacher's suit. Private collection.

5. The reaction to the Kalyvas-Marantzidis project has been forceful. In addition to the special issue of *Vivliodromio* (where the entire debate is published), see also *Eleftherotypia's* "Ios," especially "Oi Tagmatsphalites dikaionontai" ("The *Tagmatasphalites* are being exonerated)" October 26, 2003 (in two parts); "He Nea 'Sovietologia' gia ten Katoche kai ten Antistase" ("The New 'Sovietology' about the Occupation and the Resistance") May 12, 2004 (in two parts); and Kalyvas's letter to "Ios" and "Ios's" response, November 3, 2003. See also Panourgiá 2004b.

6. *Parakrátos* denotes the machinery of the underground, unacknowledged, and (thus) lethal structure of persecution, character assassination, and extermination of political dissidents that allowed the official state to maintain its modicum of legality. The *parakrátos* (translated as "deep state" in the case of Turkey) should not be confused with the paramilitary organizations and the militias, which existed in Greece (and have elsewhere in the world, such as the death squads in Latin America). The agents of the *parakrátos* certainly existed at the margins of the state. They were individuals who worked closely with the police and the gendarmerie but were not armed (as the militia and the paramilitaries were). They used crude objects (axes, axe handles, large stones, lead pipes, etc.) to carry out their operations, which were not only aimed at exterminating Leftists but also at creating and maintaining a climate of fear. As Veena Das and Deborah Poole note, paramilitaries "represent both highly personalized forms of private power and the supposedly impersonal and neutral authority of the state (2004: 14). The complete locution was *to parakrátos tes Dexias* ("the parastate of the Right"), indicating the deep commitment of the Right to maintaining power and its identification with the state (and vice versa). The existence of the *parakrátos*, like the paramilitaries, further underlines not only the fragmentation at the margins of the state but also the investment of the state in maintaining these margins. Importantly,

enumerative one, and an attempt at balancing atrocities.[5]

After the end of the civil war, military tribunals started to prosecute not only the captured DSE military but also the political branch of the Party and Leftists in general. The paramilitaries continued their terror, which set the tone of the political climate of the country as one of conflict and tension. This resulted in the murder of a number of Left and Left-leaning civilians and politicians, such as the pacifist Gregorios Lambrakis in Thessaloniki in 1963. (The Lambrakis affair, as it has come to be known, is the subject of the film *Z*, by Costa-Gavras.) The places of exile were not closed down. Quite the contrary, exile was intensified as a measure of both discipline and punishment, as we have seen. The state, through complete control of education, engaged in an even tighter production of patriotism and nationalism. In 1953, the government headed by Marshall Papagos founded the Kentrike Yperesia Plerophorion (KYP), the Greek equivalent of the CIA. According to James Becket (1970: 13), the KYP "was a subsidiary of the Langley, Virginia, parent corporation . . . and was directly financed by it." Although initially the KYP was not permitted to interfere in Greek domestic affairs but was to engage in "counter espionage activities outside of Greece" (ibid.), both the KYP and the CIA became heavily involved in Greek matters.

As Becket rightly observes, the "heavy involvement of KYP and the C.I.A. in domestic Greek affairs can be explained by their concept of the enemy. The enemy was not simply expansionist Russia but communism" (ibid.). It was back to square one of the Idiônymon. KYP and the CIA, even if they did not organize the paramilitaries, certainly abetted them. The *parakrátos* (para-state)[6] and the paramilitaries

[handwritten marginalia: but sovereignty is not at margins]

were allowed to utilize every known method of organized terror, abducting citizens in the middle of the street or in the middle of the night, or fabricating crimes and evidence.[7] One such instance, a pretext for the coup of 1967, was the case of ASPIDA (literally meaning "shield," the acronym abbreviates *Axiōmatikoi Sôsate Patrida Idaniká Dēmoratia Axiokratia*, "Officers Save Fatherland Ideals Democracy Meritocracy"). A group of Centrist army officers was accused of having formed a Left-wing, antiroyalist organization of that name, which was planning to take power through a coup. The attempt never took place and, according to the officers themselves, never had been planned. Nevertheless, the officers were tried for "treason against the Greek state" and for "following a known communist," namely, Andreas Papandreou, the son of ex-prime minister Georgios.[8]

In the crevices between the terror of the Right and the abject existence of the Left people, went on trying to live a life worth living, falling in love, dancing, going out, throwing parties, decorating Christmas trees, studying, working, swimming.

the margin allows the elasticity of being (temporarily) both inside and outside of the law, and it is therefore as fiercely contested as the center. Das and Poole have also noted this, but not the temporality of interiority and exteriority in terms of the law (see Das and Poole 2004: 15).

7. In trials of Leftists in the fifties and sixties, it turned out that policemen charged with shadowing suspects could not produce documentation because they had simply fabricated it. It is easy to dismiss this as simply one of the excesses of political power, but it reveals the state's need for an affect of legality to legitimate its actions. I am indebted to Vassilis Karydis for bringing these trial transcripts to my attention.

8. The laughable notion that Papandreou was a Communist can be explained only by the intense antidemocratic climate in Greece in the years preceding the junta, such that any and all democratic, antiroyalist and anti–Right-wing tendencies in the body politic were relegated to Communism. See the excellent account of this process in Deane [Gigantes] 1976.

7

1967–1974

Dictatorship

The Red Housecoat

On April 21, 1967, a group of colonels from the far Right, some of whom had been trained at the War College in the United States, some of whom had participated in the Tágmata Asphaleias, some of whom had been members of "X," and others of whom had been torturers in Makrónisos and Yáros, seized power from the government, using as an excuse the political instability and tension of the time, and established a dictatorship. The leader of the coup, Georgios Papadopoulos,[1] was a member of the paramilitary organization IDEA (Ierós Desmos Ellênōn Axiōmatikôn, "Sacred Bond of Greek Officers"). He was flanked by Nikolaos Makarezos and Stylianos Pattakos. Many more participated, but the three came to be the public faces of the first months of the dictatorship. James Becket made the connection between the Truman Doctrine and the junta when he wrote at the height of the latter, in 1970, "twenty years [after the Doctrine] America would find itself with an empire and Greece would find itself with a military dictatorship. The Greeks, a free people, would be subjugated by a minority armed by the United States, and the outside pressures would be American" (1970: 12).

That Friday morning of April 21, 1967, my mother did not wake us up to go to school. We woke up at our leisure, and I walked outside, where my mother, dressed in her bright-red,

1. There has been a general notion that Georgios Papadopoulos, the leader of the colonels' coup in 1967, had been a member of the Tágmata Asphaleias during the occupation. Leonidas Kalivretakis, by meticulously tracing the literature on Papadopoulos's involvement with any organization (including "X" and the Tágmata) during the occupation has shown conclusively that Papadopoulos was never involved in any organization, not out of a sense of patriotism or resistance against the Germans but because of cowardice. Even though Papadopoulos himself had not been a member of the TA, other members of the junta had such compromised lineages. Dimitrios Ioannides, the general who overthrew the colonels' junta in 1973 and brought on the most brutal phase of the dictatorship, had been a torturer on Makrónisos. Even more intriguing, the fathers of other actors of the junta had served either in the TA or in "X" during the war. Vassileios Dertiles, who had

ankle-length woolen housecoat, was standing at the crossroads in front of our house with my grandfather, looking up and down the streets. There were almost no cars about; a deafening silence reigned save for the occasional military truck going by.

I reached my mother and grandfather just in time to hear my mother joke with her father-in-law: "Do you think they would pick me up because of my red housecoat?"

"Why didn't you wake us up?" I asked her.

"There is no school today," she said, "There is a dictatorship [*egine diktatoria*, literally, "a dictatorship happened"]." My sister and I started cheering about not having school. We wouldn't understand what this meant until that evening.

participated in the mutiny of the interwar period, was the main inspiration, organizer, and first general director of the TA. His son, Nikolaos Dertiles, became a lieutenant colonel in the junta and one of its most fierce and feared torturers. He was the officer who gave the order to the tank driver outside of the Polytechnic on November 17, 1973, to drive through the main gate, thereby running over a number of students. Kalivretakis also mentions, with some reservation, the case of another torturer and collaborator of Ioannides, Lieutenant Colonel M. Pelihos, whose father, Lieutenant K. Pelihos, had also been a member of the TA (Kalivretakis 2006: 109–47).

I cannot remember my father at all on that day; he is completely absent from my memory. In the summer of 2006 I asked him how he found out that a junta had happened. "I was in the car with Spyros," he said. Spyros was an old friend and neighbor and the two of them worked at jobs very close to each other. "We left the house at 4:30 A.M., and I was driving down Vassileos Konstantinou [the main avenue that connects the area where we lived with Syngrou Avenue, off which their respective jobs were located]. Everything was very quiet, abandoned, there were no cars, no people, no buses; there were military vehicles everywhere, tanks, hardly any police. I turned on the radio. There was only classical and military music on, no news, no human voice to say anything. And from that day on we knew, every time there was classical music on the radio, that something serious had happened." He laughed at this point; everyone in the room laughed, because it was true, at that time classical music was not played on the radio except in specific programs in the evening and as accompaniment to broadcasts about serious events (a dictatorship, the death of an important political person, things of that sort).

Then he continued, "At Truman's statue there was a police car. They stopped us, or rather, we stopped to ask what was happening. They said they weren't sure. 'We don't even know,' one of them said. We said that we were going to Kalithea [the district where they worked]. 'I don't know if you can get there,' he said, and then he said, 'Why don't you turn back, go back to your homes? We are not sure what this is.' I explained to him that I was responsible for shutting down the equipment at the lab [my father worked as a chemical and mechanical engineer] and the whole plant, and that my friend had to report to the electric company where he worked. 'Try to go, what can I tell you,' he said. 'But I don't know if you are going to manage to get through to the other side [*apenanti* was the word used]. So we kept going a bit longer. We tried to go by the Stadium so that we could catch Kalirroes [Avenue] to go down to Syngrou, but they turned us around before we could get there. We pleaded with them; we wanted to go by the Stadium and get a glimpse of the palace, see if we could see anything. Impossible, impossible, they wouldn't let us. 'Go by Pangrati,' they said, a young lieutenant. 'You might be able to go across from there.' At any rate, I don't want to belabor the point [*na min sta polylogo*], we went up to Pangrati, we went through the refugee settlement [*ta prosfygika*], we tried to go by there, it was impossible."

"Did you realize what had happened?" I asked.

"Eh, after two hours on the road, with so many road blocks [*bloka*], we knew that this was a junta. But who had done it? No one was expecting it to happen then. At any rate, we realized that we wouldn't make it to Kalithea, so at some point somewhere in Dourgouti, behind Aghios Sostis [so, really, on the other side of Syngrou Avenue, about five hundred meters away from where they wanted to be, but on the wrong side] we decided that even if we did make it to Kalithea, we probably wouldn't be able to make it back, and I turned around and tried to go back to Zográphou. We couldn't go by the same roads because they were closed by that time. Everywhere we were being turned around and away. Finally I found the old streets, what streets, some goat paths they were, over on Hymettus [the mountain of Athens], and we came back from there. I think we made it back home around noon"—which explains why my father was not there when my mother was preoccupied with the potential danger posed by her red housecoat.

No one was expecting the dictatorship to happen just then, so even the members of the KKE, even the leadership of the Party, went to bed that night not suspecting anything. By the morning almost every single one of them had been arrested. Account after account of that day shows how unexpected it was for everyone, from the Palace[2] to the Party. These accounts show that even specific warnings, by people who knew that the coup would happen that night, who had specific information, went unheeded. Yet published accounts of that day have been scarce.[3] As I was researching this particular experience in the summer of 2006, the journal *Archeiotaxeio*, the flagship publication of the Archives of Contemporary Social

2. By all accounts King Konstantine and his mother, Frederika, had been preparing a coup of their own, which would have been carried out by a group of generals, not colonels, a few days before the general elections scheduled to take place on May 14, 1967. The royal family moved to Rome shortly after the April 21 coup and from Rome organized and directed a counter-coup involving the royal navy. The members of the naval forces who carried out this counter-coup were eventually arrested, tortured, and exiled just like any "common Communist [*san koinoi kommounistes*]," as one of them said (a story passed on to me by one of the members of the ASPIDA group who was in the same prison as one of the naval officers). For a personal account of the involvement of the Palace in the politics of the country before the junta and during the turbulent decade of the sixties, see Deane 1976. Deane [Gigantes] was a personal counselor to the king until shortly before the coup.

3. Accounts of that day, but also scholarly research on the junta as a whole, are scarce. Very few conferences have

History (ASKI),[4] issued a special volume on the memories of specific people of the Left from that particular day. Leonidas Kallivretakis recounts how, like me, he cheered when his mother told him that there would be no school that day, but the rest of the accounts are from people slightly to significantly older than Kallivretakis and myself, people (the older ones) who were arrested in their pajamas or (the younger ones) who were not arrested that night because they had been out with friends and had not yet returned home when the police were sent to pick them up between 2 and 3 A.M.

Antonis Liakos, who at the time was a student at the University of Thessaloniki, reports how the night before the dictatorship he and his friends were spending the wee hours discussing the dictatorship of the proletariat and when it would end in the people's republics of Eastern Europe, so that an authentic socialist democracy would be possible. Liakos remembers how, for the first time, the questions of sovereignty and applied Marxism as they were developing in the people's republics "resonated with the Greek Left and were finding a space in its journals and newspapers. The irony, of course, was that we were discussing one dictatorship as another one was happening. We left as the first tanks made their appearance in front of the White Tower and the owner of the bar said that he was closing up because a dictatorship had happened" (Liakos, 2006: 48). Liakos goes on to talk about how the cartography of the city immediately changed; how everyone who was on the Left and *charactērisménos* ("characterized, classified as such") changed his everyday itinerary, how a new conceptual map of dangerous places was immediately produced and unspokenly acknowledged. "The city that we had been crisscrossing leisurely until now stopped being the same from one day to the next. The Diagonal, the Square of St. Sophia, Aristotelous Street, the White Tower, became off limits. Crossing Egnatia Street, Tsimiske Street, was dangerous, traveling to the eastern suburbs became an adventure."

But the most important event of the day of the dictatorship, Liakos mentions, was that he missed a date with a young woman to go on a three-day trip to Chalkidike. He wonders why this sense of loss should not constitute a political moment. Why should not desire, and the loss of its fulfillment, constitute a political gesture? Even more, he wonders, why would he actually

been organized, very few studies have been published, and most of the existing information is either anecdotal or comes from the media of the time. The historian Leonidas Kallivretakis, commenting on this lacuna in Greek historical research, mentions that the National Research Institute has established a special research program with the expressed project of systematically collecting archival material concerning the political and social history of the twentieth century. Kalivretakis 2007 gives a good bibliography of memoirs, journalistic reports and accounts, and scientific studies. For an analysis of the political and ideological parameters of the junta, see Athanassatou et al. 1999; see also Clogg and Yannopoulos 1972 and Tsoucalas 1969. Poulantzas 1976 remains an important political analysis of the junta and the neo-imperialist project.

4. For all practical purposes, these are the archives of the Communist Party prior to the split of 1968, established and directed by the late Philippos Eliou, son of the late EDA deputy Elias Eliou, and one of the group of soldiers who were the last to be transported from Makrónisos when it was finally shut down in 1958.

5. As late as 1997, during a presentation at Princeton University, a famous Greek political scientist responded with contempt when a literary critic in the audience asked about the role of desire in the revolutionary process. Desire is of no importance at all, the speaker said, either for social analysis or for politics. To consider this an idiosyncratic and individual response would be to overlook: (1) the importance that the social sciences have placed on the scientificity of their discourses, with affect and desire being thought of as excluded from the scientific method and (2) the epistemological rift theories of desire had in opening up the space of analysis when desire is posited as an analytical category. On desire and the processes of delimiting it in social analysis, as well as the complexities that arise from Foucault's analysis of desire in reference to the question of race, see Stoler 1995. See also Foucault 1985.

think that they should not? Would the inclusion of desire in the revolutionary process betray a lack of political commitment? Of course, the questions that Liakos so craftily poses are rhetorical now, when it seems that we have cleared desire of the suspicion of false consciousness, when we have weeded through piles of Marxist analyses to bring to the surface the importance of desire both in Marx's own writings and in the psyches of revolutionary actors. But in 1967 desire was politically suspect.[5]

I have no clear recollection of what happened later in the day on April 21. Some time in the early afternoon, my uncle, who was a high-ranking officer in the Special Security Police, came to our house. It seemed strange to me, because he had never before come to our house during the day. He pulled out the keys that were in the keyhole on the front door. "Don't leave the keys in the door," he said, as he had said countless times previously. "And don't go out of the house after dark; do you hear me?" he said to me. "Not even downstairs to your grandmother's. There is going to be a curfew." He left.

In the early evening I remember my mother coming home (but I do not remember her having left); my father was there. She started naming names: Mimis, Spyros (the person that my father had been carrying in his car all morning), Nikētopoulos, Takis, Nikos and his parents—no women's names yet. These names of friends, which were spoken as she sat down to smoke a cigarette with my father, were repeated over and over. Where she had gone to get this information I don't know, and it's all gone from her now. At what peril and what cost she had managed to get as much as she did I don't know, either. There did not seem to be any pattern on who had been arrested other than that everyone who had been arrested had been involved with the Left and Leftist organizations or with the Center and Centrist organizations, or had held public office, such as having been a mayor, or a dignitary in the Boy Scouts, or an officer in any of the cultural associations that had sprung up between Papandreou's 1963 liberalization of politics and the day of the junta (e.g., the Union of Democratic Women, of which my mother was a member; Parergon 7.1).They had been picked up, but no one knew yet where they had been taken. And the arrests were continuing.

Both my parents were afraid. A little later, as my mother started making dinner, she introduced me to a practice that would come to organize my life for years to come, until the junta fell. At a quarter to nine in the evening, she sat

Figure 19. Photograph of the Union of Democratic Women in 1966. The lone man standing with the women of the Union is Mimis Beis, then mayor of Zográphou, later mayor of Athens. Note the wide diversity in age. Private collection.

me down in front of the radio, a fairly new one, a gift to them on their wedding day in 1957, one with the button that all Greeks knew or thought at some point would be needed: a shortwave button. My mother sat me down in front of the radio, turned it on, turned the volume down, pushed the large ivory button, and turned the dial to the right. A bit before the dial reached the end of the band, among all the screeching and garbling static, and all the unintelligible languages, my mother slowed down, listened carefully and discerned German. "You stay here and listen to it," she said. "When it says, 'And now news from Greece,' call me."

I listened to this news in German, understanding nothing, thinking of all the stories about the German occupation that I had heard over the past nine years of my life—the tortures, the executions, the bodies of the hanged dangling from trees, the security cage full of civilians that the Germans would place in front of a train engine to deter sabotage, the stories of the screaming of the tortured, the famine, the dead children in the streets, massive executions as reprisals, the

Figure 20. Photograph of a lapel pin (1965) with the letter delta (for Democracy), on which rests the profile of George Papandreou, prime minister of Greece. The pin was designed and used by the Union of Democratic Women in Zográphou, an association formed after the July events of 1965 (*Ioulianà*). Collection of the author.

collaborators, the hooded ones, treason, hard-boiled eggs in underarms, the iron vice, terror. Suddenly there was music that sounded familiar; I found out later that it was the opening to Mikis Theodorakis's *Antonis*, from his album *Mauthausen*. Then the voice came on. "Radio Station *Deutsche Welle*. And now, news from Greece," a woman's voice said in Greek, a voice that had a slight hesitation when it pronounced the letter *r*. I called my mother and was promptly sent out of the room.

I could not understand why I had been sent out of the room, and I tried to get an answer from her in the summer of 2006. "Why did you not want me to listen to the news then?" I asked.

"It was dangerous," she said. "Had anyone asked you in the street if we listened to foreign news, what would you have done?"

I pointed out that I already knew that they were listening to foreign news, the only thing I didn't know was what the news said.

"It was too dangerous," my mother said again, even more emphatically.

"It was one of the three times in my life when I saw my father carry his gun," my friend Alexandros said when I asked him what he remembered from this day.* "Are you interviewing me?" he asked. I said that I was. "Good," he said, laughingly. "Can I have my picture in the book, too?" I said that if he had one from then I would use it. "Yes, I will give you a picture from then. So, it was Sunday morning . . ."

"It was Friday morning," I interrupted him.

"Do you want my story or not?" he said.

I nodded. Of course I wanted his story, even though I knew that the beginning of it was wrong. This is the nature of fieldwork. How could I get the story if I kept interrupting him? But how could I go on pretending that I did not know that what he was saying was wrong, since I myself "had been there," I had seen it, I, too, had cheered at not having school that day? I had to be the ethnographer, but my "nativeness" kept tripping me up. As Renato Rosaldo has put it, "I didn't know if I had to put on my loin cloth or pick up my pencil and paper."[6] I decided to err on the side of my discipline, but not before one last attempt. "It was not Sunday morning," I said, "because it was a school day and every other account that we have from that day of people our age mentions exactly the same thing: cheers at not having school."

"We didn't have school that day," Alexandros said. "It was not a school day. It was Sunday, because my grandmother had gone to church,"

6. Renato Rosaldo has commented convincingly on the nuances and perplexities of maintaining a secure and fixed position in anthropological accounting, particularly in the context of the complications and complicities always inherent in the act of conceptualizing, recording, transmitting, translating, mediating, inhabiting, and living in the position of the ethnographer (Rosaldo 1989: 45).

*This particular interview was conducted in English. Alexandros grew up in Athens, where he went to school and then studied medicine at the University of Athens. After graduate work in the United States, he is currently on the faculty of a major teaching hospital there.

he continued."Your grandmother could have gone to church because she was, obviously, a very religious person," I said.

"My grandmother had gone to church because it was Sunday," he said again, "and my mother would know."

I gave him my cell phone. "Call your mother," I said.

"Let me tell you my story, and then we'll call her, but you are wrong," he continued.

I gave in for the moment. "Go on," I said, "tell me what happened."

"We were sitting down at breakfast; it was 8:15 in the morning. I remember this very well—my father was there with a glass of milk in front of him."

"What did your father do for a living?" I asked.

"He was a policeman," he said, "and at that time he was teaching at the School of the Gendarmes."

"A policeman or a gendarme?" I asked.

"A gendarme," he responded. He continued, "So, my father was putting bits of bread in his milk, and my grandmother came in. My mother said to her, 'You didn't go to church?' 'No,' my grandmother said, 'because three blocks up there are soldiers, and they said to me, 'Where are you going, little grandma?' I said, 'to church,' and one of them said, 'Go back home, grandma, there is no church today; there has been a revolution [egine epanastasis].' 'Opa,'[7] my father said and got up from the table with such force that his glass tipped over and all the milk spilled on the floor. So, for me, the memory of how the junta happened is that of spilled milk on the kitchen floor. And then, the funny thing is, we didn't know *who* had done the revolution, because there were rumors that the Left was planning a revolution, too. But we didn't know, and we didn't know if my father should go to the police station or if we should hide him in the attic [to patari]. We were looking for places to hide him. But I bet you anything, come on, let's place a bet, what will you give me when you find out that it was a Sunday, and not a Friday?"

7. *Opa* could be loosely translated "Here we go." It is an exclamation used to express high spirits, singing and dancing. But it is also used to express bewilderment, as Alexandros's father did here.

I said that it was certainly not a Sunday, but maybe it was a Saturday, the Day of Lazarus, the last Saturday before the Day of Resurrection, and maybe that was the reason his grandmother had gone to church. The dictatorship happened the week before Easter. He called his mother. She recounted the same story as he did, down to the Sunday detail. We resolved to check it out on the Web. We did. April 21, 1967, was, of course, a Friday.

"But it was not a day that we had school," he said when I called to tell him about it. "Oh, you just destroyed my childhood," he continued, jokingly. There were three times in his life, Alexandros had said, when he saw his father carrying a gun. On the day of the junta, on the day of the Polytechnic uprising (in 1973), and "the day he saw my name on the ballot of the KKE of the Interior [Parergon 7.2]. He came to the house; he put the ballot on the table. I was cooking green peas, I remember this very well. He put the ballot on the table and said, 'What is this?' 'A ballot,' I said. 'What name is this on it?' he said again. 'Mine,' I said. He left, went to the other room, got out his gun, and came up to me and said, 'Out of my house, now.' So, I got out of his house." The dictatorship had managed to split the political DNA of Alexandros's father and make a "Communist" out of his son.

The first night of the dictatorship was apparently not only a terrifying but also a bizarre event. Not only were the active members of the various political parties and smaller political groups (what in Greek are playfully called *groupouskoula*, "little groups") arrested, but so were elderly people who had been politically inactive since the end of the civil war. Since these men and women had been required to report to the police station at regular intervals for about fifteen years, they knew their neighborhood policemen, although no one would claim that they were on friendly terms with each other.[8] When the policemen went to his house to arrest him, Tzavalás Karousos mentions the hesitation and even gentleness that the first policemen he encountered showed to everyone, from the moment that they picked him up, allowing him to dress, to the police station, where the policeman on duty treated him "politely, maybe even amicably. . . . Everyone received me smiling. They even offered me coffee. They all knew me as a movie actor, because none of them had any affinity for the serious theater. . . . They searched me. They took my eyeglasses, my belt, my pen, my keychain, my money. They wrapped everything in a piece of paper and asked me to sit down. They offered me coffee again. I refused. I asked again what had happened. The response was the standard one—'We don't know anything. We are just following orders. It's others . . .'" (Karousos 1974: 24). The awkwardness of the police is palpable. For the first time since the Metaxas era the police were in the dark about political developments.

Karousos was put in a cell measuring 2 x 2.5 meters, with a barred transom on the top, along with fifteen other people: lawyers, doctors, the mayor [*proedros tes koinothtas*], two members of the city council, various entrepreneurs. He mentions that, despite not knowing what had happened or what was in store

8. The issue of recognizing a tortured intersubjective relationship between the police, the torturers, the snitches, and the objects of their charge is very complicated and not enough attention has been paid to it. The Greek situation is replete with information that could be used to examine this, from Mikis Theodorakis's comment that he came to welcome the gendarme into whose charge he had been given during his *ektopismós* at Zatouna simply because the daily requirement of reporting to the station allowed for an exchange between two human beings (*dyo ánthropoi*), to Lili Zographou's wrenching short story in which her heroine is incapable of suppressing an orgasm during her rape by a Special Security agent, to the countless accounts of tortured Leftists who have mentioned both in writing and in private interviews that occasionally, during breaks in the torture, they would feel a human connection with their torturer simply because he was there.

for them, for the moment they were in good spirits. Obviously they had the resources they needed; they knew, as Karousos says, that they "should not allow the prison to turn them upside down. Every Greek knows that. Because for decades now, half of the population has been in the prisons and the camps. Just like that, for no reason at all, simply because of their political thoughts."

Is there a way of escaping this determinism of history, a warped determinism that becomes recognized as such only once it has happened? The recognition of the repetition of history offers him a sense of familiarity, and through this familiarity it produces again, it re-produces, a collective "we," a "we" that can easily be forgotten in the lull of history, in an existence where an (almost always) imminent crisis becomes occluded by the apparition of normalcy.

In the tiny cell where Karousos was placed, there was not enough space for everyone to sit on the floor. Some stood while others sat. Karousos, tall and erect, heard a voice coming from the floor, saying: "This smells like Indonesia [referring to the 1965 Suharto coup]. American stuff."[9] Karousos recognized the man: he was a worker who had managed clandestinely to get a job at the oil refinery. The two of them had been exiled at Makrónisos and Ai-Stratis together. The worker could not procure a certificate of loyalty, and he was working undocumented. He said all this very fast, adding, "It's a good thing that the king organized [made] this dictatorship and saved me from all this [the agony of being discovered and fired]," not knowing yet, as no one did, that it was not the king who had organized the coup, that his planned dictatorship of the generals, as it came to be known, was superseded by this ridiculous dictatorship of the colonels.

"The word *Indonesia*, the case of the worker, everything darkened the place . . . We were all forty-five years old or older . . . The unknown weighed heavily on us [*mas plakonei*]" (ibid.: 25). But Karousos recognizes that this experience would not have been the same in other parts of Athens, in other parts of Greece. He lived in a very good bourgeois neighborhood, but he wonders what the situation was like elsewhere, in Piraeus, for instance, where the most committed working-class Leftists lived in well-recognized neighborhoods. He did not know that in Piraeus a small child had been arrested, along with his mother, and had been tortured in front of her so that he would give away the hiding-place of his father. He did not know that this small child had died of the torture in front of his mother. But he was himself puzzled at what had happened, and he sought refuge in doubting the

9. The reference is obviously to Suharto's 1965 coup, which was staged to indicate that it had been carried out by the Communist Party. Later on Karousos makes an even more specific reference to Indonesia. At the temporary camp at the Hippodrome, the guards demand that an old man pick up a huge barrel full of rubbish and empty it. As he tries to pick it up, it keeps slipping from his hands, spilling all the rubbish on the ground, which he then tries to pick up with his hands and put back in the barrel. After this happens a number of times, the people who are around him move to help him. At that point, Karousos says, "All the guns are turned toward us. And the soldiers from the tanks are ready to use them. We understood. It was a trap. They were trying to goad us into helping the old man so that they could claim that we had revolted and then they would kill us. Indonesia! was what we all thought" (Karousos 1974: 64).

present moment, if it were really what it seemed to be. "We are not in the time of Makrónisos any longer where, when the wind took away our tents, when the dust storm came, in the midst of the rain and the hail, we fought to put them back together in the thick darkness of the angry night. As soon as we were liberated from the camps of the Germans, we found ourselves in camps guarded by the people of the Germans, whom our allies gathered up and put above us. But there is something else, now . . . We left our jobs [to go home], and we found ourselves chained, shamelessly, without knowing whether we are to live and what's in store for us" (ibid.: 30).

What was in store for them was the temporary camp of the Hippodrome and then transport to Yáros. The army had taken over from the police by then. At the Hippodrome, Karousos noted again the age of those arrested, ranging from forty-something to the upper eighties, with some being over ninety years old. He remarked to someone there that they were all out of commission, they were too old, their arrest was nonsensical. Everybody knew everybody. Here was the leadership of the Communist Party, all of them just barely out of prison, the cadres of the Party; they all knew each other from various camps and exiles. "This is the result of this modern disease, anti-Communism," Karousos thought (ibid.: 53), turning the tables on all the medical metaphors that had been used throughout the century to describe and fight Communism.

Meanwhile, the news of the new government appeared in the newspapers, and Karousos was able to steal a glance at the paper of one of the officers. The new undersecretary of public security was T. Totomis, who had been a snitch for the Gestapo, a collaborator. He had fled the country with the Germans and had been found by the Americans, who took him with them. Twenty years later, they sent him to Greece as a high-ranking official in Tom Pappas's businesses (the same Tom Pappas who financed part of Richard Nixon's campaign, advised Spiro Agnew, and collaborated with the junta).

"It was the same, the same story," Karousos says (ibid., 79). They didn't know what would happen: collective torture or execution? "The memory of Indonesia never, not for one moment, left the camp," he writes (ibid.)

If those arrested never forgot their history, if the compounded experience of persecution, terror, and abjection never really left them, if their memory was riven by fissures that could not be sutured, the same was true for the junta. The arrested and the junta traveled across the same familiar cognitive and conceptual topography, a topography that, in turn, produced two drastically different topologies: one of extraction, the other of inclusion.

Obviously, the junta could not keep the thousands of people that it had arrested in the Hippodrome, in military camps, and in football stadia. At some point, Karousos says, it became clear that they would be transported. Indeed, military lorries were there to pick them up. With his indefatigable sense of humor, he notes, "The optimists expect Ikaria. [They say] 'They will be embarrassed to take us to Makrónisos or Yioúra. They have to take international opinion into account.' You are lucky that you haven't realized yet what American gangsterism means. The pessimists are thinking, 'Indonesia.' Most of us expected Makrónisos or Yioúra."

Then Karousos describes what has become a commonplace in the topology of crises: he engages in radical topography. In the total absence of any information, he tries to decipher the intentions of the junta by applying himself to basic geography: "Now we will see. If [the lorry] turns left, we are headed to Lavrion, so that from there we can be easily transported to Makrónisos. There is the advantage of water. It takes just half an hour for the water-transport boat to come from Lavrion. If they turn right, then we are headed to Piraeus. Yioúra, undoubtedly. We

Figure 21. Lavrion with Makrónisos in the distance, 1945. Photograph by Dimitris Harissiadis, from the exhibit catalogue *East of Attica: Photographs 1930–1970*, Benaki Museum. Reproduced with permission.

are all hoping for Makrónisos. At least from there we could see the opposite shore, we could see cars' headlights at night as they appeared and disappeared on the winding road to Athens; we could even see, during starry nights—and those are the majority in Greece—far away, behind and over the peaks of the hills of Mesogeia, the glare from the lights of Athens . . . We come out from the street. We turn right. We are going to Yioúra. Some of us still do not want to believe it. No! We might embark on Piraeus to Makrónisos. Not Yioúra! Not Yioúra! No one wants this" (ibid., 84).

The generational difference among the detainees continued to be acute. The navy ships kept transporting political prisoners, "but they never bring young ones," Karousos notes.[10] The younger ones were kept in prisons where tortures even more intense, and certainly more scientific, took place.[11]

10. Karousos stayed in Yáros until July 1967, when he was transported, still in custody, to the hospital of the Averof Prison in Athens with a massive infection. After being hospitalized for fifteen days there, he was suddenly released and allowed to seek better treatment privately. But, as he states, he had been proscribed: it was against the law to mention his name publicly or to perform his work at the national theaters. He traveled to London, Paris, and Strasbourg, where he denounced the dictatorship openly and tried to find treatment at various hospitals. He died in Paris on December 3, 1969.

11. Perikles Korovesis, one of the younger political prisoners, states that at one point Theodoros Theophiloyiannakos (one of the chief torturers and director of the Special Interrogation Unit of the Military Police, the ESA) advised him: "Talk now, because what we are doing to you is simply bar-

Figure 22. The ruins of the infirmary on Makrónisos, with the mainland and Lavrion in the distance. Photograph by the author.

baric. If you don't talk now we'll send you further in, for a more scientific treatment." It would be trite even to attempt to analyze the distinction between "barbarism" and "science" proposed in this statement. The reference to "scientific treatment" was not simply metaphorical but refers to the training of the Greek Military Police by the U.S. Army and what became the CIA in techniques of interrogation, starting from the time of the civil war.

12. Under the junta "democrats" inhabited the zone of danger heretofore occupied by Leftists, Communists, and world peace activists. "Democratically minded" citizens thus expanded the category of the dangerous citizen.

An interesting development, engendered by the junta's profound climate of suspicion, fear, and deep anti-Communism (an anti-Communism that lapsed into anti-anti-juntaism, as Clifford Geertz might have said), was that after the coup attempted by the king in December 1968 a whole group of Right-wing, royalist, high-ranking officers, primarily generals, admirals, and air-force commanders, was imprisoned on the mainland and exiled to Yáros, along with the Leftists and the "democrats,"[12] against whom they might have fought during the civil war or whom they might have helped convict and imprison only a few years before their own arrests. "I didn't have anyone to talk to, except another general," one of them said to me. "Imagine that," he continued, "what could I possibly have in common with them? What could we talk about? They wanted the breakdown of the state [*ten dialyse tou kratous*], I wanted the preservation of the king and order. But we had to eat together, and suffer together, although the gendarmes were more kind to us, they showed us the same respect that they had shown us before."

This required yet another reordering of space: where the Rightists' tents would be, where they would sit down to eat, where they would relieve themselves, so that they would not be forced to interact with the "others," would not have to expose to them their private parts, their intimate gestures. But one should mention here a recent comment by Konstantinos Metsotakis, honorary president of the Right-wing New Democracy Party, who, in a celebration for Leonidas Kyrkos, deputy of the Left-wing party Synaspismos, mentioned in public that when he himself was (briefly) arrested by the junta on April 21, 1967, he realized how "valuable it was for the bourgeois politicians to understand what the Left-wing politicians had been through thus far" (Mitsotakis 2008).

A Mistake!

A mistake! One word for the terrible reality of the present. And not for the present moment only, but of all the betrayals leading up to it over the last half-century, all the years the poet was writing: from the reckless venture of the Turkish War [1897], with the Greek troops encouraged by the British and French until the destruction of the whole Greek world of Asia Minor [1922], and up to World War II and the bloodbath and the famine of the German Occupation; and the tremendous achievements of the resistance rewarded only with the re-establishment of British colonialism and a police state, with a civil war where tens of thousands on both sides perished, and a new American military machine with its secret services the only winner (the foretaste of Vietnam), and now finally the nightmare insult of a dictatorship just when the Civil War was beginning to be forgotten, and another generation had grown up without a memory of it. *Mistake, mistake!—and our lives have changed.* (Andrews 1980: 55; at the end, Andrews cites George Seferis, "Arnese" ["Denial"])

Kevin Andrews correctly outlines the damage that the junta did in assessing that the junta managed to produce yet another generation, the generation born in the years 1955 to 1960, that has as its point of reference the civil war. And Andrews gives yet another view of Yiannis Philis's *enoteta*, this cogent unit that articulates itself on the spine of the *asphalites* and that forms the Greek experience of history.

Although, as dictatorships go, the Greek one was not particularly brutal, never achieved the levels of terror that Pinochet's did in Chile or Franco's in Spain, and certainly did not last as long as other dictatorships, just a scant seven years, this could not have been known to the people who faced the gun barrels of the military in the first few days of the junta.

"We were never afraid for our lives during the junta," I was told by Hara, a woman who was picked up in 1969 by the junta at age twenty for belonging to one of the underground Leftist resistance organizations; "it never gave us the impression that our lives were in jeopardy."

"Despite the torture?" I asked.

"Despite the torture," she responded.

I asked the same thing of an older friend, who had been exiled on Makrónisos, then on Ai-Stratis, then released and right before the junta fled to Paris. Since the end of the junta, he has held a number of positions in the public sector, and he is a revered poet, hence not an abject subject of the polity any longer. He looked puzzled as he said, "I am not sure what she means. I am still afraid; every time I go out of the house and see a policeman, I always check myself and walk quickly past him."

The junta proceeded in the midst of a rapidly growing youth movement, a movement that pushed the boundaries of the notion of generations. Once again the meaning of age and generation loomed, condensed amid an angry sexual revolution that came to index political involvement, in dancing parties, miniskirts, and long hair. Tasos Darveris, one of the students arrested by the Special Security for belonging to an antijunta organization, notes a comment made by one of the Special Security officers who was interrogating him at the Special Security Headquarters in Thessaloniki: "In previous times, the EPONitēs [a male member of EPON] would sleep right next to the EPONitissa [a female member of EPON], and he wouldn't dare think that he could touch her. Now, in 1972, if there is no fucking the organization is not moving forward" (2002: 155). The movement of resistance to the junta, although not massive, was sizable, despite the fact that it rarely resorted to armed violence and despite the fact that the only assassination that was ever attempted, twice, was that of Papadopoulos by Alekos Panagoulis (who, being a conscripted soldier, was tried by military tribunal, was sentenced to life imprisonment, and spent the rest of the junta in prison, under torture, three of those years in solitary confinement).

Every time Truman's statue was blown off its pedestal, my parents would say, "We are going to miss Takis again." Takis was an old friend of my parents, one of the defendants at the ASPIDA trial, who had been living in a semilegal state of existence—in a state of nonexistence, it would be more accurate to say—ever since the end of that trial, and certainly ever since the junta happened. Once he was describing how he had found himself in the midst of a forest fire, to which many people from the area had rushed, trying to put it out. He said that, despite all the efforts that he made to help, people, along with the firemen, would pass him by, not giving him water or letting him help put out the fire. "At some point," he said, "I saw that whatever they were doing was having no effect on the fire. I told them to cut branches from the trees and hit the fire with them, and to cut a clearing so that the fire would have no place to go. I knew all this from the army," he said, the last almost whispered.

That description was given many years ago, during the junta, at a dinner party that my parents were hosting. Takis would always appear unannounced, after midnight, so as not to be noticed by anyone, so that he would avoid putting our family in jeopardy by his presence, and, finally, so that he would not have to face two particular friends of my parents, Adam and Eucharis,[13] husband and wife. Eucharis was a co-worker of my mother's, Adam the military director of the Special Interrogation Unit of the Greek Military Police, the infamous EAT/ESA.

We never knew where Takis had been taken. He never said; neither did he speak of the tortures he had undergone, except once, when his then lover was picked up along with him. After they were both released, they came to our house on one of those name-day celebrations, appearing, as usual, after midnight. Takis started narrating this latest imprisonment with Kaity present. It was the first time that he had been arrested along with a girlfriend. They went back and forth telling the story: how they had been found, who made the arrest, how they were taken first to the Special Security and then to ESA, how the interrogation had started. They were placed in separate cells, and Kaity, being arrested for the first time, could hear the screams of those being tortured. Takis managed to send her a little note, saying not to pay attention to the screams. "This is a deranged person," he wrote. Kaity did not last long as a girlfriend, or as a prisoner—she was released unharmed.

If, in the first two-thirds of the century, the state unwittingly managed to produce scores of Leftists by placing unsuspecting citizens in the category of the suspect and the dangerous, with the junta it embarked on a new project: the creation of engineered torturers. Scientific, systematic, and methodical means were employed in an attempt to produce ranks of mindless, loyal, devoted, low-ranking, temporary torturers. The Center of Training of Military Police, the notorious KESA, was established in the military camp at Goudi. Military service was, and is, obligatory in Greece. After initial basic training at various camps, soldiers were carefully selected to be sent for further training. The selection was both psychological and physical.[14]

13. Although a pseudonym here, *Eucharis* is a real name for women in Greece, meaning full of joy and grace. In antiquity it was one of the attributes of Artemis.

14. A number of memoirs state this process in detail, and it kept coming up over and over again in the interviews that I conducted. See Katsaros 2000 and Darveris 2002. The case of Michalis Petrou is an interesting one, as Mika Haritos-Fatouros (2003) notes, not only because he was infamous for his brutality, sending a shiver down the spine of everyone who heard about him, but because of the incongruity of his social existence. Haritos-Fatouros describes how he became romantically involved with a young university student, who frequented clubs and cafés where forbidden music was played. Elaine Scarry, working with the transcripts of the trial of the junta torturers compiled by Amnesty International, pays particular attention

to Petrou (whom she does not name) as she talks about the "self-conscious display of agency" that transforms the "conversion of absolute pain into the fiction of absolute power" (Scarry 1985: 27). Petrou was famous for a ring that he wore, which every one of his torture victims mentions. The tortured would enter the torture chamber, where they would be shown the instruments of torture; then Petrou would remove his ring, stroke their hair, and start the torture. During the trial, Petrou disputed the story of the ring, maintaining that the ring was a present from his girlfriend after he had been released from the army. See also the account given by Petrou to Haritos-Fatouros of the process that resulted in his being selected to become a special interrogator.

Tall, handsome, well-built young men would be set aside for the special training, provided that they came from families with no prior political involvement, with a "clean" *certificat de civisme*. Mika Haritos-Fatouros, in her study of five torturers who were convicted after the junta, has argued that no special circumstances played a significant role in the successful training of these young men and their temporary transformation from clueless to torturers. She further argues that anyone, given the right training, can be transformed into a torturer. She mentions that, when she presented her findings at a meeting attended by Amnesty International, someone asked her if her argument was that even he, someone who worked for Amnesty International, could, given special training, be transformed into a torturer.

She replied in the affirmative (Parergon 7.3). But the state, even the most totalitarian one, can never be as successful as it wants. As one of those young men picked by the army to be trained as a torturer said (then, and again in the summer of 2005, when I interviewed him): "I entered the army in this way, and came out that way," turning over his right hand, showing first the palm, then the top, to indicate the radical change that he had undergone during the training. He went in Right-wing, and he came out Left.

This particular man, Sotiris, had studied geology in Italy, where he met an old high-school student of my mother, Katerina. That is how we met him, through her. While they were studying in Italy, they would come and visit us in Athens, bringing all sorts of gifts: news of the Red Brigades, fishnet stockings, the music of Lucio Dalla, prosciutto, posters of Antonioni's films, glittery eye shadow. They were older than me and my sister, and much younger than my parents. But there was a closeness to our family, and they would spend days with us. They were almost the adopted older children of my parents.*

When Sotiris finished his studies and came back to Greece, it was time for him to fulfill his military obligations. "Not to worry," my mother's friend Eucharis told her, "we will arrange it so that he will be kept in Athens, close to Adam." Adam was Eucharis's husband and the military director of the EAT/ESA. How can one go against the grace of power, especially when power holds the torture of torture in its hand? This was not the manufacture of consent, because there was no consent, there was sheer terror. Sotiris went to KESA, and for forty days he was tortured so that he would learn how to

---

*I have written extensively about the practice of classificatory kinship and the modalities that govern its rules and meanings in Athens (Panourgiá 1995). Katerina is a classificatory daughter of my parents.

torture others. He came to our house on his leave, and I remember that man, over six feet tall, being unable to sit on a chair from the pain.*

When time came for his release, Adam bestowed his grace again, and Sotiris was stationed at EAT/ESA, but at the moving violations office, where he had to investigate moving violations by soldiers. He kept a low profile, not revealing to anyone the particulars of how he had come to that place. Every so often, however, Theophiloyiannakos and Hatzizisis, the two chiefs of the interrogation unit of ESA, would ask him to name the names of democratic students whom he knew in Italy. He refused. He said he did not know any; he came from a poor family; he had to work in order to support himself and his brother, who was also studying there; and he had no time for socializing.

The pressure was stepped up until at one point, Katerina told me in the summer of 2005, "It became unbearable. I went to your mother and was crying, because they had become so hostile toward him that we had no idea what steps they would take next. As I was crying, Eucharis came for coffee. She saw me like this, asked why I was crying, and I hesitated to tell her. Your mother did not hesitate at all. 'They are asking Sotiris for names,' your mother said. Eucharis called Adam [Katerina started imitating Eucharis on the telephone], 'Loule [that was his diminutive], I am at Demetra's and Katerina is here and she is crying because they are asking Sotiris to give them some names from Italy.' We were looking at her, as Adam was talking to her. She took the telephone from her ear. 'Can't he give a few?' she said—apparently that was what Adam told her to ask. I motioned that no, he could not. She told Adam, 'No, he can't.' Adam said something to her. Again, she took the telephone from her ear. 'One or two? So that they'll leave him alone.' I motioned again no, he did not know any. Eucharis turned to Adam, again. 'He doesn't know any,' she said. He said something to her; she hung up and said, 'Tell Sotiris to go to see Theophiloyiannakos tomorrow to take his leave.' He went the next morning, and Theophiloyiannakos was beside himself. He started yelling at him, saying 'You thought that you were being smart? You know the Major so well and you had not said anything all this time? Then he took his revolver out, put it on his [Sotiris's] temple and ordered him out of his office. He signed his leave of absence."

What's in the act of naming, indeed, and of the admission that one knows the person who resides within that name? That the Leftist knows the Leftist, that the soldier knows the major? What is the act of acknowledging the gesture of naming? Leftists had been asked to produce the names of other Leftists, of their comrades, their contacts, by the Special Security of Metaxas and Maniadákis, by the Gestapo, by the SS, by the torturers on Yáros and Makrónisos, by the CIA collaborators of the Greek Special Security, even by

---

*See also the accounts published in Haritos-Fatouros 2003.

the most menial officer at the most menial police or gendarme station, for forty years, unendingly. It was common practice. Some gave names, some did not, but the act of naming a name has not come easily, and it has, certainly, indexed the relationship and the texture of the contact between citizens and the state. How can, then, the question "Not even one or two?" be articulated, except by a power that is so blinded by its hubris that it refuses to acknowledge that there is a plane of existence that exists in total opposition to its own, that there are other forms of life for whom the genealogy of naming names forecloses any possibility of engaging in it. This encounter is not an encounter of enemies, in the sense that Gil Anidjar (2003) has given that phrase, where the enemy is an enemy only when he has the potential of being a friend, where even if the zone of enmity always exists it is not always occupied by the same enemy. This is an encounter of radically different subjectivities, subjectivities that refuse to recognize the possibility of intersubjectivity. They are subjectivities radically incomprehensible to each other. The refusal to name names comes to Adam as an alien act. The refusal to disclose the acquaintance of Sotiris with Adam comes to Theophiloyiannakos as the same. The only recognition is that of radical *méconnaissance*.

Of course, nothing is as monolingual, monosemantic, or monolithic as it appears, not even terror. Maybe because the terror in Greece had run from the sublime usurpations of democracy of the civil-war and post–civil-war governments to the utterly ridiculous derision of parliamentarism during the junta, a common joke went: "We laughed a lot during the junta; there was pain, but there was mirth, also."[15] The colonels who were responsible for the junta were very badly educated (at a time when education was deemed to be of paramount importance and the only worthwhile pursuit) and inadequately socialized, with the result that they mangled the language and appeared clumsy and awkward in public. The junta had nothing of the glamour of the Peron, Salazar, Pahlavi, or Pinochet terrors. The mangled sentences uttered by Papadopoulos, the ridiculous hats sported by his wife, the repulsive appearance of Patakos, the pimpish look of Makarezos, the clichés produced by Ladas—all provided material for side-splitting laughter and deep contempt. All that changed, however, on November 17, 1973. Starting on November 13, a group of students, joined quickly by thousands of Athenian residents, occupied the Polytechnic building demanding freedom. The events at the Polytechnic brought about a change in the leadership of the junta when, on the night of Sunday, November 25, 1973, Demetrios Ioannides, an officer who had cut his teeth on detention, militarism, and

15. The actress Kitty Arseni pointed this out in an interview given to Stelios Kouloglou for Greek public television, ERT, on a special program on resistance to the junta. Arseni was one of the most brutally tortured prisoners during the junta. She had been arrested for trying to smuggle an audio tape with Mikis Theodorakis's latest music out of Greece. Tales of her torture circulated throughout Athens not only during the junta but for years afterward.

the fine art of torture on Makrónisos in 1947, overthrew the Papadopoulos, Patakos, and Makarezos troika and established himself as dictator.

Events had been escalating rapidly since the first day of the student uprising. University and Polytechnic students first, with thousands of high school students quickly joining them, chanting and asking the residents of Athens to join in, occupied the building of the Polytechnic on Patession Street. On Friday November 16, a bit before nine o'clock at night was the last chance to get out of the Polytechnic. The information had circulated inside and outside the Polytechnic that, after negotiating with the police, the gates to the school would be locked so that no one would be able to come in or leave. I had to go because my parents thought that I had gone to my folk-dance lesson at the Lycée of Greek Women. They would kill me if I did not come home on time. Being fifteen years old, I was too young, they thought, to participate in political acts. They did not forget that at my age they had done just the same. Quite the opposite—they were fully conscious that at my age they had done so. Every day since the beginning of the uprising I had lied through my teeth so that I could be at the Polytechnic. I would take the bus from our house to the end of the line on Academy Street, then I would walk toward Solonos Street, which was full of the "cram schools" that prepared thousands of us each year for the entrance examinations for the university, a system riddled by years of corruption, which had destroyed the educational system.[16] At Botasi Street I would walk right to get to the Polytechnic, each time with more police around, still mildly polite, trying to turn us away. The crowd felt homogeneous—thousands of high-school students who moved and acted not under the direction of their teachers but almost knowing of themselves what to do, despite disagreements as to how to proceed (offered by the Troskyists), or whether this should be happening at all (offered by the official Communist Party). Out on the streets, inside the Polytechnic, at middle-class and working-class homes, this was the moment.

The slogans were not symbolic; nothing was hidden there: "Down with the Junta"; "People Move—They Are Eating Your Bread"; "Greece of *Torturer* Greeks";[17] "Greece of Imprisoned Greeks"; "Greece of *Tortured* Greeks"; "Bread—Education—Freedom"; "General Strike." Everybody's throat hurt, voices would disappear, our parents would ask why, we would lie, we would say that we had to sing at dance class, that the weather was getting strange. On Friday November 16, as the situation started becoming more precarious, I lied even more, saying that there was an extra session at my dance class, and I got there fairly early. Hundreds of thousands of

16. Or so we thought then, having no premonition that the national educational system would be destroyed after the junta, through the populism of the (nominally socialist) PASOK government and the blatant disregard for education of the Right-wing New Democracy.

17. A play on the junta's slogan "Greece of Christian Greeks."

people had come and gone, yet tens of thousands lingered there. University and Polytechnic students had not only put together a public broadcast system to give information to the crowd outside the architecture building, where the committee coordinating the occupation of the Polytechnic was, but also an illegal radio station that the whole of Athens could hear but no one in the police or the army could shut down. "*Edo Polytechnio, Edo Polytechnio*; This is the Polytechnic, This is the Polytechnic," the voices of the students would repeat, announcing items that were needed (sutures, bandages, milk, clean water, specific medications, antiseptics); demands that the students had (freedom of assembly, of the press, of expression, academic freedom; freedom in general; down with the junta); what was happening within the school at the meetings of the coordinating committee; supplications for more people to join. Medical students were on the ready for an emergency, and economics and political theory students explained the theory of the dictatorship of the proletariat, the meaning of surplus value, and Poulantzas's analysis of fascism and the meaning of the state in Marx.

By the early evening things had escalated. Civilian and military police were everywhere, both in uniform and in plain clothes; students were being chased and clobbered; heads were bashed open; tear gas was being thrown by the police in all directions. The loudspeakers gave advice: Don't rub your eyes, use Vaseline, suck on a cut lemon, put a wet kerchief on your mouth, light fires on the street, light fires on the street. The crowd was bunching tighter and tighter, inside the school and out. There were no buses going by, no cars on the street. Traffic had completely stopped in front of the Polytechnic school. Only people were there—thousands and thousands of unarmed high-school and university students, lawyers, actors, farmers, construction workers, retirees, teachers.

The smells of the tear gas and the burning fires blend. Everything is acrid, burning your throat and your lungs. More doctors are needed, more medical supplies are needed, I wonder if I should leave and find my friends who are in medical school to see if I can find some supplies through them. I ask someone; he says that if I leave now I might not be able to come back. Everyone is afraid of *provokatores*, agents provocateurs; everyone needs to secure the school from infiltrators. There are already warnings that some of the slogans heard (such as the one for *Laokratia*: "Power to the People") are not slogans endorsed by the students. The students are careful not to reproduce party lines.

More tear gas is thrown, more students are hurt. There is no way I can find my friends now, and no way of knowing that at least two of them I will never see again. People outside the school are stoking the fires on the streets, but snipers have been firing from the balconies of the Acropol Palace Hotel right across from the school, which has been taken over by the army. I look at my watch; it's almost ten o' clock. I decide to leave. I don't have to climb over the fence; I'm thin enough to slip through it. I can hear bullets being fired, people screaming. I can't see what is happening on Patesion Street, so I start running up toward the square. About a block from the school I hear the bullet; it grazes my hair and lands on the pavement. I pick it up. I run faster until I feel a thud on my back. I fall down, as tear gas billows around me. I get up, pick up the now deflated canister. It burns my hand, but I keep it. I put it in my jeans pocket, and it warms my leg.

I am lucky, because right about this time my friend Diomedes is being killed at close range by two bullets. He is a few months older than I am, almost sixteen. I don't know about Diomedes yet, that he has been shot by members of the personal guard of the minister of public safety as he was transporting wounded demonstrators (Parergon 7.4). I run into Bótase Street. Halfway up the block is a contingent of policemen. I turn back to Stournára Street again; I am shorter, younger, and faster than they are, and I am wearing the right shoes. I keep hearing shots. I find the door to my godfather's building open. I go in, but can't go upstairs; I know better than that. If I can only make it to the square, I can pretend I am just going home from the cram school. I go outside again, walk along the wall, make a right on Zaimi Street, and it's empty. I am moving away from the Polytechnic but not far enough. At the corner another group of young students, about my age, appears. We don't speak to one another. I join them, and we walk toward the square. There we disperse. I walk up an alley, still not sure when and where the police might appear. I keep on walking; the geography I traverse is the history of this section of Athens. The entire area around the Polytechnic and the Exarcheia is where some of the fiercest battles of the Dekemvrianá took place. Most of the streets in the area have been given names of events and figures of the War of 1821, the Greek Enlightenment, the new state: Koraes, Zaimes, Loggos, Valtetsi, Arahova, Benakis, Didotos—they are here. Moving up the hill, closer to upper-class Kolonaki, most street names turn toward antiquity: Hippocrates, Homer, Pleiades, Delphoi. I know the area. I walk all the way up to Didótou Street and keep going up the hill to where my dance school is.

When I get there, at the corner stands a lone policeman. I know by now that I cannot find the medical supplies, that I need to go back home. I lie again. "Excuse me, officer, I don't want to get involved with what is happening down there. Is there a way that I can get to Zográphou from here without running into any of those?" I ask.

He sizes me up, giving me a good, long dirty look. "Are you *from* Zográphou?" he asks.

I say yes, I am, my parents and my grandparents too.

"So you must know the chief of the police station there," he says.

Yes, of course I do—he is tall, handsome, with blue eyes, a seductive bachelor many years too old for me but a friend of my mother, who is a teacher there. "Yes, I know him," I say.

"Name him," he says.

I do.

"And do you know the previous Chief?" he asks.

This is a tricky question, I think to myself. But, yes, I know him. He is my uncle (who has since been demoted for having supported the king).

The policeman grabs me by the arm and whispers to me, "Quickly, over the hill, avoid the hospitals, don't run, go home."

I start up the hill. I am too young to have an identification card yet; I must wait a few more months, if anyone stops me I can say that I am going home after my dance class. But no one stops me, no one sees me. I get to the three hospitals, I go through the garden, and from there up the main street. People are sitting inside the coffee shops here.

Now I can run home, which is exactly what I do. I get there very late and lie again. There were no buses (which is true) so I had to walk from the lycée (which is also true). They look at me, I am all in one piece. They can't ask for much more than that, and everyone goes to bed.

I share the bed with my younger sister and put my ear to the small, round red transistor that I got as a present on my name day last year. Maria Damanaki's voice alternates with that of Demetris Papachristos on Radio Polytechnic; they are student announcers for the radio. They are alone. They need more doctors, more medical supplies, more ambulances sent. They appealed to foreign embassies to send observers, but none came.[18] Young people are being shot outside the school. Ambulances take them away, but they come too late, too few. Some people already know that most of the ambulances are driven by policemen and soldiers in disguise and that, while some of them arrive at hospitals, others go straight to the Security Police. Elsewhere, the police throw smoke bombs into ambulances carrying the wounded. The station again broadcasts advice to use lemon, to keep the fires burning—but they also give the news: the tanks are coming.

At that very moment, in another part of Zográphou, at the border of Zográphou and Goudi, my friend Yiorgos, yet another medical student, is lying on the roof of his apartment

18. The question of foreign observation and documentation of torture and atrocities in Greece is neither new nor restricted to this particular instance at the Polytechnic. Becket mentions that the International Committee of the Red Cross "had a presence in Greece and had permission to visit political detainees, but they were skeptical and unresponsive on the issue of torture" (1970: xi). When cases of torture started becoming more widely known abroad and the junta started becoming anxious about this knowledge, they responded to the accusations "through Red Cross reports" (ibid.: xii). The detainees on Yioúra have also reported that the Red Cross would not only visit the island to report on its exemplary operations, but on certain occasions would participate in some forms of torture themselves. More typically, they would falsify evidence of severe disabilities caused by torture on the island, such as haemoptysis, haematemesis, fractured bones, and seizures. See Petris 1984 and Anonymous [September 1950].

building, watching the tanks leave the Goudi compound and go down to the Polytechnic. He counts them: five. He tells Katerina the next morning, who tells us, how the building shook from their treads on the pavement, how he remained motionless so that he wouldn't be seen.

The tanks arrived at the Polytechnic at 1:00 A.M. One of them positioned itself outside the gate, which was teeming with students—seated on the rails, hanging from the pillars, inside it, outside it, everywhere. The chancellor's Mercedes Benz had been placed on the other side of the gate, inside, to prevent it from collapsing.

The radio station still broadcasts, Demetris's voice is hoarse and rasping now, he can barely be heard, but he is screaming: "Soldiers, you are our brothers, soldiers you are our brothers, you will not strike against us, you will not strike against us."[19] He and Maria repeat this over and over until, at some point, they start singing the national anthem and ask everyone not to move away from their radios, to keep the radios open—and then the radio goes dead. Not a signal, nothing, just white noise.

19. Andrews, in the most intense narrative of the Polytechnic that I have read, relates that when he heard the students on the street calling the soldiers their brothers he yelled out at them: "Idiots! . . . They are not your brothers! Do you think they care for truth or justice! Six years they've been trained to kill. Run!" (Andrews 1980 [1974]: 85).

A Swedish film crew across the street from the Polytechnic was taping everything. The tank moved in, crushing the Mercedes Benz, crushing Peppi Rigopoulou's legs, as students scuttled about, incredulous. Peppi will eventually become a university professor; she will theorize the body. Demetris will become a newspaper editor; Maria will become a deputy. But right this minute no one expects any of this. Right now blood, spent bullets, hundreds of tear-gas canisters were everywhere.

A legend circulated the next morning that the soldier driving the tank refused to drive through the gate, that he was killed on the spot by his commanding officer, and that the tank was driven by the career officer himself. Nothing of the sort is true. The driver of the tank, A. Skevophylax, gave an interview (his first and only one) on November 9, 2003, on the occasion of the thirtieth anniversary of the Polytechnic. He mentions that he was a young soldier, twenty years old, serving in the tank division, and his tank was the first one to leave Goudi. He describes how he led the rest of the tanks down Alexandras Avenue, how he positioned his tank in front of the gate, how he hesitated just for a second twenty meters before the gate "to give them a chance to get out of the way," and how he drove his tank through the gate with no remorse. "Had anyone said anything to me at that moment I would have killed him, right then and there. I believed in what I was doing; I had believed what the junta was telling us, that these were dirty Communists, that they wanted to take over the country, that they were burning down Athens." After he was discharged from the army, Skevophylax got menial jobs as day laborer. "Working and living hand-to-mouth" he says, "changed my life 180 degrees. I, having been taught to hate the Communists, have voted twice for the Communist Party" (Skevophylax 2003).

Early the next morning, Katerina came to our house with the news: "The Polytechnic fell [*epese to Polytechneio*]."

"But," I said, "I have been listening to the radio; they assured us all that it would not, they said we should stay tuned . . ."

"*To Polytechneio epese*," Katerina interrupted me, with tears running down her face. She looked at me: "Did they find out?" (She meant my parents.)

I said no, they had not, that I had come home relatively early and probably they hadn't suspected anything. I said that I came back home out of concern for them.

She shook her head, saying, "You were concerned about them; I was concerned about Sotiris. If none of us had been concerned about others and we all one million of us had stayed there, maybe they wouldn't have moved in, maybe the Polytechnic wouldn't have fallen."

We went outside, where the whole city had been taken over by the army. There were tanks, soldiers, and policemen everywhere. We tried to approach the Polytechnic, but the police shooed us away. There they were, policemen in their uniforms hosing down the blood and the debris around the gate. Despite the military law that had been installed, a demonstration was taking place by the Polytechnic, this time directed at the balconies, with fists clenched and raised upward, addressing the citizens: "Last night they killed your children . . ." A few hours before, outside our house in Zográphou, a bullet shot by a soldier standing on a hill had missed my sister and my grandfather, speeding between their heads, and hit five-year-old Theodoris Dimitriou in the head. His mother was holding him by the hand, coming back from the fishmonger. She felt him go limp and tried to pick him up. When he fell to the street, without a cry or a sound, she started giving her fish away.*

Later in the afternoon, our friends who were medical students, most of them cousins and old students of my mother, started to come to our house with the news they had received from the hospitals: the police and the army had raided the hospitals, looking for the wounded, and whoever they found they took away to the Special Security Headquarters on Mesogheion Street or executed on the spot. The physicians, some physicians, tried to shield the identity of the wounded by altering the reasons for admission, the names, the ages of the wounded.[20] The curfew time was approaching. I had not heard before the dissonance created by the silence, the absence of human sounds save for the clanking of the tank treads

20. This sheltering practice by physicians created a problem for the wounded who,

*I have described this incident in greater detail in Panourgiá 1995.

and the sirens of the ambulances and police cars. Katerina could not spend the night at our house; we would have had to declare her presence to the police. She left in time to be home before sundown. My father decided to make pancakes and mountain tea.

Late Sunday afternoon, another friend, Michalis Myroyiannis, was killed by Colonel Nikolaos Dertiles as he was walking down the street at the corner of the Polytechnic, going to meet his father, who worked as a concierge at one of the apartment buildings there. Our mutual friend Pavlos came to tell us a few hours later, before the curfew. There was no mirth after the Polytechnic, and for a whole week mourning was palpable. The funerals of the dead took place, Michalis's a few graves away from Diomedes's. At the end of the week, Ioannides's counter-coup deposed Papadopoulos's junta and initiated the most brutal period of the seven-year dictatorship—which, thankfully, would last only until July 1974.

years later, tried to get compensation from the state for their mistreatment during the Polytechnic. They were unable to produce documentation that they had, indeed, been transferred to the hospital and had been treated there. See the special issue of *To Vema*, Sunday, November 18, 2003.

8

1974–2007

After History

Askesis in Forgetting

The fall of the junta, on July 23, 1974, was precipitated by a number of things: a botched attempt at a coup in Cyprus by the junta; a botched attempt at the assassination of the president of Cyprus, Makarios, by the "unionists [*enotikoi*]" of ex-Chi leader George Grivas (Parergon 8.1); the "de facto" (and long sought by the British) partitioning of Cyprus; and the fiasco of a general mobilization of the army, calling to arms against Turkey, the strongest member of the NATO alliance after the United States, the entire Greek male population between the ages of twenty and forty-five, into an army that was as ill equipped as it was untrained.[1] The fall came, as Kevin Andrews notes, "not [by] a revolution, not a riot, not a strike—no mass movement—nothing inevitable like the Polytechnic: just a noiseless and discreet withdrawal by those directly responsible, with their patriotic invitation to civilian politicians to take over" (1980: xvi). Constantine Karamanlis was recalled from self-imposed exile and under his leadership a new conservative, Right-wing party, New Democracy, was voted into power. Prime Minister Karamanlis legalized the Communist Party and established a new Constitution, one that retained severe political restrictions but was deemed to be "consonant

1. For two spellbinding first-hand accounts of the madness that was the Greek army at the time of the general mobilization see Darveris 2002 and Katsaros 2000. Both these authors had been detained and severely tortured by the junta, then, at the time of the mobilization, found themselves serving in the army. The experience of the general mobilization was ludicrous. The army did not have enough military camps to hold the reservists, so they had to pitch their tents in olive groves, on the beach, in public squares. There were not enough items of clothing to go around, so someone might be dressed in a military uniform but still wearing his personally owned flip-flops; in other cases someone might have been given army boots but no uniform, so he would wear the boots but still be dressed in beach shorts. Nor did the army have enough resources to feed all these men, so they depended on the kindness of area residents, who would cook food at home and take it to the camps. In the darkness of the junta, which still was (nominally) in power, neighborhood organizations were set up, in which block by

150

with Greek reality."[2] While guaranteeing political freedom, individual rights, and free elections, the new Constitution left the issue of accountability for the dictatorship and for Cyprus largely untouched. In an attempt to close the cycle of violence and revenge, the Greek government expected the country to engage in an exercise of forgetting, an exercise that required an almost eremitic and ascetic discipline in divesting from the past. The government took the questionable decision to prosecute only the *protaitious* ("the main culprits") of the junta, while allowing the vast majority of those who made the operation of the junta possible to exit the system without ever giving an account of themselves and their actions. There were two major trials, one that tried and convicted the main culprits, and another that tried and convicted the five torturers eventually studied by Mika Haritos-Fatouros. At the end of the trials, the then minister of defense, Evangelos Averoff, when pressed for a full disclosure of cleansing (*kátharsis*) of the armed and security forces and the public sector, replied that such a cleansing had indeed happened and that only "droplets [*stagonidia*]" of the "mad" remained. When on May 1, 1975, Alekos Panagoulis, now a deputy in Parliament, pressed the government on the issue of Cyprus and promised that "on Monday" he would make public all the incriminating evidence that he had managed to collect, which he thought would seal the case against those responsible for Cyprus, he was, curiously, killed in a car accident.[3]

block residents were entrusted with providing food and water for the reservists. But none of this was as serious as the fact that case after case of arms and ammunition would be opened to find that only the top layer would be arms or ammunition, everything below that having been replaced by rocks.

2. Andrews notes the strangeness of this turn of phrase used in the new Constitution when he writes: "The protective note in this good rough hint at a national immaturity is reminiscent of the attitude of Greece's foreign benefactors through the ages: as it were 'You are too individualistic and disorganized to rule yourselves; let us, who have the know-how and the wherewithal, govern you instead and help you to defend yourselves against our enemies. This may keep you back a bit or even permanently stunt your growth, but the longer you remain backward the longer you can profit from the generous use we make of your important peninsular location" (1980: xvi).

3. In the first years of the PASOK government, the names of a number of municipal streets (King George Street, for instance) were changed to Alekos Panagoulis Street, and with the expansion of the subway system his name was given to the station built at the place where his accident occurred. That is how Panagoulis's name circulates among the post-PASOK generation of new Athenians.

In 1981 the party of Andreas Papandreou, PASOK, a socialist party that is a member of the Socialist International, was elected with a substantial majority. When it formed a government, it engaged in the following three conciliatory gestures. (1) It decided to abolish the use of security files on citizens kept by the Greek Central Intelligence Service (KYP), and it finally incinerated the existing files at the furnace of the steel mill outside Athens in 1989. (2) It allowed the DSE fighters who had taken refuge in Communist countries to repatriate to Greece. (3) It issued pensions to all Resistance fighters. These gestures not only promised reconciliation and a (re)turn to normalcy but also

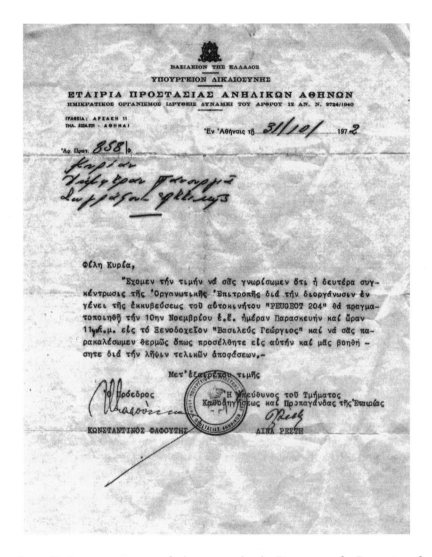

Figure 23. An announcement of a lottery run by the Department for Protection of Minors, a semi-governmental organization under the auspices of the Ministry of Justice, signed by the president of the organization and the head of the Department of Guidance and Propaganda of the department. The important point is that such a department existed.

secured the past in the furnace of the steel mill. There was no longer any trace of real accountability, no way of unpicking the skein of twentieth-century history back to when the state started to imagine and produce itself as something cohesive and self-recognizable, no fear that the actions of Venizelos, Plastiras, George Papandreou, the involvement of the Center and the implication of the Left in its own demise would ever be exposed. The Left was made, at once, both legal and forgotten.* Enforced amnesia.

With the downfall of the junta, when everyone in Greece expected complete and total catharsis,† it became apparent that neither the willingness nor the ability for such an undertaking was possible. This inability or unwillingness eroded any remaining sense of trust between the public and the state, thus enabling the most successful, long-lasting, and never-infiltrated urban guerrilla group, the Revolutionary Organization 17 November (as its full name is, or 17N), to appear on the political scene as the organization that "could and would": (1) dole out justice where justice had not been done, punishing collaborators with the junta, many of whom had previously been collaborators with the Germans; and (2) act as the perpetual enforcer of public conscience in safeguarding against corruption and exploitation of the public by a complicitous state within an irresponsible corporate sphere.

Explosive Genealogies

On June 29, 2002, coming back from dinner around 1:20 A.M., my husband and I were stopped at a traffic light on the main thoroughfare that connects the port of Piraeus to downtown Athens. At this hour, in the middle of the week, Athenian roads are almost deserted, even in the middle of the summer. As if from nowhere emerged an impressive apparition: three police cars followed by an ambulance followed by three more police cars, flanked by four police motorcycles, all with their sirens and surveillance lights on. We knew immediately that a major event had taken place, but the only event that we thought could explain such a display of care would be an accident to the prime minister or the president of the republic. We turned the radio on. Breaking news was already being broadcast: an explosion had taken place at the port, and a person had been seriously injured, apparently the detonator of the bomb. "It all points toward November 17," the announcer announced. This organization, 17N, falls somewhere between the Weather Underground (WU) and the Red Army Faction (RAF) or the Brigate Rosse in that it

---

*I am indebted to James A. Boon, who fleshed out this idea of the forgetting of the Left.

†This is the term actually used both by the democratic government that followed the junta in 1974 and by the legal apparatus that handled the trials of the dictators and their collaborators.

engaged in bombings of public and government buildings, like the WU, and in assassinations, like the RAF or the Brigate Rosse, but it did not engage in kidnappings. The two of us, secure in our knowledge of the ineptitude of the Greek police, shrugged off the claim with a laugh. "Yeah, right," we said. "As if it's *that* easy to capture 17N" (Parergon 8.2).

Of course, we could not have been more wrong. This was, indeed, 17N. Savvas Xeros and Dimitris Koufondinas, two of the main operatives of the organization, were at the port. Koufondinas served as the lookout while Xeros, attempting to place a bomb at the ticket counter of one of the shipping companies, apparently pushed the detonator a bit more forcefully than he should have. Later it was all blamed on the fact that the person who had procured the timing device, an alarm clock, was a new recruit to the ranks of the organization. Unaware of the importance of such things, instead of purchasing a sturdy, German-made metallic clock, he had bought a cheap plastic one made in China. So much for globalization and its discontents. The bomb exploded in Xeros's hands, severing completely four of the five fingers on his right hand and leaving him almost deaf and blind, with severe wounds all over his body. Koufondinas immediately called an ambulance, and he left the scene when he was certain that Xeros was being taken to the hospital. What we witnessed that night on Syngrou Avenue was Xeros's transfer from the regional hospital at Piraeus to the main trauma center in downtown Athens, less than two hours after the explosion had happened.

During the following two months, we also witnessed, to our surprise, the rapid dismantling of the Revolutionary Organization 17 November. Koufondinas was not captured by the police until he turned himself in at the end of the summer, claiming responsibility for the actions of the organization in order to continue fighting for the recognition of 17N as a *political* and not a criminal organization, on the one hand, and an urban guerrilla and not terrorist organization, on the other. The two categories were not drawn by chance. The former addressed the efforts of the liberal state to refuse to accept the political and ideological parameters that 17N had articulated for itself, as had been the state's usual practice since the introduction of the Idiônymon. The latter addressed the efforts of the parliamentary Left to deny 17N any legitimate claim to be part of the Left, and thus to claim a common kinship with the history that has made the Left both a possible and a legitimate participant in the post–Second World War political spectrum in Greece.

One of the key issues in this gesture of classification, both by the state and the calcified Left, was, of course, the fact that the Left, legal and forgotten, had finally managed to pass the dangerousness of its existence on to a different self. What were the political issues at stake in differentiating among the various forms that violence takes? Terrorism, urban guerrilla warfare, armed citizen self-defense, armed national liberation movements, political liberation

movements, partisan armed struggle, and, more recently, the antiglobaliza-
tion movement (and especially Black Bloc) are all now semantically collapsed
into "terrorism" when their tactics, objectives, political mandates, and relationship to the state, and to often-competing political ideologies, demand the
preservation of their differences.

Of course, the latest such gesture by the liberal U.S. state is the recent
morphing of the Iraqi insurgents into something that hasn't acquired its own
nomenclature yet. "I hesitate to call them 'insurgents,'" Donald Rumsfeld
announced at a news conference. "They are against a legitimate government."
When Peter Pace, the Chairman of the Joint Chiefs of Staff, said that the
U.S. military was "taking cities from the—I have to use the word 'insurgents'
because I can't think of a better word right now," Rumsfeld cut him off in
mid-sentence, saying: "Enemies of the legitimate Iraqi government—how's
that?" George W. Bush went even further the next day, creating three new categorical classifications: *Saddamists*, *rejectionists*, and *terrorists* (William Safire,
"On Language," *The New York Times Magazine*, January 15, 2006, p. 16).

The issue of terrorism has become common with reference to radical political action both outside and within the United States. In regard to Greece, especially as the Olympic Games of 2004 were approaching, terrorism became the
primary concern of the U.S. government, which sought nominally to protect
its athletic delegations but in essence to promote and protect its financial and
corporate interests. Of the urban guerrilla groups operating in Europe, none
has created more consternation for the U.S. State Department than 17N, not
only because it has assassinated a number of American citizens and dignitar-
ies but also because in 2002 it was still the longest-existing urban guerrilla
organization in Europe. It was on account of 17N's actions, specifically the
assassination in 1975 of Richard Welch, chief of the CIA station in Athens
and "a brilliant Harvard-educated classicist" (according to the Arlington
National Cemetery Web site), that the U.S. government criminalized the
public disclosure of the names of covert CIA agents (Parergon 8.3). If the
assassination of Richard Welch inaugurated 17N as an urban guerrilla group,
the assassination of British military attaché Brig. Stephen Saunders on June
9, 2000, sealed its demise.[4] British intelligence
landed in Greece for the first time since 1947
and joined forces with the U.S. security units
already in place, demanding the apprehension
of the group and its swift bringing to justice.
The symbolism could not have been clearer.
Once again, the British and the Americans were
taking over from a Greek liberal government in
policing the political landscape, again with the
total acquiescence of that government. Only

4. Stephen Saunders was assassinated on
the assumption that he was responsible for
coordinating NATO attacks on Kosovo,
an allegation that has been denied by
Great Britain but sustained by 17N in
subsequent communiqués. Saunders's
assassination took place the day before a
UN Security Council meeting that was to
mark the end of the first year of the UN
action in Kosovo.

things were a bit different this time around: 17N was a marginal political group trying to be the conscience of a country that had lost its political edge. And 17N had only marginal public support.

The dismantling of 17N has reopened a public discussion in Greece regarding a slew of old, controversial questions: the relationship of this group to the traditional Left; the relationship of the traditional Left to armed struggle, self-defense, and terrorism; the relationship of political and social memory, as experienced by the members of 17N, to their affiliation with the Left. The relationship 17N claimed with the historical past of the Left in Greece can help us to understand how the translation of history and historical experience into violent political action takes place.

The experience of the civil war has often been credited as the location in which the ideologies that animated the actions of 17N developed. The effects of such an experience are felt and lived for generations, and it is to them that 17N spoke. The thread that 17N spun between its actions, the legacy of the Nazi occupation and its collaborators, the Resistance movement, the civil war, and the Greek junta can be translated into other, homologous narratives, located in other histories, that have animated armed or otherwise violent action in the context of what we have come to accept as liberal democracies.

But these connections are not made only by 17N. At the height of the first trial of 17N, when testimony was being heard about the assassination of Pavlos Bakoyiannis—the son-in-law of the leader of the Right-wing party New Democracy and a politician in his own right, who had been trying to bring about a rapprochement between the Right and the Left—I was discussing the case with my parents in the presence of some old family friends. As I was complaining about the travesty of justice during the trial, my father, mistaking my consternation over the juridical process for support for the members of the organization, lashed out in a manner that I had not seen him use in over twenty years.

"Why did they kill Bakoyiannis?" he asked.

I said I did not know; I only knew what they had said about this particular case in their circular at the time, something that was theoretically and conceptually nebulous enough not to give a recognizable reason.

"They are no different from OPLA," my father continued. "Why did OPLA kill Maratos in '44?" he asked.

Again, I said that I had no idea why OPLA had killed Maratos. To me, Iason Maratos was just a name on a street sign on the way to my English class. I had wondered about it, but had never asked anyone. I always assumed that it had to do with the Maratos house standing at the end of the street. I promised my father that I would check in the Archives of Social History (the ASKI) to see if anything appeared there.

My father was dismissive. "You won't find anything anywhere," he said.

"They came and picked him up and killed him, and that's how our *leventes* ["brave lad," used here sarcastically] ended up in Averof."

This was the first time that I heard how my uncle Stéphanos had ended up on death row. I asked what the connection was.

"He was one of those who picked up Maratos," my father said, "and they tried him, sent him to Averof, but his father paid one hundred and thirty gold pounds to commute the sentence to life, and that's how he ended up in Yáros." This, now, made sense. He was sent to Yáros because he was too young for military service but was a convicted murderer and member of OPLA and the Party. I asked how he left Yáros, only to be told that his class was called to military service. He was transferred to Makrónisos, and from there to Grammos. The part that only those who had signed *dēlôseis* could be sent to Grammos was left out of this narrative.

I tried to find out anything I could about the Maratos case, to no avail. Several months later, around Christmas 2003, I saw an announcement in the newspaper for a book called *Ho Kokkinos Stavros (The Red Cross)*, written by Georges Maratos. I looked for it, but it did not come out for a few more months. I tried to find Maratos himself in the meantime, although I was not really sure what I could tell him in the event that I found him. As soon as the book came out, I read it in one sitting. My uncle Stéphanos's name was nowhere to be found, but the name of my other uncle, the later chief of police, appeared prominently in the book; it was he who had found the OPLA executioners and had brought young Georges Maratos to the police station, first to identify the body of his father and then to identify the main executioner. At least now I had something to go by. I called my uncle and asked about Stéphanos.

"I am not sure that he was part of that operation," he said to me. "But be careful. *Scripta manet.*"

I asked my father about it. He shrugged, saying, "What are you trying to do, now? Leave it alone. The fact is that they are both dead now, just like Bakoyiannis."

These narrativized connections constitute nodal points around which the memory of corporeal and psychological trauma organizes the articulation of historical experience and thus a conceptual platform for understanding violence against the state. If 17N produced a narrative genealogy of affinities with the revolutionary and emancipatory gestures of contemporary Greek history, this gesture did not go unnoticed by its critics, again with a twist. This twist recognizes the dialectical texture of revolution, the fact that, for every enlightening, emancipatory, and democratic gesture that it makes, there is another one, dark, oppressive, and murderous. The trial of 17N started in spring 2004 and brought to the fore the deep uneasiness in Greece about political violence.

"We didn't need this," an older friend, Popi, said about 17N. "Imagine, we have been in turmoil all our lives, it's enough."

"Did people feel safe or unsafe with 17N around?" I asked.

Another friend, Evi, responded to that. "When they were caught, I was talking with a neighbor here. I said that, finally, they had been caught, and she said to me that she never felt unsafe with 17N around. Imagine that!"

I could very well imagine that, because I had never felt unsafe with 17N around, and I said so. I said that I never felt that I would be harmed in any way. "Even after the Axarlian case?" Evi challenged.

Thanos Axarlian was a twenty-year-old man, the only untargeted victim of 17N, who was killed by rocket shrapnel when 17N tried, unsuccessfully, to assassinate the minister of finance in a busy downtown street in 1992. The truth is that even after the Axarlian case I did not feel particularly unsafe. I live in New York City, after all, and in 1992 New York City was not exactly peaceful, either. It seems that Evi's position, though, was not very prevalent, especially among Athenians. Some of them even felt an affinity with 17N's pursuit of reckless industrialists, torturers who had escaped justice, and irresponsible newspapermen with deep connections to the political establishment and the capitalist structure of the country.

Things changed, however, when 17N started targeting people whose political significance was not easily apparent or, even more disturbingly, the choice of whom belied a significant turn toward nationalism and isolationism in 17N ideology. One of those people was Bakoyiannis. This particular case created the greatest consternation, as no one could quite understand the importance that 17N placed on the possibility of such a rapprochement.

During the trial in 2004—a trial that, by all accounts, was a parody of justice, reminiscent of the trials of the Left during the 1950s, I was invited to dinner at the house of some old friends of my parents. Other people were there, too, some of whom I had not seen in many years, some of whom I did not know, and some long-time neighbors who had known the family for generations. The discussion inevitably turned to the trial, as we were watching interviews with Xeros's parents. One of those old friends, Anastasia, talked back to the television, addressing the father of Xeros, an old priest. "Yeah, and what happened to all the money that you made, and the villas that you built, you goat-priest [tragópapa]," she said.

During the trial of 17N, when asked what could possibly count as *political* motives for the actions of the organization, one of the witnesses for the defense, Giorgos Karabeliás, a book publisher in his late sixties, turned to the public prosecutor and asked: "Do you see how thick my glasses are and that I am almost blind? Do you know why I have almost lost my eyesight?"

"Because you are poor and you can't afford a good ophthalmologist," the prosecutor replied.

"No," he said, "it's because when I was born the obstetrician made a mistake that almost cost me my eyesight. But no one prosecuted him, and he knew that he wouldn't be prosecuted. So he went on delivering more children, without any fear or concern that someone might actually demand justice."

In this short exchange, what is being debated is not the eyesight of the publisher but rather conditions of social injustice and corruption that existed in Greece more than sixty years ago and that, in the eyes of the witness (so to speak), made resistance to the state not only legitimate but morally imperative.

The liberal Enlightenment state, having abandoned the mandate on which it was formed—namely, universal education, health care, liberty, and justice (we won't even touch upon the proverbial "pursuit of happiness")—needs to justify its continued existence at the level of protecting its citizens from "danger." Sometimes this danger is construed as external, other times as internal, yet other times as both.

What are the parameters that make a state categorize a portion of its citizens as "dangerous and suspicious," and what are the long-term effects of this categorization in the ways that a specific society comes to understand itself as a cultural and political entity? An examination of the role of history in the organization of everyday lived experience will point us toward a possible response to this question and will help us to elucidate the intimate but nebulous relationship between political action, political ideology, and social memory as they affect the everyday lives of citizens. Through such an examination,

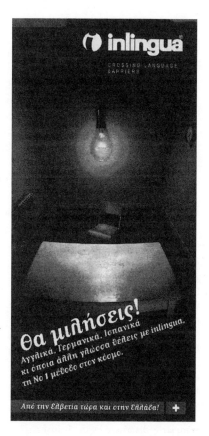

Figure 24. Advertisement for the foreign-language learning method inlingua. The caption reads: "You will talk! English, German, Spanish, and any other language you want with inlingua, the no. 1 method in the world. From Switzerland, now in Greece, too." "Speak" and "talk" are the same word in Greek (*milao*).

we can understand schematically the ways in which the experience of history, even when seemingly forgotten, organizes the ways people respond to their current lived realities, as these register "on their very bodies," as the example of the publisher Karabeliás shows. Thus, it also means to recognize and acknowledge the modes in which the experience of the body becomes translated into the experience of history through the collectivization of the memory of persecution (of going underground, of torture, of exile).

Medical metaphors have been in use since the 1930s to convey the notion that political dissidence is a (social) disease and political dissidents are infected with it, so that the intervention of a physician (a noninfected politician) capable of curing the disease becomes imperative.[5] They were extensively employed during the civil war and the dictatorship (when the whole country was deemed in dire need of being placed in a cast). Even recently, ex–prime minister Kostas Simitis declared that the country was ill and that he was the physician willing to provide a cure. All this, of course, presupposes and demands that citizens will entrust themselves to their state as one trusts one's physician. This provides us with a wider dimension for understanding the management of what Poulantzas has called "antinational" elements: the intimate relationship between political and medical discourses, whereby medical metaphors legitimate political intervention by the state under the premise of safeguarding the political body from elements that are foreign and extraneous to it and dangerous for its existence.

What is the role of violence in this? To remember Huey P. Newton, "existence is violent," so even the mere presence of citizens can be extrapolated into a violent act. But before we start addressing the question of violence, it might be instructive to think about the various discourses of "peaceful resistance." Martin Luther King and Gandhi come to mind, of course, although the pacifism of both has been questioned,[6] and, as Sally Bermanzohn et al. (2002) have shown, it has colonized Martin Luther King's image, whitewashing (so to speak) his more activist and violent past.

5. This becomes clear not only in the speeches delivered by Metaxas but also later, during the period when the camps were in full operation, in the speeches delivered by the military commanders of the camps and the politicians who supported them.

6 Gandhi, for instance, had requested that the Indians in South Africa be allowed to enlist and fight on the side of the British during the Boer War, a request that was summarily dismissed by the British.

Freud's Remnants (Parergon 8.4)

I call this stone Oedipus. It too is irregular, with deep grooves for eyes. It too rolls down with swollen feet. And when motionless it hides a fate, a reptile, my forgotten self.

I call this stone Oedipus.

For although by itself it has no meaning, it too has the shape and the weight of choice. I name it and I lick it.

Until the end of my story.

Until I understand what choice means.

Until I understand what the end means.

—*Katerina Anghelaki-Rooke, "I Have a Stone"*

There are many ethnographic moments where Oedipus turns up in an unexpected location: in testimonials by the detainees at the camps, in Lancaster's account of the Distomo massacre in 1944 (where the Germans killed all the men and set the village on fire), in a number of instances during the trial of 17N, and in journalistic accounts the figure of Oedipus raises its head, stands up on its feet, so to speak, not as the infant who envies the father and desires the mother but as the sovereign who is crushed under the weight of his responsibility and who plucks out his eyes as he encounters his accountability, the recognition that he has to account for his actions even if they were inadvertent, not intended. So far as he knew, he killed a man in self-defense, he did not kill his father; and he married the widow of a king, he did not marry his mother.

Maria Damanaki, one of the two voices of the clandestine radio during the Polytechnic uprising, now a deputy with Parliament with PASOK, prefaced a piece that she wrote about the Israeli attack on Lebanon in August 2006 with a reference to Voltaire's *Oedipus*: "on doit des égards aux vivants; on ne doit aux morts que la vèrité [we owe respect to the living; to the dead we owe nothing but the truth]."*

These ethnographic instances ask that Oedipus (the play, the myth, the cinematic account) be read again, against the grain of the expected readings, along the grain of markings on the flesh. Such a gesture allows me to think the mythical (Oedipus as the king of Thebes, the offspring of Laius and Jocasta, the brother of the Sphinx, the father of his siblings, the son of his mother) as commensurable with the political (the face whose feet and eyes come to the mind of political prisoners after torture has rendered them akin to his image). Not that we need to invent new ways of addressing the events around us, because, as Schiller noted in his letter to Goethe, "Everything is already there, so it needs only to be extricated." But we need to address the mythic again in this new mythical era that we are living. In this context, a reading of the myths that have participated in the construction of *Western* systems of subjectivities—reading, interpretation, and representation—imposes itself anew, and there is hardly a myth more definitive of the ways we have come to understand subjectivities than the myth of Oedipus. It is also in this context that the reflection upon the mythical as commensurate with the political becomes imperative.

*Damanaki 2006: 31, quoting Voltaire in Greek translation. I have used the version in Besterman 1968–1977). The quote is from Voltaire, " Première Lettre Sur Oedipe" (2d ed., 1719), 15n.

Figure 25. An engraving of a fisherman who has caught the head of Oedipus in his nets. Note the liberties taken in refashioning the myth. The engraver, A. Duvivier, is rendering a marble statue by Leon Eugène Longepied entitled "A Fisherman Catching the Head of Orpheus in His Nets," presented at the Salon des Beaux Arts in 1882, and changing the name Orpheus to Oedipus. Longepied had produced another statue depicting the same fisherman having caught Ophelia in his nets. Collection of the author.

7. The Sphinx was a monster, known from Egyptian mythology, who had the body of a bull, the nails of a lion, the wings of an eagle, and the head of a woman. In Egypt, the Sphinx was male; in Thebes, female. In Greece, the Sphinx was herself the product of the unconventional and incestuous union of two natural elements who were, structurally, a mother and a son: Echidna, the chthonic worm or snake, and her son Orthus, the dog

So, let's do what is rarely done: take a look at the myth in full. Oedipus, after leaving the Delphic oracle, killed a man at a crossroads. This is the crucial event of the myth. The myth tells us that Oedipus did not know who the man at the crossroads was. As a matter of fact, when he killed the man at the crossroads he knew as little about anything in his life or outside of it as could be possible. Before arriving at the oracle Oedipus knew that his father was Polybus and his mother was Merope, the royal couple of Corinth. But that (ephemeral) knowledge had been shaken when as a young man Oedipus was taunted by a drunkard, who told him that he was not his father's son. He asked his parents if that was true, and they, outraged, denied it. But Oedipus was not satisfied. So, without telling them anything, he set off for Delphi, to the oracle, to ask the god who, exactly, he was. Apollo sent him away, having said nothing about his lineage but having delivered the famous oracle: "You are fated to couple with your mother; you will bring a breed of children into the light no man can bear to see—you will kill your father, the one who gave you life." From there he ran away—as far away as he could from Corinth. He wandered around until, on his way to Thebes, he came upon a crossroads, where in self-defense he killed a man in a carriage coming from the opposite direction. A little further on, he encountered the Sphinx.[7]

The Sphinx was sitting on a stele atop Mount Phicium (Sphinx Mountain), and she posed the famous riddle, taught to her by the Muses, to everyone who passed by: "There walks on land a creature of two feet, of four feet, and of three; it has one voice but, sole among animals that grow on land or in the sea, it can change its nature; nay, when it walks propped on most feet, then it is the speed of its limbs less than it has ever been before."[8] Oedipus guessed correctly. *"Ánthropos,"* he said, which means human—man and woman—and the Sphinx flung herself from Mount Phicium. Upon his arrival in Thebes, Oedipus was proclaimed the savior of the city and was given Jocasta in marriage. He and Jocasta eventually had four children, two boys and two girls: Polynices, Eteocles, Antigone, and Ismene.

Jocasta had recently been widowed; her husband, Laius, had been killed—reportedly by a band of thieves at a three-road crossroads on the way to Delphi. Jocasta was the daughter of Menoeceus, one of the sons of Cadmus, the founder of Thebes, who was also the ancestor of Laius. Laius was the son of Labdacus, grandson of Cadmus and king of Thebes. When Labdacus died, Laius was still young, and his life was threatened by his uncle, who became the viceroy. According to Pausanias, Laius was given safe passage by "those who had in their best mind not to allow the genos of Cadmus to become unknown to coming generations" (Pausanias 9.5.6). Laius was offered safety in Corinth as the guest of the king of Corinth, Pelops. While in Corinth, Laius fell madly in love with the son of Pelops, Chrysippus, whom he abducted and brought to Thebes, where Chrysippus, ashamed, committed suicide. Pelops placed a curse on Laius, either to die childless or to be killed by his own son.

protecting the monstrous hunting hound Geryon. According to Hesiod she was the daughter of Chimaira and Orthus (Dawn). According to Apollodorus (as presented by Athanasiou 2008) the Sphinx was the daughter of Echidna and Typhon. In both accounts, she was the sister of the Nemean Lion, which was slain by Hercules. According to yet another version of the myth, the Sphinx is the illegitimate daughter of Laius, born before Oedipus. On the imagined meeting of mother and daughter, the Chimaira and the Sphinx, see Flaubert's *The Temptation of Saint Anthony*, where the two monsters attempt first to obliterate each other verbally and then to leave together, failing in both and parting ways at the end. For a reading of the Chimaira and the Sphinx as a means to rethink theory as it bears upon architectural practice, see Jarzombeck 1992. On the issue of female homosexuality as the danger posed by "Oedipus," especially as it pertains to the problem of the Sphinx, see Athanasiou 2008.

---

8. It would be safe to assume that only men passed by the Sphinx's corner; women never ventured outside the city wall unaccompanied. Lowell Edmunds states that this version of the riddle, by Atheneus, is the most complete one. It brings up issues of voice and animality that have systematically been excluded from analyses of Oedipus yet are constitutive of the questions posed by "Oedipus." See Edmunds 1985: 12.

After the death of his uncle, the viceroy of Thebes, Laius assumed the throne of his dead father and married Jocasta. Because Jocasta failed to become pregnant, Laius consulted the oracle at Delphi and received a warning: "You are better off without children," the oracle said, "because if you do have a son he will eventually kill you." Laius kept the oracle secret from Jocasta (who didn't much believe in oracles and seers, anyhow), but after a night of revelry and desire he coupled with her and got her pregnant. (Or Jocasta got him drunk, coupled with him, and became pregnant, unbeknownst to Laius.) When she gave birth to a boy, Laius pierced the ankles of his son with a pin and gave him to Jocasta to dispose of. She gave the boy to a shepherd to expose on Mount Cithaeron. But the shepherd took pity on the child and, instead of exposing him, he gave him away to another transhumant shepherd, from Corinth. He took the baby to his master Polybus and his wife Merope, who were childless.

So Oedipus was taken to Corinth when saved from the mountain, a generation after his father had been taken there to be saved from the usurpations of the sovereign, and it was from Corinth that Oedipus fled when he came full circle, back to Thebes, unknowingly retracing the steps of his father, through the fateful encounter at the crossroads. One day, however, when Oedipus was king of Thebes, a plague broke out in the city, and despite the purification rites that everyone performed, the plague did not go away. So Oedipus fetched the old blind seer, Teiresias (Parergon 8.5), as Jocasta's brother, Creon, consulted the Delphic oracle. The oracle came back with a command to rid Thebes of the miasma, Laius's murderer.

When Oedipus vowed to find the murderer and drive him out of the city, Teiresias identified Oedipus as the murderer, just after a messenger from Corinth came to say that King Polybus was dead and that Oedipus was the rightful heir to the throne. But Oedipus refused to go back to Corinth, out of fear of fulfilling the old oracle about marrying his mother. Oh, he shouldn't worry about that, the messenger said, since Merope was not his real mother. She had been given the baby by this very messenger, who had received it from a shepherd on the mountains of Boeotia.

A moment comes when Jocasta is convinced and also convinces Oedipus, despite the logical objections he raises initially, that he is the son she had abandoned.[9] She runs to their chamber and hangs herself, as Oedipus runs after her. When he sees that she is dead, he takes her body down and with her garment pins strikes his eyes again and again. According to the myth, he remains as king in Thebes, where he dies and is buried with great honors.

Sophocles, however, in the Athenian version of the myth, a version marked by the experience of the Peloponnesian War (Bernard Knox, introd. to Sophocles [1982]), gives us another ending. Thus blinded, Oedipus is allowed to live in Thebes until, many years later, Creon expells him. His own sons make no attempt to keep him there. Outraged at the indifference of his sons, Oedipus curses them to die at each other's hand. He leaves Thebes, blind but a seer now, with Antigone as his guide, and wanders until he arrives in Athens. There he finds refuge in the garden of the Furies and is given asylum after

9. Ahl (1991) has proposed that Oedipus was not the murderer of Laius, but that he accepts this as the truth, being convinced by the argumentation of Creon, Teiresias, and the rest, despite the fact that there is nothing that ties him to the murder. Over and above the many problems associated with Ahl's reading (exposed in Segal 1992), the main problem of Ahl's position is that he takes Oedipus to be a real person, not part of a myth. There is no real Oedipus who might or might not have killed his father.

he foretells the future of the city. He dies there and is buried in a secret place known only to Theseus, the king of Athens.

What possibilities does this myth animate, then? The myth of Oedipus, in fact, the character of Oedipus is that of a paradigmatic man who looked for a truth and accepted many, whose courage, perseverance, and intelligence guided his peripatetic life and made him a native and a stranger everywhere he went, a man who loved his wife more than he loved his mother and strove to find humanity in law and structure. What possibilities become apparent when this character is invoked in cases and under circumstance when humanity seems to be all but forgotten, and how could this character be usefully appraised as a paradigm for anthropology?

The camps in Greece stand as a paradigm for interrogating the lexical tensions of *life* and the praxes that these tensions have engendered. One of the originary metaphors that have informed the perception of *zoē* as naked life is that of Oedipus, the mythical character who was simultaneously native and stranger, offspring, parent, and sibling, king and subject, exile and dispossessed.

Oedipus has constituted the pivotal moment not only of the modern subject, as read through Hegel and Nietzsche, but also of anthropology as an interdisciplinary project. The myth of Oedipus, received by Freud through Nietzsche (even though Freud never acknowledged that he had read any of the circulating discussions on Oedipus)[10] and transformed into the universal Oedipal complex with the aid of Ernest Jones, Sándor Ferenzci, and others, made the debate between Bronislaw Malinowski and Edward Westermarck, on the one hand, and Freud, on the other, imperative. It also authorized fieldwork as the anthropological method that would become the nodal point on which a theory of humanity, a meta-knowledge of human action, could be articulated in the triangulated relationship among knowledge, truth, and method.

I do not argue that this is the beginning of fieldwork. What I argue is that this debate is perhaps the first time when specific ethnographic knowledge was presented as a critique of a theory and method (a theory of human behavior that emerged through the methodol-

10. Freud claimed in 1908, at two meetings of the Vienna Psychoanalytic Society, that he had not read anything published on Oedipus so that his judgment would not be affected. Not only then but repeatedly Freud denied that he had read any of the commentaries on Oedipus by anyone, including Nietzsche. Referring to Nietzsche in particular, Freud stated that his occasional attempts at reading Nietzsche's work "were smothered by an excess of interest" (quoted in Rudnytsky 1987: 198). The evidence, however, that Freud knew Nietzsche's pieces on Oedipus is overwhelming (see ibid.: 198–223). While studying under Brentano, Freud joined a reading group of Viennese German students that was primarily concerned with the work of Schopenhauer, Nietzsche, and Wagner. Rudnytsky notes the correspondence between Freud and his friend Edouard Silberstein, which mentions that during his first year at the university, in 1873, Freud had read Nietzsche's published work. By 1873 *The Birth of Tragedy* and the first two *Untimely Meditations* had been published, and it is in *The Birth of Tragedy* that Nietzsche's piece on Oedipus appeared.

ogy of psychoanalysis), using anthropological and ethnographic material to support itself (as Freud had done in *Totem and Taboo* and in the theoretical conclusions he arrived at through the theory of the Oedipal complex). James Boon, discussing the process of translation from ethnographic experience to anthropological writing, has mapped out the difficulties in reading, navigating, and negotiating the unmanageable contradictions, self-contradictions, self-cancellations, deep questionings, and trenchant aporias (that ought to be) present in the praxis of fieldwork. Boon moves back and forth, looking from the certainty of fieldwork as "empirical" (and naming this certainty "fallacy") to the view ("mistaken") that "cross-cultural interpretations happen empirically" (Boon 1982: 8). Focusing on the process of translation, he sees the object of anthropology (one assumes by engaging with fieldwork, but not only and exclusively with it) as being able to "make explicitly exotic populations appear implicitly familiar and explicitly familiar populations appear implicitly exotic" (ibid.: 9). Freud's Oedipalism and the Malinowskian matrilineal "facts" against the universality of the Freudian Oedipal complex (and everyone who got caught up in the battle between the two) engage in just the opposite: they maintain the exoticism of the exotic and the familiarity of the familiar.*

Here, however, Oedipus allows me to articulate a discourse on the political that is commensurate with the gestures of Oedipean specificity: questions about the fragments of the body, the emergency of biopolitical power, technologies of self and alterity, the problem of autonomy, all intimately connected with "the islands," the civil war, the dissident subject.

Oedipus, as a persona, as a character, and as a text is (still and again) appealing to the extent that he authors new renditions, translations, and adaptations of the play and the myth, which continue to appear at the beginning of the twenty-first century. At a time when the knowledge and truth sought in the modernist experience is progressively translated into apocalyptic and messianic terms (not least of all in the current discourses developed in response to 9/11 and in the articulations of a new empire), what are the key issues managed and negotiated in this narrative that make it relevant to us now? What is the type of knowledge sought through Oedipus nowadays, and how can it be culturally situated and epistemologically located to make Oedipus of interest to anthropologists and to anthropologically informed productions of knowledge? The Oedipus myth, as a comprehensive narrative that spans space and time from its pre-Homeric formulations to the present, constitutes a reflective moment on the human condition that coincides with the project of anthropology. The knowledge and the aporias negotiated by

---

*On the muddled beginnings of fieldwork, see esp. Boon's "Introduction: The Exaggeration of Cultures" (1982: 3–27).

Oedipus correspond to the fundamental principles that guide the process of anthropological investigation. In this respect, Oedipus is the first anthropologist, insofar, and only insofar, as this narrative contains the basic questions that have later come to be associated with and posed by the discipline of anthropology.[11]

Enveloped within this fiction of Oedipus as proto-anthropology is the gesture of anthropology that attempts to answer questions always already formulated outside the epistemological confines of the discipline. With my reading of the Oedipus myth as a narrative[12] (hence, as a story-line that exists in a dialectical relationship to its storyteller), I look for sites where discourses on technologies, philosophical investigations, anthropological epistemologies, and their interstices can be located and where formulations such as kinship, divinity, fate, experience, and sovereignty can be revisited. Oedipus has engendered vocabularies that have produced critical discourses about the political and the social, such as the question of the sovereign with reference to cultural praxis (in the encounter between Oedipus and the oracle). Furthermore, the philosophical foundations of the anthropological project become transparent through the questions that the Oedipean project has posed to us (and as we have inherited it from Sophocles through Hegel, Frazer, Malinowski, Irigaray, and Butler), as do the idioms that anthropology has inherited from the epistemologies that surround the character of Oedipus, such as categories of kinship, friendship, the monstrous and the human, and understandings of the divine.

One of the fundamental questions Oedipus poses for us is that of the constitution of the social subject as a product of the dialectical tension between the self and the other. In other words, the fundamental question that "Oedipus" asks us to consider is not *whether* we know who we are but *how* we know who we are, how we know who the other is, and how we negotiate these categories as they participate in the processes of identity production. When this question is posed as part of the attempt to define and delineate cultural and political formations, it acquires the urgency of political praxis. "Who is an American?" we have been asked daily since 9/11, and why some Americans are recognized as such whereas others are not is a disturbing question posed by the relatives of the fifteen hundred Americans of Middle Eastern descent

11. This proposition is just and justly as problematic as the proposition that attributes the paternity of history to Herodotus—it is just as fictional.

12. Turner (1969) proposes looking at the myth of Oedipus as a narrative that spans large segments of time, although he stays within the Lévi-Straussian analysis of Oedipus as a symbolic rather than a metaphorical text. Vernant (1996) seems to agree with Turner about the importance of thinking about Oedipus as a narrative and not simply as a play, while recognizing that Lévi-Strauss's structuralist analysis eschews the narrative in favor of mythemes (e.g., lameness, killing of the monster, patricide). This privileging of individual mythemes (e.g., incest, the monster, number and gender of siblings) against the narrative is also prevalent in folkloristic analyses, such as the ones presented in Propp 1975 and Edmunds 1995 and Dundes 1983.

who were summarily interned after 9/11, some of them still in custody or unaccounted for.

My inquiry, then, does not concern the Freudian analysis of Oedipus, not only because the inordinate volume of work devoted to it has managed to occlude the myth, but also because the psychoanalytic emphasis on Oedipus has limited the scope of other analytical possibilities to which the text lends itself. The anthropological literature on Oedipus has thus far, with minor exceptions, dealt with responses not only to Freud's claim of the centrality of the Oedipal complex to the process of identity formation but also to Freud's claim of its universality. Although responses to this analytical aspect of Oedipus are still being produced, they are not my present concern (Parergon 8.6). The problem, however, both with Freud's use of the myth and with the responses to it (from Malinowski to Parsons to Lévi-Strauss) is that none considers the myth or the play in their entirety, or as narratives. The only responses to both Freud and Lévi-Strauss that critique this narrow look at Oedipus have been articulated by the French classicists Jean-Pierre Vernant and Pierre Vidal-Naquet, who have argued convincingly that, if the Oedipus complex exists, it does not come from Oedipus (Vernant and Vidal-Naquet 1990: esp. 85–113). Of particular interest is Lacan's comment, in *Seminaire I*, that the Oedipus complex cannot be sustained if the myth is considered in its totality, precisely because the complexity of the myth, with its multiple details, overwhelms the question of just what the complex might be. Lacan's position is, of course, not separate from the importance he places on visuality and verbality. But I am primarily interested in the corpus of theoretical responses to Oedipus produced outside the space occupied by psychoanalysis: notably, the philosophical debates produced by reading the text and their importance for anthropologically informed analysis. In other words, I want to look at the anthropological response to questions posited by philosophy.

This myth, however central it has been to the theory of psychoanalysis and to the early methodology of anthropology, has not been addressed exhaustively either in psychoanalysis or in anthropology. Rather than study the myth itself, both disciplines have applied its bare contours as a framework for analysis. It is particularly startling that anthropology, a discipline uniquely positioned to analyze myth as a cultural text, has not done better here. Starting with anthropologists in the late nineteenth century (principally Frazer) and ending with the structuralists (not only Lévi-Strauss but also his critics, from G. S. Kirk and Clifford Geertz to Peter Munz) anthropology has viewed Oedipus rather reductively, merely responding to the challenges posed by Freud's interpretation. It is interesting to note that both Freudian Oedipalism and the Lévi-Straussian structuralism of Oedipus rest on a scant four pages of analysis each. The usual practice has been to look at isolated mythemes, trying to test empirically claims made by psychoanalysis. Attempts in such a direction have centered on three topics: (1) *kinship*, first by Frazer and his evolutionism alongside mythic analysis, prompting critique by functionalists such as A. R. Radcliffe-Brown and Malinowski, then incorporated into the structuralist study of myth by Lévi-Strauss, which prompted further critique by Munz and Geertz; (2) *fate*, first by Meyer Fortes in his analysis of notions of fate in Oedipus, Job, and in West Africa, and by Terence Turner in his analysis of time and structure; and (3) *incest*, primarily by William Arens and Richard Fox. Fox is the only anthropologist actually to analyze two of the plays of the Theban cycle, namely, *Oedipus Rex* and *Antigone*, but still within the parameters of the triangular formulation of kinship, incest, and parricide.[13]

In a narrative as rich as that of Oedipus, however, there might very well be found as many thematic approaches as there are epistemological, methodological, ideological, and analytical positions. Oedipus manages to complicate everything that is taken for granted and demands that it be reconsidered. Undoubtedly, the issues of incest and parricide[14] are emblematic in the analysis of the myth. The Oedipus myth, however, asks that we acknowledge and preserve the responsibility that ought to be constitutive of political power.

Aris Alexandrou, who spent January to April of 1944 in Al Dab'a and July 1948 to November 1951 on Makrónisos and Ai-Stratis, without having participated in the *emphýlios*, having become a member of the Communist youth for a short period then left, always a "Communist" for the state, never Communist enough for the Communist Party and thus an object of suspicion, in his novel *To Kivotio* (*The Mission Box*),* written from 1966 to 1972 about the last two days of the *emphýlios* and the two months afterward, brings up the question of the responsibility of the subject through the aporia of Oedipus. In a circuitous way, he brings up responsibility as a property of suicide in the context of the disciplined subject of the DSE. The entire novel revolves around a secret mission, entrusted to a number of soldiers of the DSE, to transport a sealed box from town *N* to town *K*, as if written by one

13. In classics and philosophy (from Hegel's Antigone and Oedipus to Goux 1993) the entirety of the myth, including Antigone, the legend of the Seven against Thebes, and Ismene, are considered. See Edmunds 1985 on the encounter of different disciplines with Oedipus. For a rare exception treating the myth in its entirety within psychoanalysis, see Ross 1994: esp. 94–128.

14. Pucci (1992) has ingeniously retermed the crime of Oedipus *parincest*, thus combining the horror of regicide with that of incest. As ingenious as this formulation is, however, it further underscores the lack of willingness to engage with Oedipus outside the context that Freud has produced, namely, the shorthand version of the myth as "the person who killed his father and married his mother." Pucci does bring up a question that is quintessentially anthropological, namely, how are the mother and the father conceptualized as categories of existence that become categories of kinship?

*Alexandrou 1974. For the most interesting biography of Alexandrou, see Rautopoulos 2004. On Alexandrou's position toward the Party as refracted through *The Mission Box*, see Kantzia 2003.

soldier in the form of a report that changes from being a report on the progress of the mission (before the collapse of the Democratic Front) to a report of self-criticism on the failure of the mission. At some point, the lieutenant explains that the mission is nothing more than a suicide mission, in the sense that the wounded soldiers ought to undertake responsibility for their own suicides. When it is the soldier's turn to commit suicide because he has been wounded, he starts questioning the necessity for suicide via a digression into Oedipus. The digression concerns the established wisdom about the self-blinding of Oedipus.

In a gesture that anticipates Milan Kundera's question about the act of self-blinding in Oedipus, Alexandrou takes the dialectically opposite position: Oedipus should not have blinded himself because he was not responsible for anything that had happened. He had tried to avoid fulfilling the prophesy of Apollo, had resisted following the order, only to find that fulfilling the prophesy was a prerequisite for cosmic harmony, that if Oedipus did not kill Laius, then the Creation would be unstable. Therefore, Oedipus was nothing more than an instrument in the hands of Apollo, which meant, for Alexandrou's soldier, that he was not responsible for what had happened. The soldier should not be asked to commit suicide for the same reasons that Oedipus ought not to have gouged out his eyes: neither of them is responsible for what has happened; neither of them has any agency in the course of history.[15]

The wrenching position in which Alexandrou places this (political) subject is only a refraction of the question of the political subject in the moment of *stasis*. As nothing is stable in the myth of Oedipus, so the subject in the event of *stasis* is a wavering subject, a subject that seeks to find a position that will allow her to announce the certainty with which she occupies the subjectivity of the dissident, of the fighter in a fratricidal war, of the frightened member of the party.

But such stability is impossible, as Oedipus shows us, whether in Alexandrou or in Sophocles, precisely because Oedipus reflects and complicates every certainty: the issue of the native/autochthonous and the stranger/foreigner; of home and away; of illness/disease and wellness; of dream analysis; of memory and time; of the development of the subject and its struggle with the divine; of ambivalence toward adoption; of the relationship to death and the dead; of class relations; of vision, truth, and authenticity; of the relationship to the state; of inheritance; of violence to the body, as in infanticide, parricide, suicide, rape, self-mutilation, and execution; of the violence done in power relations; of selfhood; of truth and reality; of fate, chance, and destiny; of

15. In a reading of *The Mission Box*, Dimitris Vardoulakis discusses the specter of utopia that appears in Alexandrou's political landscape, as it has been formed by his experiences as a political prisoner and a castaway of the Party. As Vardoulakis notes, for Alexandrou "power never lies with those actors called upon to decide" (2008: 3), further underlining not only the utopia of Communism but also the Oedipean utopia of responsibility.

catharsis/miasma; of purity and danger; of the construction of the biological and cultural category of the father and of the mother; of the role of the body in the formation of subjectivity; of private and public; of personal and political. As Vernant points out (1996: 331), there can be no stability in Oedipus, no stable self/other, because there is no stability in what Oedipus and everyone around him experiences as kin. But, as Vernant further states, Oedipus is a matter of responsibility (447).

Oedipus, then, is, above all a metaphor of responsibility and accountability. The myth betrays society's abstraction of the process that has constituted it as such. In this sense, I read Oedipus not as the symbolic text addressed by structuralism (from Freud to Lacan and the feminist responses to it, from Spivak to Irigaray and Butler) but as a *metaphorical* text that emerges as it participates in the process of its own metaphorization and that manages to complicate everything that it metaphorizes. What Oedipus shows us is not that "culture" (as the social formulation that engages in myth making) *can* think but that "culture" actually thinks, on the level of the conscious, producing its own metaphors. I focus on this particular dimension of Oedipus as a text that constitutes a moment of reflection upon the relationship between the mind and the body, upon problematizations of categorical thought concerning life, self, other, enemy, friend, kin, authority, truth, chance, structure, the divine, the bestial, and the human.

In this time of global cultural postmodernity, a time of movement of vast numbers of people, a time that repeatedly challenges the constants of our subjectivities, movements that are translated into different technologies of being by producing different technologies of the body—it is at this particular moment that Oedipean questions concerning the political emerge. Who is constituted as self and who is constituted as other? Should we constantly be asking the question that Oedipus asks us to? It is a question that has had a pressing importance in the history of modern Greek articulations of the political self and that right here, right now, in the shadow of Guantánamo Bay, in the darkness of the Patriot Act and the articulations of the neo-imperialist project, demands to be revisited anew.

The question that thus emerges is that of the fundamental coincidence of the experience of the fragmented body with the multiplicity of idioms that the (Oedipean) subject *is*: an infant, not *ánthropos* quite yet, not adored but exposed, sovereign but fugitive, dispossessed in his hubris and autonomous in his suffering, willing but unwitting savior, Hegel's first philosopher, Nietzsche's last philosopher, Freud's paradigmatic ego. And, also, Freud's remnants, all the points in the myth and the play that Freud ignored (consciously or unconsciously; knowingly or unknowingly): the plague in the city (as the Left was termed), the Sphinx (as Alexandros Yiotopoulos of 17N was called by the press), Oedipus's intentionality and lack thereof (Who was really responsible for the Battle of Athens, the civil war, the tribunals?), all moments articulated amid of a state of emergency: the pestilence that demands that the foreign body—the *miasma*—be removed from the city. In this discussion of the horrors of an altered body and a pestilent polis, biopolitical alterity is instantiated when the (predictably failing Aristotelian and Durkheimean) discourses of the cohesiveness of the social body are articulated.

The exiles on "the islands" saw Oedipus naked, so to speak. Beaten, tortured, and pressured to sign declarations that they were not what they claimed to be (Leftists) but something that they were not (Christian nationalists), they found themselves somatically in the place of Oedipus: with feet swollen from bastinado, eyes gouged from strikes to the head, all the while being asked to answer the unanswerable question: Are you (with us) or are you not? All the while being told the same thing: you will become human (*ánthropoi*) or you will die. So we come back to Yiannopoulos: "In order for them to make us human, they first made us into King Oedipus." The riddle of the Sphinx is reversed in this context: "Who is human?" asked the liberal state when it engaged in the first acts of the cold war. It constructed itself as the only correct answer: the human is the animal that recognizes the power of the state as the maker of the human. That is the point where the torturers of the Greek Leftists could not hear the response that they were given: we are already humans, we are already *ánthropoi*. Where did the mythological break down in that most unmythological, nay antimythological existence? Maybe the response to this question can be found in the lament of Nitsa Kanellopoulou, the wife of Panayiotis Kanellopoulos. Waiting in tears at Cava dei' Tirreni (called *Pháka*, "trap," *Phaka dei Greci*, by the Greek delegation) in September and October 1944 for transport to Greece, she said to George Seferis, "You are born *ánthropos*, just as you are born a musician" (Seferis 1986: 363).

The establishment of the modern Greek state, predicated upon the ideality of an unbroken organic history of Greece spanning ten millennia, has produced a historicity of political forms of life that in the early twentieth century demarcated the possible and the desirable from the impossible and the undesirable. The Left, from the moment of its inception as an agrarian party to its eventual materialization as a Communist Party, and all the hues of the Leftist spectrum in between, fell under the second category, that of the impossible (within the context of the Greek psyche) and the undesirable (within the context of the Greek imagination). The torturers on the islands engaged in a program of returning those (considered as) wayward and lost Leftists to the common imaginary of Greece as a capitalist entity. The bamboo sticks that fell on heads, backs, arms, legs, feet, and testicles carried the voices of the torturers with them from the first moment the Leftists arrived on the islands: you will become human or you will never leave this island alive (*Tha ginete ánthropoi i den tha fygete apo 'do zontanoí*). The implication was that

Communism transferred Communists to a being that João Biehl has called the "ex-human" (2005: 24). The islands would turn these "ex-humans" into humans again through knowledge of the good and the correct that would come by way of torture. If torture did not manage to turn them into humans again, then torture would kill them. Not alive or dead, but human or dead became the dialectic of existence on the islands, where the wounded bodies, (some of them permanently), the wounded minds (all of them permanently), and the wounded psyches of the Leftists made the metaphor of Oedipus, in the hands of Yiannopoulos, a possibility. No, this is not naked life (either in Benjamin's sense or in Agamben's). This is a tug-of-war for what is recognized as human. What makes Oedipus recognizable to Yiannopoulos, then, is what ought to make Oedipus recognizable to the anthropologist: a text on *ánthropos*, the human, and how this human makes itself intelligible to the world. Rather than Agamben's bare life and sacred man or Voglis's subject, I want to suggest *ánthropos* as the only possibility of exiting the barbed wire of the camp.

If, then, we encounter Oedipus, the mythological and theatrical figure, as the philosopher anthropologist that Sophocles and Hegel gave us, the one who, through Jean-Joseph Goux, interrogates his body as a site of accumulated cultural and philosophical aporias, as the mythologization of the metaphor of misplaced power, misplaced anger, misplaced politics, then we might be able to find ourselves, finally, in a really Oedipean universe: a universe where catharsis will engage accountability and where responsibility will interpellate the political subject. A universe where anthropology will have performed its task of opening up the human subject to the magical space that mythology has made possible for us.

Burn, Forest, Burn

There is never an end in history, despite the egregious announcements of such a possibility. When I was looking for an epilogue in the summer of 2007, Greece was facing the worst forest fires in memory and record. Three separate fire cycles managed to burn almost all the olive groves in southern Greece (in the south and western Peloponnese), vast areas of pine, spruce, and deciduous forest throughout the Peloponnese, on Euboea, in western Greece, on Mount Pelion, on islands of the Northern Aegean, on Crete, on all three mountains of Athens (Párnetha, Pentéle, and Hymettus), 73 human beings, 110 villages, thousands of homes, thousands of rare and protected species (animals and vegetation), and two of the forests that the ancient Greeks used to call "ancient": the forest on Párnetha and the forest that surrounds ancient Olympia, including Kronion Hill, the sacred hill dedicated to Zeus around which the first sanctuaries at Olympia were built in the tenth and ninth centuries B.C., touching the buildings of the Sacred Altis (the oldest organized buildings at the site), licking the museum, burning the top of the warehouse of the German Archaeological Expedition, leaving its traces on the sides of the stadium. Huddled together in front of the television set, as family, friends, and neighbors we could not stop crying, sobbing for this most emblematic of all the destructions that Greece has endured as a modern state. In the face of this destruction, the government, unable to find ways of stopping it or even managing it, resorted to communication spins: it was the fault of the wind, the fault of the drought, it was something that was happening throughout the circum-Mediterranean world—but really, the government said, through its minister of foreign affairs, Dora Bakoyianni, and the minister of public order, Vyron Polydoras, it was the doing of the anarchists, the urban guerrilla groups, and what in Europe are called antipower units, who, in this way, brought about an "asymmetrical threat" to the country.

The country responded accordingly: "asymmetrical stupidity," "asymmetrical criminality," "asymmetrical idiocy," "asymmetrical state" were only some of the responses that appeared in the leaders of newspapers, on commentaries on television, in every discussion that took place every day during the fires, over cell phones and land lines, in restaurants, over breakfast, lunch, and dinner, in the courtyards of houses, in shops, among shop owners, academics, housewives, employees in the private sector. "Is this our 9/11?" someone asked as, once again, the particular history of Greece since the Second World War came up. "χμκμχ αλλως ιχμακης" posted this comment on bavzer.blogspot .com (August 27, 2007):

The Morea [Peloponnese] had not been burned like this since the time of Ibrahim Pasha.[16] The olive trees that are burning today had been planted immediately after their destruction by the Turkoegyptians. Time goes in cycles: yesterday's enemy is nowadays in our midst: the self who has lost and forgotten the sense of worth of what it has and owns governs the country now. He is ready to leave everything fodder to much more base and personal interests. When everything that is dear and familiar is being burned by the already-familiar calamities that are endemic in us what it shows is that Greece has not been liberated yet from the civil war and its bequest, which means that the partisan state is based on relationships of submission, the lack of clear laws (Roides had already intuited something of

16. Ibrahim Pasha was the son of the Ottoman governor in Egypt and was sent to suppress the revolution in the Morea (the Peloponnese) in July 1824, with a squadron of seventeen thousand men. He was not able to penetrate the Greek navy and land on the Peloponnese until February 1825. Ibrahim's destruction of the Peloponnese has remained legendary, because of the burning of villages, olive groves, and forests, and the pillaging and rape of the population. He was stopped by the intervention of the Great Powers and capitulated to them in 1827. See Finlay 1871 for Ibrahim's expedition to the Morea.

this when he referred to the existence but not application of the laws: every law contains within it the possibility of its non-application . . .)[17] the essential absence of functioning democratic institutions in Greece.

The easy accusation of the groups of the extreme Left as being the ones not simply responsible (through negligence) but actively involved in the devastating fires by the minister of foreign affairs goes to the heart of the history of the modern Greek state and the Left: the accusation is that those groups are engaged in the active destruction of the state, an accusation that reverberates through the indictments of the Leftists from 1924 to now, through all the trials, mock trials, special tribunals, and Right-wing discourse of almost a century. The fact that the governments of the past twenty-five years (since 1981, but possibly since the post–civil-war period) have actively facilitated and supported illegal building and the plundering of public forest lands by not prosecuting illegal settlers is brushed aside as irrelevant. The fact that all governments since the Metaxas dictatorship have engaged actively in the production not of citizens, responsible and accountable to the polity, but of snitches and collaborators by rewarding them with public offices, pensions, and respectability was repeatedly brought up during the fires of the summer, primarily by cartoonists, who delivered the most acrid commentary. The political language from the postwar and junta eras was deployed again: the *dosilogoi* ("accountables and collaborators"), the *tagmatasphalites* (the Security Battalions of the German occupation), the paramilitaries, the junto-royalists, the *ethnikophrones* became again indexical of the relationship of the state to the citizens (and not the other around).

Two cartoons by Giannis Kalaitzis, both published in the daily *Eleutherotypia* after the fire at Párnetha (the fires in the region of ancient Olympia had not yet happened) rest precisely on this management of modern Greek history. One portrays the minister of the environment, George Souflias, as the wolf who has become shepherd, facing the wrath of the rest of the animals: sheep, birds, turtles. The background announces the owners

17. Emmanouel Roides (1836–1904) is one of the most important writers of modern Greece. Although he wrote almost exclusively in the official purist language (*katharevousa*), he supported the development and wide use of the vernacular *demotic*. His magnum opus is *Papissa Ioanna* (*Pope Joan*) which has been translated into many languages and recently has been retold from its purist *katharevousa* in *demotic* by Dimitris Kalokyris. *Papissa Ioanna* is a scathing critique of the Catholic Church, although it is also a veiled critique of the Greek Orthodox Church and its meddling in Greek state affairs. The book was excommunicated by the Holy Synod (a decree that was later repealed) for its critique of the Catholic Church. Roides engaged in a serious critique of the Greek state, Greek character, Greek stereotypes, and anything that he understood as being the product of intellectual laziness. His writing is tight and complex, using words that he invents or reintroduces after they had been abandoned for centuries, ironic and playful. He considered his style to be the equivalent of a calabash banging the head of the reader to wake him up, and he often compared human and animal behavior, finding the human to be lacking.

Του ΓΙΑΝΝΗ ΚΑΛΑΪΤΖΗ

Figure 26. A cartoon commenting on the role played by land speculation in the forest fires of 2007. The civil war is in the background on various levels.

of the national forest, which in the cartoon is called "*Ethnikophron* Forest of Párnetha," various small settlement cooperatives that claim ownership: the settlement of junto-royalists, of *dosilogoi*, of *hafiédes*, of the paramilitaries, of the paraecclesiastical circles. A sheep asks the wolf: "Why are you not removing the settlers who own the villas?" "Because they are a protected species," responds the wolf.

The anger, outrage, sense of helplessness, is palpable in all. Analyses, commentaries, the primacy of experience all mingle with invocations of history in an attempt to understand what is incomprehensible: How could, in the course of roughly eighty days, one-tenth of the country be burnt to charred remnants? The reporter Apostolos Diamantis, writing for the Sunday supplement of *Eleutherotypia*, dedicates his piece, a chronicle of his travel to ancient Olympia at the time of the fire, to the memory of ancestors: ancestors, without an article, definite, indefinite, possessive or not. Just ancestors. As he is approaching the area he thinks: "Nothing bad can happen to me here. Here I am protected by ancestors. By history . . . Moreas is in no need of anything; the old psyches protect him." But he finally concedes: "Only, our fathers have no water hoses, they cannot fly a CanadAir [fire fighting airplanes]. They have long been dead" (Diamantis 2007).

How can anyone, even polemically and provocatively, pronounce history dead in the celebratory spirit in which it has been done, say by Francis Fukuyama? Where is it that history cannot be found, that it is absent from the ways in which we constantly make and remake ourselves? Is there a possibility for making ourselves understood by the world outside of history? The answers to these questions have been, tentatively and hesitantly, given in the pages you have just read. There is no hopeful conclusion here, just the painful realization of what the human is and how s/he makes a world that surrounds and envelopes everything. The last words go to a firefighter who was injured in the fire at Pentéle:

And I will not forget to still call myself *ánthropos* and owe nature a big apology for all the destruction that my species has caused it.

My question is: Will the villas that you are going to build have any meaning when there is not going to be anything green around you? When the air will smell of ashes and burn your lungs? How the hell will you, up there, and we, down here, be able to breathe at all? How can I expect that a state [*krátos*] with rigged elections and prefabricated parties would create a better future out of the ashes that have filled my lungs . . . *

[handwritten: inhuman environment]

Epitaph

You died and you, too, became: the good one.
The brilliant human being, the family man, the patriot.
Thirty-six wreaths accompanied you, three homilies by vice presidents,
Seven resolutions on the wonderful services that you have rendered.
Ah, Lavrenti, only I knew what scum you were,
What counterfeit, your whole life a lie.
Sleep in peace, I will not disturb your serenity.
(I, living a whole life of silence will pay
a king's ransom for it, not the price of your sorry skin.)
Sleep in peace. As you always were in life: the good,
The brilliant human being, the family man, the patriot.

You won't be the first or the last.

—*Manolis Anagnostakis*

Understanding the past in the present, Maurice Bloch has argued, means always acknowledging that the past is not simply a matter of transmitted

---

*Philippopoulos 2007. The Philippopoulos letter circulated by e-mail throughout Greece on August 28, 2007. I am using it here as it appeared in the Sunday *Eleutherotypia*.

Figure 27. The door to the censorship office in the Yáros prison building. The label on the door means "censorship." Photograph by Apostolos Papageorgiou, used with permission.

"oral history" but equally a matter of "episodic memory" (events that are not narrated by the narrator, that are either excised or forgotten or both). Thus, Bloch argues (1998: 39), the past and its history are not a matter of "collective memory" but should include ad hoc memory, small-aside knowledge. Memory, then, even (or especially) collective memory and "oral history" cannot, do not, or (as Anagnostakis makes clear in the poem above) ought not to subjugate to their hegemony the knowledge of one by one, even if such knowledge remains private, undisclosed, and unspoken. Public knowledge of what a person or an event is or was ought not to obliterate the (possibly contradictory) private knowledge of the same.

One evening, in the summer of 2006, I was talking with my father about my uncle, the chief of Special Security after the junta, an uncle whom I loved and respected for many reasons. (He had served in the division against trafficking of antiquities in the years preceding the junta, had been fired by the junta, was gentle and kind, and inquired after me on the night of the Polytechnic.)

Just as I was asking after him, my mother's voice came from the other room. "Junta," she said, meaning that he was the embodiment of the junta.

"Junta?" I asked.

"Junta, junta," my mother responded, explaining to me, for the first time, that my uncle (her cousin) had not been fired by the junta because he was democratically minded but because he thought that the junta was not effective enough and that it had veered away from the monarchy.

Dumbfounded, I looked at my father for comment.

He nodded, "Yes."

Why had they kept up this charade all these years? "It's kinship," an anthropologist friend surmised, as I was telling the story.

But my parents had a different explanation. "It's not good to tell things like that," they said. "Forget about it now; everyone thought that he was engaged in passive resistance."

After the junta he was brought back to the police and promoted to the second-highest rank before he retired, his reputation not only intact but greatly enhanced.

How can such intimate information be turned into anthropological knowledge? Information that is of heuristic value, that cannot contribute to the development of a theory of patterns, trends, cannot produce a definitive theory of culture. Writing in this crevice, between knowledge and information, is an endeavor that finds itself faced with two risks: to naturalize one's intimate and personal experience and reproduce it as universal, and to naturalize one's familiarity with the ethical landscape and reproduce it as unproblematic. But it is an endeavor that, in recognizing its own risks and the possibilities of its own failures, engages in the production of an oblique theory of anthropological knowledge, coming at it from an angle, the angle where one recognizes the ethnographer's multiplicity of positions (nothing new in this), the subject's multiplicity of positions (nothing new in this, either), and the impossibility of any stability in any of these positions as they interrogate each other. The trenchant question of the proximity of the ethnographer to her *ethnos* has thus far organized the question of the *ethos* of ethnography. And it is precisely the *ethos* of ethnography that is at the heart of the question posited here: What sort of anthropological knowledge is produced with the intimate information of the "native" ethnographer? One could ask for Dan Sperber's solution of divorcing ethnography from anthropology as a heuristic tool to find out how one operates in the absence of the other. I think, however, that such a solution is rather like the judgment of Solomon: separating anthropology from ethnography would result in the death of both. I prefer to remain with the "uncomfortable combination" that Bloch sees in Robert Herz's ethnography in the desire to engage with and produce both a "generalizing" work and an understanding "from the inside" (Bloch 1998: 39). I want to explode the question of naturalizing the familiar.

(No, Anagnostakis did not write "Epitaph" for my uncle.)

APPENDIXES

CHRONOLOGY

1871

The Law Concerning Brigands, with provision for the prosecution of the kin of brigands and anyone who helps, supports, and abets them.

1881

Thessaly becomes part of Greece.

1910

Major agricultural strike at Kileler, in Thessaly, on March 10.

1917

Establishment of the Workers' Center in Thessaloniki.
King Constantine abdicates. King Alexander assumes the throne.
Eleutherios Venizelos forms government.
The United States enters the First World War.
The February Revolution in Russia, then the October Revolution.
Major strikes in Germany.

1918

General Workers' Union of Greece (GSEE) established.
Socialist Workers' Party of Greece (SEKE) established.
Civil war in Russia.
Communist parties of Hungary, Poland, and Germany established.
End of the First World War.
Greek Army in Istanbul, following the surrender of the Ottoman army to the Allies at the end of the First World War.

1919

First National Congress of SEKE. Decision to join the Third International.
Panhellenic general strike against the firing of exiled socialist unionists of GSEE.
Revolution in Hungary fails.
Karl Liebknecht and Rosa Luxemburg are murdered.
Founding Congress of the Third International in Moscow.
Establishment of the Communist parties of the United States, Yugoslavia, Bulgaria, and Denmark.
Weimar Republic and constitution.
Treaty of Versailles.
Greek expedition to Asia Minor.

1920

Second National Congress of SEKE. It joins the Third International. Its title changes to the Socialist Workers' Party of Greece—(Communist).
Collaboration of GSEE and SEKE-C.
Demosthenes Ligdopoulos, a leading member of SEKE, is murdered on the Black Sea.
Second Congress of the Communist International.
Major general strikes in France and Italy.
Establishment of the Communist parties of Spain, Iran, Great Britain, and France.
Establishment of the League of Nations.
Treaty of Sèvres.
The Greek army marches into the interior of Turkey. Greek defeat at Eski Sehir and Afion Karahisar.
Murder attempt against Venizelos.
Death of King Alexander. Suspicions are that he was murdered.
Venizelos is defeated in the general elections. Konstantinos Rallis forms government.
Plebiscite in favor of the return of King Constantine.

1921

Inaugural issue of *Communist Review*, the official publication of the Communist Party of Great Britain, published in May.
General strike by railroad and electrical-power workers in Greece.
The Third Congress of the Communist International is established (comprising thirteen Communist parties).
Revolt at Kronstadt by anarchist Soviet sailors, suppressed by the Bolsheviks. End of civil war in Russia.
Establishment of the Communist parties of Italy, Romania, Czechoslovakia, and China.
Albania and Ireland become independent.
The Greek army is defeated by the Turks at the Sangarius River.

1922

First Congress of SEKE.

Leading members of SEKE-C, GSEE, and Greek soldiers are imprisoned at the front for antiwar activities.

Establishment of the Association of Communist Youth of Greece (OKNE).

General strike in Italy fails.

Establishment of the USSR. Joseph Stalin becomes general secretary of the Communist Party of the Soviet Union.

March to Rome by Italian fascists. Benito Mussolini comes to power.

Asia Minor Catastrophe, following the Asia Minor Expedition.

Coup d'état by General Nikolaos Plasteras.

King Constantine abdicates and flees Greece.

King George II assumes the throne. He later declares that the most useful possession for a Greek king is a suitcase.

Trial and execution of the Six, having been accused and convicted of dragging the country into a war that cost lives and money and caused a catastrophe, at Goudi (Athens).

1923

General Strike. Greece in a state of emergency.

Armed revolts in Italy, Bulgaria, and Hamburg.

Coups d'état in Bulgaria and Spain. Failed coup d'état by Hitler.

Establishment of the Republic of Turkey. Mustafa Kemal Ataturk becomes president.

The Gregorian Calendar is adopted in Greece.

Treaty of Lausanne to end the Greco-Turkish war. Exchange of populations between Greece and Turkey.

General elections in Greece. Royalist parties abstain. Liberal Party wins elections. King George II leaves the country.

1924

SEKE faces a crisis. The "Communist Union" is formed under Avraam Benaroyia (Avraham Ben-Aruya). The "Socialist Workers' Union" is formed under Sideres. SEKE is renamed Communist Party of Greece—KKE (Greek Section of the Communist International).

General strike by tobacco workers and tobacco producers, marine workers, and railroad workers.

Lenin dies. Trotsky's positions are condemned. Stalin assumes total power.

Armed revolt in Albania.

Greece is declared a parliamentary democracy.

Failed coup by Vassileios Dertiles.

1925

Pangalos dictatorship. Strict laws of morality are imposed.
Mass movement by farmers in Thessaly and Boetia. General strike by railroad workers and civil servants.
Mass persecution of Communists by the Pangalos dictatorship.
Rizospastis (the newspaper of the KKE) founded.

1926

Pangalos is overthrown. Kondyles establishes his own dictatorship.
Dertiles and Zervas attempt a coup d'état but fail.
General elections. First Communist representatives in Parliament.
Military coups d'état in Portugal and Poland.
The United States intervenes in Nicaragua.
Agreement of neutrality and non-aggression between the USSR and Germany.
Major strike by British coal-mine workers.
Leon Trotsky, Grigory Zinoviev, and Lev Kamenev form a troika.

1927

Major strikes against the British Power Electric Company in Greece.
Strikes by tobacco workers.
The KKE expels its previous and current secretary generals (Pandelis Pouliopoulos and Pastias Giatsopoulos, respectively). The centrists of the Party resign. Communist members of Parliament are arrested and accused of treason. The Popular Party withdraws from the coalition government.
Workers' uprising in Canton. Civil war in China. Chiang Kai-shek forms a government.
Trotsky, Kamenev, and Zinoviev are expelled from the Communist Party of the Soviet Union.
Anarchists Nicola Sacco and Bartolomeo Vanzetti are executed in the United States.

1928

Fourth Congress of GSEE. Communists are expelled from the GSEE.
Centrists are expelled from the KKE.
The "Spartakos" group is formed as Left opposition to KKE.
Further strikes by tobacco workers, bakery workers, and railroad workers. Demonstrations, with many dead, in Kavala and Xanthi (in Thrace).
Venizelos returns from exile in Paris. Elections are held, with great victory for the Liberal Party. Venizelos forms a government.
Greece and Italy sign an agreement of friendship.
First five-year plan in the USSR. Development of the theory of "socialfascism."
Purges in the Communist parties of Germany, Yugoslavia, and Romania.

1929

The Idiônymon is signed into law.
GSEE becomes unionized.
KKE faces factions within its structure.
Trotsky is exiled from the USSR. Bukharin and his group are indicted and condemned.
Purges in the Communist parties of France and Czechoslovakia.
King Alexander of Yugoslavia imposes a dictatorship.

1930

GSEE is dissolved according to the provisions of the Idiônymon.
Armed revolt in Indonesia.
German reparations to countries that suffered from German aggression during the First World War.
Gandhi leads the opposition to colonial power in India.
Civil war in China intensifies.

1931

The Communist International pleads with the KKE for unity. The Central Committee of the KKE is replaced, and Nikos Zachariadis becomes secretary general.
Rizospastis is closed down after it uncovers scandals that involve the minister of justice. It resurfaces as *Neos Rizospastis*.
Arson at the Campbell Jewish settlement in Thessaloniki. On June 29, Greek Christian refugees from Asia Minor after the exchange of populations attack the Jewish quarters. Five hundred Jewish families are left homeless.
The Communist Party of Malaysia is established.
Spain becomes a republic.
Demonstrations in Cyprus against British rule.
Acute economic crisis in Germany and Austria. Devaluation of the English pound.

1932

Strike by railroad workers, bakery workers, motorists (taxi and bus drivers), and the employees of the gas company in Athens. University student movement.
The Venizelos government introduces the institution of social security (later IKA).
Elections. Panagis Tsaldares forms a government. Ten Communists are voted into Parliament. Economic crisis and financial bankruptcy in Greece.
Great famine in the USSR.
Strikes in Berlin and Belgium.
Kamenev and Zinoviev are exiled.
Conference of Lausanne, in which Great Britain, Germany, and France agreed to halt reparations imposed by the Treaty of Versailles.
National Socialists win the elections in Germany.
Franklin D. Roosevelt becomes President of the United States.
Mahatma Gandhi leads the movement of civil disobedience in India.

1933

Hitler becomes chancellor in Germany. Dissolution of political parties and persecution of Communists and Jews.

Major demonstrations in Thessaloniki meet with brutal repression by the police. Many are wounded.

Elections in Greece. Second murder attempt against Venizelos. Tsaldares forms a government again. Plasteras attempts a coup d'état but fails.

Burning of the Reichstag. Georgi Dimitrov, Bulgarian Communist and leader of the Central European section of the Comintern, is arrested in Berlin and accused of arson. During his trial at Leipzig, he delivers a defense that obligates Germany to drop the charges.

The Communist Party of Germany is pronounced illegal.

Antifascist workers' conference in France, in which many intellectuals participate.

Germany and Japan withdraw from the League of Nations.

New Deal in the United States.

Dictatorship in Austria.

1934

Sixth Plenum of the KKE underlines the "bourgeois-democratic" nature of revolution.

Municipal elections produce Communist mayors in Kavala and Serres (Macedonia and Thrace).

Balkan agreement on collaboration and mutual respect for treaties and established borders among Greece, Yugoslavia, Romania, and Turkey on February 9.

Hitler declares himself Führer. Coups d'états in Bulgaria, Cuba, and Austria.

The USSR joins the League of Nations.

Coal miners in Asturias revolt against the Spanish government. A commune is formed. On October 18, the revolutionaries surrender, and the commune is crushed by General Franco. More than two thousand workers die and over thirty thousand are jailed.

Chinese Communists start on the Long March.

Antifascist agreements are drawn up in France, Italy, and Spain.

Purges of Trotsky and other "enemies of the state" in the USSR follow the murder of Sergey Kirov, Leningrad party leader, by Leonid Nikoleyev. Trotsky is accused of being behind the murder. Kamenov and Zinoviev, accused of being implicated, are tried and executed.

1935

Sixth Congress of KKE, in which the position "that all minorities living in Greece ought to enjoy full ethnic and political equality" is adopted.

Failed pro-Venizelist coup. Venizelos flees to France. The leaders of the coup are executed. Giorgios Kondyles imposes a dictatorship. A plebiscite results in the return of King George II.

Agreements of mutual assistance between the USSR and Italy, and the USSR and France.

Italy attacks Ethiopia.

1936

Major strikes in Northern Greece. Tobacco workers' strike in Thessaloniki ends with attack by the police, leaving many dead and wounded.
Elections. Royalist parties gain a majority. Fifteen Communist deputies are voted in.
Venizelos dies in Paris. Deaths of P. Tsaldares, A. Papanastasiou, and G. Kondyles.
Metaxas imposes a dictatorship, with the support and encouragement of King George II. Thousands of Communists and Leftists are arrested, tortured, and exiled to islands. Introduction of Declarations of Repentance and Certificates of Civic Aptitude or Loyalty (*Certifats de civisme*).
Franco's coup. Beginning of the Spanish Civil War.
Axis between Germany and Italy is formed. Japan joins the Axis powers.
Arab-Jewish clashes in Palestine.

1937

Demonstrations against the Metaxas dictatorship. Cadres of the KKE (George Siantos and Costas Theos) escape from exile in Anafi. The organization Friendly Society (*Philike Hetaireia*) is formed in Athens against the dictatorship.
Moscow trials of old Bolsheviks, whom Stalin considered enemies. Many are executed or sent to labor camps in Siberia.
Antonio Gramsci dies in prison.
Papal circular against Communism.
Japan invades China.
Guernica is bombed.

1938

Many leading figures of the KKE are arrested. The secretary general of OKNE, Christos Maltezos, is murdered in the Corfu prison. Uprising against the dictatorship in Chania, Crete. It is ended within six hours.
Greece and Turkey sign an agreement of friendship.
Royal coup in Romania.
Germany annexes Austria.
Agreement among Germany, Great Britain, France, and Italy for non-aggression signed in Munich.
Moscow trials continue. Nikolai Bukharin, Alexei Rykov, and others are executed.
Trotsky forms the Fourth International.

1939

Siantos and many other leading figures of the KKE are captured.
The Communist Party of France is outlawed.
Albania is conquered by Italy and Czechoslovakia by Germany.
Madrid falls to Franco. Franco assumes power. End of the Spanish Civil War.
Molotov-Ribbentrop agreement about nonagression between the USSR and Germany.
Germany conquers Poland. Beginning of the Second World War.

1940

Konstantinos Maniadákis (chief of police in the Metaxas government) forms a "Temporary Directorship" of KKE (a shadow KKE). KKE disagrees about the nature of the war. Secretary General Zachariadis considers it a war of national liberation. The old Central Committee considers it an "intra-capitalist" disagreement.

Trotsky is murdered in Mexico.

Greece is attacked by Italy on October 28, against the advice of Hitler, and enters the war.

Italy invades Greece from Albania. Greece resists the Italian forces and makes advances into Albanian territory. Exiled Greek Communists ask to be sent to the front. The Metaxas government refuses.

The Germans conquer Denmark, Norway, Belgium, Holland, and France.

Winston Churchill becomes prime minister of Great Britain.

The Vichy collaborationist government is established in France.

Charles de Gaulle forms the "France Libre" movement.

The Battle of Britain.

1941

Greek Communists escape from the exile islands. First Resistance movements. Sixth Plenum of the Central Committee of the KKE decides to join the Resistance.

The Workers' National Liberation Front (EEAM) is formed. EEAM is transformed into the National Liberation Front (EAM).

Metaxas dies. Koryzes forms a government. The Greek government flees to the Middle East with King George II.

On April 6, Germany attacks Greece and occupies it within a week. By mid-April, the Germans are in Athens.

The Battle of Crete.

The National Democratic Greek Cooperation (EDES) and National and Social Liberation (EKKA) are formed.

The Greek government hands over all political prisoners to the Germans, who send many of them to Dachau.

A collaborationist government is formed in Athens.

Greece is under tripartite occupation: German (Crete, parts of Macedonia, some islands), Bulgarian (Northern Greece), Italian (the rest of the country). Athens is occupied jointly by German and Italian forces.

1942

Eighth Plenum of the KKE, under Secretary General Siantos (Zachariadis has been sent to Dachau).

The Greek Popular Liberation Army (ELAS) is formed.

Major strike by civil servants in Athens.

Major Resistance movement in the countryside. Aris Velouchiotes forms the first Resistance groups. ELAS and EDES cooperate in blowing up the bridge at Gorgopotamos. Many other Resistance groups are formed in the country.

British blockade of Greece. Great famine in Greece, especially Athens and other urban centers.

First battle of El-Alamein is won by the Germans in Egypt. Second battle of El-Alamein is won by the Allies.

1943

Germany plans mass mobilization of the Greek civilian population for transport to German labor camps and factories. Major demonstrations in Athens oppose this.

The Unified Panhellenic Youth Organization (EPON) is formed in Greece.

The Funeral of Kostis Palamas, the foremost Greek poet of the early twentieth century, mobilizes thousands in an antifascist demonstration.

Prime Minister Ioannis Rallis forms the Security Battalions (TA).

The Battle of Stalingrad.

Stalin dissolves the Third International.

Mass graves of Polish army officers are discovered in Katyń Forest.

Italy collapses. Germany assumes the entire occupation of Greece.

1944

Tenth Plenum of the KKE decides to form the Political Committee of National Liberation (PEEA), a noncollaborationist government of resistance.

Mutiny in the Middle East by officers of the Greek army.

The leader of EKKA, Kostos Psarros, is murdered by ELAS.

A National Council is convened by ELAS in Koryschadhes. It decides upon the "battle of the yield," so that no produce will go to the Germans.

Major advances by the Red Army. Josip Tito and his partisans form a revolutionary government.

Paris is liberated.

Agreement in Plaka, Epirus, on February 4 between EAM/ELAS and EDES to cease fighting and remain where armies were at the time of the agreement.

Agreement in Lebanon in May among representatives of all political parties of Greece and all Resistance groups to form a government of national unity in exile, comprising twenty-four ministers, six of whom come from EAM.

Agreement at Cazerta, Italy, between the government in exile and Great Britain, according to which all Greek forces will disarm and be placed under the leadership of British officer General Ronald Scobie. Participation of EAM in the next government is agreed upon. Churchill forcefully disagrees.

Athens is liberated on October 12. The Germans withdraw within a few days from the rest of the country.

A coalition government under George Papandreou is formed. EAM asks for the Cazerta agreement to be honored. Churchill and Papandreou refuse.

The December events. The British army and the RAF bomb Athens. Fifteen thousand Communists, Leftists, and members of the Resistance against the Germans are arrested and sent to a British concentration camp in Al Dab`a, Egypt, as hostages.

1945

The Varkiza agreement decrees the disarmament of ELAS. ELAS surrenders most of its armament. Leaving Athens in February, ELAS takes eight thousand hostages along. Many die; most of the others are released by March.

Eleventh Plenum of the KKE. The parliamentary way to power is chosen. Zachariadis returns to Athens from Dachau. Aris Velouchiotes dies.

Twelfth Plenum of the Central Committee of the KKE.

Popular self-defense against the paramilitaries in the countryside.

"White Terror."

One hundred and fifty young intellectuals and artists are taken to France on the *Mataroa* in December.

Yalta and Potsdam agreements.

FDR dies. Harry S Truman becomes president of the United States.

The British Labor Party wins the elections.

Atom bombs are dropped on Hiroshima and Nagasaki. Japan surrenders unconditionally.

The United Nations, the International Monetary Fund, and the World Bank are formed.

1946

The Democratic Army of Greece (DSE) is formed.

Elections in Greece. The KKE, EAM, and other socialist parties abstain, arguing that the elections were rigged from the beginning. The Right wing wins the elections. A plebiscite results in the return of King George II.

Partisans attack the gendarmerie station of Litohoron on March 30.

Exile and first executions by the Courts of the State of Emergency.

Beginning of the Greek Civil War.

Nuremberg trials.

Guerrilla warfare in Palestine.

Bulgaria and Albania become Communist countries.

1947

Yiannis Zevgos, a member of the Politburo of the KKE, is murdered.

Siantos dies.

KKE and all its "branches" are declared illegal.

Makrónisos and Yáros concentration and torture camps are established for the re-education and rehabilitation of Communists.

The Third Plenum of the KKE decides the beginning of the civil war.

A provisional democratic government is formed (the Government of the Mountain).

The Dodecannese is ceded to Greece by Italy.

King George II dies. His brother Paul ascends the throne, with Frederika as queen.

The Truman Doctrine. The Marshall Plan. Beginning of the cold war.

War in Indochina.

The Cominform is formed.

Poland and Romania become Communist.

India and Pakistan become independent and partition.

1948

Markos Vafeiades disagrees with the leadership of the KKE regarding the civil war.

Massacre of two hundred prisoners on Makrónisos from February 28 through March 1 when they refuse to sign *dēlôseis*.

American journalist George Polk is murdered in Thessaloniki. He had covered the civil war for CBS and arrives in Thessaloniki to investigate allegations that Greek officials had embezzled funds from the Marshall Plan. He is found shot at point-blank range in the back of the head. George Stakhtopoulos, a Greek Communist journalist, is accused of the murder but maintains his innocence, stating that his confession was obtained under torture. No one else has ever been accused, though an "inside job" by the Greek Right-wing is suspected.

Mass arrests and persecution continue.

Czechoslovakia, Hungary, and North Korea become Communist.

Burma gains independence.

The Berlin embargo, when the Soviets refuse access to Western forces between June 1948 and May 1949.

Mahatma Gandhi is murdered.

Israel is created as an independent nation.

KKE clashes with Tito.

Tito clashes with Stalin.

Vafeiades is accused of Titoism.

1949

Fifth Plenum of the Central Committee of the KKE takes place in Grammos (at the front line of the war).

Secretary General of GSEE Mitsos Paparegas is murdered at Special Security Headquarters in Athens.

Tito closes the borders to Greek partisans.

The DSE is defeated at Grammos and Vitsi. End of the Greek Civil War. Many members of the DSE flee to Communist countries in the north (mainly Romania, Czechoslovakia, the USSR, and Poland).

China becomes a Peoples' Republic.

Leading members of the Bulgarian and Czechoslovakian Communist parties are accused of Titoism.

Stalinism becomes a crime against the people in Yugoslavia.

Goli Otok and Sveti Grgur are established by Tito as reeducation and rehabilitation camps for Stalinists.

Indonesia gains independence.

1950

The leadership of the KKE flees to Bucharest.

Elections lead to the defeat of the Popular Party.

Sofoulis Venizelos and Nikolaos Plasteras form governments.

John Purifoy is appointed American ambassador to Greece.

Provisional Greek government headed by Mitsos Partsalides (KKE) formed.

Diplomatic relations between Greece and Yugoslavia are restored.

Gradual transfer of prisoners from Makrónisos to exile islands.
The Korean War, in which Greek volunteers fight on the side of the U.S. Army.
Malay rehabilitation and re-education camps are established.

1951

The United Democratic Left (EDA) is formed.
Major trials of Leftists and Communists, often on fabricated charges.
The Second Plenum of the Central Committee of the KKE removes Partsalides from
    the party following disagreement with Vafeiades about the role of the KKE out-
    side of Greece. His name is reinstated only in 1980.
Beloyiannis, Batses, Kaloumenos, Nikolakopoulos, Nikeforides, and many others
    are put on trial.
Municipal elections reflect the rise of the Right wing.
General Papagos forms the party of Greek Alert.
A coalition government is formed under Plasteras.

1952

Avge, the newspaper of EDA, is founded.
Nikos Ploumpides is accused by the KKE of being a double agent. The Greek police
    arrest Ploumpides.
The Trial of the Airmen, members of the Greek air force (and some civilians) accused
    in 1951 of sabotaging a Greek fighter plane as part of a KKE operation. They
    admit guilt (and one of them dies) under torture. In 1955, K. Karamantis will
    admit that the case was fabricated.
Beloyiannis, Batses, Kaloumenos, and Argyriades are executed for treason on Sunday,
    March 30.
Greece and Turkey join NATO.
The camp on Yáros is closed and its prisoners transferred to Makrónisos.

1953

Strikes against the economic policies of the government.
Trial and indictment of Ploumpides.
Greece, Yugoslavia, and Turkey sign an agreement of cooperation.
The Greek currency is devalued.
Plasteras dies.
Cambodia declares independence.
The Korean War ends.
Stalin dies. Khrushchev becomes secretary general of the Communist Party of the
    Soviet Union.
The Rosenbergs are executed in the United States on charges of treason.

1954

Ploumpides is executed in Greece. The execution is doubted by the KKE.
Mass arrests of Communists in Greece.
Tito visits Greece.

Municipal elections bring the democratic parties to municipal power.
Demonstrations support Cypriot independence.
The French are defeated in Indonesia.
A coup d'état in Guatemala is supported by the United States.
Vietnam and Laos declare independence. Ho Chi Minh rises to power.

1955

Twenty-seven leading members of the KKE escape from Vourla Prison.
General Papagos dies. Konstantine Karamanlis forms a government.
Khrushchev visits Belgrade.
Goli Otok and Sveti Grgur do not close with the destalinization of Yugoslavia.
Major demonstrations in Cyprus against the British. Martial law is declared.

1956

Sixth Plenum of the Central Committee of the KKE removes Zachariadis as secretary general, replacing him with Koliyiannis. Rapprochement of the KKE and the Yugoslav Communist Party.
Revolt in Hungary is crushed by the Soviets.
The British execute members of the decolonization movement on Cyprus (Michael Karaolis, Andreas Demetriou, and others).
Karamanlis forms the National Radical Union (ERE).
Elections in Greece. ERE wins a majority.
Demonstrations in Athens about Cyprus result in dead and wounded.

1957

Seventh Plenum of the KKE decides to expel Zachariadis from the Party.
Stephanos Sarafis, the military leader of ELAS, dies in a motor accident in Athens, hit by a sailor of the U.S. Navy.
The European Economic Union is formed.
The United Nations votes in favor of independence for Cyprus.

1958

Eighth Plenum of the Central Committee of the KKE. Ploumpides is posthumously reinstated to the Party.
EDA triumphs in elections, winning 24.5 percent of the vote.
Many leading figures of the KKE and EDA are arrested, among them Manolis Glezos.
New elections keep ERE in power.
Khrushchev and Mao meet in Beijing.

1959

Glezos and others are tried and indicted on charges of treason.
First Congress of EDA.
The Left wins again in municipal elections.

Andreas Papandreou returns to Greece.
Khrushchev visits the United States.
The first elections in Cyprus. Archbishop Makarios becomes the first president.

1960

New trials for espionage.
Major strikes by construction workers result in clashes with the police.
African decolonization movement.
Cyprus becomes a republic.

1961

George Papandreou forms the Centrist Union (EK).
Rigged elections give victory to the ERE, and Karamanlis forms a government.
Papandreou announces "uncompromising struggle" against political violations of the
    Right.

1962

Most political prisoners are released.
Papandreou's struggle results in major demonstrations and clashes with the police.
Karamanlis and the Palace clash.

1963

Queen Frederika visits London, where she is met with demonstrations by Greek
    students there.
First Marathon Peace March (Marathon-Athens), part of an international peace
    movement.
Grigoris Lambrakis, the leader of the Peace Movement in Greece, is murdered in
    Thessaloniki by paramilitary Right-wing thugs.
Karamanlis resigns and leaves Greece.
Elections give power to Papandreou's EK.
Kanellopoulos becomes the leader of ERE.

1964

Second Marathon Peace March.
Municipal elections bring EDA to municipal power.
Sofoklis Venizelos dies.
Elections give great margins to EK.
King Paul dies. Constantine II ascends the throne. He reigns under the influence of
    his mother, Frederika.
Communist leader Palmiro Togliatti dies in Italy.
The beginning of the Vietnam War.
Greek and Turkish Cypriots clash.
Khrushchev is removed from the position of secretary general of the Communist
    Party of the Soviet Union and replaced by Leonid Brezhnev.

1965

Inaugural congress of the Lambrakis Youth, the youth organization formed after Lambrakis's assassination.
Third Marathon Peace March, in March.
The July events in Athens. During a demonstration, Soteres Petroulas dies from a tear gas bomb thrown by the police.
ASPIDA trial.
Papandreou is forced to resign.
Government formed by the "Apostates."
Churchill dies.
Communists are massacred in Indonesia.

1966

Fourth Marathon Peace March.
Papandreou and Kanellopoulos reach agreement with the king to hold new elections.
The Politburo of the KKE (in Bucharest) convenes, with a delegation from the Central Committee of the Party, based in Greece.

1967

Kanellopoulos forms a government and announces elections for May 14.
On April 21, a military dictatorship in Greece is installed by the troika of George Papadopoulos, Stylianos Patakos, and Nikolas Makarezos.
The concentration camp on Yáros is reopened.
Thousands of Leftists, Communists, and Centrists are arrested, imprisoned, and exiled.
Che Guevara is murdered in Bolivia.
The Six Days' War between Israel and Arab countries.

1968

Twelfth Plenum of the Central Committee of the KKE. Split of the party to KKE and KKE of the Interior (KKE-ES.).
Panhellenic Resistance Movement (PAK) is formed.
Major trial of members of "Regas Pheraios" (the youth organization of KKE-ES.) in Athens. All are indicted and imprisoned.
First attempt against Papadopoulos by Alexandros Panagoulis. Panagoulis is captured, tortured, and kept in solitary confinement.
Papandreou dies. His funeral becomes a major antidictatorship demonstration.
May '68.
Prague Spring.

1969

Trials of resistance organizations, the Panhellenic Resistance Front (PAM) and arrests of members of the Democratic Defense.

George Seferis, poet and Nobel Laureate of 1963, makes a statement against the
    dictatorship.
Greece is expelled from the Council of Europe.
Antiwar movement in the United States.

1970

Trial of members of the Democratic Defense.
An "Advisory Council" replaces the Greek Parliament.
Salvador Allende becomes president of Chile.

1971

Seferis dies. His funeral becomes a major antidictatorship demonstration.
EOKA-B' (nationalist organization fighting for unification with Greece) is formed in
    Cyprus by George Grivas (formerly leader of "X").
War between India and Pakistan.

1972

PAK trial.
Seventeenth Plenum of the Central Committee of the KKE.
Koliyiannis is deposed and H. Florakis becomes the new secretary general of the KKE.
Bangladesh becomes independent.
"Black September," when Palestinian fighters murder members of the Israeli athletic
    delegation during the Munich Olympic Games.

1973

Major unrest in Greek universities. Students occupy the Athens Law School in
    February.
Gestures toward liberalization.
Amnesty measures for political prisoners.
A plebiscite run by the dictatorship abolishes the monarchy.
On November 17, a student uprising at the Polytechnic is crushed by the junta. By
    the official count twenty-three died, but many more dead are unaccounted for.
    There are countless wounded.
A week later, Demetrios Ioannides topples Papadopoulos and the troika to establish
    the most brutal phase of the dictatorship.
The Navy moves against the dictatorship but fails; the leaders of the movement flee
    to Italy.
Zachariadis commits suicide in exile in Siberia.
Enrico Berlinguer announces the "historical compromise" of Communism with
    bourgeois parliamentary democracy.
Pinochet overturns the Allende government in Chile and establishes a long-term
    dictatorship. Allende is murdered.

1974

The junta in Athens instigates a coup d'état in Cyprus. Turkey invades the island and it is partitioned.

The junta falls.

A coalition government is formed under Karamanlis, who returns from exile in Paris.

Greece resigns from the military branch of NATO.

Elections bring Karamanlis to premiership with the newly-formed Right-wing party Nea Demokratia (New Democracy, ND). A plebiscite establishes the form of government as a "non-royal" parliamentary republic.

Avge and *Rizospastis* resume publication. The KKE becomes legal again. A new Leftist party is formed comprising all the parties of the traditional parliamentary Left (KKE, KKE-ES, EDA).

Papandreou returns from exile and forms a new socialist party, the Panhellenic Socialist Movement (PASOK).

Revolution of the Carnations in Portugal: a peaceful revolution by the armed forces overthrows the Salazar dictatorship.

1975

New Greek constitution.

Konstantine Tsatsos is elected president of the republic.

Trial of the leaders of the dictatorship.

"Revolutionary Organization 17 November" (17N) appears, with the murder of Richard Welch at Christmastime in Athens.

Saigon falls. End of the Vietnam War.

Franco dies in Spain. Restoration of Spanish democracy. The Khmer Rouge takes power in Cambodia.

1976

Panagoulis dies in a suspicious car accident.

"Eurocommunism" is in the ascendance.

A socialist government under Mario Soares is formed in Portugal.

Communist government is formed in Angola.

Mao dies. Trial of "the Gang of Four."

1977

Fire bombings in Athens by the extreme Right.

Elections bring ND to power. PASOK is its primary opposition in parliament.

Eurocommunist parties (KKE-ES, EDA, other socialist groups) and KKE end their coalition.

Ulrike Meinhof, Andreas Baader, and Gudrun Esslin are murdered in their white cells in Stammheim Prison.

1978

Eurocommunist youth organization Regas Pheraios splits and forms B' Panhellenic.

Italian Prime Minister Aldo Moro is kidnapped and murdered by the Brigate Rosse. He had attempted a rapprochment between Communist and liberal forces.

The USSR supports a coup in Afghanistan.

1979

Student mobilizations in Athens against the extreme Right wing. The School of Chemistry is occupied by students.

Greece signs an agreement for admittance to the European Economic Union.

The USSR invades Afghanistan.

Sandinistas prevail in Nicaragua.

1980

Major clashes in Athens between students and police during the demonstration celebrating the Polytechnic uprising, leaving two dead.

Elections are won by the ND. Georgios Rallis becomes prime minister, Karamanlis president of the republic.

Greece fully rejoins NATO.

Bombing at Piazza Fontana in Bologna by fascists, leaving many dead.

1981

PASOK becomes the first socialist party to gain power in Greece, with 44 percent of the vote and the slogan "Change."

Socialists and Communists come to power in France.

Bobby Sands, a fighter in the IRA, dies during a lengthy hunger strike in Ireland.

Military law is declared in Poland following opposition to the government.

1982

Resistance to the occupation is officially recognized as "National Resistance" by the PASOK government.

Municipal elections give victory to democratic and socialist candidates.

Refugees of the civil war are allowed to return to Greece from the countries of Eastern Europe.

The Israeli army invades Southern Lebanon. There are massacres in Sabra and Shatila.

Brezhnev dies. Youri Andropov becomes the new secretary general of the Communist Party of the Soviet Union.

Socialist parties win elections in Sweden and Spain.

1983

Vafiades returns to Greece and collaborates with PASOK.

Greece agrees to allow U.S. military bases in Greece to continue to operate.

Article 4 of the Greek Constitution, regarding the restriction of the right to strike, is passed by Parliament.
Italian socialists gain power for the first time. Bettino Craxi becomes prime minister.
End of the Argentine dictatorship.

1984

PASOK wins most seats in elections for the European parliament.
Major strike by British coal-mine workers.
Andropov dies in Moscow.
Indira Gandhi is murdered in India.

1985

The border with Albania opens for the first time since 1940.
Members of PASOK resign over the direction of the movement.
Anarchist Michael Kaltezas is murdered in Athens by the police. Demonstrations ensue against the murder and police brutality.

1986

KKE-ES decides to rename itself to remove "Communist" from its title.
Beginnings of perestroika in the USSR.

1987

A split of the KKE-ES is decided during its Fourth Congress. United Renewed Left (EAR) and KKE-ES—Renewed Left are formed.
A massive political movement takes place at the universities.
Relations between church and state are strained on account of ecclesiastical real estate, which secularists claim for the state and the church wants to keep as revenue.

1988

Major strike by secondary-school teachers.
Political prisoners are freed in the USSR.

1989

The Berlin Wall falls.
The Soviets withdraw from Afghanistan.
Collapse of Communist governments in Hungary, Poland, Czechoslovakia, Romania, and the German Democratic Republic.
Pinochet falls in Chile.
The Chinese student uprising at Tiananmen Square is crushed by the Chinese government.

1990

The USSR collapses.

2002

Arrests of members of 17N. The main operative, Dimitris Koufondinas, surrenders of his own accord.

2003

The trial of 17N starts in Athens.

2004

The Olympic Games take place in Greece.

2008

Massive forest fires spur reaction from citizens. Demonstrations against the government take place in Athens.

Note: I have based this Chronology loosely on the one compiled by and published in Bournazos and Sakellaropoulos (2000).

DOCUMENTS

Document 1 (pages 204–205). A copy of a leaflet entitled *Dēmokratia: Neodēmokratikê Politikê Epitheôrēsē* (*Democracy: Neodemocratic Political Review*), Year B', no. 8, Price: 300 drachmas, presented as a publication of EDES. The lead article is entitled "To the Youth of EAM," and it rehearses the already well-known argument that EAM and the Communist Party of Greece were willing to allow Bulgaria to claim Macedonia. From a different angle, however, the article tries to convince the youth of EAM that, if Bulgaria does not annex Macedonia but instead Greece expands northward and annexes the Slavic countries, then Greece will solve its economic problems. The back page has a short analysis of events in Italy, speculating that Italy would surrender (as it did, in September 1943). It states that EDES was fighting not fascism but Italy, because Italy would always covet Greece. There are two dates on the back page, one on an announcement about the military action in Epirus of July 4, 1943, and the other on a report to the British Military Command in the Middle East about the blowing up of a bridge on the river Louros, dated July 7, 1943. I have no means of evaluating this document, because of the circumstances that surround its acquisition. One evening, in the winter of 2005, I was walking south on Amsterdam Avenue in New York City crossing at 110th Street. In the middle of the intersection, a large piece of paper caught the corner of my eye. Thinking that it might possibly be valuable to someone who had lost it, I picked it up, with the intention of trying to find its owner. What I found instead was this four-page leaflet.

ΔΗΜΟΚΡΑΤΙΑ

ΝΕΟΔΗΜΟΚΡΑΤΙΚΗ ΠΟΛΙΤΙΚΗ ΕΠΙΘΕΩΡΗΣΗ

Ἔτος Β΄   Ἀριθμὸς φύλλου 8   Τιμὴ Δρχ. 300

ΠΡΟΣ ΤΟΥΣ ΝΕΟΥΣ ΤΟΥ Ε.Α.Μ.

Ἡ συμπλήρωση τοῦ φτωχοῦ ἑλλαδίτικου χώρου ἐπιβάλει τὸ ξαναμοίρασμα τῶν ἐπιμάχων βαλκανικῶν γαιῶν. Αὐτὸ σημαίνει πὼς πρέπει νὰ πάρουν κι οἱ Ἕλληνες λίγες πεδιάδες ἀπὸ ἐκεῖνες, ποὺ ἀνήκουν στὴν φυσικὴ ἐνδόχωρα τῆς οἰκονομικῆς περιφερειακῆ ἑνότητας τοῦ Αἰγαίου καὶ τῆς Θεσσαλονίκης.

Μόνον ἔτσι θὰ μπορέσουμε νὰ ζήσουμε καλύτερα οἱ ὑποσιτιζόμενοι Ρωμηοί.

Ἐργαζόμενοι, σὰν σκυλιά, γιὰ νὰ πληρώνουμε τεράστια ποσὰ στοὺς πλουσίους Σέρβους καὶ στοὺς εὐπόρους Βουλγάρους ἴσα-ἴσα γιὰ ν' ἀγοράσουμε μόλις λίγο κρέας καὶ τὰ ὄσπρια μας, ποὺ, καθὼς ξαίρετε, ἀποτελοῦν τὰ στοιχειώδη μέσα γιὰ τὴν διατροφή μας. Δουλεύουμε σὰν εἵλωτες, γιὰ λίγο σιτάρι ὅταν οἱ Βούλγαροι κολυμποῦν μέσα στὰ δημητριακά τους· ἀμπάρια.

Αὐτὴ εἶνε ἡ πρώτη μορφὴ οἰκονομικῆς ἐκμετάλλευσης ποὺ πρέπει νὰ μᾶς συγκινήσει καὶ μᾶς ἐπαναστατήσει. Κάνουμε ἔκκληση στὰ αἰσθήματα τῶν Νέων, ποὺ ἀπὸ τὴν νοσταλγία τῆς κοινωνικῆς δικαιοσύνης, τρόβηξαν ἕως τὴν οὐτοπία, πρὸς στε γοῦν ὀρθ_ησμοῦ, νὰ προσέξουν τὸ πρόβλημα ποὺ θέτουμε καὶ νὰ ἐπιδείξουν βαθύτερη ἠθικὴ κι ἐθνικὴ συνέπεια ἀπέναντι τῆς σοσιαλιστικῆς τους ἰδεολογία.

Δὲν ὑπάρχουν μόνον τάξεις ἐκμεταλλευτικὲς κι ἐκμεταλλευόμενες.

Ὑπάρχουν καὶ Δι οἱ-Κράτη, ποὺ εἶνε φοβεροὶ ἐκμεταλλευτὲς! Ἕνα τέτοιο θῦμα οἰκονομικῆς ἐκμετάλλευσης εἶνε κι ὁ Λαός Σας «Νέοι!», γιατί δὲν Σᾶς συγκινεῖ αὐτὴ ἡ κοινωνικὴ κι ἐθνικὴ ἀδικία; Δὲν ἰσχυρίζόσαστε πὼς κάνεται «ἐθνικὸ ἀπελευθερωτικὸ ἀγώνα»; Δὲν ἀγωνίζεσθε γιὰ νὰ δοθεῖ κοινωνικὴ δικαιοσύνη στὸ Λαό μας; Γιατί σωπένετε, ὕποπτα, γιὰ τοὺς Σλάβους; Γιατί δὲν ἀγαναχτεῖτε καὶ κατὰ τῶν Βουλγάρων ὅπως κατὰ τῶν ντόπιων ἐκμεταλλευτῶν μας, (ποὺ κι αὐτοὺς πρέπει νὰ τιμωρήσουμε); Γιατί δὲν βλέπετε πὼς μόνον ἡ καθολικὴ μας ἀπελευθέρωση, δηλαδὴ καὶ ἡ ἐπίτευξη τῆς οἰκονομικῆς λευθεριᾶς τοῦ λαοῦ μας θὰ στεφανώσει τὸν ἀγώνα σας; Γιατί ἀφήσατε νὰ σκοτεινιάσει ὁ Νοῦς σας ὁ κυρίαρχος; Γιατί ἀφήνετε νὰ προστρέξετε ἀπὸ ἕναν ἄγνωστο συναισθηματισμὸ καὶ λησμονήσατε τὸν φωτεινὸ λόγισμό; Καὶ γιατὶ νὰ μὴν διαπιστώνετε τὴν φοβερὴν οἰκονομικὴν ἀνισότητα, ποὺ ὑπάρχει μεταξὺ τοῦ Ἐθνικο-Οἰκονομικοῦ μας συνόλου κι τοῦ οἰκονομικοῦ συνόλου τῶν γειτόνων μας Σλάβων, μόνο κατατρίβεσθε μὲ τοὺς λίγους πανάθλιους πλουτοκράτες μας, ποὺ εἶνε στὴ διάθεσή μας ὅ,τι ὥρα θελήσουμε; Ἀπελευθέρωση τοῦ Ἕλληνα ἀπὸ τὴν οἰκονομικὴ ἐκμετάλλευση «ἀνθρώπου ἀπὸ ἄνθρωπο» πρέπει νὰ σημαίνει, πρῶτ' ἀπ' ὅλα: Ν' ἀπελευθερώσουμε τὸν Ἑλληνικὸ Λαὸ ἀπὸ τὴν οἰκονομικὴ ἐκμετάλλευση τῶν Σλάβων, ποὺ τοῦ πουλᾶνε, πανάκριβα, εἴδη διατροφῆς· πρώτης ἀνάγκης, ποὺ τὰ

παράγουν ἴσα ἴσα οἱ πεδιάδες ἐκεῖνες ποὺ φυσικά, οἰκονομικὰ καὶ ἱστορικὰ τοῦ ἀνήκουν.

Δὲν εἶνε δυνατὸν νὰ ἐξακολουθήσουμε, καὶ στὸ μέλλον, νὰ δανειζόμεστε ἀπὸ τοὺς Ἄγγλους γιὰ νὰ πληρώνουμε τὴ διατροφή μας στοὺς Σλάβους.

Ἐναντίον αὐτῆς τῆς οἰκονομικῆς σκλαβιᾶς πρέπει νὰ ἀγανακτήσουμε, νὰ ἐπαναστατήσουμε καὶ ἀγωνισθοῦμε. Αὐτὸς εἶνε ὁ ἀληθινὸς «ἐθνικοαπελευθερωτικὸς Ἀγώνας».

*
* *

Γιὰ τοῦτο, ἐπέκταση πρὸς βορρὰν σημαίνει ὅτι:

1) Θ' ἀποκτήσουμε εὔφορα καὶ μαγοσχάματα χωράφια γιὰ νὰ πάψουμε ν' ἀγοράζουμε σιτάρι καὶ φασόλια. Κι αὐτὸ θὰ ἀνακουφίσει ἀφάνταστα τὶς λαϊκὲς μάζες, ἀφοῦ εἶνε γνωστὸ ὅτι τὰ 40 ο)ο τοῦ ἑλλήσματος στὸ ἰσοζύγιο ἐξωτερικῶν μας· πληρωμῶν ὀφείλεται στὴν ἀγορὰ τῶν σιταριῶν·

2) Θ' ἀποκτήσουμε βοσκὲς καὶ λιβάδια γιὰ τὰ ποίμνιά μας, ποὺ θὰ μᾶς δώσουν ζωοκομικὰ εἴδη σφάξιμα.

3) Ἐπέκταση πρὸς βορρὰν σημαίνει ὅτι ἕνας νέος καταναλωτικὸς πληθυσμὸς θὰ ἐνισχύσει τὶς βιομηχανίες μας καὶ ὅτι οἱ Ἕλληνες Ἐργάτες θ' ἀποκτήσουν οὐσιαστικὸ καὶ ὑψηλὸ ἡμερομίσθιο μὲ ἰσχυρὴ ἐσωτερικὴ ἀξία, ποὺ θὰ τοὺς παρέχει σταθερὴ καταναλωτικὴ δύναμη, ἀφοῦ τὰ εἴδη διατροφῆς τους θὰ τὰ πέρνουν ἀπὸ τὴν ντόπια ἀγορά μὲ ἕνα φθηνὸ ἀντάλλαγμα καὶ χωρὶς νὰ παρεμβαίνει πιὰ ἡ ἐκμεταλλευτικὴ σλάβικη ἀγορά.

4) Ἐπέκταση πρὸς βορρὰν σημαίνει ὅτι θὰ πάψουμε νὰ ἐξάγουμε τὸ εἰσερχόμενο ἀπ' τοὺς ἀδήλους πόρους, συνάλλαγμα (ἐμβάσματα μεταναστῶν μας, κέρδη ναυτιλίας, τουριστικὰ ὠφέλη) γιὰ νὰ ἀγοράζουμε τ' ἀπαραίτητα γιὰ τὴν ζωάρκεια τοῦ Λαοῦ μας. Θὰ μπορέσουμε ἔτσι ν' ἀποταμιεύσουμε κι ἐμεῖς· κι νὰ κεφαλαιοποιήσουμε τὴν ἐθνική μας ἐργατικὴ δύναμη. Θὰ μπορέσουμε νὰ διαθέσουμε, τότε, τοὺς περιωρισμένους μας πόρους ὄχι μόνο σὲ κοινωνικὲς δαπάνες ἀλλὰ καὶ γιὰ σκοποὺς παραγωγικούς.

Οἱ Ἐθνικὲς, λοιπόν, διεκδικήσεις λύνουν τὸ κοινωνικὸ ζήτημα τοῦ ἑλληνικοῦ λαοῦ καὶ ὄχι τὰ δημαγωγικὰ κηρύγματα τοῦ ΚΚΕ καὶ ἡ πατριωτικὴ δράση τοῦ ΕΛΑΣ στὴν ὀρεινὴ Ἑλλάδα.

*
* *

Αὐτὴν τὴν στιγμὴ ὅποιοι θέτουν τὸ κοινωνικὸ ζήτημα ἐπάνω σὲ ταξικὴ ἐπαναστατικὴ βάση, ποὺ προσθωθεῖ κίνευση ἐμφύλιου πολέμου καὶ διάσπαση τῆς ἐθνικῆς συνοχῆς γιὰ νὰ ἐγκαθιδρύσουν μιὰ Δικτατορία ἀκόμα πιὸ ἀποτρόπαιη, τῆς ἐπονείδιστης Γλυξιμπουργικῆς 4ης Αὐγούστου αὐτοὶ — λέμε ποὺ προετοιμάζουν ἕνα «κομματικὸ

ΤΑ ΓΕΓΟΝΟΤΑ ΣΤΗΝ ΙΤΑΛΙΑ ΚΑΙ ΟΙ ΠΙΘΑΝΕΣ ΕΞΕΛΙΞΕΙΣ ΤΗΣ ΒΑΛΚΑΝΙΚΗΣ

Ὁ Μπενίτο Μουσολίνι ἔπεσε, 20 χρόνια μετά τὴν πορεία στὴ Ρώμη, σὰν τὸν τὰπεινότερο κινηματβουλευτικὸ Ὑπουργό Μετὰ τὴν συνάντησή του μὲ τὸν Φύρερ ὑποστήριζε νά ἔκτ 1ε ἐκτ τὸ προτεινόμενο ἀπὸ τὸν Χίτλερ σχέδιο κατὰ τὸ ὁποῖο θά ἐπεμόγονα στὸν Πάδο καὶ θὰ ἔπεφναν μαζί τους ὅλι τά ἀποθέματα τῶν τροφίμων ὥστε νά ἐπιβ ηνουν τούς· ᾽ γγλοαμερικάνους μὲ τὸν ἐπισιτισμὸ 3ὸ ἑκατομ. Ἰταλῶν. Ἡ πρόταση ἀπερρίφθη διὰ ψήφων, 19 κατὰ 7 καὶ ὁ Μουσολίνι παραιτήθηκε. Οἱ Ἰταλοὶ μὲ τὸν Μπαντόλιο συνεχίζουν τὸν πόλεμο Γιατί; Ἐπειδὴ θέλουν νά πολεμήσουν γιὰ τὴν νότια Ἰταλία καὶ νά συνθηκολογήσουν μόνο ὑπὸ τὸν ὅρο νά μὴν εἰσέλθουν Ἀγγλοαμερικανικά στρατεύματα στὴν Ἰταλία καὶ μὴ γίνει ἡ Χερσόνησος τους βάση στρατιωτικῶν ἐπιχειρήσεων κατά τῆς Μέσης Ἰ υρώτης καὶ τῆς Βαλκανικῆς. Λένε: γιατί νά συνθηκολογήσουμε χωρὶς νά σταματήσουν γιὰ μᾶς τά δεινά τοῦ πολέμου ἀφοῦ τότε θά μᾶς: χτυποῦν οἱ Γερμανοί; Οἱ Σύμμαχοι ὅμως δὲν θὰ πιχωρήσουν καὶ θὰ κάμψουν τὴν Ἰταλία καὶ μὲ τὴ βία καὶ μὲ τὴν πειθώ. Ἡ Ἰταλία θά γίνει θαυμάσιο πλατ'ανόφρμο καὶ ὁρμὴ ἥρω γιά τὸν Αἷμο καὶ τά στενά ἕως τὸν Εὔξεινο Πόντο θά πλήξουν τότε ἐκ τῶν νότων τού: Γερμανοὺς καὶ θ' ἀνακουφίσουν ἀποτελεσματικά τοὺς Ρώσσους. Ὁ δρόμος, ἀπὸ τὸν Αἷμο καὶ τὴν Ἀδριατικὴ ἀνοίγει πρὸς τὴν Βουδαπέστη, τὴν Βιέννη καὶ τὴν Πράγα. Ἔτσι κατὰ τὸν ἴδιο τρόπο ποὺ ὑπερμαλαγγίσθηκε ἡ Γραμμὴ Μαζινὼ θὰ ὑπερφαλαγγισθῆ κι'ἀπ' τοὺς Συμμάχους μας «τὸ τεῖχος τοῦ Ἀτλαντικοῦ στην Εὐρώπη». Ἐν τῷ μεταξὺ οἱ Γερμανοὶ καταλαμβάνουν ὅλη τὴν πέρα τοῦ Πάδου Ἰταλία ἀρχίζοντας ἀπὸ τὴν Γένοβα, τὴν Τεργέστη καὶ τὸ Φιοῦμε.

Ἡ 8η Στρατιά ὅπου μετέχουν καὶ ἑλληνικά τμήματα ὑπάρχει βεβαιότη α ὅτι ἄν ὄχι τὸν Αὔγουστο ὅμως τὸν Σεπτέβρη θὰ κινηθεῖ κατά τοῦ Αἰγαίου καὶ τῆς Κρήτης. Ἀπὸ τοῦ Μπρίντεζι θὰ ἐξαπολυθεῖ ἴσως καὶ μεγάλη πλευροκοπικὴ κατὰ τῆς Δωδεκανήσης Ἐκστρατεία. Οἱ Ἄγγλοι μάλιστα ἀναγγέλλουν ὅτι ἀφικνεῖται στὴν «Ἑλλάδα ὁ Ρόμμελ. Τοῦτο δὲν πρέπει νά ἔχει ἄλλη σημασία παρά ὅτι οἱ Γερμανοὶ στέλνουν στὴν νότια Βαλκανικὴ τὸν ἐνδικότατο πιὰ ἐπὶ τῶν συμπτύξεων καὶ ὑποχωρήσεων Στρατάρχη τοῦ Ἐλ-Ἀλαμέϊν, τῆς Ἐλ-Ἀγγέϊλα καὶ τῆς γραμμῆς Μαρέτ.

Οἱ Ἰταλοὶ ἐν τῷ μεταξὺ διαπραγματεύονται ὅρους ἀνακωχῆς κι' ἐλπίζεται ὅτι θὰ ὑποκύψουν στὶς ἀπαιτήσεις τῶν Συμμάχων μας συνεσμότερα ἀπὸ κάθε προσδοκία.

ΙΤΑΛΟΙ ΚΙ' ΟΧΙ ΦΑΣΙΣΜΟΣ

Ἐμεῖς τὸν Φασισμὸ τὸν χτυπήσαμε ὅ αν ἦταν ὀλόρθος. Τὸν χτυπήσαμε σὰν ἦη Αὐ ούσταν. Συνεπεῖς μὲ τὴν δημοκρατική μας πιστὴ ἀντιμετωπίσαμε τὴν Πιθηνιστικὴ Φασιστικὴ τετραετία Γλύξμπουργκ -Μεταξᾶ πηγαίνοντας στὴν Φυλακὴ καὶ στὴν ἐξορία.

Τώρα ὁ Φασισμὸς εἶνε νεκρός· Ἐμεῖ, ἀσχολούμεθα μόνο μὲ τοὺς ζωντανούς.

Στὴν Κέρκυρα, στὰ Δωδεκάνησα, στὴν Πιναγ.ὰ τῆς Τήνου, στὴν Ἀλβανία καὶ στην Κρήτη δὲν ἐβλέ-

παμε Φασίστες ἀλλὰ ᾽Ιταλούς. Ἡ Ἰταλία θά ἐπιβουλεύεται πάντοτε τὴν Ἑλλάδα ἀδιάφορα ἂν θά εἶνε δημοκρατική, κομμουνιστικὴ ἢ φασιστική.

Δὲν μᾶς ἐνδιαφέρει τί θ' ἀποφασίσει ἡ Ἀγγλία γιά τὴ μεσογειακὴ τύχη τῆς Ἰταλίας. Ἐμεῖς ἔχουμε πρόθεση νά γίνουμε κύριοι τοῦ Οἴκου μας πέρα γιά πέρα μέσα στὸ Αἰγαῖο καὶ στὴ Βαλκανικὴ γιά νά κατασχηρωθμύμε ἀπὸ μελλοντικὴ ἐπίθεση τῶν Ἰταλῶν, Αἰγαῖο - Ἀλβανία—Μακεδονία—Θράκη. Ἐδαφικὰ πρὸς Βορρὰν οἰκονομικὰ πρὸς Ἀνατολάς. Ἔτσι διώχνομε τοὺς Ἰτελούς καὶ ἀποχτάμε οὐσιαστικὴ ἐθνικὴ κυριαρχία καὶ στὸ Αἰγαῖο καὶ στὴν Βαλκανική.

Ὄχι, λοιπόν, τὸν Φασισμὸ ἀλλά τοὺς Ἰταλούς πολεμᾶμε !

ΕΛΕΥΘΕΡΑ ΟΡΕΙΝΗ ΕΛΛΑΣ — Γεν. Ἀρχηγεῖον Ἀνταρτικῶν Σωμάτων - Ἐθνικαὶ Ὁμάδες Ἑλλήνων Ἀνταρτῶν—Γενικὸν Ἀρχηγεῖον (Γραφεῖον III).

Ἀνακοινωθὲν
Γιὰ τὴν πολεμικὴ δρᾶση στὴν Ἤπειρο

Κατὰ τὴν ὑπὸ ἡμετέρων τμημάτων ἐναντίον Ἰταλικῆς φάλαγγος ἐπίθεσιν παρὰ τὴν θέσιν Κακούρη τῆς 17 Ἰουνίου, ὁ ἐχθρὸς ἀπώλεσεν 6 ἄνδρας καὶ εἴχεν πολλοὺς τραυματίας. Ἐκ τῶν ἰδικῶν μας 3 ἀντάρται ἐφονεύθησαν. Τὴν 21 Ἰουνίου ἡμέτερα τμήματα προσέβαλαν ἐπιτυχῶς εἰς θέσιν Συνλό.. ἐπὶ τῆς ἁμαξιτῆς ὁδοῦ Παραμυθιᾶς—Ἰωαννίνων. Τὴν 23 Ἰουνίου ἀγορὰ συμπλικὴ ἰδικῶν μας τμημάτων εἰς περιοχὴν τοῦ χωρίου Κωσμηρὰ μεθ' ἑνὸς Ἰταλικοῦ τάγματος διαθ οντος πυροβολικοῦ καὶ ὅλμους κατέληξεν εἰς τὴν καταστροφὴν τοῦ ἐχθροῦ ὅστις φεύ αν πυρπόλησε τὸ χωρίον Πεδινή. Εἰς Ἰταλὸς ἀξιωματικὸς καὶ 8 στρατιῶται ἐφονεύθησαν. Οἱ τραυματίαι ὑπερβαίνουν τοὺς 15. Ἐκ τῶν ἡμετέρων εἷς ὑπαξιωματικὸς ἐφονεύθη. Τὴν 28 Ἰουνίου τὰ τμήματά μας συνεπλάκησαν ἐκ νέου μετὰ ἰσχυρῶν ἐχθρικῶν δυνάμεων τὰς ὁποίας ἠνάγκασαν νὰ ὑποχωρήσουν ἀτάκτως καὶ νά ἐγκαταλείψουν ἐπὶ τοῦ πεδίου τῆς μάχης 30 νεκροὺς καὶ 70 τραυματίας. Τρία φορτηγὰ αὐτοκίνητα ἀπετεφρώθησαν καὶ 10 ὑπέστησαν σοβαρὰς ζημίας.

Σ.Δ. Γενικὸν Ἀρχηγεῖον τῇ 4/7/1945
Ὁ Γενικὸς Ἀρχηγὸς Στρατηγὸς Ν Ζέρβας

ΜΙΑ ΑΝΑΦΟΡΑ
Πρὸς τὴν Βρεττανικὴν Στρατιωτικὴν Ἀποστολὴν

Παρακαλῶ ὑμᾶς ὅπως διαβιβασθῇ εἰς Κάϊρον τηλεγραφικὸς ἡ κάτωθι ἀναφορά:

Γενικὸν Στρατηγεῖον Μέσης Ἀνατολῆς.

«Ἀναφέρω ὅτι ἡ Γέφυρα Καλογήρου ἐπὶ ποταμοῦ Λούρου ἀνετινάχθη τὴν 4 Ἰουλίου ὥραν 24. Τὴν αὐτὴν ὥραν ἐπίσης ἡ ξυλίνη γέφυρα Στρεβίνα; Φιλιππιάδος. Στόπ. Τηλεγραφικαὶ καὶ τηλεφωνικαὶ γραμμαὶ ἐχθροῦ ἀπὸ Ἀμφιλοχίας μέχρι Ἰωαννίνων κατεστράφησαν ὁλοσχερῶς, ἀφαιρεθείσης μεγάλης ποσότητος σύρματος. Στόπ. Ἀπὸ 8ης ὥρας τῆς 6 Ἰουλίου συνάπτονται μάχαι μεταξὺ Ἰταλικῶν τμημάτων καὶ ἀνταρτῶν τῶν Ἐθνικῶν μας ὁμάδων. Τμήματά μου παρεμποδίζουν ἀποτελεσματικῶς κρυσταθέων Ἰταλῶν ἐπισκευῆς γεφυρῶν. Στόπ. Ἀποτελέσματα μαχῶν μέχρι τῆς στιγμῆς ἱκανοποιητικά. Στόπ.

ΕΛΕΥΘΕΡΑ ΟΡΕΙΝΗ ΕΛΛΑΣ 7/7/43
Ὁ Γενικὸς Ἀρχηγὸς Στρατηγὸς Ν. Ζέρβας

MAKRONISOS HOLDS A HOPE TO GREEKS

Army's Center for Retraining
Ex-Communists, 'Associates'
a Post-Rebellion Factor

MAKRONISOS, Greece, Aug. 21
—On this barren island opposite Sunium (Cape Colonna), where Byron scratched his name on a famous ancient temple to Poseidon, and across from the little lead mining village of Lavrion, the Greek Government is conducting its first experiment in mass de-communization.

This is confined to the political re-education of young men drafted to the colors who upon investigation are shown to have had asso-ciations with Communists, making them poor security risks. The island also contains prisons and camps for civilian suspects but this correspondent only visited the military establishments of the three Special Battalions being trained here.

According to Government officials many thousands of young recruits have passed through here and been "purified," later going to the regular armed forces where they have served well. Most of them have been mixed in with other units, but two regiments made up entirely of Makronisos graduates have been integrated into the army.

After-Effects Sought

Certainly a visit to Makronisos is an unusually interesting experience. Capt. Eustace Poulantzas, of the National Social Education section of the General Staff, served as the writer's guide.

Captain Poulantzes said a major effort was now being made to

Document 2 (above and opposite). "Makrónisos Holds a Hope for Greeks": article published by Cyrus Leo Sulzberger in The New York Times, August 21, 1949, p. 4, a week before the collapse of the DSE at Vitsi. The article was written after Sulzberger, accompanied by his Greek wife, Marina Tatiana Lada, who acted as translator, visited Makrónisos. Sulzberger asked to speak with some of the incorrigibles on the island, and Konstantinos Despotopoulos was brought out from "the Wire" to speak with him. Despotopoulos has noted that when he entered the office of the director of the camp, he saw "not only the Director, but also an American journalist and a lady [acting] as interpreter. He posed various questions. I dared both to go beyond the questions and to develop my more general thoughts about what was then happening in the rest of Greece and in the world, as much as the circumstances and the presence of the director there allowed me, and even beyond. When the interview was over, the foreign journalist addressed me with very sympathetic words and announced his name. He was the famous journalist of the *Times* of New York, Sulzberger. And the until-then interpreter introduced herself to me in a familiar tone: 'Mrs. Sulzberger, that means Marina Lada, Soteriadou's cousin, friend of Mrs. Ioanna Tsatsou, and your friend'" Despotopoulos 2006a: 35). Mrs. Ioanna Tsatsou was the sister of the poet (and later Nobel Prize Laureate) George Seferis and wife of the philosopher Constantine Tsatsos, who was, of course, a friend of Despotopoulos, and whose chair at the Faculty of Philosophy Despotopoulos had filled.

spread word through the country that the youths trained here were good patriots when they emerged, so that they would be received in friendly fashion when they returned to their home villages and would not be ostracized and again driven into Muscovite organizers' hands.

What this correspondent saw of that aspect of Makronisos was impressive. However, on a visit of this sort one cannot be 100 per cent convinced and there are certainly some disparities in the official statements.

For example, the writer has been told there are 25,000 persons on the island. He has also been told there are 10,000 men, 8,000 men and 7,000 men in the Special Battalions.

The writer asked to see some unconverted Communists, of whom it is admitted they exist. One officer suggested bringing a certain prisoner from "the Wire." When the writer inquired what this was, one officer said it was a barbed-wire enclosure where such die-hards were kept.

Other officers denied there was such a "Wire." Still others gave various figures as to the number of men incarcerated.

On the basis of these contradictions, it is this writer's impression that all the young men who "go along" with their re-education—which appears to be the vast majority—are extremely well treated and are prepared for the Regular Army life and eventual return to a peaceful Greece—provided too much bitterness against their past associations does not prevail in their villages.

Commander From Sparta

The acting commander of the island today was Maj. Mikhail Kourakos. A dour-looking man from Sparta with twenty-five years' experience as a Regular Army officer, his face lights up in smiles when he discusses his task here.

Major Kourakos, after the fight-ing of 1940-41. joined a resistance group called ES. For a brief time he served with the Communist-led Elas, but split when he found out its political ties. As a result. he says. his mother was decapitated, two nephews slain and his house burned down by Communists.

"As a man I am naturally bitter against Communists," he said. "But as a Greek officer I must work for Greece and national unity.

"When I think of my past misfortunes, I sometime have a sick feeling. but when I see these boys go away cured, I feel perhaps I have prevented from happening to others what happened to me and my family. I have suffered so much I cannot really hate any more and I feel my greatest mission is to prevent future tragedies."

Certainly the most interesting man this writer talked with was tiny, bespectacled, bald Prof. Constantine Despotopoulos. 36. former member of the faculty of the University of Athens. Dr. Despotopoulos sent word from the theoretically nonexistent "Wire," where he is kept because he refuses to sign a "recanting" document, that he would talk with the writer, but would "not sign anything."

He had been discharged from the university and then sent to Icarea, although, he said, he was not a Communist. When his class was mobilized, he came to Makronisos because his record showed he had been in Icarea.

Again denying he was a Communist, Professor Despotopoulos refused to reply to specific questions as to how he was treated behind "the Wire," or whether he thought Makronisos a good or bad institution for others.

He said he remained a friend of War Minister Panayotis Kanellopoulos, who also used to be an Athens University professor, despite the fact that Mr. Kanellopoulos now heads the branch of the Government that keeps him not only on Makronisos but behind "the Wire."

Υπεύθυνος Δήλωσις

Ο κάτωθι υπογεγραμμένος Στουραΐτης Γεώργιος του Αναστασίου εκ Κερατέας αττικής νυν κρατούμενος εις τας Εγκληματικάς Φυλακάς Κερκύρας.

Δηλώ υπεύθυνος και εξ ιδίας πρωτοβουλίας ότι ουδέποτε υπήρξα κομμουνιστής και ούτε εσυμπαθώ τας υπό του κομμουνισμού πρεσβευομένας ιδεολογίας καθόσον θεωρώ το κομμουνιστικόν κόμμα ως προδοτικώς εξυπηρετούν ξένα συμφέροντα και εσατανικώς εργαζόμενον διά την εξαφάνισιν παντός εθνικιστικού στοιχείου προς εξαφάνισιν της τελικής επικυριαρχίας του εις την προσφιλή μου πατρίδα και τελείαν υποδούλωσίν της εις τους Σλάβους. Δι' ο και είμαι προθυμότατος να ενταχθώ εις τας εθνικάς δυνάμεις και να πολεμήσω τούτους μετά του μεγαλυτέρου φανατισμού.

Εν συνεχεία δηλώ ότι ως γνήσιος Έλλην με πατριωτικά αισθήματα ήμην παρών εις τας εκάστοτε προσταγάς της πατρίδος μου έτοιμος να χύσω το αίμα μου διά την τιμήν και ακεραιότητα ταύτης πολεμήσας κατά την κατοχήν εναντίον των Γερμανοϊταλών ως κατατάνιος ενταχθείς εις τας αντάρτικας ομάδας του ΕΛΑΣ. όπως και τόσοι άλλοι μη γνωρίζοντες τους εγκληματικούς και καταχθονίους σκοπούς των. Εκ τούτων δε ως αντελήφθην τους προδοτικούς των σκοπούς αμέσως απεχωρίσθην τούτων μετά την ομάδος μου αποκηρύξας το κόμμα τούτο ως προδοτικόν κ.λ.π. διά δημοσιεύσεώς μου εις τας Αθηναϊκάς εφημερίδας της 19 Σεπτεμβρίου 1946 καθώς και δι' ετέρας δημοσιεύσεώς μου εις τας ίδιας εφημερίδας 22-23/5/48 εστιγμάτιζα τους δυστυχώς παρασυρομένους κομμουνιστάς του αειμνήστου υπουργού της Δικαιοσύνης Χ. Λαδά.

Document 3 (above and opposite). A declaration of repentance, found in the archives of the Municipality of Markopoulo. It is signed by Georgios Stouraitis from Keratea (a town southeast of Markopoulo, on the Attican peninsula), who had been imprisoned on Corfu. I am grateful to Stamates Methenites, the local historian in Markopoulo, who drew my attention to it. Reproduced with permission.

φωνάζω καὶ καλῶ ὅλους τοὺς παρασυρμένους νὰ ἐγκαταλείψουν τοὺς ἐαρηοβόλους κομμουνιστάς καὶ τὴν ἀρρώ-
στεια ποὺ ἔχουν εἰς τὴν ψυχή των καὶ νὰ ἐπανέλθουν εἰς τοὺς
κόλπους τοῦ ἔθνους. Ὅλοι στὴ δουλιά γιὰ τὴν πατρίδα
καὶ γιὰ τὸ Βασιλέα, ὅτι γνωρίζει ὁ καθένας ἀπρόσωπα καὶ ἀράγ-
ματα σὰν Τέλειος Ἕλληνας νὰ σπεύδει νὰ τὰ καταγγίζη εἰς
τὰς ὑπευθύνας ἀρχάς.
Ὅλοι στὰ ὅπλατα γιὰ τὴν πατρίδα μας καὶ γιὰ τὸ Βασιλέ-
ιας.
ἡ νέοι στὰ ὅπλατα, ἡ γέροι στὴ δουλιά, ἡ διανοούμενη δυὸ
λόγια γιὰ τὴν ἄβυσσο, ἡ νέες μητέρες καὶ ἀδολφὲς γιὰ τοὺς
μαχωμένους Στρατιῶτες μας, ἰδι ἀγαπών πραγματικά
τὴν πατρίδα τὴ Θρησκεία καὶ τὴν οἰκογενιά τους ὡς δράλον
τὸ καθίκων τους, φανιτε ἀντάξιοι τῆς ἑλληνικῆς ἱστορίας
ἔστησα δηλῶ ἐδῶ τὸ λόγω τῆς ἀνθρωπίνου καὶ οἰκογενια-
κῆς τιμῆς ὅτι εἶχεν εἰς Θέλην εἰς τὴς ἰδιοτικότερη
τοῦ μίρους καὶ τῆς μαχριάς καὶ ἀπάνω τὴν περι-
φερειάν μου νὰ θέσω ἐν συναγερμῶ καὶ ἰδι σαφὸς πολλῶν
ἀπαντας τοὺς κατοίκους τοὺς δυνάμενους νὰ φέρουν
ὅπλα καὶ νὰ εξ-τυπόνεωφε καταλέφραζα τοὺς ἀνάνδρους
σαούδοκους κομμουνιστάς καὶ καταστροφῆς τῆς
ἱστορικωτάτου πατρίδος καθὼς καὶ τοὺς μὴ δυνάμενους
νὰ φέρουν ὅπλα νὰ ὑποστηρίξουν καὶ αὐτοὶ τὸν ἀγῶνα μὲ
ὁποιοδήποτε μέσον.

Ζήτω τό ἔθνος
Ζήτω ὁ Βασιλεύς
Ἐθεωρήθη διὰ τό   Ζήτω ὁ ἔνδοξος ἑλληνικός Στρατός
μνημεῖον τῆς ὑπογραφῆ   Ἐν Φυλακαῖ Κερκύρας 10/10/48
Ὁ Διευθυντὴς τῶν ἐγκλημάτων   Ὁ ὑπεύθυνος Δηζών
Φυλακαὶ Κερκύρας   Γεζουράζης

C
O
P
Y   MAKRONISSOS ISLAND - THE GREEK DACHAU
     ───

        If there is a remnant of civilization, every man and
woman must raise their voices vigorously protesting against the
abominable crimes that brought up the slaughters and criminals
of the Greek government on the political transported persons of
the Makronissos island.

        They do inflict horible corporal tortures on the prison-
ers in order to compel them to sign the "declaration" some thing
which constitues an insult for the human dignity.

        One of these hangmen, the L/nant Rados who is a character-
istic type of sadique, declared openly to them that if they go on
to insist refusing to sign, they shall all be killed.-

        5 of the soldiers of the greek governmental army, ocular
witnesses of these scenes of horror got mad. An 75 years old man
NIKITIDIS by name of KILKIS's district of origin, has "commited
suicide" after having been tortured for hours,

        Yet a score of other prisoners have been assacinated.

        After these horrible tortures the men who insisted to re-
fuse to sign are forced to burden a load of -' kilos of pebble and
run during all the day If exhausted fall down, the hangmen beat
them with bambou sticks in such a manner that they become infirm
for all their life. The well known author DIMITRI PHOTIADIS, who
has been transported since 19 months.althogh he had no political
action and without a setence, suffered the same tortures.-

        Shuddering nights of terror succeed the other without ar-
rest since 15 days in this new Dachau of Greece which surpassed
that of Hitler. If this S.O.S..reaches in your hands please communicate it to the U.N.O. giving at the same time the most wide
publicity.-

Athens 2nd December 1949

Document 4. An anonymous letter that made its way out of Makrónisos, entitled "Makronissos Island—the Greek Dachau." The letter found its way to Upton Sinclair, who passed it on to *The Nation,* with a note placing the magazine at liberty to use the letter if it wished. *The Nation* did not publish it. Found in *The Nation* archives at the Houghton Library, Harvard University. Reproduced with permission.

PARERGA

Parergon 1.1

Of course, the occupation was by the Germans, the Italians (until 1943, when Mussolini collapsed), and the Bulgarians, but the locution commonly used implicated only the Germans, referring only occasionally to the Italians and, at least in southern Greece, almost never to the Bulgarians. Nikos Doumanis (1997) has dealt with the different ways in which the occupation by the Italians has been remembered in the Dodecanese, especially in relationship to the memory of the Germans. He argues that the Italian occupation has been passed on as a relatively peaceful encounter, whereas the memory of the German occupation has been the exact opposite: as the most brutal, savage, barbaric, and fearful experience in modern Greek history. This is also my experience as a subject of this history: the stories told about the Italian occupation have usually been rather innocuous and sometimes humorous.

One such story was told me by a man who grew up in Crete, Manolis. Manolis was born after the war, but the story, he says, is one that his mother would often recount as he was growing up to make him laugh: "Our house had been taken over by the Italians as a Commandatura. My mother and my father were confined to one bedroom and the Italians had the rest. The Commandante was a very gentle man, a classicist, who spoke perfect ancient Greek and who usually communicated with my mother in his own version of modern Greek. One day he went to my mother and, in Greek, asked for a *kochliarion* [the ancient Greek term for "spoon"]. My mother said 'But, Giovanni, you know, I don't speak Italian.' To which he responded, '*Ma donna mia Margarita* [in Italian], *Hellenika milo, koutali thelo* [in modern Greek].' ["But dear Mrs. Margarita, I speak Greek, I want a spoon"]."

The incident is of importance mainly because it is an example of what theories of language ideology describe, where the deployment and reception of specific registers of a language circumscribe the political and social position of the speaker. On language ideology in general, see Woolard and Schieffelin 1994. On language ideology within the specificity of the Greek example, see Tsitsipis 1999. But the incident is equally important as yet another example of the relationship of Western Europeans, in general, to modern Greece. For them, modern Greece usually exists only as the symptomatic site of Greek antiquity (see Herzfeld 1982a; Danforth 1984; Gourgouris 1996; Leontis 1995; Panourgiá 1995, 2001, 2004a). Importantly, too, my Cretan friend was told this experience from the Italian occupation as a funny story. By contrast, being Cretan and remembering accounts of the Battle of Crete in 1941 and the brutal retaliations of the Germans throughout the occupation, he always shivered at the thought of the Germans.

In light of this historical experience, the current relationship of the Cretans with the Germans—and the other way around—becomes particularly interesting. When visiting Crete, on a number of occasions I have repeatedly been shown locations of remembrance of Greek and German encounters, such as the German cemetery, the place where the Commandatura had been, and the famous "bird," a small statue of an eagle sitting atop a pillar whose beak had been broken because, my interlocutor said, "people believed that the Germans had hidden golden sovereigns there." She continued, "When Manolis [her grandson] goes to school I want him to learn German," a desire that I also heard voiced by a number of other Cretan women.

When I asked her daughter-in-law, a young woman from Athens, about this, she shrugged her shoulders, saying, "I have no idea; don't ask me. This is her own thing."

To engage with this fully would require its own research, but I can at least mention here that all the women who expressed this admiration for the German language and wanted their grandsons to learn it came from Right-wing families.

Crete is also the primary destination of German tourists, and German tourists are considered by most Cretans to be the best tourists they can have. As one hotel owner mentioned to me a few years back, they are clean and orderly, they pay their bills, and they never make noise. In light of that, however, one should also consider the following story, recounted by Eleni, who visited Rethymno with a group of Athenian friends a few years ago: "I had not been in Crete in a few years, and I had never stayed at a resort before. This time we were participating in a conference, and early one morning we were woken up by the voice of a German physical education coach yelling "*Schnell, schnell*" as she coached a group of German tourists doing gymnastic exercises on the lawn outside my window. It reminded me of all the films about the war and the occupation that we were watching as children."

This dissonance between the experience of the two occupations cannot be dismissed as making the Italian occupation an object of nostalgia as opposed to the barbarity of the German occupation. First of all, it is now widely understood (as seems to have been the case at the time, too) that the Italian soldiers who fought during the war and became occupying forces did so under duress, having been conscripted into the army by and under the fascist dictatorship of Mussolini. This knowledge was widely shared at least by the Leftists and the anti-Metaxas Greeks, in connection with the knowledge that the Italian Leftist and Communist movement had suffered as harshly under Mussolini as their Greek counterparts had under Metaxas. Therefore the Italian occupying forces, by and large, were encountered as themselves existing in fear of fascism, unlike the German forces, who are still viewed as willing participants. Had the Italian occupation been the only one, we would probably hear about Italian atrocities more often. But by contrast with the Germans, who occupied Greece at the same time, the Italian presence in occupied Greece became a refuge for memory. What I mean by "refuge for memory" is that, in light of the German barbarity, the brutality of the Italian occupation (accompanied by a high level of inefficiency, incompetence, and haphazard operations that drew the scorn of the Germans) came to be a mnemonic space of humanness, with all its frailties and weaknesses. It came to be a space where memory could take a breath, where memory could seek refuge from the atrocities that have been burned onto it. In all of my interviews and encounters with the different generations of Greeks who experienced the war and the occupation, I have not come across even one narrative of Italian brutality, although Philip Deane (pseudonym for Philip Tsigantes) mentions that his uncle, Ioannes Tsigantes, the leader of Midas, one of the minor Resistance groups under the direct guidance of the British Foreign Office, was brutally executed by an Italian patrol detail when he was caught burning incriminating evidence of the organization in his stove.

Such stories are rare, however. More typical is a story told by a woman whom I interviewed in the winter of 2004. She had been born in a small village on the mainland of Greece in early 1942. As she recounted: "My mother said that in '43 (it must have been '43 because I was just crawling)—my parents had bought the house just a couple of years earlier—they [occupying soldiers] came to the village looking for an *andártēs* [a partisan] who had been hiding there. So they came in and looked for him, the Italian soldier first. We were just standing and crawling there, and my father was behind the door, my mother next to him. As the Italian came in, my father picked up a piece of wood to hit him behind the head, but my mother pulled him away. The Italian saw him and turned his gun on him, right on his forehead, and then said, in Italian it must have been, pointing toward us, 'Bambino, bambino,' meaning that he would have killed him had we not been there. The Italian left, and not half an hour later the Germans came in and burned our house." I have encountered narratives of Italian arrogance, as when the Italians decreed that in Athens schools would teach Italian in fulfillment of the foreign language requirement, or when they requisitioned the house of a family friend, who came from a long line of revolutionaries of the 1821 War of Independence, then took all the relics that had been left in the house and had not already been taken by various museums (letters from the government, the great-grandfather's sword, all sorts of documents).

That narratives of Italian compassion are more common than narratives of brutality is especially noteworthy given that there are *no* narratives of compassion by Germans (although there is at least one account, in Skroubelos's *Bella Ciao*, of a German who collaborated with the Greek andártes and procured ammunition for them). This might seem to invite explanation by attributing to Greece an Italophilia and Germanophobia before the war. But we have no evidence of this. Quite the contrary, the well-established philhellenism of the Germans had produced an affinity for Germany among at least the economic and intellectual elite of the country (aided, one would imagine, by the ties of the royal family of Greece to the German royal families). Indeed, many Greek intellectuals and academicians had been educated in Germany in the interwar period and were completely baffled by the German invasion. On the issue of German and Greek intellectual relations before, during, and after the war, see Fleischer 2003: 87–121.

Parergon 1.2

I do not invoke the notion of DNA lightly. Although a trope, the deployment of a metaphorical DNA as index of the political experience of exclusion ought not to be taken as *simply* a trope, because it attempts to capture the segmentary classifications, produced in Greece, that separate the "Communists" (and the "Leftists") from the nationalists within a constructed context of both symbolic and actual kinship. What I mean by this is that the Greek state has, from the beginning of the Leftist movement, articulated a thought about the Left that rests, on the one hand, upon understanding kinship as a purely biological category and, on the other, on a notion that social and political behavior are overdetermined. In other words, the Greek state expressly expected members of families (nuclear and extended) to share social and political ideologies, an expectation that is reflected in all legislation concerning social dissidence from 1871 (the Law on Brigandage) on. It is also reflected in the surprise that was expressed when such expectations did not materialize (as, for example, when the child of a Right-wing family grew to be a Leftist, or the child of a Leftist became Right wing).

Kyriakos Athanasiou, a biologist and the son of a Communist who died in 1948 at the age of 32, having been lynched by the paramilitaries while in government custody during the civil war, has written an account of being the "son of a brigand [*Yios Symmoritou*]." Athanasiou mentions how, of all the slurs that his neighbor at his village would hurl at him and his brother when they were little boys ("bastards [*bástarda*]," "criminals [*kakoúrgoi*]," "dirty Communists [*vrōmokommounistés*]"), the one that hurt him most was "dirty Communists." "Maybe because I understood that it hid a truth," he writes. "I felt it as a heavy curse. Something that you get in your genes. But what nonsense am I saying? 'Genes.' As if one could have heard the term at six years old. Even Watson himself probably did not know it at the time. Maybe it was during those days that he first uttered it. Somewhere at Cambridge. There, where Europe, in the mid-fifties, was entering a new epoch, when humanity in general was entering its new epoch. But not Mavromati [his village]. Not Greece" (Athanassiou 2003: 10).

This medical metaphor, which organizes the experience of his history, recurs in his life. During the junta he was drafted into the army to fulfill his obligation for military service. He was summoned to the Office of Security and Indoctrination (the infamous A2). There, with his file open in front of him, the officer in charge asked questions: What did his mother do? Where was his brother right now? What had he studied? At some point, Athanasiou mentions, he had "optical contact with a particular point in the file . . . 'Son of a brigand,' 'dead,' or 'executed,' or something of this sort. It's as if you are being told that from birth you carry the microbe of cholera. And that they know it. That was the first time in my life that I realized that each human [*ánthropos*] is not only what he appears to be, what he thinks he is. You are not only what you have done by yourself for yourself, what they taught you or you have learned in your life . . . You are always something else. You carry within you some others. Your kin [*tous dikous sou*]. What they were. What they did or what was done with them. You also carry what happened to them and what they went through . . . My father's torturers had also killed a part of me . . . I will always be a constant threat to the security of the country [*khōra*]. I have always been a miasma, the son of a brigand, the nephew of brigands" (ibid.: 24–25).

If the position of the state has been that Communism is something that is carried within one's line of kinship, the Left has produced a different narrative of itself as a political subjectivity. The Left's position has been that one *becomes* a Leftist, engaging in a process of becoming and self-inauguration in the Foucauldian sense of subjectification, where the formation of the subject always includes the experience of the body (in other words, the formation of the Leftist as a social and political subject is always already circumscribed by the experience of the violence of the state upon the body of the Leftist). As Dimosthenis Dodos mentioned in a message sent to the Electronic List for the Study of the Civil War in Greece, "one decides to belong to the Left through torturous personal trajectories and positionalities" (February 7, 2007; used with the kind permission of Dodos; my translation).

I do not make the distinction between Leftists and nationalists lightly, recognizing full well that what for the Greek state between the 1920s and the 1980s was axiomatically accepted as truth—namely, that "communist" and "nationalist" were mutually exclusive self-ascriptions—was simply not so for the Communists, who considered themselves to be both internationalists and nationalists. On the meaning of the term *dikos* ("my own, member of my family, someone beloved, someone with whom I identify") see Panourgiá 1995.

Parergon 1.3

The line comes from Takis Sinopoulos's poem "To Nesi tou Thanatou" ("The Island of Death"), from his 1957 collection *Metaihmio II* (Takis Sinopoulos, *Sylloge I* [*Collection I*]; Athens: Hermes, 1986).

The Island of Death

Flesh and light you breathed into the golden rocks
I heard the voice of the sea the wood's voice.
Different voices at midday.
The sandy sea-shore torched
And to the west of the rocks
The hands and the legs and the bodies
There the seaweed nursed
On the sun

Farther away dry stone walls yet farther the gardens
Under the sun motionless
Under the sun.
                    I heard the voices. I couldn't
Tell what they wanted.
I was only guessing the message.
The island was gathering up
The nails black on the body of the sea.

With flesh yes and with flesh still I yelled.
You place it against death
And it battles.
                    I was looking for you
My fingers crushing everywhere
On stones and on light.
The blood spurted from the wound.
                    I was looking for you what was I looking for?
You were you weren't you were leaving you were vanishing. I said hit me
On the face on the teeth and on the eyes hit me.
Break my body the strength

Because the voices are calling me.
On the rock I sat.

The voices were coming their heads were coming
White and I was chasing them away with my staff.
They buzzed they brought messages—
The hands nailed from the light
Salt light silence.
I heard all the voices
That favored the whisper.
Dream shaken by the wind—and I was going
To the water of the rock to wash
The hands and the face
For the blood to go away.

The blood does not leave the island. With flesh yes
Fighting death fighting
With you my dead the dead
The wood the sails—
Voice of the dead voice of the wood and of the sea
On the sandy island
Your own voice
Wasn't heard anywhere
Not the voice of denial
But human voice
Of fear or of annihilation
As I came out from the dream
And I was going where was I going?
These were hands
My hands your hands the hands of the dead
And the island in the sun
And the island on the seabed
And the sandy seashore
In the sun sharp rocks
Golden rocks

Whatever I heard only I know.
Because the dead hear only the language
of the dead.

Parergon 1.4

I fully acknowledge how problematic this collective "we" is, for, as Derrida notes, "who could ever venture a 'we' without trembling?" (2001). But it is a "we" that attends to the writing of mourning (and still mourning, of things not that much different from in my *Fragments*; Panourgiá 1995). I am writing of the gestures of mourning, gestures that can be deciphered only through the exploration of deflected accounts, practices, narratives, and self-presentations that I am trying to trace in this present project. This is mourning that most often does not appear as such, does not cry out its melancholia, for a *khōra* (that happens to be my *khōra*, also, my place) where justice forgot to happen, where the pain of existence got flattened into discourses of entitlements and acquiescence, where the seduction of capitalist comforts (even when never attained and realized, even when eternally suspended as desire) has completely dislocated what one of my interlocutors noted (lamenting its loss), namely, the ethos of poverty as a cultural value. "Poverty [*ftōhia*] and friendship [*philía*] are what kept us together," said this person, who has gone from being a barefoot village boy to a multi-millionaire restaurant owner. Therefore it is precisely in the name of friendship, as Derrida says, in that there is no "we" without or outside of friendship, that the utterance of "we" presupposes a friendship that allows, asks, and demands to share the burden and the responsibility of mourning, that this "we" that I invoke here wants to be heard.

Wendy Brown complicates and problematizes the use of "we" in different ways when she invokes the collectivity of the "we" in her discussion of mourning the revolution. Without a trace of hesitation (and rightly so), Brown speaks of the inclusiveness of the "Left" (my quotation marks) in socialism, in the antiwar movement, in a feminist revolution that "carried the promise of remaking gender and sexuality that itself entailed a radical reconfiguration of kinship, sexuality, desire, psyche and the relation of private to public" (Brown 2003: 8). Brown deploys this "we" in the face of mourning for the feminist revolution that has failed, for the emancipatory promise of that project, and it is a "we" that needs to be uttered and articulated in the face of so many carefully constructed fragmentations of identities that refuse to undertake the responsibility of a "we."

In Jean-Luc Nancy's terms, we should not take this "we" as being " 'composed' of subjects," neither is it "a subject" as part of a process of a narrative of a self, and hence it does not necessarily posit or transcend the "aporia of all 'intersubjectivity'" (Nancy 2000: 75). But Nancy suspends the idea of the "one" and "with" in the colloid that produces the "we," in that no "we" exists unless it exists as the one being "with-one-another." In other words, the "we" presupposes and understands that all who comprise it are specific "ones" existing with other "ones" (2000: 76).

Elephantis (2008 [1997]) brings the entire question of "we" into sharp focus in the case of Greece (but, one would suspect, within a far wider context, and certainly with Derrida in mind) when he posits this "we" as a question in reference to the legacy of the October Revolution. Which "we," Elephantis asks? "The radicals and socialists of the end of 1910, the Communists of the decade of the twenties, the socialists, the antifascists of the interwar period, of the antifascist war, the EPON, EAM, ELAS of the Resistance [the Leftist youth, civilian, and military organizations of the Resistance], the captains [military leaders of ELAS], the fighters of the emphýlios, the exiled and imprisoned, the Leftists of EDA [the coalition of the Left between the 1950s and the 1970s], the fighters against the junta, the ones who revered the Soviet Union, the Trotskyists, the Archive Marxists, the peasantists, the libertarians, those who considered the de-Stalinization of 1956 to be the 'true' vision of communism, the Zachariadists [loyal to the Secretary General of the Communist Party of Greece, Nikos Zachariadis], those who followed the 'Rebirth,' the Maoists, the Guevarists, the Lambrakides [followers of the assassinated Grigoris Lambrakis, members of the World Council for Peace], the Eurocommunists, members of the Communist Party of Greece (KKE) and its youth (KNE) after [the split of the Party in] 1968, those agreeing with 'the movement,' the ecologists, the feminists, the members of Synaspismos [the new coalition of parties of the Left], the partisans who fled to the countries of Eastern Europe, the exiled, the imprisoned, the 'movement,' the rest of the Left, the dēlôseies [those who signed declarations of repentance], those who denounced others, those who were 'rehabilitated,' the dead?" (42). But there is nothing stable in the categories that Elephantis gives, and he knows it. As he says, there are real, actual people who inhabit these categories; they are not just ghosts or specters of existence. He knows full well, as he says, that "there is no continuous 'we,' unchanged by time." He recognizes that the history of the terms that he has produced is a history that belies uniformity and homogeneity but that nevertheless is the history of the current Leftists, sometimes grouped together, often fragmented, through the enchantment of friendship and the bitterness of betrayal, mourning for a better world that could not have come.

In any case, however, an act of mourning can be claimed behind every "we" that is uttered. The "we" is intimately connected to the work of mourning, and it is precisely this mourning that I am invoking here.

Parergon 1.5

I recognize perfectly well the dangers that lurk in this universalism, as I recognize the utterance itself as a universalizing gesture. I do hope, though, in the course of these pages to show how this universalism slides between its own totalizing discourse and the particularity of specific and individual experiences. Ánthropos (in the plural, ánthropoi) is the term deployed in the narrative discourses of the experience of history that I am researching—as an existential category, not simply a biological one. In Greek the process of socialization, of making a child part of a social community, a social animal, is conflated with the process of "making one human [kánō to paidi ánthrōpo]," bringing one up from the realm of animality (as a biological being) into the realm of humanity, thus bringing one from the realm of no responsibility to the world of recognition of utter responsibility. *Ánthropos* is the biological animal that has been brought up to recognize the responsibility of its actions. Gayatri Chakravorty Spivak in 2001 commented on this concept of "making a child human" as a common locution in India, also. We will see how this existential attribution was denied to the Leftists in Greece when their fundamental humanity was explicitly denied to them, especially when, under torture, they would be told that through torture (and its educational effect) the torturer would make them human (*tha se kano ánthropo*).

Foucault argued in 1966 that the deployment of the term *ánthropos* as a concept that places a particular animal (the human animal) within the temporal specificity of its course of development happens at the moment when labor, language, and biological life become a constellation of existence, produce a new form of life, and are "unified around and constitute a would-be sovereign *subject*" (as Rabinow notes in 2003: 13). But Foucault (and Rabinow, through his reading) are concerned with the history of *ánthropos* as "the logos of modernity" (Rabinow 2003: 15). What concerns me here are the ways in which the concept of *ánthropos* is used on the local level, by social actors, and how in its plasticity, indeterminacy, and hesitancy it becomes politicized. In other words, I am concerned with how the concept *ánthropos* is constantly contested and redefined precisely because its porousness lends itself to such fluidity.

Parergon 1.6

Krátos is only one of the four constitutive elements of the political in contemporary (post-eighteenth century and post–1821 War of Independence) Greece. The other three are *éthnos* (inadequately translated as "nation"), *laós*, and *khōra* ("country"). Schematically speaking, *éthnos* describes the totality of Greeks and Greekness anywhere in the world, without geographical or temporal restriction. It encompasses the presumed *psyche* and *pneuma* (spirit, *Geist*) of Greekness, what used to be "Greek," and what *is* Greek outside of the geography of the country (which includes the diaspora). It is a designation that includes the totality of the kinship lines that allow for the articulation and recognition of the utterance "I am Greek." *Laós* is the term for the living masses, the populace, that comprise the country who, when granted voting privileges, are transformed into *polites* ("citizens"). *Khōra* has become complicated by Derrida's development of the concept as it appears in Plato's *Timaeus*, though elsewhere in the Platonic dialogues the term bears the uncomplicated notion of space that it still retains in modern Greek. Gadamer and Vassilis

Kalfas, however, give to the Timaean *khōra* the horizon of space that participates in the relationship between *paradeigma* ("paradigm") and image, thus
bringing the term to mean what is translated as "country": the horizon that
determines and contains the idea, the image, of what a *khōra*, a country, is.
Khōra, then, is the term used to denote the geographical space that contains
resident citizens, containing *krátos*, the state, without occupying the space
connoted by *éthnos*. The literature on the Greek nation and Greek nationalism is vast, and I cannot reproduce it here. See Skopetea 1988, Leontis 1995,
Gourgouris 1996, Tsoukalas 1999, Liakos 2005. On the Platonic concept of
khōra as presented in the *Timaeus*, see Derrida 1995 and Gadamer 1980; the
definitive work on the corpus of commentaries on the *Timaeus* remains the
introduction and commentary in Kalfas 1995.

Parergon 1.7

Asinēn te refers to a Homeric Hymn and a poem by George Seferis. The only
textual information that exists about Asine is the Homeric catalogue of ships
that participated in the Trojan War. Seferis wrote his poem after visiting
Asine in the summer of 1938 and finished it in Athens in January 1940. I have
used the translation by Edmund Keeley and Philip Sherrard.

The King of Asine

Asinēn te . . .

ILIAD

All morning long we looked around the citadel
starting from the shaded side, there where the sea,
green and without luster—breast of a slain peacock—
received us like time without an opening in it.
Veins of rock dropped down from high above,
twisted vines, naked, many-branched, coming alive
at the water's touch, while the eye following them
struggled to escape the tiresome rocking,
losing strength continually.

On the sunny side a long empty beach
and the light striking diamonds on the huge walls.
No living thing, the wild doves gone
and the king of Asine, whom we've been trying to find for two years now,
unknown, forgotten by all, even by Homer,
only one word in the Iliad and that uncertain,
thrown here like the gold burial mask.

You touched it, remember its sound? Hollow in the light
like a dry jar in dug earth:
the same sound that our oars make in the sea.
The king of Asine a void under the mask
everywhere with us everywhere with us, under a name:
"*Asinēn te . . . Asinēn te . . .*"
and his children statues
and his desires the fluttering of birds, and the wind
in the gaps between his thoughts, and his ships
anchored in a vanished port:
under the mask a void.

Behind the large eyes the curved lips the curls
carved in relief on the gold cover of our existence
a dark spot that you see traveling like a fish
in the dawn calm of the sea:
a void everywhere with us.
And the bird that flew away last winter
with a broken wing:
abode of life,
and the young woman who left to play
with the dogteeth of summer
and the soul that sought the lower world squeaking
and the country like a large plane-leaf swept along by the torrent of the sun
with the ancient monuments and the contemporary sorrow.

And the poet lingers, looking at the stones, and asks himself
does there really exist
among these ruined lines, edges, points, hollows, and curves
does there really exist
here where one meets the path of rain, wind, and ruin
does there exist the movement of the face, shape of the tenderness
of those who've shrunk so strangely in our lives,
those who remained the shadow of waves and thoughts with the sea's
        boundlessness
or perhaps no, nothing is left but the weight
the nostalgia for the weight of a living existence
there where we now remain unsubstantial, bending
like the branches of a terrible willow-tree heaped in permanent despair
while the yellow current slowly carries down rushes uprooted in the mud
image of a form that the sentence to everlasting bitterness has turned to stone:
the poet a void.

Shieldbearer, the sun climbed warring,
and from the depths of the cave a startled bat
hit the light as an arrow hits a shield:

"Asinēn te . . . Asinēn te . . ." Would that it were the king of Asine
we've been searching for so carefully on this acropolis
sometimes touching with our fingers his touch upon the stones.

—Asine, summer '38—Athens, Jan. '40

Translation by Edmund Keeley and Philip Sherrard, George Seferis, *Collected Poems* (Princeton, N.J.: Princeton University Press, 1995: 134–36).

Parergon 1.8

There is a startling reverberation here with the oath required of all Athenian citizens after the end of the civil war of 404 to 401 B.C., which erupted among Athenians after Spartans defeated Athens in 404 B.C. and burned the Long Walls, the wooden walls that had been built in the middle of the fifth century B.C. around Athens and Pireaus to connect and protect the two parts of the city. The oath demanded that citizens not recall the misfortunes caused by the civil war. The exhortation *mē mnēsikakein* ("do not hold grudges," literally, "do not hold onto bad memories") was, as we will see, completely forgotten by the later Greeks of the modern civil war. But then modern Greek politicians are not held accountable to the same code of ethics as the ancients. Although the directive against remembering past misfortunes was rigorously applied to the Left in the 1950s, it was certainly not required of the rest of the political spectrum, especially the Right, whose governments (local and national) engaged in many mnemonic rituals (both religious and secular) at sites throughout Greece where battles between the Left and the government forces had taken place. Not until the 1990s did the Left engage in a few commemorations of its own, primarily on the exile islands and at Grammos, the place of the final defeat of the Democratic Army.

Nicole Loraux emphasizes that the oath was taken on an individual rather than a collective basis: "I shall not recall misfortunes—*Ou mnēsikakēsō*," an active verb individually uttered that drew each citizen into the vortex of city politics, into the vortex of the polis (2006: 149). Loraux further reminds us that the discourse on amnesty (thus the demand that certain acts become forgotten) was originally associated with the fine imposed on Phrynichus (2006: 148). Phrynichus, one of the earliest tragedians, composed a tragedy entitled *Miletus Captured* shortly after the city of Miletus, one of the members of the Ionian League in Asia Minor, was captured and sacked by the Persians in 503 B.C. The Persians brought such devastation on the city that Athens (the metropolis of this colony) also mourned. When the tragedy was taught in Athens, the audience wept, and Phrynichus was fined for having reminded the Athenians of *oikeia kaká* (familial—or familiar—misfortunes). On the civil war of 404 to 401 B.C., Loraux 2006 remains indispensable.

Parergon 1.9

At least one commentator has used the terms the "first civil war (December 1944)" and the "second civil war (1946–1950)." See Papadopoulos 1967: 7. The trajectory of the "rounds" metaphor is not an uncomplicated one. This metaphor permeates most of the postjunta historiography dealing with the civil war. The terms are always in quotation marks, yet have never been attributed to a specific source. I have managed to trace the use of the terms to John Iatrides's *Revolt in Athens* (1972), but even there they are in quotation marks. Correspondence with Iatrides yielded the following explanation: "As far as I can remember, I used the term 'second round' simply because that's what we called it at that time. I don't remember finding the term in any of the sources I used but I'll check and will let you know what I find. The quotation marks were my own choice, thinking that readers might otherwise think the numbering was somehow formally established. In one of his many books and manuscripts, [Chris] Woodhouse writes approvingly of calling the *Dekemvriana* the second round."

When I asked Iatrides what he meant by "we called it at that time," he responded: "By 'called it at that time' I meant before the 1960s (when I was working on *Revolt in Athens*) and by 'we' I had in mind family, friends, colleagues in the Greek army and government, and others in Greece and here who were interested in the civil war and with whom I discussed it. It had nothing to do with the State Department or British official views. As for Woodhouse, there is nothing on 'rounds' in *Apple of Discord* but *The Struggle for Greece* (published in 1976) is divided into three sections called 'rounds.' I am almost certain he used the terms much earlier, perhaps in unpublished writing, but if so I was not aware of it when I used 'Second Round.' Again, I simply cannot remember what prompted me to use it other than it seemed to be the natural thing to do! I checked my sources for *Revolt in Athens* and can't find 'rounds' anywhere. Perhaps I was reacting to Foivos Gregoriades's *Istoria tou Emfyliou Polemou*, whose subtitle is *To Deftero Antartiko*" (Iatrides, personal communication, e-mail message, November 1, 2006). I am indebted to Iatrides for taking the time to look into this question and for sharing with me his thoughts on it, and for giving me permission to publish his comments.

Parergon 1.10

The Archive Marxists (*Archeiomarxistés*) were a group of intellectuals within the Communist Party that appeared some time in 1918 (and were certainly recognizable by 1919) in the Communist Union (a secret group within the Socialist Labor Party, SEKE, in Greece; SEKE later became the Communist Party of Greece, KKE). When the Communist Union was dissolved, some of its members started publishing a periodical, *Archeia Marxismou (Archives of Marxism).* During the first years of International Trotskyism, the Archive Marxists of Greece were the largest and most robust section of the Trotskyist movement. In 1924 the Archive Marxists organized the Archeiomarxist Organization, with Dimitrios Yiotopoulos (known by his pseudonym Witte) as its leader. Yiotopoulos was a chemist by profession and Leon Trotsky's secretary. In July 1930, the Archeiomarxist Organization applied for admission to the International Left Opposition (which later became the Fourth International). In October 1930 the organization changed its name to the Bolshevik-Leninist Organization of Greece. In 1934 the organization split away from the Trotskyist movement, never becoming part of the Fourth International.

The basic project of the Archive Marxists was education and indoctrination into Marxism and Leninism, by making available the writings of Marx and Lenin. The group made these works available in a number of different European languages, some of them (badly and hastily) translated into Greek. However, reading in any language in the beginnings of the twentieth century was limited to the better-educated portions of the population, leaving the working-class and agrarian Stalinists at a disadvantage (as Margaret Kenna has pointed out, 2003: 120). The Archive Marxists, however, insisted that before the Party opened up its ranks the uneducated workers had to be educated and trained. A split with the main Party was inevitable, as the Party was heavily invested in swelling its ranks and stomping out the false consciousness of intellectuals. By the time of the Metaxas dictatorship (1936) the Archive Marxists were persecuted equally by the Communist Party and by the dictatorship. On the Archive Marxists see Kenna 2001 and 2003; Noutsos 1992 and 1993. On Yiotopoulos, see Trotsky 1978; on the Greek Trotskyists and the Fourth International, see Trotsky 1979; on Greek Trotskyism within the context of the international Trotskyist movement, see Alexander 1991.

Parergon 1.11

An excellent account by women inmates on death row who witnessed their comrades being taken out to be executed can be found in Hart 1999. The lyrics of the song are an exercise in allegory and analogy:

Sten steria den zei to psari
oute anthos stin ammoudia
ki oi Souliotises den zoune
dihos tin elefteria

Ehete geia vrysoules
loggoi, vouna, rahoules
ehete geia vrysoules
ki eseis Souliotopoules

A fish cannot live on land
nor can a flower on the sandy seashore
and the Souliot women
cannot live without freedom

Good-bye little fountains
ravines, mountains, slopes
good-bye little fountains
and you little Souliot women

This translation diverges from the one published by Hart, who erroneously takes the suffix *–poules*, a diminutive of the main noun or adjective, to mean "little bird." As Hart mentions (and as everyone in Greece knows), in nationalist (which means official) historiography the song has been classified as a folk song on the claim that it was sung by the women of Souli as they jumped from cliffs rather than be captured alive by the advancing Ottoman army during the siege of 1827. Everything in the song contradicts this official claim. The fact that it rhymes (which Greek folk songs do not), its rhythm, and its melody (which would have placed it among the island songs, not the Epirot ones) betray some later, outside, and scholarly intervention.

Being a physical education teacher, Demetra had to teach this song and its dance to her high-school students. I asked her what that meant for her. "In the beginning a day did not go by that I would not think of the women at Averof," she said. "In time I forgot." For three exhaustive accounts of the involvement of nationalist scholarship (and even propaganda) in the construction of a seamless national narrative that includes folklore, literature, and the dimensions of the law, see Lambropoulos 1988, Herzfeld 1982a, Gourgouris 1996.

Parergon 1.12

Ektopisis, or *ektopismós*, has been translated into English as "banishment." See Voglis 2002 on the institution of *ektopismós* during the civil war, and Kenna 2001 for an example of *ektopismós* prior to the civil war, specifically, the islands of Anafi. Many other places were used before the civil war for *ektopismós*: the islands of Folegandros, Aghios Efstratios, and Gavdos; also Katouna and Kalpaki. In the latter, prisoners were forced to water wooden electricity poles "until they sprout leaves," a form of torture that is not immediately recognizable as such but is homologous to the equally humiliating question that white voting officials used to pose to blacks who tried to register to vote before the Civil Rights Act of 1963: "How many bubbles are there in a bar of soap?" The impossibility of an answer, like the impossibility of the task of watering a wooden electricity pole, added insult and humiliation as part of the process of exclusion from the social body. Later on, on Makrónisos, prisoners were asked to catch flies and present them to the authorities.

Banishment has often been conflated with exile, denoting the physical removal of the exiled to another place but giving special emphasis to the fact that she is banished from her familiar surroundings, her environment, and her friends and relatives. I prefer, however, to leave the term untranslated, while I acknowledge that *ektopismós* is not coterminous with exile—the common term for that is *exoria*—so as to retain the emphasis on place, *topos*. *Ek-topismós* is literally the removal of an individual from her physical *and* thematic context, and it was effected for a set period of time (although it could always be extended at the discretion of the local security committee). In addition, it was taxonomized into two different protocols, which eventually became intertwined:

(a) *Judicial ektopismós (Dikastike ektopisis)*, a measure added onto a legal sentence and effected after the end of a prison term at a place determined by the court as part of the sentence. This was reserved for counterfeiting, animal theft and animal killing, use of narcotics, contraband activities, espionage, evading the tax on alcohol, and (of most interest to us), for transgressions of the Third Resolution and of Law 509/1947, which delineated security measures taken to safeguard the state, the form of government, and social stability. It was conceived as a precautionary measure to avert new crimes.

(b) *Administrative ektopismos (Dioiketike ektopisis)*, a precautionary measure taken by the local security committees against those suspected of possibly engaging in illegal acts in the future against public order and security. The security committee decided not only the length of the exile but also how long the exiled would be considered dangerous.

A number of laws established *ektopismós* as an administrative measure, such as the 1871 Law Concerning Brigandage, Law 19/4/1924, which established the committees of public security, Law 98/1946 on *ektopismós* of the families of military deserters, etc. Law 51/1947 added a number of restrictive provisions that delineated the specific living conditions of the exiled. The writer of the entry on *ektopismós* in the 1964 edition of the Papyros-Larrousse encyclopedia did not fail to note that "*ektopismós*, either as a sentence or as an administrative measure, is dangerous, judging from its results; in no way does it act as a precaution, but it destroys the exiled both socially and professionally. Especially as an administrative measure, where the exiled is deprived of the securities of the legal process, it often acquires a character that is opposed to the founding principles of modern law . . . as it stands against Article 5 of the international Convention of Rome."

Ektopismós was a remnant from antiquity, both Greek and Roman (*hyperória*: "beyond the borders"), where it was reserved for serious crimes, especially those against the security of the state. Whereas *exoria* constituted a sentence for a crime already committed, *ektopismós* was a purely precautionary measure. The *ektopisménoi* ("the exiled," *ektopisthéntes* in the linguistic purist version, *kathareuousa*, used at the time) were not only removed *from* a specific place, the one that constituted them as political and social beings, but they were moved *to* another place, always remote and minimally accessible, and always with strict orders not to come into contact with the native population (where it existed), so that the physical body of the exiled citizen would be effectively desocialized and depoliticized. *Ektopismoi* were effected at a number of places, mainly remote islands in the Aegean, with Agios Efstratios (Ai-Stratis), Anafi, and Gavdos among the principal ones. Ai-Stratis and Anafi were used again as places of exile during the civil war and afterward. Gavdos became famous during the trial of 17N because two of the main persons who were charged as operatives of the organization, Dimitris Koufondinas and Angeliki Sotiropoulou, used to take their vacations there.

Ektopismós is the official term used by the state in legislation and in sentencing, whereas *exoria* comes from common parlance. The latter focuses not on *topos* but on limits and borders. A common locution using *exoria* is the phrase *zoun sten exoria tou Adam* ("they live in Adam's exile"), used to refer to someone who lives far away from what is understood as a neighborhood, or a context. The locution, with its reference to the exile from Paradise, also underlines the undesirability of the situation, the fact that *exoria* is not undertaken voluntarily but is, rather, an act of punishment located within the power (*pouvoir*, not *puissance*) of the sovereign for an act of insubordination, of questioning the arbitrariness of the law (and the legislator). The noun *exoria* is produced from the locution *ektos orion*. *Oria* denotes the limits (physical, conceptual, imaginary, or phantasmatic) of a place, an action, or a thought; in legal terms, it indicates the displacement of a person outside national borders. The *exorisménoi* (*exoristhéntes* in *kathareuousa*) were sent outside the limits of their context, outside the confines of their existence, and they never did so willingly.

The Greek notion of exile is close to the articulation Edward Said has given us in his "Reflections on Exile": the "unhealable rift forced between a human being and a native place, between the self and its true home," whose "essential sadness can never be surmounted" (2000 [1984]: 173). Exile should thus be distinguished from both self-exile and the condition of a refugee. Self-exile is ultimately a matter of agency (keeping in mind, constantly, the impossibility of true choice as a paradigm for action), where the self-exiled "takes the road of exile"(as the Greek expression is) as an alternative to annihilation, whether physical or political. A refugee is part of a massive and rapid forced exodus to a location that is not only alien and undetermined but also physically outside the national boundaries of his homeland. My position here is both linguistically and conceptually stricter than the one proposed by

Liisa Malkki, who blurs the exile and the refugee in the case of the Hutu in Burundi (Malkki 1995).

The Argentinean term *incile*, as the opposite of *exile*, another judicial measure at the disposal of the state, is an interesting counterpoint. There the convicted is not allowed to leave his place, rather than being banished elsewhere. It is akin to the Greek *kat'oikon periorismos* ("home confinement"), except that in the Greek case the meaning is literal (one cannot leave one's house), whereas in the Argentinean case it applies to the country.

Parergon 1.13

Some of the main points in the Idiônymon (Law 4229/1929) bring out, as in a bas relief, the argument concerning the preemptive persecution of ideas and the process of constituting the category of the "dangerous person":

> For quite a while now, a minority that seeks the violent overthrow of the established social status quo by disseminating its principles and attracting followers, often through essays and underground means, has put in danger the security of society. The protection of society from the actions and methods of this minority is imperative. Such protection would not involve the prosecution of sociological, philosophical, or economic principles and ideas, because such an act would contradict the very bases of democracy, but it concerns ideas that, being based on the violent overthrow of the social system and (through that) on the imposition of a minority constitute a danger for the quiet of citizens.
>
> To all this there has been added another dangerous class of people, who, obviously being instigated from abroad, support ideas regarding the separatism of certain areas of the country, using excuses related to those that support the overthrow of the social status quo. What is absent from our legislation is a precautionary prosecution of the preparation for such overthrow, which puts in daily danger the quiet and serenity of citizens. . . .
>
> It would, however, be remiss [*átopon*] to let go unpersecuted an obvious gesture that, for the time being, is restrained to procuring followers but nonetheless will become dangerous for the security of the public. To this end, the submitted bill of law is restricted to the prosecution of the dissemination of such ideas of violent overthrow, because for the more serious cases the already-existing laws are adequate. Under this law, special harshness is reserved for those employed in the public sector, in any branch and at any rank, who, by being instruments of the State and managing its operations, place in grave danger the substance of society by participating in such a movement. To this end, their dismissal from

their post is automatic in the event that they are convicted [of the crime of participation]. Their temporary dismissal, though, shall be based on the discretion of their local committee, in the event that their remand in custody is based on the suspicion of such involvement. . . . Because of the special nature of the crimes dealt with in this bill and the danger to public order that is often created by them, it has been deemed right to recognize explicitly the possibility of remand in custody in the case when there has not been a *flagrante delicto* arrest, and the District Attorney does not find it prudent to arrest by direct order on account of the need to collect of further evidence or for other reasons and the remand in custody, in the case of misdemeanors, cannot be effected without additional reasons according to the existing legislature, and for this particular reason to make impossible release upon bail, an act that would put in jeopardy the measures taken by the authorities in order to safeguard the quiet of citizens. . . .

Educators, even when they have not committed any act punishable by this law, who nevertheless engage in the propagation of Communist principles or insult the idea of the Homeland or the national symbols are irrevocably dismissed from their posts after the decision of their home committees.

As Voglis has noted (2002: 36), the Idiônymon inaugurated two measures that proved to be foundational for the later treatment of the Left in Greece. First, the law, although it did not make special provisions for political prisoners (therefore they were not exempt from forced labor, nor did they have any special allowances or treatments), made it explicit that they ought to be kept "in a special prison or in a special department of a prison," thus opening the way for the special internment camps. Second, one of the provisions of the Idiônymon was that, if a prisoner petitioned for early release, the prisoner would have to declare that he or she had "repented" and would refrain from any further political activity, a measure that provided precedent for the eventual introduction of the *dēlôseis metanoias* of the Metaxas government.

Parergon 1.14

The first historical accounts of the dictatorship of August 4 are Spyros Linardatos, *How We Arrived at August 4*, published in 1965, and his *August 4*, published in 1966, both in Athens. These publications mark the beginning of serious historical analysis of the circumstances that made the transgressions and excesses of the political system in Greece possible, by exposing the myth that the liberal democratic parties had maintained up to that point, namely, that they had opposed the Metaxas dictatorship. Linardatos showed, through meticulous, impassioned research, the complicity of liberal democracy with the structures of the state involved in constructing the Left as its enemy a priori and the processes through which the democratic parties sustained and even aided the persecution of the Left by the dictatorship. The Metaxas dictatorship, because it was construed as having resisted the Italian invasion, avoided the scrutiny of historical research (which, after the occupation and the civil war was taken up exclusively by the winners—the Right and the Center—and was preoccupied with those two events) until the relatively calm period of the early 1960s, when the exiled and interned Leftists started coming back. Even now, scholarship on the dictatorship is limited and usually falls under the wider context of research on political exclusion.

The work of Nicos Poulantzas stands out here, as he was able to show that, despite the fact that the dictatorship has been recorded in local and collective memory as a "fascist" formulation that had close ties with Nazi Germany, in actuality its political affinities were with Franco's Spain and particularly Salazar's Portugal. Thanassis Sfikas mentions that, during an interview with a French newspaper in September 1936, Metaxas "willingly accepted a favorable comparison of his regime with that of Salazar in Portugal. Later on, in private, he agreed that the similarities between the two regimes were greater than with any other" (Sfikas 2006: 21).

Spyros Marketos has successfully shown how the Metaxas dictatorship falls within a wider context of bourgeois totalitarian imaginary (Marketos 2006). Marketos argues that the international financial collapse of the late 1920s led the bourgeois classes to seek calmness and security, which they perceived as being available in the totalitarian ideologies of the time. He further argues that part of the seductiveness of the Metaxas regime for the Greek bourgeoisie was aesthetic. His argument highlights the delicate relationship between liberal democracy and "mild" authoritarian regimes, on the one hand, and the explosiveness of the relationship between liberalism and the Left, on the other. Metaxas's fascism (which fell within the scope of a European bourgeois aesthetic that defined manners and savoir faire as politics), Marketos argues, provided the country—ravaged by war, the Asia Minor expedition of 1919 to 1922, the subsequent exchange of populations following the 1923 Treaty of Lausanne, and the subsequent economic crash—with a seductive aesthetics that blotted the misery of the country out of the bourgeois imaginary.

Parergon 1.15

The Metaxas regime has been described, formulaically, as a junta or as a dictatorship. Strictly speaking, it was neither a junta nor a dictatorship, since it did not come to power as the result of a military coup-d'état, nor did it seize power at the end of a war. In April 1936, Metaxas was given the premiership by the king, George II, with the consent of the political parties in Parliament, for a period of five months. The two political parties of the Right (*Laiko Komma*) and the Center (*Komma Phileleutheron*) could not form a government on their own, and it became clear that the vote of the Communist Party was necessary for the formation of a coalition government. The Communist Party came to agreement with the other two parties on electing the president of Parliament, with the understanding that Metaxas (whose own political party, the *Kómma Eleutherophrónōn* had received 3.4 percent of the popular vote at the general elections in January 1936) would not be supported by the king past his five-month mandate. Political unrest did not cease, and, especially after the massacre of May 9 in Thessaloniki, a number of strikes by different sectors took place. A general strike was announced for August 5. On August 4, Metaxas visited the Palace with a plan detailing the suspension of a number of articles of the Constitution and the dissolution of Parliament, a plan that the king approved. Metaxas moved on both points of his plan, and his dictatorship was thus established. The Metaxas regime, however, had all the characteristics of a dictatorship: the complete militarization of the state, brutal suppression and persecution of the opposition, a populist labor project, and the shameless appropriation of plans made by previous governments as actions of the dictatorship (such as the claim to have established the Social Security Fund, a project that had been initiated about a year prior to Metaxas).

Parergon 2.1

Epitaphios does not have the singular meaning "epitaph," as one might expect from the usage of the term in antiquity. In modern Greek, *epitaphios* is the replica of the sepulcher of Christ that is carried around the parish and venerated on Good Friday evening, in the reenactment of the transport of Christ's dead body from Golgotha to the tomb. It is also the term used for the lament (*epitaphios threnos*) of Mary, not as the mother of god, but as a mother whose child has been executed. For a description of the procession and the lyrics of the lament, see Panourgiá 1995.

Parergon 2.2

Yiannis Ritsos's *Epitaphios* is emblematic of the new relationship that the state was producing with its intellectuals and artists, what in Greece is called *diannöese* (and could be translated as "intellectuality"). Metaxas, with his severe anti-intellectualism and populism, managed to produce the body of the intellectuals as anti-Metaxians, not because they were engaged in any sort of resistance to his attempts at totalitarianism but because they were involved in artistic production that was not actively supportive of the dictatorship. Metaxas's anti-intellectualism was not formulated in a vacuum, as he had witnessed the development of a new modality of artistic production that was actively engaged in social and cultural critique in the poetry of C. P. Cavafy, Konstantinos Karyotakis, and Nikos Kazantzakis (in his *Odyssey*). This appeared during the last years of the 1920s and echoed the melancholy of the Asia Minor Catastrophe of 1922, the bankruptcy of the bourgeoisie, and a critique of the establishment. In a sense, the introspective intellectualism of the 1920s not only prepared the space for the Surrealist, symbolicist, and hellenocentric introspection of the "generation of the thirties" but also presaged Metaxas's position toward intellectualism in general. Unlike elsewhere, where dictatorial regimes were openly supported by intellectuals and literary figures (such as Martin Heidegger, Gottfried Benn, Gabriele d'Annunzio, Ezra Pound, Louis-Ferdinand Celine, Luigi Pirandello, Knut Hamsun, and C. S. Lewis, to name a few), in Greece there is no such open artistic collaboration, and Metaxas's journal *Neon Kratos* (*New State*) never managed to attract serious submissions.

The "generation of the thirties," which included both of the Greek Nobel Prizewinners for poetry, George Seferis and Odysseus Elytis, was not a movement but an orientation. It included poets (apart from Seferis, Elytis, and Ritsos, also George Sarandaris, Nikos Engonopoulos, Andreas Embeirikos, Nicholas Calas), novelists (Helias Venezis, Stratis Myrivilis, Kosmas Politis, Yiorgos Theotokas, Aggelos Terzakis, Melpo Axiotou, Ioanna Tsatsou), painters (Spyros Vassileiou, Hatzikyriakos-Ghikas, Yiannis Moralis, Yiannis Tsarouchis), essayists and literary critics (Linos Politis, Konstantinos Dimaras, Zisimos Lorentzatos), architects (Dimitris Pikionis, Aris Konstantinidis), choreographers (Rallou Manou, Zouzou Nikoloudi), actors and directors (Karolos Khun), musicians (Menelaos Palladios, George Sicilianos), photographers (Voula Papaioannou, Nicholaos Tombazis), German-educated philosophers (Constantine Tsatsos, Evaggelos Papanoutsos, Ioannis Theodorakopoulos), folklorists (Angeliki Hadjimichali and Dora Stratou), classicists (Ioannis Kakridis), and, by association, Lawrence Durrell and Henry Miller. All of them—managed, organized, and (more importantly) conceptualized as a lose unit by George Katsimbalis (the prototype for Henry Miller's *The Colossus of Marousi*)—navigated Metaxism without siding with the dictatorship, precisely because Metaxas a priori considered the arts to be fundamentally opposed to his project. Ritsos's *Epitaphios*, however, was the first book of modern Greek *poetry* to be burned in public as dissident. This happened in 1938 in a central spot in Athens, along with five hundred other books—ironically at Hadrian's Gate, named for a Roman emperor who supported and sheltered the arts and letters. Among the banned books and littérateurs were Leo Tolstoy, Maxim Gorky, and Sophocles's *Antigone*. Ritsos, a member of the Communist Party by 1938, started writing more symbolic poetry after the pyre, so that his writings could get past the censorship office (where Seferis was stationed for some time). The poetic gestures of Cavafy, Karyotakis, Varnalis, and Kazantzakis produced an air, an environment, within which literature and critical thought came to signify a dangerous zone that could be inhabited and populated by everyone (Leftist or Centrist) who was not engaged or implicated in actively supporting the dictatorship. Some of these artists, however, became active supporters of the oppressive postwar governments and their methods of reproducing the body politic (as did Myrivilis, Venezis, and Konstantinos Tsatsos). Karen Van Dyck has commented on the employment (and deployment) of "paralogy" (a logos and a discourse that exist outside the margins of logic but are performed as a new kind of logic) in literary works produced under the Metaxas dictatorship, such as those by Tsatsos and Seferis, in which both those "poets and the regime all espoused 'Greekness'" (Van Dyck 1998: 50). The bibliography on the generation of the thirties (especially in literature) is vast, but as a general overview Vitti 1971 remains indispensable. For approaches that are more critical, see Lambropoulos 1988, Gourgouris 1996, Leontis 1995.

Parergon 2.3

Certificats de civisme is the felicitous translation given by Stavros Papadopoulos (1967) for these certificates. The Greek term is *koinonika phronemata*, literally meaning "social thoughts," what really constitutes the characteristic qualities of the citizen, of the person who is obliged to serve the civic sphere and be indebted to it for her existence as a social subject. *Phronēsis* is a term that has been deeply excavated by philosophy and, more recently, social science. In various works by Plato, *phronēsis* is presented as one of the four cardinal virtues, being a poetic (as in creating, constructing) force of human well-being, one that is cognizant of what is good and what is bad, one that allows the human to evaluate what can be done and what ought not to be done. In Aristotle's *Nicomachean Ethics*, *phronēsis* correlates to age, but in either case, Plato's or Aristotle's, it transcends the meaning "knowledge." *Phronema* (*phronemata* in the plural), then, becomes the *nous*, the mind, the disposition that combines desire, will, and intention and develops with the acquisition of knowledge and the accumulation of experience. *Phronēsis* then produces *phronema*, which in turn animates and organizes action, as it provides the context of knowledge, prudence, and will, which are the principles behind action. The certificates of political *phronemata*, then, sought to address this particularity in the constellation of political action in Greece, underlining questions of intent and desire. The certificates are not unlike, in their conception, the Certificates of Loyalty introduced in the United States with the 1940 Smith Act.

Voglis 2002 and Herzfeld 1998 argue that the *dēlōseis metanoias* are conceptualized along the lines of the Christian notion and practice of repentance. I do not disagree entirely with this analysis, but I think that something beyond Christian affect organized the logic of repentance for Maniadákis. He repeatedly brought up the strength of rational thought in the effort to rehabilitate the Leftists, claiming that if Communism could take Communists away from the nation, then nationalism could bring them back, so long as the conditions that made them turn to Communism in the first place were met (such as poverty and social inequality). See Lymberiou 2005; Anonymous 1937.

On *phronēsis* in the social sciences, see Flyvbjerg 2001, in which Flyvbjerg calls for the abandonment of a social science based on the epistemologies of the "objectivist" hard sciences, a turn away from the desire to be predictive, and a focus, instead, on "context, practice, experience, intuition, and practical wisdom," all of which he reads as constitutive of Aristetelian *phronēsis*. See also Geertz 2001 for a review of Flyvbjerg.

Parergon 2.4

The submarine has remained unidentified to this day, but the strong suspicion has been that it was Italian. Count Galeazzo Ciano, Italian minister for foreign affairs and Mussolini's son-in-law, made the following diary entry on the day: "A Greek vessel has been sunk by a submarine of unidentified nationality. The incident threatens to become serious. As for me, I consider the intemperance of De Vecchi [one of the fascist leaders] at the bottom of it. I confer with the Duce [Mussolini], who desires to settle this incident peacefully. It was not necessary. I suggest sending a note to Greece. This will place the question on a diplomatic plane" (1947: 284). We certainly cannot take Ciano's diary to be innocent, not only because the innocence of diaries is (and ought to be) always suspect, but also because Ciano himself mentions at various points in his diary that Il Duce wanted him to be keeping a diary for posterity. On August 17, 1940, Ciano mentions that Dino Alfieri, minister of propaganda, ambassador to the Holy See, and ambassador to Germany, had "an interesting conference with von Ribbentrop [Nazi minister for foreign affairs]," where it was mentioned "that an eventual [Italian] action against Greece is not at all welcome at Berlin" (ibid.: 285). Despite Mussolini's desire to "teach the Greeks a lesson," it is obvious to Ciano that a war with Greece will not be an easy one and also "that even in German opinion the war is going to be hard. The Duce himself has dictated our counterproposal. Naturally, we accept the Berlin point of view, even as regards Greece. In fact we put back in the drawer the note [of declaration of war against Greece] that we had already prepared" (ibid.: 285). On August 22, Ciano mentions that Mussolini has decided to postpone indefinitely any action against Greece and Yugoslavia. Apparently the Metaxas government believed that an appeal to the Germans would stave off the Italians. Ciano mentions that, according to von Ribbentrop, the Greek minister of foreign affairs "had tried to knock on the doors of Berlin but was harshly treated. Von Ribbentrop did not receive him and told him it would be more useful to speak with Italy, since Germany is in perfect accord with us about everything" (ibid.: 287). See Dubish 1995 on the importance of the celebration on Tenos in the official narrative produced by the Greek state about its destiny as a metaphysical entity.

Parergon 2.5

The phrase comes from George Seferis's entry in his diary for Friday, September 22, 1944, written at Cava dei Tirreni, as a member of the Greek government in exile. He writes:

> Today is a week since we first got here.
>
> Peculiar, peculiar: there are various people who leave Greece (even *now*) and come here. All these gentlemen, who come (as they say) from the belly of the fighting nation, do not make us better, they make us worse.
>
> As night fell there is a blackout. Someone tells me this. In Macedonia, andártes killed some Germans. Reprisals: The Germans took six young women, raped them, and then slaughtered them on the graves of the killed. Chthonic adorations of orthodoxies. (Seferis 1986: 359)

Parergon 2.6

"Haxion Esti Anagnosma Tetarto" ("Worthy It Is: Fourth Reading"), "The Field with the Nettles," by Odysseus Elytis:

> On one of those sunless days of that winter, a Saturday morning, cars and motorcycles surrounded Lefteris's small tenement, with the tin windows and the open sewers. And with wild voices *ánthropoi* with leaden faces and hair straight like straw came. And they ordered all men to gather at the field with the nettles. And they were armed head to toe, the mouths of their guns facing low to the side of the crowd. And a great fright came over the children, as it so happened, almost all of them had some secret in their pocket or their psyche. But there was no other way, and, giving honor to their necessity, [they] took their place in the line, and the *ánthropoi* with leaden faces, hair straight like straw, and short black shoes unfolded barbed wire around them. And they cut the clouds in two, until sleet started falling, and jaws found it difficult to keep teeth where they belonged, so they would not leave or break.
>
> Then from the other side slowly appeared The One with the Erased Face, who raised a finger and the hours shivered on the large clock of the angels. And whomever he happened to stand in front of, others

would grab by the hair and drag on the ground, stepping on him. Until the moment came to stand in front of Lefteris. But he did not move. He only raised his eyes slowly and got them at once so far away—far into his future—and the other felt the jolt and leaned back in danger of falling. And enraged, he made a motion to lift the black cloth from his face so he could spit right onto his face. But Lefteris still did not move.

Right at that moment, the Great Foreigner, the one who was following with three chevrons on his collar, resting his hands on his midriff, sneered: there, he said, there are the men who want to change the course of the world! And without knowing, the poor wretch, that he was speaking the truth, he struck him on the face with his whip three times. For a third time Lefteris did not move. Then, blinded with the little effect that his power had on him, the other one, not knowing what he was doing, pulled out the revolver and blasted him on his right ear.

And the children were very frightened, and the *ánthropoi* with leaden faces and hair straight as straw and short black shoes turned to wax. Because the shacks came and went, and at places the tar paper fell and there appeared far away, behind the sun, women crying, kneeling on an empty field, full of nettles and black thick blood. While the great clock of the angels struck precisely twelve o'clock.

Parergon 2.7

See Fleischer 1986 and 2003. Mazower also gives a short and succinct description of the role and the operations of the Tágmata. He states:

> During the first years of the Occupation, when Greece had been largely administered by the Italians, the Greek police had helped the resistance. Many *Gendarmes* had even joined the guerrillas in the mountains rather than serve under the despised Italians. After September 1943, however, the Germans took over the whole of Greece and the SS took over policing duties. In keeping with the reinforced Nazi anti-Communism of the closing stages of the war, the SS encouraged Greek collaborators to set up auxiliary anti-Communist militias against the resistance, and even formed what would later become known as 'death-squads' which used counter-terror strategies, indiscriminately killing civilians to dissuade them from supporting EAM. (Mazower 1997: 131)

The categorization of the Italians by Mazower as "despised" should not surprise us and should not be thought of as contradictory to the more general disposition in Greece toward the Italians during the occupation. The status of the Italians as an occupying force exists only in comparison to the Germans. Therefore, a hierarchy of dispositions ought to be taken into account: the

Italians were despised, the Germans hated, the Tagmatasphalētes (being collaborators) loathed.

The most comprehensive work to date on the TA is Kostopoulos 2005.
For an attempt (roughly since the mid 1990s) to show the complexities of the
processes that made this institutionalized collaboration with the Germans
possible from an ethical viewpoint (but which, in all actuality, only reiter-
ates the arguments produced by the collaborationist government of Ioannis
Rallis, namely, that the violence produced by the Left, whether EAM or as
ELAS, was more sustained and organized than the violence produced by the
Germans), see S. Kalyvas 2003, S. Kalyvas and Marantzidis 2004, S. Kalyvas
2006. The argument proposed by Kalyvas rests on the novel *Orthokostá*, published in 1994 by Thanassis Valtinos, which attempts a balanced presentation
of the experience of the Resistance and the creation of the TA.

In *Orthokostá*, as in Kalyvas's texts and in the original circulars and memo-
randa used by Rallis, Valtinos argues that villagers in the Argolid, where he
grew up, resented the brutal German reprisals caused by partisan actions and
turned to the TA to ask for protection. The irony that anyone would turn to
the Germans for protection while under German occupation is, of course, part
of what makes fiction valuable. Literature can and does engage in philosophical inquiry and does produce knowledge, but we should not expect literature
to produce information. We should expect literature to take the poetic license
that it needs in order to produce the environment that it needs in order to
elicit the emotional response by the reader that is the defining moment of
the act of reading literature. The work of the novelist is done when she can
produce torrential feelings in her reader. No one can hold a novelist to the
epistemological standards of academic disciplines. But beside the question of
the potential differences between information and knowledge and what sort
of each literature produces, the main problem with Kalyvas using Valtinos's
novel is that Kalyvas does not have the disciplinary tools to engage with a
work of literature on the level of the literary. For a more detailed development
of this argument, see Panourgiá 2004b. For a review of Kalyvas 2006, see
Panourgiá 2008c. For an ingenious critique of Valtinos through literature, see
Voulgaris 2004. For a critique of the politics of Valtinos's original argument,
see Elephantis 2008. For a critique from the viewpoint of literary criticism,
see Calotychos 2000.

Parergon 2.8

The physician Petros Kokkalis, born in Levadeia in 1886, was educated at the
University of Athens and then studied surgery in Switzerland and Germany.
He returned to Greece in the late 1920s, where he became the director of the
City Hospital and, later, of the Third Surgical Clinic at the Evangelismos

Hospital in Athens. He took a teaching post at the School of Medicine at the University of Athens, where he rose to the rank of full professor. In 1942 he was dismissed from his post at the university and joined the Resistance. He not only became a member of the PEEA, as minister of education, but he also fought in the civil war and held the office of minister of health in the Provisional Government. Sometime during the civil war, Kokkalis left Greece, first for France, and he eventually sought refuge in Romania and then East Germany. He took a teaching post at Humboldt University and became a member of the Berlin Academy. He lived in exile until his death in 1962.

His son, Socrates Kokkalis, born in 1939, returned to Greece under the amnesty granted to political refugees by the George Papandreou government in 1963 and received Greek citizenship in 1965. Eventually Socrates Kokkalis became one of the richest and most influential Greek citizens, initially by manufacturing and providing parts and services for the Greek network of telecommunications, acquiring the first mobile telecommunications services, then running the lottery trade, and, finally, expanding to the old Communist countries after 1989. Kokkalis established a TV and a radio station, and he bought (and still owns) the football team Olympiakos. Educated in East Germany and Moscow, Kokkalis was accused by the Greek state of having been an agent for the East German secret service Stazi, an accusation of which he was eventually acquitted. In 1997 Kokkalis established the Kokkalis Program in Southeastern European Studies at the J. F. Kennedy School of Government at Harvard University. In 1998 he established the Kokkalis Foundation, a charitable organization concerned with promoting the study of modern Greek political formulations. He is thought of as the Bill Gates of Greece.

Perhaps ironically, given Petros Kokkalis's position toward the involvement of the United States in Greek politics and domestic affairs, the street that flanks the American Embassy, was named by the Greek state after him: Hodos Petrou Kokkali.

Parergon 3.1

These phrases come from Seferis's diary entry for Saturday, December 30, 1944 (1986: 382–83). He writes:

> Killings, refugees, cold, and that barking of the machine gun. In the morning telegram from London. The King appoints [archbishop] Damaskenos as viceroy. The political intelligencia [word transliterated in the original] has gone bankrupt everywhere in Greece.
>   I met Damaskenos briefly, since I came back. He has the secure wisdom [*phronemada* in the original] of the peasant, which is, at least, a

point of strength. He is democratic, not fanatical; this is an advantage, too. We went to see him.

We asked him how the regency suits him; he responded with the following parable:

> When I was young, my school was in another village, an hour and a half away from mine. At some point they bought me new shoes [*tsarouchia*] for Easter. I put them in my knapsack and started for school wearing my old ones, so that I wouldn't damage them. Every now and then I would take them out, caress them, and be proud of them. That day it took me three hours to get to school. The regency is like my new shoes.

He was lying in bed, and he seemed disproportionately large for that room. His eyes sparkled as he told the story; he was in good spirits [*eihe kefi*]. He does not know any foreign language, save that when he was exiled in Salamis he learned by heart a French dictionary, I suppose to kill time.

The archaeologist who continues to think that the amputated bodies are nothing more than broken statues etc., etc.

Parergon 3.2

The line is from a folk song, whose lyrics were adapted to the realities of Al Dab`a. The original song, from the islands, was a love song (of sorts) about a woman who owned a fishing boat. It was adapted by Vassilis Tsitsanis early in 1945 and was recorded in 1946 by Tsitsanis and Stratos Payioumitzis.

Tha sas po mian historia	I will tell you a story
Apo ten aihmalosia	From captivity
—varka yialo—	—boat by the shore—
Kapoia mera tou polemou	One day of the war
(den to pisteva pote mou)	(I would never have believed it)
—varka yialo—	—boat by the shore—
Hoi Egglezoi mas kyklosan	The English rounded us up
Me ta tanks kai mas tsakosan	With their tanks they captured us
—varka yialo—	—boat by the shore—
Mas eperan ta roloyia	They took our wristwatches
Me to xylo, me ta logia	By force or by persuasion
—Varka yialo—	—boat by the shore—

St' autokineta mas valan
Kai ten piste mas evgalan
—varka yialo—

In the lorries they put us
And we suffered much
—boat by the shore—

Sto Goudi kais to Hasani
Ki apo kei gia to limani
—varka yialo—

At Goudi and at Hasani
And from there to the port
—boat by the shore—

Mas evalan sto papori
Kai gia to Port-Said plore
—varka yialo—

They put us in the boat
And they took us to Port Said
—boat by the shore—

Mas eferan sten El Ntampa
Kai sten plate mas mia stampa
—varka yialo—

They brought us to El Ntampa
On our back they put a stamp
—boat by the shore—

Mas edinan te vdomada
Dyo koutalia marmelada
—varka yialo—

They gave us two spoonfuls of marmalade
Once a week
—boat by the shore—

Mas edinan kai fystikia
Pou 'tane yia ta katsikia
—varka yialo—

They gave us peanuts
That you use to feed the goats
—boat by the shore—

Mas edinan kai mia stala
Sympepyknomeno gala
—varka yialo—

And they gave us a drop
Of condensed milk
—boat by the shore—

Den xehnousan hoi Egglezoi
To helleniko trapezi
—varka yialo—

The English would not forget
The Greek cuisine
—boat by the shore—

Kai mas dinan taktika
Kai mpizelia araka
—varka yialo—

And they fed us regularly
Peas
—boat by the shore—

Den to teloume to gala
Oute kai ten marmelada
—varka yialo—

We don't want the milk
Nor the marmalade
—boat by the shore—

Mono theloume na pame
Piso sten glykeia Hellada
—varka yialo—

The only thing we want
Is to go back to sweet Greece
—boat by the shore—

Another version, recorded in New York by George Katsaros and Stella Kay (Standard F-9014-B) mentions the campaign as one of exile specifically, both in its title *They Took Us to Exile*, and in the lyrics.

Kai mas pegan exoria	And they took us to exile
Makrya apo ten Athena	Away from Athens
—varka yialo—	—boat by the shore—

Parergon 3.3

The presence of Iannis Xenakis on the *Mataroa* is contested. Although the story that Xenakis had left on the *Mataroa* circulated in Athens until I was a university student in the late 1970s, including that he was still recovering from a wound inflicted during the Dekemvrianá by a British shell, which cost him his left eye, both Nelli Andrikopoulou and Xenakis's biographer, Nouritza Matossian, say that he was not on the boat. According to them, after he was wounded he was found by his father (or by the National Greek Army; it's not entirely established) and taken to the hospital, where he stayed until March 1945. In the summer of 1946 he finished his studies at the Polytechnic School, at the School of Engineering. He then fled to France in 1947, after he had been conscripted into the army, had been asked to sign a *dēlôseis*, had refused, and was given safe passage by one of the recruiting army officers so as to be saved from being sent to Makrónisos. Xenakis himself never talked about this experience.

Cornelius Castoriadis, Mimika Kranaki, and Nelli Andrikopoulou are the only ones from the *Mataroa* group who have written or spoken publicly about the experience. In 1950 Kranaki wrote a small essay in *Temps modernes* with the title "Journal d'exil," which she later expanded and contextualized in her seminal *Philhellenes* (1992). Recently she republished the essay in a bilingual (Greek and French) edition under the title *"Mataroa" in Two Voices: Pages of Emigration* (2007). As Dimitris Papanikolaou has noted in a review, "the *Mataroa* became mythical, to the extent that we assumed that every Greek who had a career in France after the War had left *in that boat*" (2008: 30).

The account provided by Castoriadis is of great interest. In an interview for *Agora International* during the Colloque de Cerisy in 1990, Castoriadis spoke about his involvement in the Resistance movement during the occupation, his interpretation of the Dekemvrianá (which, in a strange twist, he calls a Stalinist coup-d'état, as if the Communist Party had been the official government of Greece in 1944 or as if ELAS were the national army), and his own trajectory, which brought him to be included among the 150 young intellectuals awarded the fellowship, "120 young leftists and people who had just graduated from the Polytechnic," says Castoriadis (1990: 4). Castoriadis had studied philosophy at the University of Athens with the "neo-Kantians" Panayiotis Kanellopoulos, Konstantinos Despotopoulos, and Constantine Tsatsos, who had studied law and philosophy in Germany in the interwar period (ibid.: 3). During the occupation, Castoriadis says, they were discussing Hegel's *Logic* and Kant's *Prolegomena*.

By all accounts, travel to Paris was a traumatic experience. Food was scarce and travel precarious, although, as Kranaki (2004) reports, there was great camaraderie among the fellows. They subsisted on galettes and handouts from peasants wherever the train stopped. Arriving in Switzerland, where, as Castoriadis mentions, there had been a rumor that the government had announced in December 1943 they might have to ration chocolate (1990: 3), they were handed chocolates. As Castoriadis reports, having lived with the sight of dead bodies strewn in the streets of Athens during the famine of 1941 to 1942, they arrived in France to find that "people were laughing, eating sausages, drinking wine. One rediscovered one's self in Paris" (ibid.: 4). See Andrikopoulou 2007, Castoriadis 1990, and Kranaki 1950, 1992, 2004, 2007. See also the review of *Philhellenes* in Gourgouris, 1994, and the reviews of Andrikopoulou 2007 and Kranaki 2007 in Papanikolaou 2008. On Xenakis, see Matossian 1986. I am indebted to Papanikolaou, who pointed out to me the inconsistencies regarding the passage of Xenakis to France.

Parergon 4.1

A line from Eleni Vakalo's poem "Threnody" (translated by Nikos Spanias, 1994: 160):

I want to speak of the great silence

That has no moon in its sky
That has no horses to send off the cortège
That has been forgotten by the river

I want to speak of our bitter
Unforgetting heart

They set Distomon on fire and put Morea to the knife
I want to speak of the destruction that crushes us

The dead one was brought to us
Wrapped in a red blanket
And a handful of jasmines
And the sorrows of night
They brought is closed shutters

A knife made of steel
To pierce the bark of trees
To make sky and sea
Incarnadine

This silence I love
This our heart I know

Parergon 5.1

This is the first line of the song "Apones Exousies" ("Heartless Powers"), with lyrics written by Michalis Cacoyiannis and music by Mikis Theodorakis. The song is part of the record *Sten Anatole* (*To the East*), which circulated in November 1974 and was dedicated to the memory of the students who participated in the Polytechnic uprising in November 1973. This dedication summons up the specter of the civil war and the persecution of the Left as background for the Polytechnic.

Parergon 5.2

President Harry S Truman's address before a joint session of Congress, March 12, 1947, reads as follows.

Mr. President, Mr. Speaker, Members of the Congress of the United States:

The gravity of the situation which confronts the world today necessitates my appearance before a joint session of the Congress. The foreign policy and the national security of this country are involved. One aspect of the present situation, which I wish to present to you at this time for your consideration and decision, concerns Greece and Turkey.

The United States has received from the Greek Government an urgent appeal for financial and economic assistance. Preliminary reports from the American Economic Mission now in Greece and reports from the American Ambassador in Greece corroborate the statement of the Greek Government that assistance is imperative if Greece is to survive as a free nation. I do not believe that the American people and the Congress wish to turn a deaf ear to the appeal of the Greek Government.

Greece is not a rich country. Lack of sufficient natural resources has always forced the Greek people to work hard to make both ends meet. Since 1940, this industrious and peace loving country has suffered invasion, four years of cruel enemy occupation, and bitter internal strife. When forces of liberation entered Greece they found that the retreating Germans had destroyed virtually all the railways, roads, port facilities, communications, and merchant marine. More than a thousand villages had been burned. Eighty-five per cent of the children were tubercular. Livestock, poultry, and draft animals had almost disappeared. Inflation had wiped out practically all savings. As a result of these tragic conditions, a militant minority, exploiting human want and misery, was able to create political chaos which, until now, has made economic recovery impossible.

Greece is today without funds to finance the importation of those goods which are essential to bare subsistence. Under these circumstances the people of Greece cannot make progress in solving their problems of reconstruction. Greece is in desperate need of financial and economic assistance to enable it to resume purchases of food, clothing, fuel and seeds. These are indispensable for the subsistence of its people and are obtainable only from abroad. Greece must have help to import the goods necessary to restore internal order and security, so essential for economic and political recovery.

The Greek Government has also asked for the assistance of experienced American administrators, economists and technicians to insure that the financial and other aid given to Greece shall be used effectively in creating a stable and self-sustaining economy and in improving its public administration. The very existence of the Greek state is today threatened by the terrorist activities of several thousand armed men, led by Communists, who defy the government's authority at a number of points, particularly along the northern boundaries. A Commission appointed by the United Nations Security Council is at present investigating disturbed conditions in northern Greece and alleged border violations along the frontier between Greece on the one hand and Albania, Bulgaria, and Yugoslavia on the other.

Meanwhile, the Greek Government is unable to cope with the situation. The Greek army is small and poorly equipped. It needs supplies and equipment if it is to restore the authority of the government throughout Greek territory. Greece must have assistance if it is to become a self-supporting and self-respecting democracy.

The United States must supply that assistance. We have already extended to Greece certain types of relief and economic aid but these are inadequate. There is no other country to which democratic Greece can turn. No other nation is willing and able to provide the necessary support for a democratic Greek government. The British Government, which has been helping Greece, can give no further financial or economic aid after March 31. Great Britain finds itself under the necessity of reducing or liquidating its commitments in several parts of the world, including Greece.

We have considered how the United Nations might assist in this crisis. But the situation is an urgent one requiring immediate action and the United Nations and its related organizations are not in a position to extend help of the kind that is required. It is important to note that the Greek Government has asked for our aid in utilizing effectively the financial and other assistance we may give to Greece, and in improving its public administration. It is of the utmost importance that we supervise the use of any funds made available to Greece; in such a manner that each dollar spent will count toward making Greece self-supporting, and will help to build an economy in which a healthy democracy can flourish.

No government is perfect. One of the chief virtues of a democracy, however, is that its defects are always visible and under democratic processes can be pointed out and corrected. The Government of Greece is not perfect. Nevertheless it represents eighty-five per cent of the members of the Greek Parliament who were chosen in an election last year. Foreign observers, including 692 Americans, considered this election to be a fair expression of the views of the Greek people.

The Greek Government has been operating in an atmosphere of chaos and extremism. It has made mistakes. The extension of aid by this country does not mean that the United States condones everything that the Greek Government has done or will do. We have condemned in the past, and we condemn now, extremist measures of the right or the left. We have in the past advised tolerance, and we advise tolerance now.

Greece's neighbor, Turkey, also deserves our attention. The future of Turkey as an independent and economically sound state is clearly no less important to the freedom-loving peoples of the world than the future of Greece. The circumstances in which Turkey finds itself today are considerably different from those of Greece. Turkey has been spared the disasters that have beset Greece. And during the war, the United States and Great Britain furnished Turkey with material aid.

Nevertheless, Turkey now needs our support.

Since the war Turkey has sought financial assistance from Great Britain and the United States for the purpose of effecting that modernization necessary for the maintenance of its national integrity.

That integrity is essential to the preservation of order in the Middle East.

The British government has informed us that, owing to its own difficulties [it] can no longer extend financial or economic aid to Turkey.

As in the case of Greece, if Turkey is to have the assistance it needs, the United States must supply it. We are the only country able to provide that help.

I am fully aware of the broad implications involved if the United States extends assistance to Greece and Turkey, and I shall discuss these implications with you at this time.

One of the primary objectives of the foreign policy of the United States is the creation of conditions in which we and other nations will be able to work out a way of life free from coercion. This was a fundamental issue in the war with Germany and Japan. Our victory was won over countries which sought to impose their will, and their way of life, upon other nations.

To ensure the peaceful development of nations, free from coercion, the United States has taken a leading part in establishing the United Nations. The United Nations is designed to make possible lasting freedom and independence for all its members. We shall not realize our objectives, however, unless we are willing to help free peoples to maintain their free institutions and their national integrity against aggressive movements that seek to impose upon them totalitarian regimes. This is no more than a frank recognition that totalitarian regimes imposed on free peoples, by direct or indirect aggression, undermine the foundations of international peace and hence the security of the United States.

The peoples of a number of countries of the world have recently had totalitarian regimes forced upon them against their will. The Government of the United States has made frequent protests against coercion and intimidation, in violation of the Yalta agreement, in Poland, Rumania, and Bulgaria. I must also state that in a number of other countries there have been similar developments.

At the present moment in world history nearly every nation must choose between alternative ways of life. The choice is too often not a free one. One way of life is based upon the will of the majority, and is distinguished by free institutions, representative government, free elections, guarantees of individual liberty, freedom of speech and religion, and freedom from political oppression.

The second way of life is based upon the will of a minority forcibly imposed upon the majority. It relies upon terror and oppression, a controlled press and radio; fixed elections, and the suppression of personal freedoms.

I believe that it must be the policy of the United States to support free peoples who are resisting attempted subjugation by armed minorities or by outside pressures. I believe that we must assist free peoples to work out their own destinies in their own way. I believe that our help should be primarily through economic and financial aid which is essential to economic stability and orderly political processes.

The world is not static, and the status quo is not sacred. But we cannot allow changes in the status quo in violation of the Charter of the United Nations by such methods as coercion, or by such subterfuges as political infiltration. In helping free and independent nations to maintain their freedom, the United States will be giving effect to the principles of the Charter of the United Nations.

It is necessary only to glance at a map to realize that the survival and integrity of the Greek nation are of grave importance in a much wider situation. If Greece should fall under the control of an armed minority, the effect upon its neighbor, Turkey, would be immediate and serious. Confusion and disorder might well spread throughout the entire Middle East.

Moreover, the disappearance of Greece as an independent state would have a profound effect upon those countries in Europe whose peoples are struggling against great difficulties to maintain their freedoms and their independence while they repair the damages of war.

It would be an unspeakable tragedy if these countries, which have struggled so long against overwhelming odds, should lose that victory for which they sacrificed so much. Collapse of free institutions and loss of independence would be disastrous not only for them but for the world. Discouragement and possibly failure would quickly be the lot of neighboring peoples striving to maintain their freedom and independence.

Should we fail to aid Greece and Turkey in this fateful hour, the effect will be far reaching to the West as well as to the East. We must take immediate and resolute action.

I therefore ask the Congress to provide authority for assistance to Greece and Turkey in the amount of $400,000,000 for the period ending June 30, 1948. In requesting these funds, I have taken into consideration the maximum amount of relief assistance which would be furnished to Greece out of the $350,000,000 which I recently requested that the Congress authorize for the prevention of starvation and suffering in countries devastated by the war.

In addition to funds, I ask the Congress to authorize the detail of American civilian and military personnel to Greece and Turkey, at the request of those countries, to assist in the tasks of reconstruction, and for the purpose of supervising the use of such financial and material assistance as may be furnished. I recommend that authority also be provided for the instruction and training of selected Greek and Turkish personnel.

Finally, I ask that the Congress provide authority which will permit the speediest and most effective use, in terms of needed commodities, supplies, and equipment, of such funds as may be authorized.

If further funds, or further authority, should be needed for purposes indicated in this message, I shall not hesitate to bring the situation before the Congress. On this subject the Executive and Legislative branches of the Government must work together.

This is a serious course upon which we embark.

I would not recommend it except that the alternative is much more serious. The United States contributed $341,000,000,000 toward winning World War II. This is an investment in world freedom and world peace.

The assistance that I am recommending for Greece and Turkey amounts to little more than 1 tenth of 1 per cent of this investment. It is only common sense that we should safeguard this investment and make sure that it was not in vain.

The seeds of totalitarian regimes are nurtured by misery and want. They spread and grow in the evil soil of poverty and strife. They reach their full growth when the hope of a people for a better life has died. We must keep that hope alive.

The free peoples of the world look to us for support in maintaining their freedoms.

If we falter in our leadership, we may endanger the peace of the world—and we shall surely endanger the welfare of our own nation.

Great responsibilities have been placed upon us by the swift movement of events.

I am confident that the Congress will face these responsibilities squarely. (The Avalon Project, Yale University, 1997, http://www.yale .edu/lawweb/avalon/trudoc.htm)

Parergon 5.3

The United States Army Military Group–Greece, which was part of the U.S. Mission for Aid to Greece, was established on May 24, 1947, and was placed under the command of James Van Fleet, after the personal intervention of General Marshall. Translating the Truman Doctrine into practice, the U.S. Mission was charged with providing operational advice to the Greek National Army. Later in 1947, the Joint Military and Advisory and Planning Group (USJMAPG) was created, "with the mission of providing the Greek military with aggressive assistance in operations and logistical support," as described by Paul Braim, Van Fleet's biographer (Braim 2001: 162). The USJMAPG had an initial staff of ninety-nine officers, eighty enlisted men, and a number of advisors who were assigned to all branches of the military, at the level of division headquarters. According to Braim, Van Fleet acquired almost complete control over military operations of the Greek Army, to the extent that, when

Van Fleet visited Makrónisos in 1948 and was shown repentant Communist soldiers by General Bairaktares, the latter said, "General, here is your army."

Braim's biography of Van Fleet ought to be taken judiciously in matters that have to do with the situation on the ground in Greece before the emphýlios and Van Fleet's involvement. For instance, Braim mentions that "near the end of the war the Communists concealed their identity under the title National Liberation Movement, or EAM" (2001: 158), whereas EAM was established in 1941, the first year of the war, a scant six months after the Axis forces occupied Greece. Furthermore, he mentions that with the beginning of the emphýlios the Greek National Army had an added disadvantage over the DSE, the fact that it "was worn out from years of fighting the Germans" (2001: 161), when there had been no National Army to fight the German occupation and the brunt of the resistance against the Axis had been carried largely by the military branch of EAM, ELAS, largely the same army that the newly reconstituted Greek National Army was now fighting. But his material pertaining to Van Fleet is largely taken from Van Fleet's personal notes and is indispensable for documenting Van Fleet's personal disposition toward Greece and the emphýlios.

Parergon 5.4

When the Greek government petitioned the U.S. government for an increase in the National Army, the U.S. ambassador to Greece, Henry Grady, refused to consider the request. He wrote to the secretary of state on November 22, 1948:

> The key to success according to [this] thinking is always more: more men, more money and more equipment. We have today in Greece an armed forces reorganization of 263,000 men, which is fed with American purchased daily rations of 4,200 calories, clothed with American purchased uniforms, equipped with American arms, transported by vehicles and pack animals supplied by America and trained and advised in operations by American and British officers. Supporting the land army is heavy artillery, an air force and navy.
>
> This armed force has been unable to make appreciable progress . . . against a bandit organization of some 25,000 men fed with what they could steal or buy locally, clothed in remnants, armed with old weapons . . . transported on their own, or their donkey's legs, and trained by their own leaders. . . . Bandit land army is not backed by a single airplane, heavy gun or naval vessel. In view of the fact that we have [already] increased size and equipment of Greek armed forces, during which time strength of bandit forces has remained proportionately constant to that of Greek army, and as we have not achieved greater security

by these actions, it seems to me that we are not justified in [applying] the old method of increasing again the size and the equipment of armed forces. (Quoted in Nachmani 1990: 17)

Pharmakes (2006) states that even during the Battle of Athens the equipment of ELAS was dismal, especially compared with that of "X." He says that ELAS's equipment, because it had been pillaged from the retreating Italians and Germans, was haphazard and not interchangeable, so that two ELAS fighters fighting side by side could not share ammunition because their weapons were of different makes. Nachmani also mentions that the United National Special Committee on the Balkans (UNSCOB) observers learned not to record in their reports the weapons that they witnessed being used by the DSE because they were of U.S., Nazi, and British make, so that the fiction of Balkan material support to the DSE would have collapsed.

Parergon 5.5

Gilles Deleuze, in "Desert Islands" (2004) engages in a radical deconstruction of the notion of the "desert" island by invoking the lack of recognition by the European traveler/settler of the humanity already existing there. He is primarily thinking of the European travel literature of the Enlightenment and emphatically not referring to actually desert islands—places where only the most tenuous life can be sustained, given scant rainfall, for only a couple of months a year, places that have no aquifer or have only an aquifer that holds contaminated or undrinkable water. Deleuze is speaking of the construction of the desert as part of a discourse that has sustained colonialism. I am speaking of actually desert (not deserted, even metaphorically) islands. Michael Taussig (2004) has captured not only the horror of actually desert islands as colonies for undesirables (Poulantzas's "antinationals") but also the complicity between the management of undesirable life and capitalist ventures, especially in the way in which he erects the problem of offshore operations not as simply an economic but a political one. The only one of the islands of exile not truly a desert island is Trikeri, which in 1947, and still today, is sparsely populated and desolate, but not desert.

An eerily similar environment is found in Goli Otok (meaning "Naked Island") and Sveti Grgur, two uninhabited islands, really "two rocky reefs" (as Banac calls them) in the northern Adriatic near the island of Rab, off the coast of Croatia. After his break with Stalin and the Cominform, Tito decided that the new country needed to purge itself of Stalinist elements (the very Stalinist elements that had made the Resistance possible, had exacted heavy losses from the German army, and had brought Tito's dream of socialism to fruition). Tito's containment discourses made Goli Otok into the iconic and exemplary space of re-education. The methods used there were

similar to the ones used on Makrónisos and Yáros: torture, the handling
of stone, psychological warfare, the creation of a paternalistic relationship
between authority and detainees. (On Makrónisos, this took actual verbal
form when the detainees were made to cry out to the visiting King Paul, "You
are our father.") As the Serbian philosopher Svetozan Stojanovic, a member of
the Praxis group, pointed out in 1972: "Although the struggle against domestic Stalinists was and still is justified, explicitly Stalinist methods of struggle
against them offer ample testimony" to the fact that Yugoslav resistance to
Moscow had for a long time the contours of Stalinist anti-Stalinism (Banac
1989: 244).

Spyros Asdrahas has developed an interesting, even if ultimately uncon-
vincing, theory that the island complex of the Aegean is an aggregate city.
Taking as his starting point the medieval and Renaissance cities of Western
(i.e., non-Ottoman) Europe, Asdrahas explores the "individualized organi-
zational forms of the Archipelago" that were produced by its "fragmentary
nature" and that allowed it to "survive throughout the long years of Turkish
rule. Those forms—each a retreat into the self of the archipelago—were typical of urban structuring" (Asdrahas 1985: 236). Asdrahas locates this "urban
complex" of the archipelago not in the fact that the routes between the two
poles of the east-west axis of the Mediterranean went through the islands
of the archipelago, but rather "in the constant to-ing and fro-ing of people,
goods and ships from one island to another, in an economic osmosis" (ibid.:
238). Asdrahas mentions the "islands' obligation to maintain vigilance over
the seas and to keep in touch with fires by night and pillars of smoke by day"
(ibid.: 239).

As seductive as this proposition is, life on the ground bespeaks a different
reality. Asdrahas bases his argument primarily on the economic and intellectual exchanges that were afforded to the islanders through the merchant
marine. However, the retention of local identities by the islanders themselves
(the Kalymnian, for instance, being distinct from the Lerian, to the extent
that as late as 1981 a woman from the island of Leros married to a Kalymnian
man was known in the Kalymnian capital, Pothia, as "the Lerian [*he Leriá*]")
or the distinctiveness accorded to each island in folk songs invite a different
reading: if we play along with Asdrahas's notion of the archipelago as a "uni-
fying sea or plain-like expanse," then the distinctiveness of each island would
point to the metaphor of villages in a plain and not a city (should one wish to
preserve a metaphor, though Asdrahas does not metaphorize but concretizes
the image of the archipelago as city).

Nowhere does this question of the archipelago become more painfully
complicated than in the testimonials of prisoners on Yáros. Some of the
few instances of literature on Yáros come from Andreas Nenedakis, in his
1964 book *Apagoreuetai* (*It Is Forbidden*) and scattered in various of his

short stories. Nenedakis was a lawyer and writer who participated in the Mutiny of the Middle East (when Greek soldiers and officers demanded that the government in exile include representatives of the Resistance and were arrested and imprisoned in British military prisons across the Middle East and North Africa). After the end of the war, Nenedakis returned to Greece, where he was arrested as a Communist and sent first to Yáros and later to Makrónisos. Michael Herzfeld published an ethnographic critical biography of Nenedakis in 1997, in which he brings to the fore the immense complexities that made up Nenedakis as a political and literary figure who had become a legend among people who had served in the Middle East, on Yáros, and on Makrónisos. In 1977, for instance, when Nenedakis's niece Eirene and I were asked to help establish a cultural association in our neighborhood that would be named after Kostis Palamas (the major Greek poet whose funeral during the occupation was followed by hundreds of thousand of Athenians as an act of resistance against the Germans, who had prohibited large congregations of people), I told my grandfather, who had fought in the Middle East from 1942 to 1944, that the two of us were working together. I remember the awe in my grandfather's eyes when he said to me: "She's Nenedakis's niece."

Writing of Yáros, Nenedakis emphasizes the deep alienation that the prisoners on the island felt at knowing that they were in the midst of an archipelago. He relates how the prisoners would see, far away, commercial liners sailing from island to island, twice a week, "to other worlds. Farther away from you are other islands. . . . Other humans, just like you, live there. Humans who wake up without being cursed, without being beaten with whips. Humans who board a ship, travel, speak with each other, sleep, wake up, walk. . . . And when they sail past Yioúra they might even ask about this island. They might have heard about the prisoners. They must have heard something, it's impossible not to . . ." (Nenedakis 1964: 165).

Parergon 5.6

Banac reports that the first boats carrying Cominformists embarked for Goli Otok and Sveti Grgur in July 1949 and that "by February 1951 eight groups of a total of 8,250 inmates had been shipped there" (Banac 1989: 248). Matthew Mestrovic notes that Aleksander Rankovic, member of the Yugoslav Politburo starting in 1940 and minister of the interior and head of military intelligence under Tito, at a speech in 1952 claimed that 13,700 persons had been sentenced as Cominformists, of whom 7,531 had already been released (in Markovski 1984: xi). Goli Otok, now a tourist attraction, remained open until 1989, ten years after Sveti Grgur had been closed down. Goli Otok was used for men, Sveti Grgur for women. Initially Goli Otok was used during the First World War by the Austro-Hungarian Empire for Russian prisoners of war. With the Tito-Stalin schism, during the *Informiro* that lasted from 1948 to 1956 Stalinists or anyone who was suspected of being a Stalinist, of sympathizing with the Soviet Union, or even of reading Soviet or Russian literature was sent to the islands. After the normalization of relations between Tito and the Soviet Union, Goli Otok was used as a prison for anti-Communist national-ists, and yet later it was used as a prison for juvenile delinquents.

Mestrovic reports that Goli Otok was chosen in 1948 by "someone, it is not known who . . . as the place of detention for 'Cominformists'" (in Markovski 1984: ix). Milovan Djilas, Vice President of Yugoslavia in Tito's government, stated, however, that the Politburo, or the Secretariat, never made any decision about the camp. The decision was made by Tito himself and implemented by the state security under Rankovic (Djilas 1985). Djilas states, moreover, that not only did no one know about the establishment of the camps but there was no legal act on which it was based. He further notes that only later was a law passed to provide the necessary framework for this "obligatory socially useful labor" (ibid.: 235). One could be tempted to think of this gesture by Djilas as an attempt to exonerate himself, especially since his fall out of favor with Tito in 1954. Djilas's son Aleksa is equally certain that neither his father nor anyone other than Tito and Rankovic knew anything about the decision, and he thinks that the idea may have come from Rankovic (Aleksa Djilas, personal communication, April 2007).

There is no question, I think, that Djilas felt remorse about the camp, though he recognized the reasoning that made it possible. He writes, "we had to cripple the Stalinists and the Cominformists—initially, perhaps, by setting up a camp, in order to avoid the appearance of confusion and forestall outside intervention that could link up with domestic inner-party opposition" (Djilas 1985: 236). For Djilas, the existence of the camp and the program of re-education and rehabilitation was a point not only of shame but of "unimagi-nable humiliation" (ibid.: 245) and "defeat and disgrace" (ibid.: 237). His critique of the islands has two levels: first, the perceived need for the camps indexed the (ultimate) defeat of the Yugoslavian Communist experiment as a form of ethical living; second, and intimately related to the first, it marked the defeat of the new humanism that Yugoslavian communists wanted to produce. The sovereign decision on the islands dehumanized not only the interned but the entire Yugoslav population. As Djilas writes, "the way we dealt with those arrested and their families—that was something else again. There was no need to behave as we did. That conduct sprang from our ideo-logical dogmatism, from our Leninist and Stalinist methods, and, of course, in part from our Balkan traditions of reprisal" (ibid.: 236). He concludes, "Goli Otok was the darkest and most shameful fact in the history of Yugoslav Communism" (ibid.: 245). See also Banac 1989; for the most comprehensive examination of Goli Otok in the Anglophone literature, see Lukic 2007.

Parergon 5.7

Venko Markovsi, who was imprisoned in Goli Otok as an unrepentant Stalinist, managed to smuggle a number of letters out of the place. These were later collected and published. His Letter Eight describes the island as he first encountered it. He writes: "Until 1948 no one even knew that such a place existed. . . . The island is nothing but rocks, rocks that are enveloped in a spectral silence during our blood-red sunsets. . . . On Goli Otok human beings are reduced to things, to numbers. . . . From dawn to dusk a sorrowful train of people moves back and forth across the desert that is Goli Otok. Their eyes are sunken; their hands have been broken in inhuman toiling. . . . Each of these shadows is a loose page torn from a shattered life. . . . On Goli Otok it was largely the prisoners themselves—those apostates who had submitted utterly to the will of the authorities—who were used to break the others, to destroy the honor and decency that they were trying to preserve" (Markovski 1984: 30–32). Dejan Lukic, reading the account of Goli Otok by Milinko B. Stojanovic—who has called "the whole camp of Goli Otok . . . one big tragic theater" (quoted in Lukic 2007: 103)—has noted how "the islands are indeed spaces where utopias both begin and end" (ibid.: 105). By deploying the notion of utopia in reference to the islands, Lukic manages to capture the bipolarity inherent in any project of national re-education and rehabilitation by bringing together the promise of utopia (if the re-education project were to succeed—a success that was impossible precisely because of the conceptualization of rehabilitation as part of a project of utopia) and the destruction of any utopian possibility by the very conceptualization of the need for rehabilitation. In other words, utopia cannot exist or be achieved by employing antiutopian means.

Although Tito (or Rankovic) may have come up with the idea of these camps on his own, the parallels with Greek re-education camps for Stalinists are interesting, indeed chilling. Is it possible that Tito had heard about Makrónisos and Yáros from the fighters of the retreating Democratic Army, in 1948 and 1949? Of course, he might also have used other models, say from the Stalinist USSR or Czarist Russia.

Parergon 5.8

Stratis Bournazos is correctly hesitant about the accuracy of this attribution, since it is found only in the circular *Skapaneus*, published by repentant soldiers on Makrónisos. Kanellopoulos himself did not dispute that he had anointed Makrónisos as the New Parthenon until after the fall of the junta, in 1973. Bournazos mentions that, when Kanellopoulos was asked by the newspaper *To Vema* in 1983 what was the gravest mistake of his life, Kanellopoulos responded that it would have been to call Makrónisos the New Parthenon, had he actually done so (Bournazos 2000: 128–29).

The philosopher of law and member of the Academy of Athens Konstantinos Despotopoulos, a friend of Kanellopoulos and later teacher of Cornelius Castoriadis, was sent to Makrónisos because in 1945 he had accepted an invitation from the minister of finance, George Kartalis, to head the Youth Association for Greek-Soviet Friendship, despite the fact that Despotopoulos had no Left leanings. The association caused him to be accused of Communism, and he was sent to Makrónisos in 1947. He remained there for three years, until 1950, and he was known as the Associate Professor (*Hyfegetes*). While Despotopoulos was on Makrónisos, Kanellopoulos and the royal couple of Greece, Paul and Frederika, accompanied by (or accompanying) General Van Fleet visited the island, and Kanellopoulos gave the disputed interview to *Skapaneus*. A few weeks later Cyrus Leo Sulzberger, the foreign correspondent for *The New York Times* visited Makrónisos and interviewed Despotopoulos about the conditions on the island. (See the Appendixes for the full article by Sulzberger). Many years later, in 2006, Despotopoulos mentioned in a short prepublication piece from his autobiography that when, a few days after the visit, he read the interview with Kanellopoulos in *Skapaneus*, he found it to be an apology for Makrónisos. According to Despotopoulos, Kanellopoulos's statement "embellished with the fine language of the Minister and charismatic writer" was nothing more than the official position on Makrónisos. He started by referring to the history of Greece—"Greece, who at other times has given to humanity the Parthenon and Saint Sophia, Plato and Aristotle, Aeschylus and Sophocles"— to underline the present situation, where "she has found herself, over the past two years and more, in the tragic position where her children have taken up arms against her. She was obligated, then, to establish this camp in order to return her wayward children to her bosom." Thus, Despotopoulos claims, happened the confusion, when "a ruthless eavesdropping [*echotheras*] journalist extracted the word *Parthenon* from its context and presented it as if it had been uttered to characterize Makrónisos" (Despotopoulos, 2006a: 37). In this way, Despotopoulos relieves Kanellopoulos (posthumously) of the accusation of having coined the term "New Parthenon."

Parergon 5.9

Dionysis Savvopoulos used the tune of "Hark! The Herald Angels Sing" for the lyrics of his song "On Makrónisos, Then" for the film *Happy Day* (1976), by Pantelis Voulgaris, an adaptation of the novel *Loimos* (*The Plague*), by Andreas Fraggias, which is based on the experience of Yáros and Makrónisos.

Parergon 5.10

Nenedakis mentions that on December 6, 1947, the day of St. Nicholas, when all the occupants of a tent on Yioúra were sitting outside it, listening to screams coming from the penitentiary, a small bird sat in front of them and looked them "straight in the eye. We were dumbfounded. It was the first time that we had seen such a living thing here. It was a bird. . . . With small wings. With little eyes that brightened up when they looked at us, and it jumped up and down in front of our tent." Someone looked for bread crumbs to give to the bird, but none could be found because the bread had not been apportioned yet. The encounter was interrupted when one of the wardens came up to the tent, saw the bird, and started hitting with his stick everyone and everything that he could see in front of him, so that the entire scene ended in a frenzy of torture (Nenedakis 1964: 75–77).

Parergon 5.11

Lucius Sulla was a Roman general from 95 B.C. until 78 B.C. He was born in 138 B.C. and died in 75 B.C. In 82 B.C. he was appointed dictator (*rei publicae constituendae causa*) by the Senate, later approved by the Assembly. There was no set limit on time in office. This was a high honor for Sculla, since he was reintroducing an institution that had existed over a century earlier, when a dictator had been appointed in times of extreme political danger to the city, but only for a six-month period and only with the approval of the Senate and the Assembly. Sulla instituted a practice of exterminating his political opponents and banishing their relatives and anyone who would defend them in public or be found to have sheltered them in private. Their children would be banished for thirty years if they declared their relationship to their parents. Sulla passed an act granting him immunity for all his past and future acts and giving him the power of life and death, confiscation, colonization, founding or demolishing cities, and taking away or bestowing cities at his pleasure, according to Plutarch (1916: 433). The reference to Sulla's banishment of eighty thousand of his political enemies to Yáros comes from Anonymous 1950: 85, which is a survey of the conditions of the exiles on Yioúra and a historical account of the island. I have not been able to confirm the information in any of the published biographies of Sulla that I have consulted. This does not mean that the information is necessarily inaccurate, though the number of eighty thousand remains highly questionable. Yáros is a large island, but on only a small portion of it can one actually stand, as it is mountainous and precipitous. That would seem to preclude the possibility of such a large concentration of people under normal circumstances. Circumstances at Yáros have never been normal, however, and it is not inconceivable that Sulla might have sent his political prisoners there for specific periods of time, so that this seemingly improbable number does not refer to simultaneous coexistence.

Parergon 5.12

The composer Mikis Theodorakis, who was detained on Makrónisos, has said that the legendary wind there would pick up the papers on which his poems were written, hurl them around, and impale them on the barbed wire that separated the cage of the incorrigibles from the rest of the prisoners.

Parergon 5.13

In 1942, this song had been composed about the children who were being sent to Dachau. I am indebted to Apostolos Papageorgiou, who sent it to me.

Katoche, 1941 (Gavriel Marinakes)

Katoche '41, ta paidakia ta kaemena
Tremouliazoun mes' stous dromous, nestika kai tromagmena

Hola tous skeletomena, peinasmena kai presmena
ap' ta spitia tous ta pairnan kai ta stoivazan sta trena.

Sto Dachau ta pegainan kai ta kanane sapouni
kai ta piata tous eplenan, hotan trogane hoi Hunoi

Occupation 1941 (Gavriel Marinakis)

Occupation in '41, the poor little children
are shivering in the streets, unfed and frightened.

All of them skin and bones, famished and bloated,
They would take them from their homes and pack them up in trains.

They would take them to Dachau and turn them into soap
To wash their dishes, when the Huns were eating.

Parergon 5.14

A pamphlet with the same title has been attributed to a member of the KKE, but I have not been able to locate its text or the pamphlet itself to see if it is the same as the one sent to Sinclair. Here is the text of the petition (I have kept the original spelling and punctuation):

If there is a remnant of civilization, every man and woman must raise their voices vigorously protesting against the abominable crimes that brought up the slaughters and criminals of the Greek government on the political transported persons of the Makronissos island.

They do inflict horrible corporal tortures on the prisoners in order to compel them to sign the declaration some thing which constitutes an insult for the human dignity.

One of these hangmen, the L/nant Rados who is characteristic type of sadique, declared openly to them that if they go on to insist refusing to sign, they shall all be killed.—

5 of the soldiers of the greek governmental army, ocular witnesses of these scenes off horror got mad. An 75 years old man NIKITIDIS by name of KILKIS's district of origin, has "commited suicide" after having been tortured for hours.

Yet a score of other prisoners have been assacinated.

After these horrible tortures the men who insisted to refuse to sign are forced to burden a load of—[the weight is not mentioned] of pebble and run during all the day If exhausted fall down, the hangmen beat them with bambou sticks in such a manner that they become infirm for all their life. The well known author DIMITRI PHOTIADIS, who has been transported since 19 months. although he had no political action and without a setence, suffered the same tortures.—

Shuddering nights of terror succeed the other without arrest since 15 days in this new Dachau of Greece which surpassed that of Hitler. If this S.O.S. reaches in your hands please communicate it to the U.N.O. giving at the same time the most wide publicity.—

Athens 2nd December 1949

(MS Am 2302 [4147], Sinclair, Upton, 1878–1968. Correspondence, 1938–1949. 1 folder. The Houghton Library)

I would like to thank the Houghton Library at Harvard University for permission to publish this letter.

Parergon 5.15

There cannot and ought not to be an analytical approach to comparing atrocities. Yet one must look at how they are articulated. The question is not whether the Greek paradigm is "the same" or "comparable" to the German one. Greeks who were taken to Dachau and Auschwitz and then to Yáros and Makrónisos seemed to think that there was a horrific comparison to be made on two levels. First, as prisoners in Germany they could still retain their fundamental alterity from the authorities: "We are Greeks; they are

Germans." Second, they recognized that the German project was ultimately
an enumerative one: so many Jews, so many Gypsies, so many Communists,
so many homosexuals. The Greek project, by contrast, aimed to reconfigure
the mind. Therefore, on one level its regime of enumeration was indefinite,
whereas on another level it was completely metaphysical.

Hannah Arendt has posited this question precisely: "Who would dare to
measure and compare the fears human beings experienced?" (1994 [1953]:
298). When describing the German reprisals after a group of Dutch Jews in
Amsterdam attacked a detachment of German security police in 1941, however, Arendt herself falls into a discourse of comparing terrors. She writes
that in reprisal to the attack 430 Jews were arrested, "and they were literally
tortured to death, first in Buchenwald and then in the Austrian camp of
Mauthausen. For months on end they died a thousand deaths, and every
single one of them would have envied his brethren in Auschwitz, and even
Riga and Minsk. There exist many things considerably worse than death,
and the SS saw to it that none of them was ever very far from their victims'
minds and imagination" (1963: 12). Tony Judt has compared atrocities when
he compared the warders on Makrónisos and their disciplinary practices to
those of the "Romanian Communist techniques in the prison at Pitesti in the
same years, albeit marginally less vicious" (2005: 505), an interesting assessment if one keeps in mind that the vast bibliography on Makrónisos has not
been translated into English, so someone who cannot read Greek can hardly
engage in comparing atrocities on such a microlevel.

Parergon 5.16

Phálanga (in the feminine) is the term used in Greece for bastinado, the practice of strapping a prisoner to a bed or a plank and, with shoes on or off, hitting
the bottom of the feet until they swell and bleed and the flesh becomes pulp,
so that the person cannot walk or even stand, sometimes for weeks. When it is
done by an experienced torturer, the damage is not permanent, and, after the
tortured has recovered, there are no detectable traces of it. In the hands of less
experienced or careless torturers, however, the damage is often permanent and
ranges from swollen feet to fractured or shattered tarsal bones.

The term originally referred to the wooden contraption that held feet during the beating, and, according to Greek historian Kyriakos Simopoulos, it
comes from the Arabic *falaq*, through the Turkish *falaqa*. Simopoulos has
traced the use of *phalangas* (in the masculine) to the Ottoman Empire, where
it was used as early as the seventeenth century as a means of either punishment
or extracting information and confession. The first mention of the torture
is attributed to a scholar from the Morea (the Peloponnese), Christophoros
Angelos, who was accused of espionage in Athens in 1607 and was subjected
to *phalangas*. According to Simopoulos, Angelos described the torture in a

book that he published ten years later in England. Angelos later became a professor of Greek at Trinity College, Cambridge. He used to show his scars from the *phalangas* there. When *phalangas* was administered as a punishment, it was given as a set number of strokes, and it required both an executioner and a colleague who would count them. The person being punished would then have to pay both the executioner and the counter.

Scattered accounts of the use of *phalangas* are found in various travelers' accounts from the Cyclades, Athens, and Constantinople. Simopoulos states that during the Greek War of Independence *phalangas* was the mildest form of torture, applied to swindlers and disobedient soldiers. It was the preferred punishment for professionals in the service of the public (such as bakers, grocers, and millers) who were discovered to have weighted scales. It was also occasionally announced as a possible punishment for anyone caught throwing household rubbish into the street. After Greek independence, with the advent of banditry, *phalangas* was often used by bandits as a form of torture and extortion. The oncologist and medical folklorist Gerasimos Rigatos (2005) has published an etching attributed to the late-nineteenth-century artist and illustrator Gustave Doré in which a group of Greek bandits submit one of their hostages to *phalangas*.

Phalangas was used, both during the Ottoman Empire and during the War of Independence, to punish students. Nineteenth-century Greek literature is replete with examples of the use of *phalangas* (or *pheleka*, or *phelekoxylo*) by teachers. Simopoulos mentions a school rhyme collected by the folklorist Georgios Megas (quoted in Simopoulos 2003: 460n348) that refers to *phalangas* as a disciplinary measure:

Arxon, heir mou agathê
Grápson grámmata kalá
Mê dartheis kai paideutheis
Kai ston phálanga valtheis

Start, my good hand,
Write good letters,
Lest you be beaten and tortured
And put on the *phálanga*.

Another poem, found in a codex from Epirus dated 1815, was recited in chorus by the students:

Afēsé mas, kyr Dáskale,
Na páme eis ton oikon mas
Na kalospernêsōmen
Kai aúrion tachý
Opoios mên érthē glêgora

Tha fágē eis ta pódia
Ravdiá eikositéssera
Kai to mikró pros dôdeka

Let us, Teacher, Sir,
Go home tonight
To have a good evening
And tomorrow [we return] in haste
Whoever does not come early
Will receive twenty-four hits
On the feet
And the youngest of all
Close to twelve (in Simopoulos 2003: 459, and n346)

Simopoulos mentions that *phalangas* was abolished as a punishment for children in Greece at the end of the War of Independence by Edict 2210, August 28, 1829 (460).

In the twentieth century the term *phálanga* (in the feminine) was synechdochically used for the beating itself, done by policemen or military personnel, since the *phalangas* (the instrument, in the masculine) had fallen into disuse. The feet now were usually bound by the strap of the torturer's gun and beaten with a bamboo stick (or often with a metal rod or pipe). One of the people I interviewed, who had been tortured by Special Security during the junta, mentioned that at times the pain from the strap became as excruciating as the pain from the bamboo.

The pain from *phálanga* is so deep that it can efface intense pain that follows it. One of the students who was arrested during the junta for belonging to an antijunta student organization reported that after he had been tortured with *phálanga* "upstairs" (a small shed on the roof of the Security building, where torture took place during the first years of the junta), he was dragged downstairs to his cell, since he could not walk. On the way, the wardens hit him so hard in the mouth that they broke all his front teeth. He said he did not realize that his teeth were gone until much later, because the pain in his feet was so intense that he did not feel the pain of the broken teeth. The connection between swollen feet and Oedipus is painfully obvious (even if it had not been made by Yiannopoulos). On the history of *phálanga*, see: Simopoulos 2003; Rigatos 2005: 356–57. For references on Christophoros Angelos, see Simopoulos 2003: 452.

Parergon 6.1

This is a reference to the song by Loukianos Kelaidones that I wrote about earlier (Panourgiá 1995), but now I want to look at the fifties not as they produced the middle-class generation of youth that came of age in the fifties and sixties (and thus produced the political and cultural landscape of modernity in Greece) but as they produced abject political spaces in the context of the Truman Doctrine and with the aid of the Marshall Plan. On a certain level, the doctrine and the plan secured the survival of the new middle class while giving it a certain power and authority. The term *post–civil war*, of course, can be taken as only a temporal marker, referring to the date when the actual fighting was over. In other words, there is nothing "post" regarding the civil war in Greece, perhaps even now.

Parergon 6.2

In the report that Mark Ethridge, the U.S. delegate to UNSCOB, submitted in May 1947 with his findings about outside involvement in the civil war and Communist Party actions, he mentioned that he found very little evidence to support the Greek government's claims. See US/NA 501, BC-Greece/ 4-847. This is also shown by Nachmani (1990), who has researched exhaustively all the sources of the period. The views that Ethridge presented in the report, however, are complicated by the private accounts that appear in the book that his wife, Willie Snow, wrote about her impressions of Greece, Bulgaria, and Yugoslavia when she visited her husband in 1947 (Snow 1948). She unwittingly shows how Paul Porter (the head of the U.S. economic mission to Greece), her husband, members of the various foreign postwar and recon-struction delegations to Greece, members of the Greek government and the Greek aristocracy, and members of the various relief organizations informally and in social settings reinforced each other's convictions about a Communist plot and the role of international Communism in shaping the landscape of Greece immediately after the war.

In an interview that Ethridge gave in 1974 to Richard McKinzie, he men-tions how, on the basis of intuition, he urged President Truman to make a declaration on account of Greece (which later became the Truman Doctrine). McKinzie mentions how, by February of 1947 (about a month before the British announced their intention of pulling out of Greece), Ethridge had sent a dispatch to the United States in which he said that it *appeared* to him that there was going to be an all-out Communist push to take over the gov-ernment. McKinzie asked Ethridge whether he had any evidence of this or it was his own personal assessment. Ethridge seemed to flounder: "Yes, yes. Well, they were having demonstrations in Athens the whole time, and they broke up a couple of meetings of the Commission with their demonstrations outside. And I walked out of a Commission meeting, saying, 'If you people can't keep order there's no use in us going on.' . . . Yes, you could *sense it, you could sense it.* They were *going to try* an all-out push and the Truman Doctrine prevented it" (my emphasis). Ethridge visited the Balkans to study the post-war situation for the U.S. Department of State in 1945; he was U.S. delegate to the UN commission of investigation to study the Greek border disputes in 1947; he was U.S. representative on the UN Conciliation Commission for Palestine in 1949; and he was the chairman of the U.S. Advisory Commission on Information from 1948 to 1950. His oral history interview with McKinzie took place in Moncure, North Carolina, on June 4, 1974, for the Harry S Truman Presidential Library.

Parergon 7.1

George Papandreou, who had won the elections in 1964 with a 53 percent majority, was driven to resign on July 15, 1965, after intense meddling in the political affairs of the government by King Constantine II and his mother, Queen Frederika, and their support by Panos Kokkas, publisher of the newspaper *Eleutheria* (*Freedom*). The Palace managed to install a number of short-lived governments following the dismissal of Papandreou, which were supported by the twenty-five apostate members of the EK (Enosis Kentrou, Center Union), an event that came to be known as the Apostasy. A time of great political upheaval followed the Apostasy, with political assassina-tions, intensified political violence, state repression, and manufactured tri-als. Major strikes and demonstrations in Athens ended in police brutality. The demonstration of July 21, 1965, resulted in the death of the university student Soteres Petroulas when he was hit by the canister of a smoke bomb. A week later, on July 27, a major strike and demonstration organized and led by the union of construction workers turned downtown Athens into a war zone. The Apostasy, and the governments that it supported, made the junta of 1967 possible. Among the apostates were: the later leader of the Right-wing New Democracy Party and prime minister, Konstantinos Mitsotakis, who is still considered to be the leader of the apostates; Theophanis Rentis (the son of Konstantinos Rentis, who was implicated in the Beloyiannis execu-tion); Elias Tsirimokos, member of the Resistance, secretary of justice in the PEEA government of 1944, and then exiled to Makrónisos, who in August 1965 constituted a pro-royalist government, which failed to gain a vote of confidence and was dismantled.

The Union of Democratic Women was formed as a (small and local) cen-ter of resistance to escalating political corruption, violence, and violation of the democratic rule of law by women ranging from employees in or retirees from various branches of the private and the public sector, to housewives, to women who were informally helping in their husbands' private medical and law practices. Interestingly enough, the women who formed the Union, some of them members of the Left during the emphýlios, seemed to have forgotten or forgiven Papandreou's role in establishing the camps on Makrónisos and Yáros and in the persecution of the Left. Or, as one of these women mentioned to me recently, Papandreou in 1964 presented a chance for a liberal democracy in the face of the rapidly advancing Right wing and its political excesses.

The Union was local, and the women either had known each other since childhood or, for those who had moved to the area as a result of marriage, had been acquainted through their husbands. By all accounts, there was an astonishing level of familiarity among them, resulting in friendships that have lasted until now. The Union was involved in various cultural and charity projects, from organizing poetry readings to running a soup kitchen, which was still in operation in the 1960s, for the children of the victims of the emphýlios. As one of these women mentioned in a recent interview, when the Union was closed down a few days after the junta in 1967, they all thought that this was a temporary suspension of operations and anticipated that the Union would resume operation after the fall of the junta. "But," she said, "with the fall of the junta things were so changed, we were all so tired and exhausted, we were older, and with the creation of PASOK we had no reason to run an organization just for women."

Parergon 7.2

After much friction over the practice of socialism and as a result of the deep divisions that appeared within the KKE after the emphýlios concerning questions of responsibility and accountability for the results of the war, the Party split in 1968. The KKE of the Interior (KKE-ES.) was formed by the majority of the members of the Central Committee, who had been living clandestinely in the country after 1949, whereas the remaining members of the Central Committee had been living as political refugees in Eastern Europe. Poulantzas reports that the split of the Party was, in effect, the final triumph of Soviet interventionist tactics: "the Soviets succeeding in splitting the Party in the way that [Santiago] Carillo [Solares] prevented them from doing so" in Spain (1976: 161). The split [*he diaspase*, as it is known in Greece] has been a particularly traumatic event and experience for members of both Parties. It solidified divisions that had been present within the Party and the movement from the beginning, certainly since 1936. It also further aligned the Party with and subordinated it to the Soviet Union, at a time when Communist parties in Europe had started questioning such dependency and developing a more flexible interpretation of the practice of Marxism than the dogmatic orthodoxy being produced by the Soviets. The only European Communist party that kept the same orientation toward the Soviet Union was the French.

Of course, historical conditions and disagreements about orthodoxy notwithstanding, it would be safe to say that what finally did the party in was the fact that it (its members) had lived in the shadows of legality, in a climate of fear and paranoia, since 1936. In many ways the plan of Maniadákis and Metaxas succeeded in the end. The Greek bibliography on the split, in the form of Party analyses and accounts by both parties, is vast and impossible to reproduce here.

Parergon 7.3

Haritos-Fatouros 2003: xx. Her work on the psychological parameters that make the production of a torturer possible remains unique and ground break-ing, primarily because it is based on a methodological and systematic study of the torturers, reverberating with Fanon 1963 and the theory of torture in Vidal-Naquet 1998. She interviewed five of the main torturers brought to trial by the Greek state after the fall of the junta. Thirty-six torturers, officers and soldiers of the armed forces, were brought to trial, including Odysseas Angelis (the vice-president of the republic under the junta), Anastasios Spanos, Nikolaos Hatzizeses, Theodoros Theophiloyiannakos, and Michalis Petrou. Many more escaped trial. The parameters she takes into account are almost exhaustive: the socioeconomic background of the family, educational status, whether the torturers had been mistreated as children, whether they had par-ticularly strict or harsh fathers, whether they had been orphaned early. There was nothing remarkable about their backgrounds, she concludes. They came from reasonably stable families; their parents had not been unreasonably strict; none of them had been abused or even mistreated as a child; they were not affluent, but they were not below the poverty line; no family was particu-larly involved with extreme political parties; and none of the five men could be classified as "authoritarian personalities." In short they exhibited none of the psychosocial pathologies that are usually associated with such cruelty. What Haritos-Fatouros does not note, however, is that none of them came from a Left-wing family. One could argue that the sample was biased, since men from Left-wing families would never have been able to produce a "clean" *certificat du civism*, but one has to wonder if a torturer from a Left-wing fam-ily could have been created within the specific environment in Greece.

There are some accounts of torture during the junta, primarily in the form of memoirs. There are also a couple of reports addressed to the international community, one being Dreyfus 1969, on the trial of members of the youth organization of KKE (Es.). Another documentation of the tortures is Becket 1970. Becket gives a partial list of people tortured by the junta to date, a list of some of the persons killed and where, and the names of torturers and places of torture. He also documents the methods of torture applied.

Parergon 7.4

As Diomédes's father said at the one-year memorial of Diomédes's death: "he was hit by two bullets, one through the heart, the other straight through the body, by bullets fired at close range, face to face, between 9:45 and 10:00 o'clock Friday night, November 16th, 1973, and was carried dead to the First Aid Station and then to the Morgue, where I eventually laid eyes on him chopped up for autopsy in the refrigerator. It was over the radio and then the television that I first learned my son was dead. . . . Several employees led me into the refrigeration chamber and drew out a shelf. On it lay Diomedes, dead. I found him handsome. . . . Here, I thought, is the thoroughbred offspring of my family, my only begotten son. One of those boys who exist in many, many families and are the backbones of nations—here, with a hole through his heart and the coroner's gash from neck to groin. I controlled my reflexes. Most of all I felt the need to speak to him. 'Diomedes, help me to be worthy of you'—the words came out on their own accord. Because it was not our habit to embrace each other, I kissed his hair. . . . Diomedes's funeral was arranged for Monday, November 19th. At the Cemetery many young people came up to me and slipped pieces of paper into my pockets . . . : 'I was with him . . .' 'Killed at this spot . . .' I was afraid of arrests, of the danger to these young. I found an excuse—the boy's mother in a state of collapse—and postponed the funeral at the last minute. . . . The day he was buried my anxiety was correct; three of his schoolmates were arrested and carried off first to Doirani Prison, then to the Security Police in Mesogheion Street." The eulogy would not have been published had it not been for the persistence of Kevin Andrews, who got it from Yiannis Komninos, Diomedes's father (Andrews 1980 [1974]: 300–301).

Parergon 8.1

In brutally schematic terms, Cyprus became a protectorate of Great Britain in 1878, when Great Britain bought the island from the Ottoman Empire at the Congress of Cyprus. The protectorate status ended when the Ottoman Empire attacked the Entente Powers in 1914, during the First World War. As a result, Great Britain annexed Cyprus and offered to cede it to Greece (fulfilling the hope of Greek Cypriots) in return for Greece's participation in the war on the side of the Allies and for launching an attack on Bulgaria. Greece refused. Great Britain declared Cyprus a Crown Colony in 1925 under an oppressive constitution that did not grant Cypriots the right of participation in the government. Resistance to the colonial administration of the island and expressed desire for unification with Greece started in earnest in 1931. During the Second World War, Cypriots joined the British army and fought alongside British soldiers. Pressure for unification mounted during the years after the war, until King George of Greece declared in 1945 that Cyprus desired unification and that Greece was willing to proceed. Great Britain refused. Resistance escalated, meeting with violence on the part of Great Britain, in measures ranging from raids to executions, assassinations, and outright murder of the *agonistes* ("fighters") as they came to be known.

George Grivas, a Cypriot and the ex-chief of "X" in Greece, returned to Cyprus in 1955 to organize the decolonization of the island, independence, and (eventually, although not openly stated at that point) union with Greece. To that end, on April 1, 1955, he formed the organization EOKA (Ethnike Organosis Kyprion Agoniston, National Organization of Cypriot Fighters), which carried out guerrilla operations against British targets, primarily tactical sabotage of British installations, assassinations, and general interruption of the flow of administration. In 1959, given the promise of independence as Great Britain bowed to international pressure, Grivas dismantled EOKA.

The independence of Cyprus was ratified in 1960, and Archbishop Makarios, who had headed the political branch of EOKA, was elected first president. He had abandoned unification with Greece as an objective. Greece and Turkey were placed as guarantors of the Cypriot Republic, keeping armed forces there at a ratio of three to two, while both *enosis* ("unification") and *taksim* ("partition") were prohibited.

Grivas returned to live in Greece. In 1971, with the support of the Greek junta, he returned to Cyprus to organize EOKA-B, with the explicit aim of effectuating union with Greece. While EOKA was accepted and approved by the majority of the Cypriot and Greek populations as an anticolonialist organization, EOKA-B was immediately recognized for what it was: a fascist organization that did not hesitate to terrorize civilians, persecute and assassinate socialists, and create a climate of intense fear for anyone supporting independence against *enosis*. The organization carried out two assassination attempts against President Makarios.

When Grivas died in January 1974, EOKA-B came under the direct power of Dimitris Ioannidis (who had overthrown Papadopoulos in the intrajunta coup of November 25, 1973, after the Polytechnic uprising). He installed Nikos Sampson as the new leader of the organization. On July 15, 1974, EOKA-B, in a plan approved by the junta and carried out by Sampson with the help of the Cypriot National Guard, organized a coup against Makarios, overthrew him, and installed Sampson as President of the Cypriot Republic.

This was considered a casus belli by Turkey and was quickly followed by an invasion of the island. Turkey occupied 38 percent of the island, displaced two hundred thousand Greek civilians, relocated sixty thousand Turkish residents from Anatolia to the northern part of the island, and thus forced an illegal partition.

Parergon 8.2

The case of 17N makes painfully apparent the deep anthropological aporia of disclosure, since it brings to the level of consciousness of the ethnographer (but also into the sphere of conscience, hence that of deontology and ethics) the fundamental epistemological difficulty of our discipline: To disclose or not? To tell or not? And if to tell, to tell what? Sherry Ortner, writing on the difficulties encountered by ethnographers working on resistance, warns against a number of pitfalls that need to be avoided in resistance studies, one being "sanitizing politics" rather than preserving the danger that politics poses (1995: 177), another being "thinning culture" rather than thickening description (181). These warnings aim to further problematize an area of ethnographic research that is already heavy with its own moral and ethical aporias.

Edward Said, in his thoughtful interrogation of anthropology as a discipline, opens this painful sore when he brings to our attention the tensions present in Richard Price's and James Scott's work on ritual in secret societies and peasant strategies of resistance, respectively. Price reflects thoroughly and genuinely on whether to publish details of secret ceremonies entrusted to him, and Scott discusses "foot-dragging" by peasants as a strategy of resistance to authority. Said comments appreciatively on the wrenching questions articulated by Price and Scott concerning "publication of information that gains its symbolic power in part by being secret" (Price quoted in Said 2000 [1988]: 310) or reading peasant comportment of "footdragging, lateness, unpredictability, non-communication" (Said about Scott, ibid.: 310) as passive resistance to the authority of a distant and demanding state. He identifies it as a *political* problem, which positions the anthropologist in front of the "theoretical paradoxes and aporias faced by anthropology" (ibid.).

I have wrestled over what to do with nonpublic information about 17N and have decided to address only what is publicly known and transmitted by and about the organization. For an account of the organization (prior to its dismantling) see Kassimeris 2001; see also the published communiqués by the organization in Anonymous 2002. For a view of 17N that reproduces the arguments made by the Greek state, the U.S. State Department, and Scotland Yard, see Papachelas and Telloglou 2002; for a critique of Papahelas and Telloglou, see Grivas 2003. See also Anonymous (n.d.b) for an attempt to show that Alexandros Yiotopoulos was not the leader of 17N and that his trial was predetermined and politically expedient, in an effort to effect his release.

Parergon 8.3

"Plamegate" probably would not have happened without this initial assassination by 17N. Plamegate was one of the many political scandals of the George W. Bush administration. Members of Bush's close circle (by all accounts Vice President Dick Cheney) disclosed the name of CIA agent Valerie Plame in retribution for Plame's husband, Richard Wilson, having exposed the administration's lies regarding the acquisition of yellowcake by Iraq from Nigeria to produce nuclear and chemical weapons.

The established opinion is that disclosing names of CIA agents was criminalized in the wake of the Welch assassination, given the publication of names of CIA agents in Agee 1975. This position has been claimed by the legal expert Floyd Abrams during an event at Columbia University. Abrams (or George H. W. Bush, for that matter) does not refer to Agee's 1975 book, which does not mention Welch's name at all, but rather to a list of names of CIA agents that Agee published in 1975, in an issue of the magazine that he had founded, *CounterSpy*. This did include Welch's name but had him still stationed in Peru (where he was stationed before his transfer to Athens). In his 1987 *On the Run* (132), Agee notes that Welch's name had already been published in 1968 in an East German book by Julius Mader, under the title *Who Is Who in the CIA*, and that it was published again in November 1975 in the Athens Anglophone daily *Athens News*. Agee further mentions that Welch's cover had been exposed a number of times before the *CounterSpy* article "by Mader in 1968, [the] Peruvians in 1974, and *CounterSpy* and the *Athens News* in '75—and who knows how many other times in between" (1975: 133), so that its inclusion in *CounterSpy* was not the first disclosure. On a certain level, all this discussion about the publication of Welch's name concerns only the CIA and the U.S. Intelligence Identities Protection Act introduced by then CIA Chief George H. W. Bush and passed into law. It has very little to do though with the Welch assassination.

A close look at the transcripts of the 17N trial shows that 17N itself stated very clearly that they never knew of (let alone looked at) *CounterSpy* or the *Athens News*. What 17N has said is that they followed their targets around and established their identity. The identity of Richard Welch was widely known in Greece in 1975 and did not require any special research, all the more so since the CIA used the same house as the CIA station chief's residence (Agee 1987: 133). What might not have been known in Greece at the time is that Welch had been stationed in Greece before, in 1951, before being transferred to Cyprus from 1960 to 1964, Guatemala from 1966 to 1967, Guyana from 1967 to 1969, and Peru from 1972 to 1973.

Parergon 8.4

In a different version, this segment has appeared in Panourgiá 2008a.

Parergon 8.5

The Sphinx's sexual indeterminacy is not the only example of sexual indeterminacy in the narrative. Equally confusing is Teiresias, who, although born male, was transformed into female when as a child he watched two snakes copulating at a crossroads on Mount Cithaeron. He killed the female with his shepherd's staff and was immediately transformed into a woman. Teiresias spent seven years as a woman, during which time she had intercourse with men, until she witnessed two snakes copulating again. She again killed one of them—this time the male—and was transformed back into a man. Teiresias was asked to testify during a quarrel between Zeus and Hera about which of the sexes experienced greater sexual pleasure. The woman, opined Teiresias, and not by a little but ninefold. An enraged Hera, determined to prove to Zeus that women had been shortchanged in their sexuality, blinded Teiresias, but Zeus gave him unique powers of divination and prophecy and seven times the lifespan of mortal men.

Loraux asks why Hera should be outraged by such an answer. She suggests that what enraged Hera was the fact that Teiresias's response (based on personal experience and not mere speculation) went against the position that Hera (as "guardian of the orthodoxy of marriage," in Loraux's words, 1997b: 10) held: namely, that women ought to be content with the level of sexual pleasure afforded to them within the context of marriage and reproduction. Loraux further argues that the response given by Teiresias indicates that women, by experiencing nine times the sexual pleasure that men do, pay more attention to the qualities of Aphrodite than to the demands of Hera. Loraux's reading of Teiresias is a highly unorthodox one. Rather than following the myth given above regarding the blinding of Teiresias, Loraux focuses on a version developed by the Hellenistic librarian and poet Callimachus. In Callimachus's version, Teiresias was blinded when as a child he accidentally glimpsed the naked body of Athena as she was undressing to bathe in a stream. In either case, Teiresias is blinded as a man for having witnessed the scene of the woman. Through Callimachus's reading, Loraux can place the soma of the woman within the man's field of vision as a dangerous object that will both deprive him of sight and grant the gift of seeing, thus complicating not only analyses of female sexuality in Athenian social life but also (and, perhaps, more importantly) the question of knowledge itself. See Loraux 1997b.

Parergon 8.6

The latest such undertaking was by Suzette Heald (1994). She engages in a critique of the Freudian theorization of the Oedipus complex by presenting alternative material from Gizu ritual male circumcision. Heald's gesture echoes Malinowski (who tried to prove that the complex presupposes a patrilineal descent system and foreclosed its possibility within a matrilineal one) and Anne Parsons (1970), who proposed triangulating Freud's and Malinowski's positions by presenting yet another complication in kinship structure, one that she observed in Naples. Unlike Freud's late-nineteenth-century Vienna, where the patrilineal family rested on the distance between the parents, on the one hand, and the son and the father, on the other, or Malinowski's early-twentieth-century Trobrianders, where the matrilineal family rested on ignorance about the father's contribution to reproduction and closeness to the mother's brother, Parsons shows that in working-class Naples kinship was experienced through the proximity between the mother and the son, and the distance between them and the son's wife. Melford Spiro tries to synthesize all existing anthropological responses to the Freudian universalist model by crediting Malinowski with having managed to teach "every (anthropological) schoolboy" that the Oedipus complex "is not found in the Trobriands and, by extrapolation, in other societies whose family structures do not conform to that of the Western type" (1982: 1). Allen Johnson and Douglass Price-Williams (1996) attempt an anthropological approach (which becomes a folkloristic enterprise) to the Freudian position on Oedipus by supplying folktales from around the world that deal with incest. The main problem with their approach is that, instead of looking at the myth of Oedipus as a culturally specific narrative and analyzing it as a cultural text, the two authors (the former an anthropologist/psychoanalyst and the latter a psychiatrist) take Freud's reading and look for other folktales around the world that refer to incest, thus reducing Oedipus to something more restrictive and narrow than even Freud had produced.

The most comprehensive account of Oedipus in anthropology is Paul 1985. For an astute review of the question of Oedipus in anthropology, see Weiner 1985.

WORKS CITED

Abu-Lughod, Lila. 2000. *Veiled Sentiments. Honor and Poetry in a Bedouin Society.* Los Angeles: University of California Press

Agamben, Giorgio. 1991. *Language and Death: The Place of Negativity.* Trans. Karen E. Pinkus, with Michael Hardt. Minneapolis: University of Minnesota Press.

———. 1998. *Homo Sacer: Sovereign Power and Bare Life.* Trans. Daniel Heller-Roazen. Stanford, Calif.: Stanford University Press.

———. 2000. *Means Without End: Notes on Politics.* Trans. Vincenzo Binetti and Cesare Casarino. Minneapolis: University of Minnesota Press.

———. 2002. *Remnants of Auschwitz: The Witness and the Archive.* Trans. Daniel Heller-Roazen. New York: Zone Books.

———. 2004. *The Open: Man and Animal.* Trans. Kevin Attell. Stanford, Calif.: Stanford University Press.

Agee, Philip. 1975. *CIA Diary: Inside the Company.* New York: Stonehill.

———. 1987. *On The Run.* Secaucus, N.J.: L. Stuart.

Agier, Michel. 2002. " Between War and City: Towards an Urban Anthropology of Refugee Camps." Trans. Richard Nice and Loïc Wacquant. *Ethnography* 3, no. 3: 317–41.

Ahl, Frederick. 1991. *Sophocles' Oedipus: Evidence and Self-Conviction.* Ithaca, N.Y.: Cornell University Press.

Alexander, Robert J. 1991. *International Trotskyism, 1929–1985: A Documented Analysis of the Movement.* Durham, N.C.: Duke University Press.

Alexandrou, Aris. 1974, *To Kivotio.* Athens: Kedros.

———. 1996. *The Mission Box.* Trans. Robert Christ. Athens: Kedros.

Alivizatos, Nicos C. 1981. "The 'Emergency Regime' and Civil Liberties, 1946–1949." In *Greece in the 1940s: A Nation in Crisis*, ed. John Iatrides, 220–29. Hanover: University Press of New England.

Anderson, David. 2005. *Histories of the Hanged: Britain's Dirty War in Kenya and the End of Empire.* London: Weidenfield and Nicholson.

Andrews, Kevin. 1980. *Greece in the Dark.* Amsterdam: Adolf M. Hakkert.

Andrikopoulou, Nelli. 2007. *To Taxidi tou* Mataroa, *1945: Ston Kathrefte tes Mnemes* (The Journey of the *Mataroa*, 1945: On the Mirror of Memory). Athens: Hestia.

Angelakopoulos, Yiorgos Har. 2005. *381 Camp: El-Ntampa* (Camp 381: Al Dab'a). Athens: privately published.

Anghelaki Rooke, Katerina. 2008. *The Scattered Papers of Penelope.* Ed. and Introd. Karen Van Dyck. London: Anvil Press.

Anidjar, Gil. 2003. *The Jew, the Arab: A History of the Enemy.* Stanford, Calif.: Stanford University Press.

———. 2004. "Terror Right." *The New Centennial Review* 4, no. 3 (Winter 2004): 35–69.

Anonymous. [N.d.]a. *Oi Prokyrexeis, 1975-2002: Ola ta Keimena tes Oraganoses* (The Communiques: All the Texts by the Organization). Athens: Kaktos.

———. [N.d.]b. *To Chroniko mias Proapofasismenes Enohes-Katadikes* (The Chronicle of a Predetermined Conviction of Guilt). Athens: Epitrope gia ten Apeleutherose tou Alekou Yiotopoulou.

———. 1937. *Ho Kommounismos sten Hellada* (Communism in Greece). Athens: Ekdoseis "Ethnikēs Hetaireias."

———. [September 1950]. *Yioúra: Matomene Vivlos* (Yioura: Bloodied Bible). Athens: Ekdotikos Oikos Gnoseis.

———. 1967. *Yioúra: Liberté pour la Grèce.* Paris: François Maspero.

———. 2002. *17N, Oi Prokeryxeis 1975–2002: Ola ta Keimena tes Organoses; 621 Onomata, Anafores, kai Stochoi* (17N, the Communiques 1975–2002: All the Texts of the Organization; 621 Names, References, and Targets). Athens: Kaktos.

———. 2003. *Makrónisos: Historikos Topos* (Makrónisos: Historical Place). Vols. 1 and 2. Athens: Syghrone Epoche.

———. 2006. *Makrónisos: Historikos Topos* (Makrónisos: Historical Place). Vol. 3. Athens: Syghrone Epoche.

Antonakes, Michael. 1996. "Christ, Kazantzakis, and Controversy in Greece." In *God's Struggler: Religion in the Writings of Nikos Kazantzakis,* ed. Daren Middleton and Peter Bien, 23–36. Macon, Ga.: Mercer University Press.

Apostolopoulou, Natalia. 1997. *Perephanes ki Adoulotes: (a) He Gynaika sten Antistase, (b) He Gynaika ston Metapeleftherotiko Diogmo (Phylakes-Exories), (c) He Gynaika ston D.S.E., (d) He Gynaika Homeros tes Juntas* (Proud and Free: [a] The Woman in Resistance, [b] The Woman in the Post-Liberation Persecution (Prisons-Exiles), [c] The Woman in the Democratic Army, [d] The Woman as Hostage of the Junta). Athens: Ekdoseis Entos.

Arendt, Hannah. 1963. *Eichmann in Jerusalem: A Report on the Banality of Evil.* New York: Viking Press.

———. 1968. *The Origins of Totalitarianism.* New York: Harcourt.

———. 1994. "Mankind and Terror." Speech, in German, for RIAS Radio University, March 23, 1953. Trans. Robert and Rita Kimber, in Arendt, *Essays in Understanding, 1930–1954: Formation, Exile, and Totalitarianism,* 297–306. New York: Schocken Books.

Arens, W. 1986. *The Original Sin: Incest and Its Meaning.* Oxford: Oxford University Press.

Aretxaga, Begoña. 2000. "A Fictional Reality: Paramilitary Death Squads and the Construction of State Terror in Spain." In *Death Squad: The Anthropology of State Terror,* ed. Jeffrey Sluka, 46–70. Philadelphia: University of Pennsylvania Press.

————. 2005. "The Intimacy of Violence." In *States of Terror: Begoña Aretxaga's Essays*, ed. Joseba Zulaika. Introd. Kay B. Warren. Reno: Center for Basque Studies, University of Nevada.

Argyriou, Alexandros. 2000. "He Pezographia Peri Makronisou kai Merika Parepomena" (Prose Writing about Makrónisos and Some Attendant Issues). In *Historiko Topio kai Historike Mneme: To Paradeigma tes Makronisou* (Historical Place and Historical Memory: The Paradigm of Makrónisos), ed. Stratis Bournazos and Tassos Sakellaropoulos, 245–59. Athens: Philistor.

Arlington National Cemetery Website. http://www.arlingtoncemetery.net/rwelch .htm, accessed October 3, 2006.

Asad, Talal. 2005. "Where Are the Margins of the State?" In *Anthropology in the Margins of the State*, ed. Veena Das and Deborah Poole, 279–89. Santa Fe: School of American Research Press.

Asdrahas, Spyros. 1985. "The Greek Archipelago: A Far Flung City." In *Maps and Map Makers of the Aegean*, ed. Vasilis Sphyroeras, Anna Avramea, and Spyros Asdrahas, trans. G. Cox and J. Solman, 235–48. Athens: Olkos Ltd.

Athanasiou, Athena. 2005. "Technologies of Humaness, Aporias of Biopolitcs, and the Cut Body of Humanity." *differences: A Journal of Feminist Cultural Studies* 14, no. 1: 125–62.

————. 2008. "Anamneses of a Pestilent Infant: The Enigma of Monstrosity, or Beyond Oedipus." In *Ethnographica Moralia: Experiments in Interpretive Anthropology*, ed. Neni Panourgiá and George E. Marcus, 77–96. New York: Fordham University Press.

Athanassatou, Yianna, Alkis Regos, and Serafim Seferiadis, eds. 1999. *He Diktatoria 1967–1974: Politikes Praktikes–Ideologikos Logos–Antistase* (Dictatorship 1967–1974: Political Practices–Ideological Discourse–Resistance). Athens: Kastaniotis.

Athanassiou, Kyriakos. 2003. *Yios Symmoritou* (Son of a Brigand). Athens: Ekdoseis Vivliorama.

Aust, Stefan. 1987. *The Baader-Meinhof Group: The Inside Story of a Phenomenon*. Trans. Anthea Bell. London: The Bodley Head.

Baerentzen, Lars, John Iatrides, and Ole Smith, eds. 1987. *Studies in the History of the Greek Civil War, 1945–1949*. Copenhagen: Museum Tusculanum.

Balta, Athanassia. 1989. "He EON: Propaganda kai Politike Diafotise" (EON: Propaganda and Political Indoctrination). In *Praktika A' Diethnous Synedriou Syghrones Historias, He Hellada 1936–1944: Diktatoria–Katohe–Antistase* (Proceedings of the First International Conference of Modern History, Greece 1936–1944: Dictatorship—Occupation—Resistance), ed. Hagen Fleischer and Nikos Svoronos, 70–76. Athens: Kastaniotes.

Banac, Ivo. 1989. *With Stalin Against Tito: Cominformist Splits in Yugoslav Communism*. Ithaca, N.Y.: Cornell University Press.

Bataille, Georges. 1993. *The Accursed Share, Volumes II and III*. Trans. Robert Hurley. New York: Zone Books.

Becket, James. 1970. *Barbarism in Greece: A Young American Lawyer's Inquiry into the Use of Torture in Contemporary Greece, with Case Histories and Documents*. Foreword by Senator Claiborne Pell. New York: Walker and Company.

Berger, Peter L. 1974. *Pyramids of Sacrifice: Political Ethics and Social Change.* London: Penguin.

Bermanzohn, Sally Avery, Mark Ungar and Kenton Worcester, eds. 2002.*Violence and Politics: Globalization's Paradox.* London: Routledge.

Besterman, Theodore, ed. 1968–1977. *Oeuvres complètes de Voltaire/Complete Works of Voltaire: Correspondence and Related Documents.* Geneva: Voltaire Foundation.

Biehl, João, and Torben Eskerod. 2005. *Vita: Life in a Zone of Social Abandonment.* Berkeley: University of California Press.

Bien, Peter. 2006. *Kazantzakis: Politics of the Spirit.* Vol. 1. Princeton, N.J.: Princeton University Press.

Bietak, Manfred. 1996. *Avaris, the Capital of the Hyksos: Recent Excavations at Tell el-Dab`a .* London: The British Museum Press.

Birtles, Bert. 1938. *Exiles in the Aegean: A Personal Narrative of Greek Politics and Travel.* Trans. Yiannis Kastanaras. Introd. David Close, Alkes Regos. Athens: Philistor.

Bloch, Maurice. 1998. *How We Think They Think: Anthropological Approaches to Cognition, Memory, and Literacy.* Boulder, Colo.: Westview Press.

Boon, James A. 1982. *Other Tribes, Other Scribes: Symbolic Anthropology in the Comparative Study of Cultures, Histories, Religions, and Texts.* Cambridge: Cambridge University Press.

————. 1990. *Affinities and Extremes: Crisscrossing the Bittersweet Ethnology of East Indies History, Hindu-Balinese Culture, and Indo-European Allure.* Chicago: University of Chicago Press.

Bournazos, Stratis. 2000. "To 'Mega Ethnikon Scholeion Makronisou' 1947–1950" (The "Great National School of Makrónisos," 1947–1950]. In *Historiko Topio kai Historike Mneme: To Paradeigma tes Makronisou* (Historical Place and Historical Memory: The Paradigm of Makrónisos), ed. Stratis Bournazos and Tassos Sakellaropoulos, 115–47. Athens: Philistor.

Bournazos, Stratis, and Tassos Sakellaropoulos, eds. 2000. *Historiko Topio kai Historike Mneme: To Paradeigma tes Makronisou.* (Historical Place and Historical Memory: The Paradigm of Makrónisos). Athens: Philistor.

Bowman, Steven. 2008. *The Agony of Greek Jews, 1940–1945.* Stanford, Calif.: Stanford University Press.

Braim, Paul. 2001. *The Will to Win: The Life of General James A. Van Fleet.* Annapolis, Md.: Naval Institute Press.

Brossat, Alain. 1996. *L'épreuve du désastre: Le XXe siècle et les camps.* Paris: Albin Michel.

Broussalis, Kostas. 1997. *He Peloponnesos sto Proto Antartiko, 1941–1945: Apeleftherotikos agonas kai emphylia diamache* (The Peloponnese During the First Andartiko, 1941–1945: Struggle for Liberation and Civil Dispute). Athens: Paraskenio.

Brown, Wendy. 2003. "Women's Studies Unbound: Revolution, Mourning, Politics." *Parallax* 9, no. 2: 3–16.

Butler, Judith. 1990. *Gender Trouble.* New York: Routledge.

————. 2004. *Precarious Life.* London: Verso.

Caillois, Roger. 1959. *Man and the Sacred.* Trans. Meyer Barash. Glencoe, Ill.: The Free Press.

Calotychos, Vangelis. 2000. "Writing Wrongs, (Re)Writing (Hi)story? 'Orthotita' and 'Ortho-graphia' in Thanassis Valtinos's *Orthokosta.*" *Gramma* 8: 151–67.

———. 2003. *Modern Greece: A Cultural Poetics.* New York: Berg.

Cameron, Alister. 1968. *The Identity of Oedipus the King: Five Essays on the 'Oedipus Tyrannus.'* New York: New York University Press.

Castoriadis, Cornelius. 1990. "Entretien d' Agora International avec Cornelius Castoriadis au Colloque de Cerisy." http://www.agorainternational.org/CCAIINT/pdf, accessed January 23, 2007.

Chege, Michael. 2004. "Mau Mau Rebellion Fifty Years On." Review Article. *African Affairs* (2004): 103, 123–36.

Chouliaras, Yiorgos. 2003. "Politismos kai Politike: Emphylios Polemos kai 'Politistike Anasygkrotese' sten Hellada" (Culture and Polics: Civil War and "Cultural Reconstruction" in Greece.) In *He Hellada '36–'49: Apo ten Diktatoria ston Emphylio, Tomes kai Syneheies* (Greece '36-'49: From the Dictatorship to the Civil War, Ruptures and Continuities), ed. Hagen Fleischer, 428–39. Athens: Kastaniotes.

Ciano, Galeazzo. 1947. *The Ciano Diaries 1939–1943: The Complete, Unabridged Diaries of Count Galeazzo Ciano, Italian Minister for Foreign Affairs, 1939–1943.* Ed. Hugh Gibson. Introd. Sumner Welles. Garden City, N.Y.: Garden City Publishing Co., Inc.

Clastres, Pierre. 1989. *Society Against the State: Essays in Political Anthropology.* Trans. Robert Hurley, with Abe Stein. New York: Zone Books.

Clifford, James. 1986. "On Ethnographic Allegory." In *Writing Culture: The Poetics and Politics of Ethnography*, ed George E. Marcus and James Clifford, 98–122. Berkeley: University of California Press.

Clogg, Richard, and George Yannopoulos, eds. 1972. *Greece under Military Rule.* New York: Basic Books.

Close, David. 1995. *The Origins of the Greek Civil War.* London: Longman.

Close, David, ed. 1995. *The Greek Civil War, 1943–1950: Studies of Polarization.* London: Routledge.

Clutterbuck, Richard L. 1963. "Communist Defeat in Malay—A Case Study." *Military Review* 43 (September): 63–78.

———. 1966. *Long War: Counterinsurgency in Malaya and Vietnam.* New York: Praeger.

———. 1973. *Revolution in Singapore and Malaya, 1945–1963.* London: Faber.

Collard, A. 1989. "Investigating Social Memory in a Greek Context." In *History and Ethnicity*, ed. Elizabeth Tonkin et al., 89–103. London: Routledge.

Cramer, Douglas. 2006. "Dachau 1945: The Souls of All Are Aflame." *The Self-Ruled Antiochian Orthodox Christian Archiodocese of North America.* http://www.antiochian.org/souls-aflame, accessed September 22, 2006.

Dalianis-Karambatzakis, Mando A. 1994. *Children in Turmoil During the Greek Civil War 1946–49: Today's Adults, A Longitudinal Study on Children Confined with Their Mothers in Prison.* Stockholm: Karolinska Institutet, University of Lund.

Daloukas, Manolis. 2005. *Hellenike Rock: Historia tes neanikes koultouras apo tin Genia tou Chaous Mehri ton Thanato tou Pavlos Sideropoulos. 1945–1990* (Greek Rock and Roll: The History of Youth Culture from the Generation of Chaos to the Death of Pavlos Sidiropoulos 1945–90). Athens: Agkyra.

Damanaki, Maria. 2006. "Enas Athlios Polemos" (A Vile War). *Eleutherotypia*, August 20, 2006, p. 31.

Damianakos, Stathis. 1987. *Paradosi Antarsias kai Laikos Politismos* (The Tradition of Mutiny in Folk Culture). Trans. G. Spanos. Athens: Plethron.

———. 2005. *Hethos kai Politismos ton Epikindynon Taxeon stin Hellada* (Ethos and Culture of the Dangerous Classes in Greece). Introd. Spyros Asthrahas. Athens: Plethron.

Danforth, Loring. 1984. "The Ideological Context for the Search for Continuities in Greek Culture." *Journal of Modern Greek Studies* 2, no. 1: 53–85.

Daniel, Valentine E. 1996. *Charred Lullabies: Chapters in an Anthropography of Violence*. Princeton, N.J.: Princeton University Press.

Darveris, Tasos. 2002. *Mia Historia tes Nyhtas: 1967–1974* (A Story/History of the Night: 1967–1974). Athens: Vivliopelagos.

Das, Veena, and Deborah Poole, eds. 2004. *Anthropology in the Margins of the State*. Santa Fe: School of American Research.

Deane, Philip (Gigantes). 1976. *I Should Have Died*. London: Hamish Hamilton.

Deleuze, Gilles. 2004. *Desert Islands and Other Texts, 1953–1974*. Los Angeles: Semiotext(e).

Deleuze, Gilles, and Félix Guattari. 1983. *Anti-Oedipus: Capitalism and Schizophrenia*. Preface by Michel Foucault. Minneapolis: University of Minnesota Press.

Derrida, Jacques. 1976. *Of Grammatology*. Trans. Gayatri Chakravortry Spivak. Baltimore: Johns Hopkins University Press.

———. 1987. *The Truth in Painting*. Trans. Geoffrey Bennington and Ian McLeod. Chicago: University of Chicago Press.

———. 1995. *On the Name*. Ed. Thomas Dutoit. Stanford, Calif.: Stanford University Press.

———. 2001. *The Work of Mourning*. Ed. Pascale-Anne Brault and Michael Naas. Chicago: University of Chicago Press.

———. 2005. *Rogues: Two Essays on Reason*. Trans. Pascale-Anne Brault and Michael Naas. Stanford, Calif.: Stanford University Press.

Despotopoulos, Konstantinos. 2006a. "Makrónisos, To Agos tis Hellenikes Politeias: Apomnemoneumata Konstantinou Despotopoulou gia ten Periodo apo ton Oktovrio 1947 eos ton Ioulio 1950" (Makrónisos, the Miasma of the Greek State: Memoirs of Konstantinos Despotopoulos of the Period October 1947 to July 1950). In *Makrónisos, Historikos Topos* (Makrónisos, A Historical Place), 3:23–42. Athens: Syghrone Epohe.

———. 2006b. *Anapoleseis, Volume B 1940–1960* (Memoirs 1940–1960). Athens: Papazisis.

DeWitte, General J. L. 1943. Letter of Transmittal to the Chief of Staff, U.S. Army, June 5, 1943, "Final Report: Japanese Evacuation from the West Coast 1942." Headquarters Western Defense Command and Fourth Army, Office of the Commanding General, Presidio of San Francisco, California, Chapters 1 and 2. Washington: U.S. Govt. Printing Office. The Virtual Museum of the City of San Francisco/Western Defense Command and Fourth Army Wartime Civil Control Administration. www.sfmuseum.net/hist9/evactxt.html. Accessed December 20, 2004.

Diamantis, Apostolos. 2007. "Homo Sapiens: Monoi me tis stahtes" (Homo Sapiens: Alone with the Ashes). *E* of *Eleftherotypia*, Sunday, September 2, pp. 21–22.

Dillon, Michael. 1997. "Otherwise than Self-Determination: The Mortal Freedom of *Oedipus Asphaleos.*" In *Violence, Identity, and Self-Determination*, ed. Hent de Vries and Samuel Weber, 162–86. Stanford, Calif.: Stanford University Press.

Djilas, Milovan. 1985. *Rise and Fall*. San Diego: Harcourt, Brace and Jovanovitch.

Doumanis, Nicholas. 1997. *Myth and Memory in the Mediterranean: Remembering Fascism's Empire*. New York: Palgrave MacMillan.

Doxiadis, Constantine A. 1946. *Ai Thysiai tes Hellados eis ton Defteron Pagkosmion Polemon* (The Sacrifices of Greece in the Second World War). Quadrilingual edition. Athens: Society for the Survival of the Greek People.

Dreyfus, Nicole. 1969. *Les étudiants grecs accusent*. Paris: Maspero.

Dubisch, Jill. 1995. *In a Different Place: Pilgrimage, Gender, and Politics of a Greek Island*. Princeton, N.J.: Princeton University Press.

Durkheim, Emile. 1952. *Suicide: A Study in Sociology*. Trans. John A. Spaulding and George Simpson. Ed. and Introd. George Simpson. London: Routledge and Kegan Paul Ltd.

Edmunds, Lowell. 1985. *Oedipus: The Ancient Legend and Its Later Analogues*. Baltimore: Johns Hopkins University Press.

———. 1991. "Oedipus in the Twentieth Century: Principal Dates." *Classical and Modern Literature: A Quarterly* 11, no. 4 (Summer): 317–24.

Edmunds, Lowell, and Alan Dundes, eds. 1995. *Oedipus: A Folklore Casebook*. Madison: University of Wisconsin Press.

Elephantis, Angelos. 2002 [1994]. "Orthokosta." In *Mas Peran ten Athena . . . Xanadiavazontas merika shmeia tis Historias 1941–1950* (They Took Athens from Us . . . Rereading Some Points in History 1941–1950), 281–94. Athens: Vivliorama.

———. 2008 [1997]. "He Oktovriani Epanastasi ki 'Emeis'" (The October Revolution and "Us"). In *Angelos Elephantis: Enthemata, Emvoliasmoi, kai Strateuse: Paremvaseis gia ten Aristera* (Angelos Elephantis: Insertions, Inocculations, and Commitment: Interventions on the Left), ed. Yiorgos Stathakis, 39–46. Athens: He Avge.

Elkins, Caroline. 2005. *Britain's Gulag: The Brutal End of Empire in Kenya*. London: Jonathan Cape.

Elytis, Odysseas. 1959. *Axion Hestin*. Athens: Ikaros.

Ethridge, Mark. 1947. *The Department of State Bulletin*. US/NA 501, BC-Greece/4-847. May.

Fanon, Frantz. 1963. *The Wretched of the Earth*. New York: Grove.

Farakos, Gregores, ed. 2000. *Dekemvres tou '44: Neotere erevna—Nees Proseggiseis* (December of 1944: Latest Research—New Approaches). Athens: Philistor.

Fernandez, James. 1972. "Persuasions and Performances: Of the Beast in Every Body . . . and the Metaphors of Everyman," *Daedalus*, special issue "Myth, Symbol, and Culture" (Winter): 39–61.

Finlay, George. 1871. *History of the Greek Revolution*. Edinburgh: William Blackwood.

Fleischer, Hagen. N.d. *To Stemma kai he Swastika: He Hellada tes Katohes kai tes Anti-*

stasis (The Crown and the Swastika: Greece in the Occupation and Resistance). Athens: Papazisis.

———. 1986. "He Nazistike Eikona gia tous (Neo-)Hellenes kai he Antimetopise tou Amahou Plethysmou apo tis Germanikes Arches Katohes" (The Nazi Impression on [Neo]Hellenes and the Treatment of the Civilian Population by the German Occupation Forces). In *Afieroma ston Niko Svorono* (Tribute to Nikos Svoronos), ed. Hagen Fleischer. Rethymnon: University Press.

———. 1995. "The National Liberation Front (EAM), 1941–1947: A Reassessment." In *Greece at the Crossroads: The Civil War and Its Legacy*, ed. J. Iatrides and Linda Wrigley, 49–89. State College: Pennsylvania State University Press.

———. 2003. "Strategikes Politismikes Dieisdyseis ton Megalon Dynameon kai Hellenikes Antidraseis, 1930–1960" (Strategies of Cultural Infiltration of the Great Powers and Greek Reactions, 1930–1960). In *He Hellada '36–'49: Apo ten Diktatoria ston Emphylio, Tomes kai Syneheies* (Greece '36–'49: From the Dictatorship to the Civil War, Ruptures and Continuities), 87–120. Athens: Kastaniotes.

Fleming, Amalia. 1973. *A Piece of Truth: The Full Story of Lady Fleming's Personal Encounter with Imprisonment and Torture at the Hands of the Greek Military Regime That Is Still Officially Supported by the United States.* Boston: Houghton Mifflin.

Flyvbjerg, Bent. 2001. *Making Social Science Matter: Why Social Inquiry Fails and How It Can Succeed Again.* Cambridge: Cambridge University Press.

Fortes, Mayer. 1983. *Oedipus and Job in West African Religion.* Cambridge: Cambridge University Press.

Fotopoulos, Mimis. 1984 [1964]. *El Ntampa Homeros ton Egglezon: Chroniko.* (Al Dab'a: Hostage of the English, a Chronicle). Athens: Syghrone Epoche. 3d ed.

Foucault, Michel. 1966. *Les Mots et les choses.* Paris: Gallimard.

———. 1974. "On Attica: An Interview." *Telos*, no. 19 (Spring): 154–62.

———. 1978. "About the Concept of the Dangerous Individual in Nineteenth-Century Legal Psychiatry." Trans. Carol Brown. *International Journal of Law and Psychiatry* 1, 1–18. Later published in a new translation by Alain Baudot and Jane Couchman with the title "The Dangerous Individual," in *Michel Foucault: Politics, Philosophy, Culture, Interviews and Other Writings 1977–1984*, ed. Lawrence D. Kritzman (London: Routledge, 1990), 125–52.

———. 1979. *Discipline and Punish: The Birth of the Prison.* Trans. Alan Sheridan. New York: Vintage.

———. 1985. *History of Sexuality. Vol. I: An Introduction.* New York: Vintage.

———. 2003. *Society Must Be Defended.* New York: Picador.

Fox, Richard. 1993. "The Virgin and the Godfather: Kinship Versus the State in Greek Tragedy and After." In *Anthropology and Literature*, ed. Paul Benson, introd. Edward M. Bruner, 107–51. Urbana: University of Illinois Press.

Franceschini, Alberto, and Giovanni Fasanella. 2004. *Che Cosa Sono le Brigate Rosse: Le radici, il presente—Chi erano veramente i brigatisti e perche continuano a uccidere* (What Sort of Thing Were the Red Brigades: The Origins, the Present—Who the Brigands Really Were and Why They Continue to Kill). Afterword by Justice Rosario Priore. Milan: RCS Libri S. A Greek edition by Nikos Kleitsikas includes a consideration of the Greek involvement (Nikaia: Ekdoseis "Direct").

Freud, Sigmund. 1965 [1900]. *The Interpretation of Dreams.* Trans. James Strachey. In The Standard Edition of the Complete Psychological Words of Sigmund Freud, 4:292–94. London: Hogarth.

———. 1967 [1939]. *Moses and Monotheism.* Trans. Katherine Jones. New York: Alfred A. Knopf.

———. 1973. *Introductory Lectures on Psychoanalysis.* Trans. James Strachey. Hammondsworth, Middlesex: Penguin.

———. 1985. *The Complete Letters of Sigmund Freud to Wilhelm Fliess, 1887–1904.* Ed. and trans. Jeffrey Moussaieff Masson. Cambridge: Harvard University Press.

———. 1989 [1913]. *Totem and Taboo: Some Points of Agreement Between the Mental Lives of Savages and Neurotics.* Ed. and trans. James Strachey. Introd. Peter Gay. New York: Norton.

Gadamer, Hans-Georg. 1980. "Idea and Reality in Plato's *Timaeus.*" In Gadamer, *Dialogue and Dialectic: Eight Hermeneutical Studies on Plato,* trans. and introd. P. Christopher Smith, 156–93. New Haven, Conn.: Yale University Press.

Geertz, Clifford. 2001. "Empowering Aristotle." *Science* 293, no. 6 (July): 53.

Geladopoulos, Philippos. 1994. *Makrónisos: He Megale Sfage, 29 Flevare–1 Marte 1948* (Makrónisos: The Great Massacre, February 29–March 1 1948). Athens: Ekdoseis Alpheios.

Georgatos, Dionysis. 2003. "To Syrma tes Apomonoses" (The Wire of Solitary Confinement). In *Makrónisos, Historikos Topos* (Makrónisos, A Historical Place), 2:44–47. Athens: Syghrone Epoche.

Gerolymatos, André. 2004. *Red Acropolis, Black Terror: The Greek Civil War and the Origins of Soviet-American Rivalry, 1943–1949.* New York: Basic Books.

Gheith, Jehanne. 2007. " 'I never talked': Enforced Silence, Non-Narrative Memory, and the Gulag." *Mortality* 12, no.2 (May 2007): 160–75.

Gide, André. 1950. *Two Legends: Oedipus and Theseus.* New York: Alfred A. Knopf.

Girard, René. 1979. *Violence and the Sacred.* Trans. Patrick Gregory. Baltimore: Johns Hopkins University Press.

———. 2004. *Oedipus Unbound: Selected Writings on Rivalry and Desire.* Ed. and introd. Mark R. Anspach. Stanford, Calif.: Stanford University Press.

Gitlin, Todd. 1967. "Counter-Insurgency: Myth and Reality in Greece." In *Containment and Revolution: Western Policy Towards Social Revolution, 1917 to Vietnam,* ed. David Horowitz, preface by Bertrand Russell, 140–82. London: Anthony Blond.

Goldhill, Simon. 1984. "Exegesis: Oedipus (R)ex." *Arethusa* 17, no. 2: 177–201.

Gourgouris, Stathis. 1994. "Review of Mimika Kranaki, *Philellenes.*" *Planodion* 21 (December): 591–95.

———. 1996. *Dream Nation: Enlightenment, Colonization, and the Institution of Modern Greece.* Stanford, Calif.: Stanford University Press.

———. 2006. "Today—Communism and Poetry Without Compromises." Unpublished ms. In the possession of the author.

Goux, Jean-Joseph. 1993. *Oedipus, Philosopher.* Trans. Catherine Porter. Stanford, Calif.: Stanford University Press.

Greenberg, Mitchell. 1994. *Canonical States, Canonical Stages: Oedipus, Othering, and Seventeenth-Century Drama.* Minneapolis: University of Minnesota Press.

Grigoriadis, Foivos N. N.d. *To Antartiko: ELAS, EDES, EKKA* (The Brigandry: ELAS, EDES, EKKA). Athens: Ekdoseis K. H. Kamarinopoulou.

Grivas, Kleanthes. 2003. *Anti-Fakellos 17N: He Tromokratia sten Hellada—Kritike stous A. Papachela kai T. Telloglou* (Anti-File 17N: Terrorism in Greece—A Critique of A. Papachelas and T. Telloglou). Athens: Kaktos.

Grosz, Elizabeth. 1994. *Volatile Bodies: Toward a Corporeal Feminism.* Bloomington: Indiana University Press.

Goffman, Erving. 1963. *Stigma: Notes on the Management of Spoiled Identity.* Englewood Cliffs, N.J.: Prentice-Hall.

Hamilakis, Yiannis. 2002. " 'The Other Parthenon': Antiquity and National Memory on Makrónisos." In special issue "Greek Worlds, Ancient and Modern," ed. Gonda Van Steen, *Journal of Modern Greek Studies* 20, no. 2: 307–39.

Haritos-Fatouros, Mika. 2003. *The Psychological Origins of Institutionalized Torture.* London: Routledge.

Hart, Janet. 1996. *New Voices in the Nation: Women and the Greek Resistance.* Ithaca, N.Y.: Cornell University Press.

———. 1999. "Tales from the Walled City: Aesthetics of Political Prison Culture in Post-War Greece." *Comparative Studies in Society and History* 41, no. 3: 482–509.

Hay, John. 1978. *Oedipus Tyrannus: Lame Knowledge and the Homosporic Womb.* Washington: University Press of America.

Heald, Suzette. 1994. "Every Man a Hero: Oedipal Names in Gizu Circumcision." In *Anthropology and Psychoanalysis: An Encounter Through Culture,* ed. Suzette Heald and Ariane Deluz, 184–210. London: Routledge.

Heald, Suzette, and Ariane Deluz, eds. 1994. *Anthropology and Psychoanalysis: An Encounter Through Culture.* London: Routledge.

Herzfeld, Michael. 1982a. *Ours Once More: Folklore, Ideology, and the Making of Modern Greece.* Austin: University of Texas Press.

———. 1982b. "When Exceptions Define the Rules: Greek Baptismal Names and the Negotiation of Identity." *Journal of Anthropological Research* 38, no. 3 (Fall): 289–302.

———. 1998. *Portrait of a Greek Imagination: An Ethnographic Biography of Andreas Nenedakis.* Chicago: University of Chicago Press.

Hionidou, Violetta. 2004. "Black Market, Hyperinflation, and Hunger: Greece 1941–1944." *Food and Foodways* 12: 81–106.

———. 2006. *Famine and Death in Occupied Greece, 1941–1944.* Cambridge: Cambridge Univesrity Press.

Hobsbawm, Eric. 1965. *Primitive Rebels: Studies in Archaic Forms of Social Movement in the Nineteenth and Twentieh Centuries.* New York: W. W. Norton.

Hondros, John. 1983. *Occupation and Resistance: The Greek Agony, 1941–1944.* New York: Pella.

Horkheimer, Max, and Theodor W. Adorno. 1990. *Dialectic of Enlightenment.* Trans. John Cumming. New York: Continuum Books.

Hubert, Henri, and Marcel Mauss. 1964 [1898]. *Sacrifice: Its Nature and Function.* Trans. W. D. Halls. Foreword by E. E. Evans-Pritchard. Chicago: University of Chicago Press.

Humphreys, S. C. 1978. *Anthropology and the Greeks*. London: Routledge & Kegan Paul.

Iatrides, John. 1972. *Revolt in Athens: The Greek Communist "Second Round," 1944–1945*. Princeton, N.J.: Princeton University Press.

———. 1980. *Ambassador MacVeagh Reports: Greece, 1933–1947*. Princeton, N.J.: Princeton University Press.

———. 2005. "Revolution or Self-Defense? Communist Goals, Strategy, and Tactics in the Greek Civil War." *Journal of Cold War Studies* 7, no. 3 (Summer): 3–33.

Iatrides, John, ed. 1981. *Greece in the 1940s: A Nation in Crisis*. Hanover, N.H.: University Press of New England.

Iatrides, John, and Linda Wrigley, eds. 1995. *Greece at the Crossroads: The Civil War and Its Legacy*. State College: Pennsylvania State University Press.

Iliou, Philippos. 2005. *Ho Hellenikos Emfylios Polemos: He Embloke tou KKE* (The Greek Civil War: The Involvement of the Communist Party of Greece). Athens: Themelio.

Iosef, Andreas. 2006. "Den Skotôneis Anthrôpo gia tis Politikés tou Pepoithêseis" (You Don't Kill a Human for His Political Beliefs). In *Martyries gia ton Emphýlio kai ten Hellēnikê Aristerá* (Witness Accounts of the Civil War and the Greek Left), ed. Stelios Kouloglou, 285–89. Athens: Estia.

Jambresic Kirin, Renata. 2004. "The Retraumatization of the 1948 Communist Purges in Yugoslav Literary Culture." In *History of the Literary Cultures of East-Central Europe: Junctures and Disjunctures in the Nineteenth and Twentieth Centuries*, vol. 1, ed. Marcel Cornis-Pope and John Neubauer, 124–32. Amsterdam: John Benjamins.

Jarzombeck, Mark. 1992. "Ready-Made Traces in the Sand: The Sphinx, the Chimaira, and Other Discontents in the Practice of Theory." *Assemblage*, no. 19 (December): 72–95.

Johnson, Allen W., and Douglass Price-Williams. 1996. *Oedipus Ubiquitous: The Family Complex in World Folk Literature*. Stanford, Calif.: Stanford University Press.

Jones, Ernest. 1954 [1949]. *Hamlet and Oedipus: A Classic Study in the Psychoanalysis of Literature*. New York: Doubleday.

Judt, Tony. 2005. *Postwar: A History of Europe since 1945*. New York: Penguin.

Kalfas, Vassilis. 1995. *Platon, Timaeus: Introduction, Translation, Commentary*. Athens: Polis.

Kalivretakis, Leonidas. 2006. "Georgios Papadopoulos: Tagmata Asfaleias kai 'X'" (Georgios Papadopoulos: Security Batallions and "X"). Special issue dedicated to April 21, 1967, *Archeiotaxio*, May 2006: 105–47.

———. 2007. "Heptaetia: Sovaro Elleimma sten Historike Ereuna" (The Dictatorship: Serious Omission in the Historical Research). *Ta Nea (Vivliodromio)*, April 21, 2007.

Kalyvas, Andreas. 2005. "The Sovereign Weaver: Beyond the Camp." In *Politics, Metaphysics, and Death*, ed. Andrew Norris, 107–35. Durham, N.C.: Duke University Press.

Kalyvas, Stathis. 2003. "Poioi Fovountai ten Epistemonike Ereuna tes Historias mas?" (Who Are Those Who Are Afraid of the Scientific Study of Our History?) *Vivliodromio Ta Nea*, November 8, 2003, p. 31.

———. 2006. *The Logic of Violence in Civil War*. Cambridge: Cambridge University Press.

Kalyvas, Stathis, and Nikos Marantzidis. 2004. "Nees Taseis ste Melete tou Emphyliou Polemou" (New Trends in the Study of the Civil War) *Vivliodromio Ta Nea*, April 20, 2004, p. 10.

Kantzia, Emmanouela. 2003. "Literature as Historiography: The Boxful of Guilt." In *Modern Greek Literature*, ed. Gregory Nagy and Anna Stavrakopoulou, 115–32. London: Routledge.

Karagiannakidis, Thymios. N.d. "Selides Anamneseon" (Pages of Memories). Unpublished memoir.

Karakasidou, Anastasia. 1997. *Fields of Wheat, Hills of Blood: Passages to Nationhood in Greek Macedonia, 1870–1990*. Chicago: University of Chicago Press.

Karliaftis, Loukas. 1991. "From Acronauplia to Nezero: Greek Trotskyism from the Unification Conference to the Executions." *Revolutionary History* 3, no.3 (Spring): 24–37.

Karousos, Tzavalás. 1974. *Yáros: He Prosopike Empeiria Enos Exoristou* (Yaros: The Personal Experience of an Exile). Athens: Pleias.

Karrer, Alexis. 2004. *El-Ntampa He Historia Mias Homerias Hexenta Hronia Meta* (Al-Dab`a the History of a Captivity: Sixty Years Later). Athens: Entos.

Kassimeris, George. 2001. *Europe's Last Red Terrorists: The Revolutionary Organization 17 November*. London: Hurst.

Katsaros, Stergios. 2000. *Ego o Provokatoras, o Tromokrates: He Goeteia tes Vias* (I the Provocator, the Terrorist: The Seduction of Violence). Athens: Mavre Lista.

Kazantzakis, Nikos. 1965. *Hoi Aderphophades* (The Fratricides). Athens: Ekdoseis El. Kazantzaki.

Kenna, Margaret E. 1991. "The Social Organization of Exile: The Everyday Life of Political Exiles in the Cyclades in the 1930s." *Journal of Modern Greek Studies* 9, no. 1: 63–81.

———. 2001. *The Social Organization of Exile: Greek Political Prisoners in the 1930s*. Amsterdam: Harwood Academic.

———. 2003. "Recollecting Difference: Archive-Marxists and Old Calendrists in an Exile Community." In *The Usable Past: Greek Metahistories*, ed. K. S. Brown and Yannis Hamilakis, 105–29. Lanham: Lexington Books.

Kenyata, Jomo. 1971. *Suffering Without Bitterness: The Founding of the Kenyan Nation*. [Nairobi]: East African Publishing House.

Kerényi, Karl, and James Hillman. 1995. *Oedipus Variations: Studies in Literature and Psychoanalysis*. Woodstock: Spring Publications.

Koronios, Kostas. 2001. *Anamneseis apo ten Makroniso* (Memories from Makrónisos). Athens: Ekdoseis Didymoi.

Kostopoulos, Tasos. 2005. *He Aftolokrimene Mneme: Ta Tagmata Asfaleias kai he Metapolemike Ethnofofrosyne* (Self-Censored Memory: The Security Battalions and Postwar National Consciousness). Athens: Philistor.

Kouloglou, Stelios. 2006. Interview with Nikos Pharmakes for the Greek Public

Television Station (ERT) Series *Reportage Horis Synora* (Reportage Without Borders), October 2.

Kouloglou, Stelios, ed. 2006. *Martyries gia ton Emphýlio kai ten Hellēnikê Aristerá* (Witness Accounts of the Civil War and the Greek Left). Athens: Estia.

Koulouris, Nikos. 2000. *Hellenike Vivliographia tou Emphyliou Polemou 1945–1949: Autotele Demosieumata* (Greek Bibliography on the Civil War 1945–1949: Monographs). Athens: Philhistor.

Kranaki, Mimika. 1950. "Journal d'exil." *Tempes Modernes.* July, 326–40.

———. 1992. *Philhellenes*. Athens: Ikaros.

———. 2004. *Autographia* (Autography). Athens: Ikaros.

———. 2007. *'Mataroa' se Dyo Fones: Selides Xenitias*. (*Mataroa* in Two Voices: Pages of Emigration). Athens: Benaki Museum.

Kristeva, Julia. 1982. *Powers of Horror: An Essay on Abjection*. Trans. Leon S. Roudiez. New York: Columbia University Press.

Lacoue-Labarthe, Philippe. 1978. "Mimesis and Truth: Review Essay of René Girard, 'Système du Délire' and *La Violence et le Sacré*." *Diacritics*, March 1978: 9–23.

Lambropoulos, Vassilis. 1988. *Literature as National Institution: Studies in the Politics of Modern Greek Criticism*. Princeton, N.J.: Princeton University Press.

———. 2006. "Farewell to the Revolution" Unpublished ms. In the possession of the author.

Lambropoulou, Demetra. 1999. *Graphontas apo ten Phylake: Opseis tes Hypokeimenikotetas ton Politikon Kratoumenon 1947–1960* (Writing from Prison: Facets of Subjectivity of the Political Prisoners 1947–1960). Athens: Nefeli Historia.

Lancaster, Osbert. 1949. *Classical Landscape with Figures*. Boston: Houghton Mifflin.

Laqueur, Walter, ed. 2004. *Voices of Terror: Manifestos, Writings and Manuals of Al Qaeda, Hamas, and Other Terrorists from Around the World and Throughout the Ages*. New York: Reed Press.

Lear, Jonathan. 1999. *Open Minded: Working Out the Logic of the Soul*. Cambridge: Harvard University Press.

Lefort, Claude. 1986. *The Political Forms of Modern Society: Bureaucracy, Democracy, Totalitarianism*. Cambridge: Polity Press.

Leontis, Artemis. 1995. *Topographies of Hellenism: Mapping the Homeland*. Ithaca, N.Y.: Cornell University Press.

Lévi-Strauss, Claude. 1963. *Structural Anthropology*. Trans. Claire Jacobson and Brooke Grundfest Schoepf. New York: Basic Books.

———. 1983. *The Way of the Masks*. 2d ed. Trans. S. Modelski. London: Jonathan Cape.

Lewey, Guenter. 2000. *The Nazi Persecution of the Gypsies*. Oxford: Oxford University Press.

Liakos, Antonis, 1988. *He Emphanise ton Neanikon Organoseon: To Paradeigma tis Thessalonikis* (The Emergence of Youth Organizations: The Paradigm of Thessaloniki). Athens: Lotos.

———. 2005. *Pos Stochastekan To Ethnos Aftoi Pou Ethelan Na Allaxoun Ton Kosmo?* (How Did Those Who Wanted to Change the World Think about the Nation?). Athens: Polis.

———. 2006. "To Hameno Rendez-vous" (The Lost Rendezvous). *Archeiotaxio* 8 (May): 47–49.

Liapés, Vaios. 2003. *Agnostos Theos: Horia tes anthropines gnoses stous Prosokratikous kai ston* Oidipoda Tyranno (Unknown God: The Limits of human knowledge in the Pre-Socratics and *Oedipus Tyrannus*). Athens: Ekdoseis Stigme.

Linardatos, Spyros. 1965. *Pos Eftasame stin 4e Avgoustou* (How We Arrived at August 4). Athens: Themelio.

———. 1966. *He 4e Avgoustou* ([The Regime of] August 4). Athens: Themelio.

Lincoln, Bruce. 1991. *Death, War, and Sacrifice: Studies in Ideology and Practice*. Foreword by Wendy Doniger. Chicago: University of Chicago Press.

Lloyd, David, and Paul Thomas. 1998. *Culture and the State*. New York: Routledge.

Loizos, Peter. 1996. "Perspectives from an Earlier War." In *War, Exile, Everyday Life: Cultural Perspectives*, ed. Renata Jambrešic Kirin and Maja Povrazanovic, 293–303. Zagreb: Institute of Ethnology and Folklore Research.

Longinovic, Tommislav Z., et al. 2004. "1948. Introduction: The Culture of Revolutionary Terror." In *History of the Literary Cultures of East-Central Europe: Junctures and Disjunctures in the Nineteenth and Twentieth Centuries*, ed. Marcel Cornis-Pope and John Neubauer, 107–32. Amsterdam: John Benjamins.

Loraux, Nicole. 1986 [1981]. *The Invention of Athens: The Funeral Oration in the Classical City*. Trans. Allan Sheridan. Cambridge: Harvard University Press.

———. 1997a. "La guerre dans la famille." *CLIO* 5: 21–62.

———. 1997b. *The Experiences of Tiresias: The Feminine and the Greek Man*. Trans. Paula Wissing. Princeton, N.J.: Princeton University Press.

———. 2006. *The Divided City: On Memory and Forgetting in Ancient Athens*. Trans. Corinne Pache, with Jeff Fort. New York: Zone.

Lotringer, Sylvère, and Christian Marazzi, eds. 1980. *Autonomia: Post-Political Politics*. Special issue, *Semiotext(e)* 3, no. 3.

Lukic, Dejan. 2007. "Inscriptions of the Apparitional: Interrogating Ex-Yugoslavia." Ph. D. dissertation, Department of Anthropology, Columbia University.

Lymberiou, Theodoros M. 2005. *To Kommounistiko Kinema sten Hellada*. Tomos A (The Communist Movement in Greece. Vol. A). Athens: Papazeses.

Lyotard, Jean-François. 1977. "Jewish Oedipus." *Genre* 10: 395–411.

McClintock, Michael. 1992. *Instruments of Statecraft: U.S. Guerrilla Warfare, Counterinsurgency, and Counterterrorism, 1940–1990*. New York: Pantheon.

McNeill, William. 1947. *The Greek Dilemma: War and Aftermath*. Philadelphia: J. B. Lippincott.

Mahaira, Eleni. 1987. *He Neolaia tes 4es Augoustou* (The Youth of August 4). Athens: IAEN.

Mahairas, Evaggelos. 1999. *Piso apo to Galanoleuko Parapetasma: Makrónisos, Yioúra, ki alla Katerga* (Behind the Blue-and-White Screens: Makrónisos, Yioúra, and Other Dungeons). Ed. Aggelos Sideratos. Introd. Giorgos Petropoulos. Athens: Ekdoseis Proskenio.

Makryiannis, Ioannes. 1972. *Apomnemoneumata* (Memoirs). Introd. Tassos Vournas. Athens: Tolides.

Malinowski, Bronislaw. 1965 [1927]. *Sex and Repression in Savage Society*. New York: Meridian Books.

Malkki, Liisa. 1995. *Purity and Exile: Violence, Memory, and National Cosmology among Hutu Refugees in Tanzania.* Chicago: University of Chicago Press.

Mamdani, Mahmood. 2006. "Mau Mau: Understanding Counter-Insurgency." Review article of Caroline Elkins, *Imperial Reckoning: The Untold Story of Britain's Gulag in Kenya,* and David Anderson, *Histories of the Hanged: The Dirty War in Kenya and the End of Empire. Africa Review of Books/Revue africaine des Livres,* March: 7–9.

Mangakis, George-Alexander. 1997 [1972]. "Letter to Europeans." In *An Embarrassment of Tyrannies: Twenty-five Years of Index on Censorship,* ed. W. L. Webb and Rose Bell, 25–38. London: Victor Gollancz.

Manousos, Demetres. 2005. *Yioúra: "To Aparto Kastro" Ston Emfylio kai te Junta* (Yioúra: The Unconquered Castle During the Civil War and the Junta). Athens: Entos.

Manthoulis, Roveros. 2006. *To Hemerologio tou Emfyliou Dichasmou 1900–1974: Xenes Epemvaseis, Diktatories, Polemoi, kai Emphylioi Polemoi* (The Diary of the Emphýlios Schism 1900–1974: Foreign Interventions, Dictatorships, Wars, and Civil Wars). Introd. Stelios Kouloglou. Athens: Kastaniotes.

Maratos, Georges. 2003. *Apagoreutikon Apoplou* (Sailing Ban). Athens: Hestia.

———. 2004. *Ho Kokkinos Stavros* (The Red Cross). Athens: Hestia.

Marcuse, Harold. 2001. *Legacies of Dachau: Uses and Abuses of a Concentration Camp, 1933–2001.* Cambridge: Cambridge University Press.

Margaris, Nikos. 1966. *Historia tes Makronisou* (History of Makrónisos). Athens: Dorikos.

Margarites, Giorgos. 2001. *Historia tou Hellenikou Emfyliou Polemou 1946–1949* (History of the Greek Civil War 1946–1949). 2 vols. Athens: Ekdoseis Vivliorama.

Marketos, Spyros. 2006. *Pos Filisa ton Mussolini: Ta Prota Vimata tou Hellenikou Fasismou* Tomos 1 (How I Kissed Mussolini: The First Steps of Greek Fascism). Vol. 1. Athens: Vivliorama.

Markovski, Venko. 1984. *Goli Otok, The Island of Death: A Diary in Letters.* Boulder, Colo.: Social Science Monographs.

Marx, Karl. 1999 [1846]. *On Suicide.* Ed. and introd. Eric. A. Plaut and Kevin Anderson. Trans. Eric. A. Plaut, Gabrielle Edgcomb, and Kevin Anderson. Evanston, Ill.: Northwestern University Press.

Matossian, Nouritza. 1986. *Iannis Xenakis.* London: Kahn and Averill.

Mazower, Mark. 1993. *Inside Hitler's Greece: The Experience of Occupation, 1941–44.* New Haven, Conn.: Yale University Press.

———. 1997. "Policing the Anti-Communist State I: Greece, 1922–1974." In *The Policing of Politics in the Twentieth Century: Historical Perspectives,* ed. Mark Mazower, 129–51. New York: Berghan Books.

Mazower, Mark, ed. 2000. *After the War Was Over: Reconstructing the Family, Nation, and State in Greece, 1943–1960.* Princeton, N.J.: Princeton University Press.

Mbembe, Achille. 2003. "Necropolitics." Trans. Libby Meintjes. *Public Culture* 15, no. 1: 11–40.

Methenites, Stamates Dem. [2007]. *To Markopoulo ton Mesogeion: Hodoiporiko stous Aiones* (Markopoulo of Mesogeia: Itinerary Through the Centuries). Markopoulo: Nikos Lymberis.

Middleton, Daren, and Peter Bien, eds. 1996. *God's Struggler: Religion in the Writings of Nikos Kazantzakis*. Macon, Ga.: Mercer University Press.

Mikedakis, Emmanouela. 2007. "Renouncing the Recent Past, 'Revolutionising' the Present and 'Resurrecting' the Distant Past: Lexical and Figurative Representations in the Political Speeches of Georgios Papadopoulos (1967–1973)." Ph. D. dissertation, University of New South Wales.

Minh-ha, Trinh T. 1989. *Woman, Native, Other: Writing Postcoloniality and Feminism*. Bloomington: Indiana University Press.

Mitsotakis, Konstantinos. 2008. Speech in honor of Leonidas Kyrkos. *Eleutherotypia*, April 18.

Nachmani, Anikam. 1990. *International Intervention in the Greek Civil War: The United Nations Special Committee on the Balkans, 1947–1952*. New York: Praeger.

Nancy, Jean-Luc. 2000. *Being Singular Plural*. Trans. Robert D. Richardson and Anne E. O' Byrne. Stanford, Calif.: Stanford University Press.

NARA / ALIC / Japanese Relocation and Internment During World War II / Documents and Photographs Related to Japanese Relocation During World War II. http://www.archives.gov/research_room/alic/reference_desk/military/japanese-internement. html, accessed December 24, 2004. National Archives / Archives Library Information.

National Security Archive. 2008. "New Kissinger 'Telcons' Reveal Chile Plotting at Highest Levels of U.S. Government." *National Security Archive Electronic Briefing Book No 255*. Posted September 10, 2008, at http://www.gwu.edu/nsarchiv/ NSAEBB/NSAEBB255/index.htm, accessed September 11, 2008.

Neilson, Brett. 2004. "*Potenza Nuda?* Sovereignty, Biopolitcs, Capitalism." *Contretemps* 5: 63–77.

Nenedakis, Andreas. 1964. *Apagoreuetai: To Hemerologio tes Yiouras* (It Is Forbidden: The Yioúra Diary). Athens: Themelio.

Nikolakopoulos, Elias. 2007. "Ho Hartes ton Eklogon: Adeles hoi epiptoseis son pyrkagion" (The Electoral Map: The Repercussions from the Forest Fires Are Silent). *Ta Nea*, Saturday, September 1–2, 2007: 20.

Noutsos, Panayiotis. 1992. *He Sosialistikē Sképsē stēn Helláda apo to 1875 ōs to 1974*. Tomos 2: *Idées kai Kiniseis yia tēn Oikonomikē kai Politikē Orgánōsē tēs Ergatikēs Táxēs, 1907–1925* (Socialist Thought in Greece from 1875 to 1974. Vol. 2: Ideas and Actions for the Economic and Political Organization of the Working Class, 1907–1925). Athens: Gnosi.

———. 1993. *He Sosialistikē Sképsē stēn Helláda apo to 1875 ōs to 1974*. Tomos 3: *He Hedraiosē tou Marxismou-Leninismou kai hoi Apoklinouses he hoi Heterogeneis Epexergasies 1926–1955* (Socialist Thought in Greece from 1875 to 1974. Vol. 3: The Establishment of Marxism-Leninism and Variant or Heterogeneous Elaborations, 1926–55). Athens: Gnosi.

Oikonomakos, Nikos. 2006. *Sevah o aristeros: Anamneseis hexi dekaetion, 1930–1990* (Sinbad the Leftist: Recollections of Six Decades, 1930–90). Athens: Hestia.

Oikonomides, Phoevos. 2005. *O Dekemvres tou '44 kai he diethnes semasia tou* (December 1944 and Its International Significance). Athens: Orpheas.

Ogot, Bethwell A. 2005. "Review Article of David Anderson and Caroline Elkins,

Britain's Gulag: The Brutal End of Empire in Kenya." Journal of African History 46: 493–505.

Ortner, Sherry. 1995. "Resistance and the Problem of Ethnographic Refusal." *Comparative Studies in Society and History* 37, no. 1: 173–93.

Panourgiá, Neni. 1995. *Fragments of Death, Fables of Identity: An Athenian Anthropography.* Madison: University of Wisconsin Press.

———. 2001. "Review of Bastéa, *The Creation of Athens: Planning the Myth.*" *Journal of Modern Greek Studies* 17, no. 4 (October): 293–99.

———. 2002. "Interview with Clifford Geertz." *Anthropological Theory* 2 (December): 421–31.

———. 2004a. "Colonizing the Ideal: Neo-classical Articulations and European Modernities." *Angelaki* 9, no 2: 166–80.

———. 2004b. "Ho Hagios Velouhiotes kai ta Tagmata Asphaleias" (Saint Velouchiotis and the Security Battalions). *Vivliodromio,* "Dialogos gia ten Historia" (Dialogue on History) series. *Ta Nea.* Saturday-Sunday, October 2, 10. Rept. in *Dialogos gia ten Historia: 18* Eidikoi Syzetoun gia ten Via ston Helleniko Emphylio (Dialogue on History: 18 Experts Discuss the Question of Violence in the Greek Civil War) *Ta Nea,* December, 34–35.

———. 2008a. "Fragments of Oedipus: Anthropology at the Edges of History." In *Ethnographica Moralia: Experiments in Interpretive Anthropology,* ed. Neni Panourgiá and George E. Marcus, 97–112. New York: Fordham University Press.

———. 2008b. "Desert Islands: Ransom of Humanity." *Public Culture* 20, no. 2: 395–421.

———. 2008c. "Review of Stathis Kalyvas, *The Logic of Violence in Civil War.*" *Historein* (Fall): 192–97.

Papachelas, Alexis, and Tassos Telloglou. 2002. *Fakelos 17N* (17N File). Athens: Hestia.

Papadimitriou, Despoina. 2006. *Apo ton Lao ton Nomimofronon ston Ethnos ton Ethnikofronon: He Synteretike Sképse sten Hellada 1922–1967* (From Law-Abiding People to Nationally Minded Nation: Conservative Thought in Greece 1922–1967). Athens: Savvalas.

Papadopoulos, Stavros. [1967]. "Avant-propos." In *Yioura liberté pour la Grèce.* Paris: François Maspero.

Papa-Karteres. 2003. *Anamneseis apo to Vouno. Ioulios 1947–Maes 1949* (Memories from the Mountain. July 1947–May 1949). Athens: Ekdoseis Vivliorama.

Papanikolaou, Dimitris. 2008. "He Kivōtós tōn Hellênōn" (The Arc of Greeks). *Ta Nea,* January 4: 30.

Papatheodorou, Yiannis. 2000. "He 'Pyknokatoikemene Eremia' ton Poieton tes Makronisou" (The "Densely Populated Wilderness" of the Poets of Makrónisos). In *Historiko Topio kai Historike Mneme: To Paradeigma tes Makronisou* (Historical Place and Historical Memory: The Paradigm of Makrónisos), ed. Stratis Bournazos and Tassos Sakellaropoulos, 227–45. Athens: Philistor.

Parker, Robert. 1983. *Miasma: Pollution and Purification in Early Greek Religion.* Oxford: Oxford University Press.

Parsons, Anne. 1970. "Is the Oedipus Complex Universal? The Jones-Malinowski Debate Revisited and a South Italian 'Nuclear Complex.'" In *Man and His Culture: Psychoanalytic Anthropology after 'Totem and Taboo,'* ed. Werner Muensterberger, 331–85. New York: Taplinger.

Pasolini, Pier Paolo, and Oswald Stack. 1979. *Pasolini on Pasolini: Interviews with Oswald Stack.* Bloomington: Indiana University Press.

Patrikios, Titos. 1993. *Synehes Horario: Diegeseis* (Continuous Labortime: Narratives). Athens: Kedros.

Paul, Robert. 1985. "The Oedipus Complex in Cultural Anthropology Today." *Reviews in Anthropology* 12: 353–60.

———. 1991. "Freud's Anthropology: A Reading of the 'Cultural Books.'" In *The Cambridge Companion to Freud,* ed. J. Neu, 267–87. Cambridge: Cambridge University Press.

Petrakis, Marina. 2005. *The Metaxas Myth: Dictatorship and Propaganda in Greece.* London: Tauris Academic Studies.

Petris, Yiorgos, introd. 1984. *Yioúra: Hypomnema Kratoumenon Pros ton Hypourgo Dikaiosynes tes Kyverneseos Plastera.* (Yioúra: Memorandum of the Detainees to the Minister of Justice of the Plasteras Government). Athens: Ekdoseis Gnosi.

Pharmakes, Nikos. 2006, Interview with Nikos Kouloglou, *Reportage Horis Synora* (Reportage Without Borders). ERT (Greek National Television), October 2.

Philippopoulos, Nikos. 2007. "Letter from a Firefighter." *Epsilon Eleftherotypia,* September 2, 2007: 8.

Phillis, Yannis A. 2006. *Mia Stagona ston Cheimarro* (A Drop in the Torrent). New York: Seaburn Press.

Plutarch. [1916]. *Parallel Lives: Alcibiades and Coriolanus. Lysander and Sulla.* Trans. Bernadotte Perrin. Cambridge: Harvard University Press.

Poulantzas, Nicos. 1976. *The Crisis of Dictatorships: Portugal-Greece-Spain.* Trans. David Fernbach. London: NLB.

———. 2000 [1978]. *State, Power, Socialism.* New ed., introd. Stuart Hall. London: Verso.

Propp, Vladimir I. 1975. *Edipo alla Luce del Folclore: Quattro studi di etnografia storico-strutturale.* Turin: Einaudi.

Pucci, Pietro. 1992. *Oedipus and the Fabrication of the Father: 'Oedipus Tyrannus' in Modern Criticism and Philosophy.* Baltimore: Johns Hopkins University Press.

Rabinbach, Anson. 1997. *In the Shadow of Catastrophe: German Intellectuals Between Apocalypse and Enlightenment.* Berkeley: University of California Press.

Rabinow, Paul. 2003. *Anthropos Today: Reflections on Modern Equipment.* Princeton: Princeton University Press.

Ramphos, Stelios. 1996. "Poietike Techne ston *Oidipoda Tyrannon:* O Prologos kai He Parodos" (Poetic Art in *Oedipus Tyrannus:* The Prologue and the Parodos). *Indiktos* 5 (June): 306–25.

Rautopoulos, Dimitris. 2004. *Aris Alexandrou: Ho Exoristos* (Aris Alexandrou: The Exiled). Athens: Sokoli.

Rezan, Maria. 2006. "Oute oi Germanoi den Ektelousan Kyriake" (Even the Germans Did Not Carry Out Executions on Sunday). In *Martyries gia ton Emphýlio kai ten Hellēnikê Aristerá* (Witness Accounts of the Civil War and the Greek Left), ed., Stelios Kouloglou, 281–85. Athens: Estia.

Rigatos, Gerasimos A. 2005. *Lexico Iatrikes Laographias: Meri kai Leitourgies tou Somatos; Sympromata kai Patheseis; Therapeutika Mesa kai Therapeutes* (Dictionary of Medical Folkore: Body Parts and Fuctions; Symptoms and Diseases; Therapeutic Means and Therapists). Athens: Veta.

Rocco, Christopher. 1997. *Tragedy and Enlightenment: Athenian Political Thought and the Dilemmas of Modernity.* Berkeley: University of California Press.

Roper, Lyndal. 1994. *Oedipus and the Devil: Witchcraft, Sexuality and Religion in Early Modern Europe.* London: Routledge.

Rosaldo, Renato. 1989. *Culture and Truth: The Remaking of Social Analysis.* Boston: Beacon Press.

Ross, John. 1994. *What Men Want: Mothers, Fathers and Manhood.* Cambridge: Cambridge University Press.

Rudnytsky, Peter L. 1987. *Freud and Oedipus.* New York: Columbia University Press.

Said, Edward. 2000 [1984]. "Reflections on Exile." In Said, *Reflections on Exile and Other Essays,* 173–87. Cambridge: Harvard University Press.

———. 2000 [1988]. "Representing the Colonized: Anthropology's Interlocutors." In Said, *Reflections on Exile and Other Essays,* 293–317. Cambridge: Harvard University Press.

Sarafis, Stephanos. 1980. *ELAS: Greek Resistance Army.* Trans. Sylvia Moody. Introd. Marion Sarafis. London: Merlin.

Scarry, Elaine. 1985. *The Body in Pain: The Making and Unmaking of the World.* New York: Oxford University Press.

Schmitt, Carl. 2004 [1963]. *The Theory of the Partisan: A Commentary/Remark on the Concept of the Political.* Trans. A. C. Goodson. East Lansing: Michigan State University Press.

Seferis, George. 1986. *Meres D' 1 Genare 1941–31 Dekemvre 1944* (Days D January 1, 1941–December 31, 1944). Athens: Ikaros.

Segal, Charles. 1986. *Interpreting Greek Tragedy: Myth, Poetry, Text.* Ithaca, N.Y.: Cornell University Press.

———. 1992. *"Sophocles' Oedipus: Evidence and Self-Conviction,* by Frederick Ahl." *The Classical World* 86, no. 2 (November-December 1992): 155.

———. 2001. *Oedipus Tyrannus: Tragic Heroism and the Limits of Knowledge.* Oxford: Oxford University Press.

Selton, Lt. Col. Robert W. 1966. "The Cradle of US Cold War Strategy." *Military Review,* August: 68.

Seneca, Lucius Annaeus. 1998. *Oedipus.* Freely translated and adapted by Michael Elliot Rutenberg. Wauconda, Ill.: Bolchazy-Carducci Publishers, Inc.

Sfikas, Thanassis. 2006. "He Ideologia tes 4es Avgoustou" (The Ideology of August 4). *Eleutherotypia (Vivliotheke),* August 4: 20–21.

Sharp, Lesley. 2002. *The Sacrificed Generation: Youth, History, and the Colonized Mind in Madagascar.* Berkeley: University of California Press.

Shaw, Ian. 2000. *The Oxford History of Ancient Egypt.* Oxford: Oxford University Press.

Simopoulos, Kyriakos. 2003. *Vasanistiria kai Exousia: Apo ten Hellenoromaike arhaioteta, to Vyzantio kai ten Tourkokratia os ten epohe mas* (Torture and Power: From Greco-Roman Antiquity, Byzantium, and the Turkish Occupation to Our Epoch). Athens: Ekdoseis Stahy.

Skevophylax, A. 2003. "Mila o Odigos tou Tanks" (The Driver of the Tank Speaks). Interview for the Sunday magazine of *To Vema*, special issue "Reportage," November 9.

Skopetea, Helle. 1988. *To Protypo Vasileio kai he Megale Idea: Apopseis tou Ethnikoou Provlematos sten Hellada (1830–1880)*. (The "Model Kingdom" and the Megale Idea: Views on the National Problem in Greece, 1830–1880). Athens: Polytypo.

Slattery, Dennis Patrick. 2000. *The Wounded Body: Remembering the Markings of Flesh*. Albany: State University of New York Press.

Smith, Ole. 1984. "The Memoirs and Reports of the British Liaison Officers in Greece, 1932–1944: Problems of Source Value." *Journal of the Hellenic Diaspora* 11, no. 3 (Fall): 9–32.

Snow Ethridge, Willie. 1948. *It's Greek to Me*. New York: Vanguard Press.

Sofsky, Wolfgang. 1997. *The Order of Terror: The Concentration Camp*. Trans. William Templer. Princeton: Princeton University Press.

Sophocles. [1982]. *The Three Theban Plays: Antigone, Oedius the King, Oedipus at Colonus*. Trans. Robert Fagles. Introd. Bernard Knox. New York: Viking Penguin.

Spanias, Nikos, ed. and trans. 1994. *Resistance, Exile, and Love*. New York: Pella Publishing.

Spiro, Melford E. 1982. *Oedipus in the Trobriands*. Chicago: University of Chicago Press.

Spivak, Gayatri Chakravorty. 2001. "Moving Devi." *Cultural Critique* 47 (Winter 2001): 120–63.

Staveris, Elias. 2001. *Glaropholia: Makronisi 1948–1949* (Seagull Nest: Makrónisos 1948–1949). Athens: Philistor.

Stephens, William N. 1962. *The Oedipus Complex: Cross-Cultural Evidence*. New York: The Free Press of Glencoe, Macmillan Co.

Stocking, George W., Jr. 1983. "The Ethnographer's Magic: Fieldwork in British Anthropology from Tylor to Malinowski." In *Observers Observed: Essays on Ethnographic Fieldwork*, ed. George W. Stocking, Jr., 70–121. Madison: University of Wisconsin Press.

———. 1986. "Anthropology and the Science of the Irrational: Malinowski's Encounter with Freudian Psychoanalysis." In *Malinowski, Rivers, Benedict and Others: Essays on Culture and Personality*, ed. George W. Stocking, Jr., 13–50. Madison: University of Wisconsin Press.

Stoler, Ann Laura. 1995. *Race and the Education of Desire: Foucault's History of Sexuality and the Colonial Order of Things*. Durham: Duke University Press.

———. 2002. "On the Uses and Abuses of the Past in Indonesia: Beyond the Mass Killings of 1965." *Asian Survey*. 42, no. 4 (July-August): 642–50.

Sutton. David. 2001. *Remembrance of Repasts: An Anthropology of Food and Memory*. New York: Berg.

Svoronos, Nikos. 1982. *Episkopise tes Neohellenikes Historias* (Survey of Modern Greek History). Trans. Aikaterine Asdraha. Athens: Themelio.

Tacitus. 1942 [109 A.D.]. *The Complete Works*. Ed. and introd. Moses Hadas. Trans. Alfred John Church and William Jackson Brodribb. New York: Random House.

Taussig, Michael. 2004. *My Cocaine Museum*. Chicago: University of Chicago Press.

Theodoratou, Liana. 2006. "Manolis Anagnostakis and the Love of Writing." Unpublished ms.

Theodorou, Victoria, ed. 1996. *Gynaikes Exoristes sta Stratopeda tou Emfyliou: Chios, Trikeri, Makrónisos, Ai-Stratis 1948–1954* (Women Exiles to the Camps of the Civil War: Chios, Trikeri, Makrónisos, Ai-Stratis 1948–1954). Athens: Ekdoseis Kastaniotis.

Trotsky, Leon. 1978. *Oeuvres Mars 1933/Juliet 1933*, vol. 1. Paris: Études et Documentation Internationales.

———. 1979. *Writings of Leon Trotsky: Supplement 1929–1935*. New York: Pathfinder Press.

Tsitsipis, Lukas. 1999. *A Linguistic Anthropology of Praxis and Language Shift: Arvanitika (Albanian) and Greek in Contact*. Oxford: Oxford University Press.

Tsoucalas, Constantine. 1969. *The Greek Tragedy*. London: Penguin.

———. 1981. "The Ideological Impact of the Civil War." In *Greece in the 1940s: A Nation in Crisis*, ed. John Iatrides, 319–43. Hanover, N.H.: University Press of New England.

Tsoukalas [sic], Constantine. 1999. *Koinonike Anaptyxe kai Kratos* (Social Development and the State). Athens: Themelio.

Turner, Terence S. 1969. "Oedipus: Time and Structure in Narrative Form." In *Forms of Symbolic Action*, ed. Robert F. Spencer, 26–68. Seattle: American Ethnological Society.

Vakalo, Eleni. [1994]. "Threnody." In *Resistance, Exile, and Love*, ed. and trans. Nikos Spanias, 160. New York: Pella Publishing.

Van Boeschoten, Riki. 1997. *Anapoda Chronia: Syllogike Mneme kai Historia ston Ziaka Grevenon* (Troubled Years: Collective Memory and History in Ziakas Grevenon). Athens: Plethron.

Van Dyck, Karen. 1998. *Kassandra and the Censors: Greek Poetry since 1967*. Ithaca, N.Y.: Cornell University Press.

Van Steen, Gonda. 2005. "Forgotten Theater, Theater of the Forgotten: Classical Theater in Modern Greek Prison Islands." *Journal of Modern Greek Studies* 23, no. 2 (October): 335–97.

Vardinoyiannis, Vardis, and Panayiotis Aronis. 1996. *Oi Misoi sta Sidera: Otan Anoixan oi Varies Ambares ki Ekleisan Mesa tous to Miso Ethnos* (Half of us Behind Bars: When the Heavy Doors Opened and Enclosed in Them Half the Nation). Athens: Philistor.

Vardoulakis, Dimitris. 2008. "The Greek Utopia: Aris Alexandrou's *The Mission Box*." Unpublished paper.

Varikas, Eleni. 2003. "Le figure du Paria: Une exception qui confirme la règle." *Tumultes* 21–22: 87–107.

Varon, Odette. 2003. "Apo tin EON sten EPON, 1936–1946: Mnemes kai Viomata apo Dyo Neanikes Organoseis" (From EON to EPON: Recollections and Experiences from Two Youth Organizations). In Hagen Fleischer, *He Hellada '36–'49: Apo ten Diktatoria ston Emphylio, Tomes kai Syneheies* (Greece '36–'49: From the Dictatorship to the Civil War, Ruptures and Continuities), 150–65. Athens: Kastaniotes.

Vernant, Jean-Pierre. 1996. *Entre mythe et politique.* Paris: Seuil.

Vernant, Jean-Pierre, and Pierre Vidal-Naquet. 1990. *Myth and Tragedy in Ancient Greece.* Trans. Janet Lloyd. New York: Zone Books.

———. 2001. *Oedipe et ses mythes.* Paris: Complexe.

Vervenioti, Tassoula. 2000. "Left-Wing Women Between Politics and Family." In *When the War Was Over: Reconstructing the Family, Nation, and State in Greece, 1943–1960*, ed. Marc Mazower, 105–22. Princeton, N.J.: Princeton University Press.

Vidal-Naquet, Pierre. 1998. *Torture dans la république (1954–1962).* Paris: Minuit.

Villefosse, Louis de. 1950. "Makronissos, laboratoire politique." *Les Tempes Modernes*, 1287–99.

Vitti, Mario. 1971. *Historia tes neohellenikes logotechnias* (History of Modern Greek Literature). Athens: Odysseas.

Voglis, Polymeris. 2000. "Between Negation and Self-Negation: Political Prisoners in Greece, 1945–1950" In *When the War Was Over: Reconstructing the Family, Nation, and State in Greece, 1943–1960*, ed. Marc Mazower, 73–91. Princeton, N.J.: Princeton University Press.

———. 2002. *Becoming a Subject: Political Prisoners During the Greek Civil War.* New York: Berghan Books.

Voltaire. 1968–1977 [1719]. "Première Lettre sur Oedipe." In *Oeuvres completes de Voltaire/Complete Works of Voltaire: Correspondence and Related Documents.* Ed. Theodore Besterman, 1:15n20. Geneva: Voltaire Foundation.

Voulgaris, Kostas. 2004. *He Partida: H ena Paihnidi Logotehnias kai Historias* (The Round; or, A Game of Literature and History). Athens: Vivliorama.

Weiner, Annette B. 1985. "Oedipus and Ancestors." *American Ethnologist* 12, no. 4: 758–62.

Weston, Kath. 1998. *Long, Slow Burn: Sexuality and Social Science.* New York: Routledge.

White, Hayden. 1978. "Ethnological 'Lie' and Mythical 'Truth.'" Review of René Girard, *Violence and the Sacred. diacritics*, March 1978: 2–9.

Woolard, Kathryn A., and Bambi Schieffelin. 1994. "Language Ideology." *Annual Review of Anthropology* 23: 55–82.

Yannas, Prodromos. 1994. "Containment Discourse and the Construction of Post–World War II Greece." *Thetis* 1: 117–28.

Yiannopoulos, D. Yiorgos. 2001. *Makronissos: Martyries Enos Foititi 1947–1950* (Makrónisos: Testimonials of a University Student 1947–1950). Athens: Vivliorama.

INDEX

In this index "f" after a number indicates a separate reference on the next page, and "ff" separate references on the next two pages. A continuous discussion over two or more pages is indicated by a span of page numbers, e.g., "57–59." *Passim* is used for a cluster of references in close but not consecutive sequence.